RENAISSANCE EUROPE

Renaissance Europe

Age of Recovery and Reconciliation

DE LAMAR JENSEN Brigham Young University

D. C. HEATH AND COMPANY
Lexington, Massachusetts   Toronto

To my wife, Mary, and to our children,

Jonna Lu, Marde, Brad, Emily, and Christine

COVER PHOTO: A detail from Domenico Ghirlandaio's "Zacharias in the Temple," depicting (from left to right) Marcilio Ficino, Christoforo Landino, Angelo Poliziano, and Demetrius Chalcondilas, all noted fifteenth-century humanists. (Editorial Photocolor Archives, Inc.)

Published simultaneously in Canada.

Printed in the United States of America.

International Standard Book Number: 0-669-51722-4

Library of Congress Catalog Card Number: 80-80547

Preface

My quest in the following pages may be as impossible a dream as that of the ingenious knight of La Mancha when he went out with lance and shield to overthrow evil. Yet, however short of our goals we may fall, any success, however small, is a victory not to be discounted. The purpose of *Renaissance Europe* (and its companion, *Reformation Europe*) is to present the civilization of Europe during those times as a whole in all of its varied colors and hues—its violence and compassion, hatred and love, destructiveness and creativity—in a way that the reader may comprehend its complexity and understand its important lessons. For history does teach by example, and in no other period of history are the examples more relevant and instructive for our time.

The age of the Renaissance—from approximately the middle of the fourteenth century to the middle of the sixteenth (1350–1550)—was a time of great change and diversity, a dynamic period of discovery, exploration, and expansion, not only in geography but also in politics, economics, religion, art, and science. It was an age of reform, one in which many old ideas and institutions were challenged and changed. The parallels between Renaissance and contemporary history are more than superficially striking, not so much in collateral events as in the similarity of their effects.

Reflect, for example, on the parallel between the "informational revolution" of our day, a product of sophisticated electronic technology, and the dramatic impact of printing in the Renaissance; or on the correlation between the rise of Renaissance monarchies and the modern emergence of new nations. And who cannot recognize the related philosophical implications of the discovery of the New World and the explorations of outer space—which may yet disclose commensurate economic and political consequences?

It is my hope that readers of this volume will catch the spirit and meaning of the dynamic age of Renaissance, or "rebirth"; sense the creative power of Michelangelo and Dürer; understand the political problems and challenges of Lorenzo the Magnificent and Isabel of Castile; feel the moral courage of Wyclif and John Hus; experience the excitement of the discoveries of Columbus and Copernicus; cultivate a thirst for knowledge like that of Leonardo da Vinci and Pico della Mirandola; and appreciate the fortitude of millions of human beings who lived, worked, fought, built, suffered, and died during that epoch. Their lives have enriched our own in countless ways.

Suggestions for Further Reading

The short bibliographical essays following each chapter have been written to assist the student in making purposeful selections of additional reading material, either for more extensive study or for enjoyment—or both. I feel that this is better achieved by a limited number of good books, accompanied by brief comments or evaluations, than by long impersonal lists of authors and titles.

To keep these bibliographies as brief and functional as possible, the following criteria have been used: (1) Despite the enormous amount of important historical literature in foreign languages, only works written in English or translated into English are included. (2) Source materials are not included, except in certain cases in which the modern work contains particularly useful documents. (3) In order to make these bibliographies as current as possible, the most recent works are cited. Those written before 1960 are included only if they have been reissued in later editions or are of unique value. (4) First priority has been given to full-length books, but shorter essays and journal articles are sometimes included when these are the best, or only, studies of a particular topic.

Acknowledgments

I gratefully acknowledge my debt to the many others who have preceded me in summarizing this period of history and to those who have collected documents, published monographs and articles, written reviews, and presented lectures and papers. Their work is invaluable for anyone wishing to understand history and appreciate its great relevance and significance today. To the many colleagues, teachers, students, friends, and members of my family who have assisted me individually or collectively, I express particular thanks, especially to a generation of interested and challenging students at Brigham Young University, with whom I have shared ideas and from whom I have learned much over the years. Several colleagues and other experts have read parts or all of these chapters and have given priceless advice and suggestions for their improvement. I need not mention them by name, but they know of my gratitude.

Having been able to incorporate into this volume some of the information and interpretations gained while doing research in Europe on more specialized studies supported by grants from the Institute of International Education, the Rockefeller Foundation, the National Endowment for the Humanities, and most recently from the Guggenheim Foundation, I gratefully acknowledge their interest and help. I also wish to express appreciation to the editors and others at D.C. Heath for their expert advice and assistance, particularly Ann Knight, Bryan Woodhouse, and Dorothy Williams. Finally, and most importantly, my wife and children have endured, without complaint, many inconveniences and frustrations, as a direct result of the time I have devoted to this book over a period of many years. My daughter Christine has also assisted me in preparing the index.

DE LAMAR JENSEN

Contents

List of Maps

The Meaning of
The Renaissance

HE "RENAISSANCE" is a term with many meanings. To Jacob Burckhardt, the nineteenth-century Swiss historian and art critic who marked the starting point of all modern interpretations of the Renaissance with his great *Civilization of the Renaissance in Italy* (1860), it was the spirit of self-discovery and fulfillment, of recognition of human worth, and a dynamic outpouring of artistic activity. It was also the beginning of modern times, for Renaissance Italy was "the first-born among the sons of modern Europe." Since Burckhardt's time, many have criticized his interpretation, some justly and others unjustly. He did overemphasize the cultural break between the Middle Ages and the Renaissance and failed to recognize the equally marked distinctions between Renaissance society and the modern industrial world. History, after all, is both continuity and change. He probably laid too much stress on individualism and secularism as Renaissance characteristics and not enough on its deep religious content. Yet his recognition of the dynamic nature of Renaissance society and its cultural grounding in classical literature and art is well founded and important.

Many subsequent assessments have concentrated on aspects of the Renaissance controversy, such as economic and social history and the history of science, that were generally neglected by Burckhardt. The great Dutch historian Johan

Huizinga saw the Renaissance—in France and the Netherlands at least—as the decline of medieval culture. George Sarton criticized the Renaissance humanists' lack of interest in science, and Lynn Thorndike accused them of setting back the progress of science a hundred years or more. More recently, Robert Sabatino Lopez has emphasized the financial recession and stagnation of early Renaissance economy. In a different vein, Hans Baron sees the key to Renaissance culture in the "civic humanism" of early fifteenth-century Florence; Wallace Ferguson finds it in the predominance of Italian urban life; B. L. Ullman in the high level of poetic achievement; Robert Ergang defines its as the secularization of society; and Denys Hay recognizes it as an overall style of living.

There is truth and value in all of these interpretations. Yet the problem of the Renaissance is compounded by the use of the term in so many different ways. Most scholars would agree that *Renaissance* implies something of all of these, not just a "rebirth," as the word suggests. But the difficulty arises when we start being specific as to the exact ingredients and their proportions. What characteristics distinguish Renaissance man, woman, art, thought, politics, or poetry from their medieval counterparts? Or are these arbitrary labels employed by the historian to facilitate organizing and explaining the past? *Renaissance* is partly that. But I believe it also has meaning in terms of thought, expression, attitude, and style.

To begin with, the Renaissance was a period of time, like any other, during which people revealed their character, personality, feelings, and aspirations by what they thought and did. But the Renaissance was also unique in many ways. In addition to common features it shared with earlier and later periods, it had distinct characteristics as well. These characteristics, revealed in certain attitudes, institutions, and creations, did not originate or terminate at any precise date. Therefore, it is impossible to impose a rigid time frame on the period. Nevertheless, by the latter half of the fourteenth century (the 1300s), as Europe was gradually recovering from the heaviest ravages of the Black Death, many of these Renaissance characteristics were coming into play. Some of them had started decades or even centuries earlier; some would not appear until many years later. Yet by the time of Petrarch's and Boccaccio's deaths (in 1374 and 1375, respectively), as their disciples were carrying the ideals of humanism into all parts of Italy, the spirit of the Renaissance was beginning to manifest itself on a large-enough scale to distinguish it as a major movement, not just the expression of a few isolated writers or artists of genius. Its manifestations were most pronounced in Italy from the late fourteenth to the early sixteenth centuries (roughly 1375 to 1525) and in the rest of Europe from the late fifteenth to the early seventeenth centuries (roughly 1475 to 1625). It was bounded by crises, at one end by the Black Death (1348–51) and at the other by the devastating Thirty Years' War (1618–48).

What was the philosophical framework of this period, and the essence of its spirit? Part of it was an outlook on life that encouraged a higher regard for human attributes and destiny and a greater appreciation of physical beauty—both manmade objects and those seen in nature. Related to this attitude was a growing consciousness of people as beings in time as well as space, an awareness of the dimension of history and mankind's place in it. This awareness justified the promotion of literature and scholarship to better understand the past, and suggested the continuing role and responsibilities of people in society.

Not only were people historical beings but also political ones, citizens whose privilege and duty it was to participate actively and directly in government. Such notions of participation are best illustrated in the Italian city-states, but also reveal a broader shift away from the medieval concept of *Respublica Christiana*—the notion of a single commonwealth composing all of Latin Christendom—toward the establishment of territorial or national states, larger than the local jurisdictions of the medieval nobles yet smaller than the whole of Europe. With this change came new institutions of government and a new outlook on the nature and dynamics of international relations and the techniques of diplomacy. Political relations were also affected by the fluidity and range of expanding commercial relations, which brought Renaissance Europeans into closer contact with one another and with the wider world.

All of these developments took place within the context and laws of the institutionalized church. But many of these ideas ran counter to some of the traditional practices and beliefs of the church as interpreted by those exercising ecclesiastical authority, and tension began to develop that eventually led to conflict and upheaval all over Europe.

Obviously, no single feature of Renaissance times adequately describes the age. How could it, when even a single life is too complex to summarize, let alone an entire civilization—especially a civilization so rich in contrasts? Yet through the maze of conflict and contradictions, some features seem to stand out like prominent mountain peaks as landmarks to guide us to a better understanding of the age. One of these is embodied in the term *recovery* in both its meanings—"to recuperate from some unhappy condition" and "to regain something that has been lost."

In the first sense, the Renaissance was an age of recovery from the calamitous fourteenth century, which was "a violent, tormented, bewildered, suffering and disintegrating age," according to Barbara Tuchman's vivid description, "a time, as many thought, of Satan triumphant." The Renaissance was an era of recuperation from the consequences of the Black Death, which had wiped out more than one-third of the total population, and the crisis of faith and despair associated with it; from war and political disorder bordering on chaos; and from devastating economic depression. It was also a time of gradual adjustment to the colder, wetter weather and shorter growing seasons of the so-called Little Ice Age that began in the fourteenth century.

From the final quarter of that century on, Italian sources repeatedly refer to recovery and revival, and a distinct consciousness of having survived a holocaust and now being part of a period of rebuilding. In their recovery from the crises, many survivors established a tradition of courage and resolution that carried them forward into a new life, a rebirth, so to speak.

Succeeding generations took pride in their achievements and in those of their ancestors, whose surrounding monuments reminded them of ancient sacrifices and glories. Increasingly aware of its own historical heritage, the Renaissance age sparked a rebirth of the classical spirit, a recovery of the ancient Greco-Roman culture that had once civilized the Mediterranean world. This recovery and restoration of classical literature, art, and ideas was a motivating feature of the Renaissance search for the meaning of life and pervaded all activities from politics to philosophy. The classics were seen as relevant to contemporary society and were made an intimate part of Renaissance letters.

Moreover, the recovery of classical antiquity was taken as a step in the broader reconciliation of the diverse aspects of human life and thought. The Renaissance humanists hoped to reconcile and harmonize the ancient world with the present, pagan philosophy with Christian theology, scholarship with faith, action with contemplation. The ideal of the "well-rounded individual," or the "complete man," was the realization of a broad integration of the many paradoxes and contradictory ingredients that make up human beings. The spirit of the Renaissance emphasized not only human dignity and worth, but also the composite human nature and its capacity to harmonize its contradictions and reconcile society, nature, and God. Obviously, these goals were seldom reached, but they represented values and motivations that gave some coherence to the period, despite its remarkable diversity.

Finally, a feature of the Renaissance that gave further meaning and cogency to the age was its spirit of growth and expansion. Although the characteristics I have described appeared first in Italy during the late fourteenth century and reached their fullest expression there in the fifteenth (the *quattrocento*, or 1400s), some of these ideals and values spread to other parts of Europe and provided a classical component to European style from the late-fifteenth to the mid-seventeenth centuries. This was a time of dramatic political, economic, geographical, and intellectual expansion, when new worlds were being discovered and explored, and new horizons were first viewed. It was also a period of intense religious bigotry, personal cruelty, and wholesale destruction, as well as a time of spiritual devotion and deep artistic sensitivity. Above all, it was a time of change—an age of boldness, innovation, and revolution. New concepts and techniques of government, diplomacy, economics, and religion were injected into the traditional life-style and thought of western Europe.

Yet men and women of the Renaissance sought desperately to harmonize and synthesize these contradictions and to retain the unified, integrated, and orderly universe their predecessors had thought they lived in. Although different from the medieval period, even antagonistic to it in some ways, the age of the Renaissance tried to reconcile the Ancient World with the Middle Ages and link them into a larger synthesis. It aspired to end not only the dichotomy between paganism and Christianity but also that between heaven and earth, and to create a world of consistency and concord. This Renaissance reconciliation reached its climax in the early sixteenth century with giants like Leonardo da Vinci, Pico della Mirandola, Desiderius Erasmus, Albrecht Dürer, Baldassare Castiglione, Sir Thomas More, and Raphael Sanzio. Then its very foundations were shaken by the Reformation, and a new era of stress and upheaval ensued. Even after that, the thread of reconciliation and synthesis was not entirely broken, and the search for stability and order was continued in the seventeenth century.

Suggestions for Further Reading

GENERAL: RENAISSANCE AND REFORMATION

The age of the Renaissance and Reformation has been the subject of many good books, from Henry S. Lucas's long-standard, *The Renaissance and the Reformation*, 2nd ed. (New York, 1960) to Charles G. Nauert's latest, very brief, *The Age of Renaissance and Reformation* (Hinsdale, 1977). They all have strengths and weaknesses. S. Harrison Thomson, *Europe in Renaissance and Reformation* (New York, 1963) is especially strong on Eastern Europe, although too heavy and encyclopedic. V.H.H. Green, *Renaissance and Reformation: A Survey of European History between 1450 and 1660*, 2d ed. (London, 1965) is a fast-moving political history but gives insufficient attention to cultural and intellectual matters. More balanced is Lewis W. Spitz, *The Renaissance and Reformation Movements* (Chicago, 1971). Other surveys include P. J. Helm, *History of Europe, 1450–1660* (New York, 1964), and M. L. Bush, *Renaissance, Reformation and the Outer World* (London, 1967).

Three sound but very short summaries are J. Russell Major, *The Age of the Renaissance and Reformation: A Short History* (Philadelphia, 1970); A. G. Dickens, *The Age of Humanism and Reformation* (Englewood Cliffs, 1972); and J.F.H. New, *Renaissance and Reformation: A Short History*, 2nd ed. (New York, 1977). Richard L. DeMolen, ed., *The Meaning of the Renaissance and Reformation* (Boston, 1974) is a collection of eight essays on broad topics of the period. Robert M. Kingdon, ed., *Transition and Revolution: Problems and Issues of European Renaissance and Reformation History* (Minneapolis, 1974) includes useful selections of source readings. Another excellent introduction, more general than its title suggests, is Donald J. Wilcox, *In Search of God and Self: Renaissance and Reformation Thought* (Boston, 1975).

THE RENAISSANCE

Reliable accounts of the Renaissance alone include Wallace K. Ferguson, *Europe in Transition, 1300–1520* (Boston, 1962), a solid if somewhat imposing study; Robert Ergang, *The Renaissance* (Princeton, 1967), which sees the Renaissance as a secularization of life, thought, and culture; Denys Hay, *Europe in the Four-teenth and Fifteenth Centuries* (New York, 1966), a keen analysis of Renaissance society by one of its leading authorities; and Ernst Breisach, *Renaissance Europe, 1300–1517* (New York, 1973), a very good coverage of all aspects of Renaissance life. A splendid little book with many useful illustrations is Margaret Aston, *The Fifteenth Century: The Prospect of Europe* (New York, 1968) in the Harcourt Brace History of European Civilization Library, edited by Geoffrey Barraclough. Eugene F. Rice, *The Foundations of Early Modern Europe, 1460–1559* (New York, 1970), and De Lamar Jensen, *The Renaissance World* (St. Louis, 1979) are briefer general summaries.

A solid series on cultural and social history in Renaissance Italy, edited by J. R. Hale, includes John Larner, *Culture and Society in Italy, 1290–1420* (New York, 1971), which describes the interaction between literature, art and society; Peter Burke, *Culture and Society in Renaissance Italy, 1420–1540* (New York, 1972), which is especially good on the social institutions of Renaissance Italy and their relationship to the great artists and writers; and Oliver Logan, *Culture and Society in Venice, 1470–1790* (New York, 1972), an engaging study of Venice's golden age. Peter Laven, *Renaissance Italy, 1464–1534* (London, 1966) sees the age in terms of change and reorganization in the whole of Italy.

Finally, a number of collected essays provide some of the most important insights into the age. Among the best of these are Charles S. Singleton, ed., *Art, Science and History in the Renaissance* (Baltimore, 1967), a product of the Johns Hopkins Humanities Seminar; J. H. Plumb, ed., *The Horizon Book of the Renaissance* (New York, 1962), sumptuously illustrated, as is Denys Hay, ed., *The Age of the Renaissance* (London & New York, 1967). E. F. Jacob, ed., *Italian Renaissance Studies* (London, 1960) is a tribute to Cecilia M. Ady. Anthony Molho and John Tedeschi, eds., *Renaissance: Studies in Honor of Hans Baron* (Dekalb, 1971), and J. G. Rowe and W. H. Stockdale, eds., *Florilegium Historiale: Essays Presented to Wallace K. Ferguson* (Toronto, 1971) contain more valuable essays.

RENAISSANCE INTEPRETATIONS

The classic interpretation of the Renaissance is Jacob Burckhardt's *The Civilization of the Renaissance in Italy* (1860 and many editions since). The standard analysis of this and other interpretations is Wallace K. Ferguson, *The Renaissance in Historical Thought: Five Centuries of Interpretation* (Boston, 1948). More recent views and debates can be found in Denys Hay, *The Italian Renaissance in Its Historical Background* (Cambridge, 1961), which sees the Renaissance as a growing and changing series of attitudes and ideas, and in the essays published in Tinsley Helton, ed., *The Renaissance: A Reconsideration of the Theories and Interpretations of the Age* (Madison, 1964); Wallace K. Ferguson, *The Renaissance: Six Essays* (New York, 1962) and *Renaissance Studies* (New York, 1970); Denys Hay, ed., *The Renaissance Debate* (New York, 1965, 1976); Robert Schwoebel, ed., *Renaissance Men and Ideas* (New York, 1971); and Karl H. Dannenfeldt, ed., *The Renaissance: Basic Interpretations*, 2nd ed. (Lexington, 1974), in the D. C. Heath Problems in European Civilization series. George C. Sellery, *The Renaissance: Its Nature and Origins* (Madison, 1950, 1962) is a very critical essay showing that the Renaissance was simply an evolution of medieval society. In *The Renaissance in Perspective* (New York, 1973) Philip Lee Ralph places the Renaissance in the broader perspective of Western history and culture.

CHAPTER ONE

The Medieval Heritage

ESTERN CIVILIZATION has roots reaching far into the past, roots that connect it with the rich artistic and intellectual heritage of the ancient Greeks, with the fertile religious tradition and literature of the Hebrews, with the legal thought and expressive language of the Romans, and with the ideals and primitive brutality of the freedom-loving Germans. To these divergent ingredients, and many more, were added the spiritual zeal of devotional Christianity that, perhaps more than any other single factor, welded these elements into a new civilization with its own distinctive arts, institutions, and ways of life and thought. This process of amalgamation took place over a period of many centuries during the era commonly known as the Middle Ages. By the eleventh and twelfth centuries, most of the features of this European civilization had been integrated into a functional, organized, and growing society.

Manorial Life and Economy

The society of the Middle Ages was divided into well-defined classes, each with distinctive obligations, duties, rights, and symbols. This stratification was not as rigid as the caste structure of India, but it was extremely difficult to move vertically between classes in medieval Europe. The division was especially marked between the peasant (worker) class and the noble (warrior) class, even though the two were highly dependent on each other. The middle class, too, composed largely of

craftsmen, merchants, lawyers, and the practitioners of other urban professions, was dependent on the peasants for sustenance and on the nobles for protection. All classes looked to the clergy for their spiritual needs. Thus the entire social order rested on a system of interdependent relationships existing within and among the classes.

The most basic relationships, next to the family itself, centered around the self-sufficient agricultural community known as the manor. Each manor was composed of a number of peasant households clustered together in crude shelters around the nucleus of a church, mill, blacksmith shop, wine press, and other facilities. Nearby was the manor house, or castle, where the lord of the manor lived, usually a knight or higher-ranking nobleman, or a bishop. Surrounding the village proper lay the manorial fields, pasture lands, and forests.

The cultivated lands were in large, open fields producing the crops required as food and clothing for everyone associated with the manor and for sale in nearby towns. These fields were divided into narrow

strips for cultivating. All of the land was worked by the peasants, some of it for themselves and their families, the rest for the manorial lord. Because artificial fertilizers were unknown and available animal manure was insufficient, the only practical method of revitalizing the soil was to let it lie fallow for at least a year. Thus a two-field rotation was generally practiced by tilling half the strips each year and letting the other half lie fallow. Two important innovations of the late Middle Ages greatly increased the efficiency and productivity of manorial estates in northern Europe. These were the invention of the heavy, wheeled plow with a moldboard to turn over the soil, and the development of the three-field system of crop rotation. With the three-field system, two fields were planted, one usually in winter wheat, harvested in July, and the other planted in some kind of spring grain that was harvested in the fall. The third field lay fallow. By these methods, agricultural production was increased by one-third and the quality of the crops also improved.

In addition to the cultivated fields, other kinds of land usually belonged to the manor: untilled pasture lands, used in common by all the villagers for grazing animals; lowland meadows from which a small amount of grass and swamp hay could be gathered for winter feed; and outlying forested areas where fish and game generally abounded. These forest lands, however, unlike the pastures, belonged exclusively to the manorial lord, and poaching by the peasants was a serious offense, often punished by death. Peasant rights in the forests were restricted to firewood and berry gathering, and for pasturing their semiwild pigs.

The social status of medieval peasants was hardly enviable, yet they did have rights as well as obligations. The most common condition of peasants in central and northern Europe was serfdom, a status less onerous than slavery but still far from freedom. Specific duties were required of serfs, yet they possessed certain rights and, if we use the term very loosely, privileges. Serfs could not leave the manor on their own volition, could not engage in "outside" economic activities, and could not marry without the permission of the lord. Servile taxes, both in money and kind, were also owed, and they were usually oppressive and always bore the stamp of social inferiority. Of course, serfs were also required to labor long hours under difficult conditions in the manorial fields, most of the time on the lord's land, the *demesne*. In addition to this regular labor, serfs were expected to perform "boon-work," or seasonal work, for the lord at various times of the year when it was needed. On the other hand, serfs were permitted to hold some of the land themselves and devote part of their time to cultivating it. Their tools, animals, huts, and clothing were considered their own, but of course they were not free to dispose of them or remove them from the manor. The lord was obliged to defend the serfs and provide refuge in his castle to all villagers in times of enemy attack. Thus, serfs were politically, socially, and economically bound to the manor, but they were guaranteed the necessities of life: food, clothing, shelter, and protection.

The status of peasant women was unenviable. They had few rights and almost no freedom, being always under the jurisdiction of either their fathers or husbands, and obliged to labor alongside them in the fields. Here there was very little sexual discrimination. Women were expected to work long and hard. They tilled the soil and planted crops, cut hay and threshed grain, harvested grapes and gathered wood, just as the men did. But, in addition, they also performed all of the household labors for their families: cooking, spinning, weaving, clothes-making, and mending. Fortunate were those peasant wives who had daughters too young to marry or work in the fields, because to them could be delegated some of the perennial household chores.

Families lived in huts made of sticks, mud, and straw (wattle and daub) with a clay floor and thatched roof. Huts usually had no more than two rooms, one for cooking, eating, and other household industries, and the other for sleeping. The simple but nutritious fare of the peasant table consisted of bread made from barley or rye, supplemented with oats. Wheat, the aristocrat of cereal grains, was the staple only for the well-to-do peasants and the higher classes. To this were added many varieties of vegetables—beans, chick-peas, leeks, onions, cabbage, lettuce, and beets—along with cheese, fish, occasional meat (usually pork), and honey, chestnuts, mushrooms, and wild fruit gathered from the forests, all of which were washed down with ample portions of water or crude, homemade wine.

This highly integrated manorial community did not exist uniformly in all parts of medieval Europe. In the Mediterranean basin, where the soil is thin and rainfall light, smaller, very loosely organized hamlets and farms were more common, along with large estates with very primitive agriculture and servile labor. Likewise, in northern England and Scotland, Ireland, and Scandinavia, agricultural production was less tightly organized. In eastern Europe, particularly the Polish flatlands, hunting and food gathering were only gradually replaced by agriculture and stock raising on small, peasant-owned lands. In the fourteenth and fifteenth centuries, however, these succumbed to large feudal reserves owned by the nobles and tilled by agricultural servants whose status was akin to serfdom.

Even in the European heartland of northern France and western Germany, where the manorial economy prevailed, there were variations and exceptions to the pattern just outlined. For example, in many medieval manors, some freemen also lived and participated as an integral part of the system. These freemen were distinguished from the serfs by their right to dispose of property, to move from one manor to another, to sue in the royal courts, and to marry as they chose. Many feudal services were not required of them, and they were frequently assigned supervisory positions on the manor. One such freeman might be designated by the lord as bailiff, to supervise the work of the manor and maintain the lord's accounts.

Manorialism underwent many changes in the late Middle Ages; with the altered conditions brought about by the growth of towns, the revival of a money economy, commercial and industrial development, and the rise of territorial states, many serfs were gradually transformed into free peasants. This process was well along by the end of the fifteenth century, although in some parts of eastern Europe and in Russia serfdom lasted until the late nineteenth century.

The Growth of Trade and Towns

One of the important developments of the eleventh and twelfth centuries was the expansion of trade and the accompanying growth of towns. After several centuries of almost no long-distance trading, commerce began to revive in the Mediterranean, especially an active East-

West trade with Moslem lands and a new maritime trade centering in the Baltic and North Sea area. Soon these regions were linked by overland and inland water routes, and commercial exchange started to become an integral part of European life. Some of the impetus for this commercial activity came from the Christian counteroffensive against Islam and the establishment of bases in the Levant following the First Crusade. The gradual improvement of agricultural production resulted in some food surpluses in the West, and the increase in population also contributed to the spread of trade. The center of this commercial expansion was Italy, where the coastal towns were ideally located to capitalize on the economic opportunities. As Mediterranean commerce expanded, a network of trade routes crisscrossing Europe also developed: north and south along the Rhone and Rhine waterways; overland from Paris to Vienna and radiating from there to Leipzig, Cologne, and the North Sea; to Danzig and Riga on the Baltic and Kiev in the east.

For several centuries, the centers of international trade were the great medieval fairs. These were held at regular intervals at the crossroads of the trade routes, at Geneva, Lyon, Medina del Campo, Frankfurt, Bruges, Bergen-op-Zoom, and the four great fairs of England. Champagne, in northeastern France, with its series of fairs lasting almost the year around, was the greatest of them all. At these fairs, merchants from all over Europe exchanged goods, money, gossip, and news, stimulating the process that was to grow into an organized business of international trade. The heyday of the European fairs was the twelfth and thirteenth centuries. After that, they declined in importance as the numerous commercial towns themselves became year-round fairs and centers of the new commercial capitalism.

Closely related to the expansion of commerce, and stimulated by it, was the growth in the size and number of towns throughout Europe, especially in Italy and the Low Countries. Some of these were of Roman or earlier origin; others were seats of bishoprics; many were fortified settlements dating from the early Middle Ages; some were born out of the necessities of commercial expansion. Whatever their beginnings, the towns experienced dramatic growth from the twelfth century on.

With access to the trade routes, and partially protected from the devastations of feudal warfare by charters from the nobles or the king and by the erection of protective walls, these towns were the focal point of all kinds of commercial activity engaged in by the growing class of merchants. The merchants did not fit well into the accepted niches of medieval society; they were despised by the nobles, distrusted by the priests, and envied by the peasants. Nevertheless, they continued to prosper and increase in importance. Part of the merchants' success was due to the favor they found with the monarchs, many of whom recognized the value of friendship with the moneyed class. Perhaps more of their success can be attributed to their organization into guilds for the purpose of exercising monopolistic control over the marketing and business activities of the towns. The merchant guilds not only set the rules of commercial practice and regulated the conduct of all transactions but also frequently dominated the town governments, particularly in Italy.

Craft guilds also participated in the organization and supervision of business activities. They were more numerous than the merchant guilds, each regulating the affairs of the practitioners of a single handicraft industry, such as bakers, butchers, shoemakers, tailors, weavers, apothecaries, candle makers, carpenters, stonemasons, goldsmiths, and so forth. The craft guilds maintained strict rules governing the production, quality, and price of goods; these rules also controlled the number of people working at each trade. The nucleus of the handicraft industry was individual craftsmen-specialists (masters in the guild) with their shops, tools, and technical ability. These artisans bought the necessary raw materials from merchants, and then with their personal skills and those of the apprentices and journeymen working with them, turned the raw materials into finished products for sale to the local market. Before being admitted to full membership in a guild as masters, aspiring young craftsmen had to spend many years (six to ten, depending on the trade) as apprentices in a shop, where they worked without wages for room and board while they were taught the

MEDIEVAL CRAFTSMEN AT WORK. *These illustrations from a Nuremberg guild book show a pewterer turning a jug on a hand lathe (which actually took two people to operate) and a shoemaker finishing a pair of one-piece leather shoes. (The Bettmann Archive, Inc.)*

rudiments and skills of the trade. Upon the approval of the guild, they advanced to the rank of journeymen and could work in a shop for wages until the guild saw fit to admit them as masters.

The merchants of the Middle Ages thought of their occupation as a means of making a living, not as a way to increase their wealth. They were encouraged in this attitude by the church, which taught that all economic endeavor should be conducted according to Christian principles. The price charged for the sale of goods, therefore, should be determined by the moral principle of "just price," that is, an amount that would provide an adequate livelihood for the seller but not a lucrative profit. This, of course, prohibited taking interest on money loaned. On the same grounds, the church taught that workers should receive wages no higher than would allow them to support themselves and their families in a custom appropriate to their social position. Yet despite the strictures of the church, and the seeming resignation of peasants and the willingness of nobles to accept the bounds prescribed by their class, merchants tended to feel less fettered by those prescriptions. Eventually, these urban businesspeople developed a very different attitude toward the accumulation of wealth, thereby laying the foundations of modern free-market capitalism.

Despite the growing wealth of a few merchant entrepreneurs, life in a medieval town was far from luxurious. In fact, for most of the urban population, it was less comfortable, less sanitary, and more dangerous than life on the manor. Streets were extremely narrow, dark, and dirty, and filled all day with milling people and animals. Houses were small and crowded; public buildings were better made and more spacious, but equally vulnerable to fires, disease, and disorder. Vagrancy and lawlessness were widespread. Still, some opportunities existed for the townspeople (the *bourgeoisie*) that were not available to the country serfs. They were, in most cases, protected by the town charters from the impositions of the landed nobles and guaranteed at least a taste of self-government.

Feudalism

Just as serfs were beholden to their manorial lords for labor and service, who in turn were obligated to their serfs for livelihood and protection, the entire noble class was interlinked by contractual bonds of mutual obligation known as *vassalage* or *feudalism*. In the absence of a strong central government capable of maintaining law and order, particularly after the collapse of Charlemagne's empire in the ninth century, feudalism provided the cohesion that held society together during the last five centuries of the Middle Ages. Broadly speaking, feudalism was a social, political, military, and economic system, marked by the wide dispersal of property and political authority, and composed of mutual rights, duties, and interdependence.

In this system, a weaker nobleman might choose to commend his services and allegiance to a stronger one in return for the latter's promise of protection. The arrangement began with the ceremony of homage and fealty, by which the prospective vassal placed his clasped hands between those of his protector, declaring that he wished to become his man and pledging his faith as a vassal to his lord. He was then raised to his feet, kissed by his lord, and given a Bible or sacred relic on which he took an oath to confirm his promise.

The feudal contract was mutual and imposed obligations on both parties. The vassal agreed to serve his lord. This usually meant military service, either his own person as a mounted knight, if he belonged to that order of nobility, or the service of a specified number of knights if he was of higher rank and possessed vassals of his own. Another service a vassal was expected to give was *consilium*, that is, advice and counsel when summoned to his lord's court.

For his part, the lord owed his vassals protection and maintenance. He was obliged to come to their aid when they were unjustly attacked, and in general to defend them against their enemies. Maintenance refers to the lord's duty to provide his vassal with the means for giving service, either by maintaining him at court or by investing him with some source of revenue, known as a *fief* (Latin *feodum*, or *feudum*, from which the term *feudalism* is derived). Usually the fief consisted of a landed estate or manor, but it could vary all the way from a single castle without land to a territory half the size of France. A fief might even consist of some special duty, office, or right; but most often it was the tenure of land. It carried with it the right to judge and administer the laws within that territory and to govern the people who lived there. The process of division and distribution of fiefs to numerous vassals and subvassals is known as *subinfeudation*. This practice usually led to all sorts of complications and contradictions. By subinfeudation, a knight became the vassal of one nobleman and the lord of another. Or he might be the vassal of two or more lords at the same time, holding different fiefs from each one. After 1066, the duke of Normandy—Normandy being the fief he held as a vassal of the king of France—was himself the king of England.

Kingship in the Feudal System

The role of the king in the feudal system calls for some special comment. Kingship in Europe stemmed from Germanic traditions, in which the most courageous and effective fighter was proclaimed king by his peers. Early medieval monarchs were also warrior kings and fit perfectly into the hierarchical structure of feudalism. Theoretically, the vassal-lord relationship extended in orderly steps from the simple knight up through the ranks of counts, barons, and dukes to the king at the apex of the hierarchy. Such a concept was compatible with the prevalent religious view of the hierarchical universe in which all things had their appropriate rank and status. Consequently, the person of the king took on a special religious aura in later medieval Europe. He was not only the highest-ranking secular lord in the realm, but also the church-anointed vicar of God. In the coronation ceremony, he was consecrated by a bishop or archbishop of the church, symbolizing his acceptance by God as well as men. But the solemn coronation oath, which he was required to take, also reinforced the two-way contractual nature of medieval kingship, just as that of all other vassal-lord relationships, for in it he made a promise to protect the church, maintain peace, and do justice to all. If he subsequently violated this oath in any way, the contract was broken and his vassals were no longer obligated to obey him.

Furthermore, despite the sanction of the church, the king's authority was no greater than that of any other feudal lord who had to rely on the willingness of his vassals for material strength. The independent power of the dukes and barons was great enough that the king could expect their loyalty and service only when it benefited them, as well. Remembering that subvassals owed their loyalty to their lords, not directly to the king, and that even his own tenants-in-chief (immediate vassals) frequently had obligations and interests that were contrary to his, it is easy to see why medieval monarchs were very limited in real power. They were suzerains, not sovereigns. Power, as well as jurisdiction, was dispersed and fragmented.

Just as the actions of the king were restricted by feudal contract, so were they regulated by custom. The laws the monarch administered were the laws prescribed by custom and locality; his duty was to administer them justly. Furthermore, adjudication was not the prerogative of the king alone; every feudal lord was expected to summon his vassals as a court of law to hear litigation and to pronounce judgment on their peers. Obviously, since feudal courts were the executors of local laws and customs, medieval Europe was a hodgepodge of conflicting legal practice and jurisdiction. It is little wonder that feudal justice was arbitrary and capricious. An offense punishable by a small fine in one locality might be subject to the death penalty only a few miles away. Most often, cases in the early feudal courts were decided by ordeal, or battle, a practice that served strength more than justice. However, with the gradual revival and spread of written Roman law from the twelfth century on, and the establishment in England of the common law (common to the whole realm), the administration of justice became more equitable and consistent.

Warfare and the Nobility

Another condition that made feudalism so uncertain and disorderly, in addition to the absence of central government, was the nobility's unflagging propensity for war. "Gentle knights were born to fight," said the chronicler Froissart. War was ingrained into them from birth. It was

KNIGHTS PREPARING TO JOUST. *This miniature from Froissart's* Chronicle *depicts the jousts of Saint-Inglevert, near Calais, where in 1389 a team of French knights challenged all comers to a contest of skill during a period of thirty days. (Harl. 4379, f. 23v.) (Reproduced by permission of the British Library)*

their heritage, their education, their livelihood, and even their pleasure; usually, it was also the cause of their death. Since the feudal bonds of loyalty and obligation were vertical rather than horizontal, nothing prevented peers from pouncing on one another at the slightest provocation. Private warfare raged almost continuously throughout the Middle Ages and, with the military commitments occasioned by widely interlacing vassalage and subinfeudation, frequently enlarged into huge encounters resulting in great loss of life and physical destruction. The clergy tried to mitigate the brutality of feudal warfare by the so-called Peace Movement, which they hoped would set some limits on the conduct of war. One such proposal was the "Peace of God," a pronouncement forbidding fighting on the lands of the poor or the church, and protecting the lives of noncombatants. This effort was reinforced by another, known as the "Truce of God," which called for the cessation of hostilities during holy days and weekends. Although these measures were ineffective except when supported by the more powerful lords, they did produce some pauses in the otherwise incessant warfare of medieval Europe.

When not engaged in combat, noblemen were often rehearsing and practicing for it, either in frequent jousts and tourneys (which sometimes were almost as bloody as real battles), or in private military exercises. Hunting was another favorite sport that tested and sharpened their military skills.

At other times, especially in winter, noblemen might be found enjoying the protection and primitive comforts of castle life. High stone walls punctuated by parapets, platforms, and towers, and girded by a deep moat as protection against attack, enclosed the castle proper. Even inside, the narrow, slit windows, thick walls, and deep window seats were reminders of its fortress function. Rooms were cold and damp, with the only light coming from a lamp or flickering torches set in the wall. The center of activities was the great hall where the lord and his retainers, guests, and courtiers held court, ate and drank, and amused themselves with music and merriment. Hand-woven tapestries hung from many of the walls, where they provided both decoration and much-needed warmth. Food, remarkable more for its quantity than its quality, consisted mostly of bread, highly spiced meat of many kinds, and wine. The dress of most of the nobles consisted of homespun woolen clothes, spartan and coarse by later standards. But for the very highest ranks of nobility it was costly and exclusive, consisting of delicately woven woolens from Flanders, crisp linens from Reims, and shining silks from Lucca, Cyprus, or even Damascus. Along with glittering jewelry and a large retinue of retainers, these fine clothes provided appropriate symbols for the class-conscious military elite. They also emphasize the stark contrast between the nobility's refined appearance and their bloody profession.

In the twelfth century, the very exclusiveness of the nobility helped to reduce somewhat the gap between manners and conduct, as the character of warfare was modulated by the ideas of chivalry. The elitism of knighthood gave rise to a code of military courtesy that held the virtues of honor, loyalty, and generosity in as high repute as bravery and prowess. A knight would never take unfair advantage of his adversary, whether by stealth or surprise; he would not strike an unarmed opponent or cruelly take the life of a fallen foe; he would always be loyal to his lord and his friends. Other ingredients of chivalry were added by the church, such as protecting the weak and poor, defending the church, and fighting for righteous causes. The creation of the Knights Templar and the Hospitallers of Saint John reflects the chivalric ideal of uniting arms and faith in a holy cause. But holy or otherwise, warfare continued to be brutal and destructive.

A final stage in late-medieval chivalry was reached in the special role assigned to women who, because of their supposed meekness, compassion, and humility, were esteemed above the highest nobles. Only through his lady could the chivalrous knight receive or reflect these virtues, just as she benefited from his strength and valor. Because it was believed that women were by nature more fragile and defenseless than men, they should be given special courtesy and respect. A knight could serve a lady and in her honor perform deeds of merit and valor, compose songs and poems, and agonize over her beauty and purity. She stood above him in social plane (not only in theory but also in fact, since she was likely the wife of his lord), and by his acts of devotion, service, and unrequited love, he was lifted to a higher plane himself. This notion of courtly love was widely celebrated by the troubadours of southern France and quickly spread to most of Europe. Yet, although the rules of chivalry placed women on the highest pedestal, the realities of medieval life often reduced them to a mundane and humdrum existence. Somewhat freer than her peasant counterpart, the noblewoman was still linked to the fortunes and caprices of her husband, and spent most of her life inside the castle walls. She could inherit a fief, but could not rule it except through her husband. She enjoyed equal rank with him in relation to his vassals and servants, but in relation to him she was subservient and without rights.

Christianity and the Catholic Church

Interwoven into the entire fabric of medieval Europe was the all-important church. After centuries of development and refinement, Christian cosmology pictured a structured and orderly universe, designed, organized, and minutely controlled by a just and omnipotent God. At the center of this universe was the earth, around which, in their respective crystalline spheres, rotated the sun, the planets, and the stars. Not only were the heavenly bodies, in their immutable and eternal orbits, unable to alter or affect their course, but humans also were ordained to a certain status and function while on earth and could do little to change their lot. Any sin brought retribution from God and quick punishment from his temporal instrument, the church.

Even a person's supremely important relationship to God and to life after death was an institutionalized matter rather than an individual concern. People believed in the dual nature of man, composed of matter and spirit, and in the primeval disobediences of Adam and Eve, which had brought all humanity to a fallen state. These things made it impossible to achieve salvation without the redemptive grace of God, and that, according to the theory, was not bestowed outside the organized structure of the church. Therefore, it was necessary for the church not only to provide the means for salvation but also to remind its wayward charges of their duties and responsibilities to God and to each other. For this purpose, creeds that could be recited frequently by the lay members were created, as well as a program of prayers and ceremonies designed to remind the lay members of God and assist them in contemplating and serving him. The channel of divine grace, and thus the key to salvation, was the elaborate sacramental system of the church, consisting of seven recognized sacraments: baptism, confirmation, marriage, ordination, penance, eucharist, and extreme unction.

In addition to its sacramental function, the ordained clergy also provided many educational, philanthropic, and social services to medieval society, and governed the church through an elaborate hierarchy that organized all members of the clergy into a chain of command and responsibility, ranging from the pope at the top through the archbishops and bishops to the widely scattered parish priests at the bottom.

The papacy constituted a special and unique institution at the head of the church. It had gradually evolved through the early centuries of the Christian era to become the powerful papal monarchy of the tenth to thirteenth centuries. By then, its elaborate administrative structure was extensive and efficient. The *curia* was composed of the pope and all of the cardinals functioning as an executive council, the chancellor, treasurer, and other officers; the *chancery*, which handled all papal correspondence; the *datery*, which drafted indulgences, absolutions, and dispensations; the *rota*, which handled legal matters; and the *camera*, the financial department with its continent-wide tax-collecting structure and sophisticated credit system. To extend its administrative arm into all Christendom, the papacy made extensive use of legates and nuncios, who had been delegated the power to represent the pope wherever they were sent.

Monasticism

Paralleling this ecclesiastical structure were the orders of monks and nuns, whose primary function was to provide the means for a more ascetic and personal expression of Christian piety. They were governed by the *regula* (rule) of their respective orders, and took upon themselves formal vows of poverty, chastity, and obedience. Medieval monasticism had evolved through a long history of ascetic expressions since the third century, when early hermits took literally Christ's injunction to "Go and sell that thou hast and give to the poor." With the institutional direction given to it by Saint Benedict in the sixth century, monasticism became one of the most characteristic features of medieval Christianity. The primary function of monks and nuns was to insulate themselves from the sins of the world through prayer, meditation, study, and work, thereby promoting their own and others' salvation. Despite the personal orientation of the monastery, it became one of the most socially useful medieval institutions, providing medical and hospital care for thousands, preserving and transmitting the literary and cultural heritage of the past, giving shelter and sustenance to the weary traveler, and advancing the rudimentary science of agriculture.

Corruption followed institutionalization, however, and monasticism was soon in need of correction and reform. In the tenth century, a widespread revitalization began in France and Germany under the auspices of several reforming abbots who set out to improve the discipline and administration of their respective monasteries and revive the spiritual aims of monasticism. The most famous and effective of these came from the monastery of Cluny, north of Lyon, whose monks stressed service, devotion, piety, and a return to the strict observance of the Benedictine rule. The Cluniac reforms had a revitalizing effect throughout the church. A century later, the Gregorian reform movement infused a new ascetic devotionalism into monastic life, and in the mid-1100s, Saint Bernard of Clairvaux, a remarkably devoted and energetic Cistercian monk, led a partially successful crusade to increase monastic asceticism and promote piety and love, not only in the monasteries but in the church at large as well.

The mendicant (begging) friars, first organized in the thirteenth century, had a somewhat different orientation from the earlier monks. Instead of seclusion in monasteries, they sought to carry the message of Christian love and charity into the world. The first of these orders was the Franciscan, or Friars Minor, founded by Saint Francis of Assisi early in the thirteenth century to care for the needs of the poor and carry the consoling words of Christ to the lowly. It is fitting that Saint Francis was the founder of the friars, for his own life was one of simple devotion to God and unselfish service to humanity. Shortly thereafter, the Castilian priest and student Saint Dominic founded the Dominican order, or Friars Preachers, whose primary mission was to study, learn, and teach the Christian doctrines to all the world. Tightly organized and earnestly devoted to their cause, the Dominicans spread over Europe, teaching not only as mendicant travelers but also soon occupying chairs of philosophy and theology in most universities. Franciscans, also, flocked to the universities and became active upholders of doctrinal purity against heresy.

Medieval Thought and the Universities

The church was the principal educational institution of the Middle Ages. The monasteries, especially, were refuges for medieval scholars, many of whom copied manuscripts and contributed to the preservation of classical as well as Christian learning. Gradually, the church began to establish grammar schools, especially for training future clergymen. The first of these were monastic and cathedral schools, teaching basic reading and writing in Latin and promoting the liberal arts. The cathedral school at Chartres was one of the most famous and attracted young students from all over Europe.

One distinctive and important contribution of the Middle Ages to the modern world is the university. This institution developed in the twelfth and thirteenth centuries out of the earlier cathedral schools as eager young men flocked to the great centers to receive instruction at the feet of famous teachers. In time these student-teacher groups received formal charters from rulers (or the pope) giving them certain guild rights of self-government and immunity from the civil law. This led to many clashes between "town and gown," but was the foundation of one of the distinctive characteristics of the university, its autonomy.

Among the earliest recognized universities of the West were Bologna, where the study of Roman law attracted students from all over Europe; Salamanca, a center of language study as well as theology; Paris, which received its charter from Philip Augustus in the year 1200 and soon became the center of theological studies; and Oxford, founded by a nucleus of students from Paris.

The arts curriculum in most of the universities consisted of the widely accepted seven arts and sciences making up the *trivium* (grammar, rhetoric, and logic) and the *quadrivium* (arithmetic, geometry, astronomy, and music). For the advanced student, the universities offered more specialized training in the fields of theology, medicine, or law. The growth of universities in the late Middle Ages was symptomatic of the expanding horizons of Latin Christendom and of the increased motivation for intellectual growth. By the end of the fifteenth century, no less than eighty reputable universities in Western Europe and several in the east (particularly at Prague and Cracow) were providing advanced education for thousands of people.

The medieval university was also the birthplace of the intellectual movement known as scholasticism, which was intimately associated with the theological and cosmological concepts of the Catholic church. In essence, scholasticism was the attempt by the great schoolmen to reconcile the numerous doctrines of Christian belief with human reason and with the authority of honored philosophers of the past. To the scholastics, it was not a matter of setting up reason as superior to faith, but rather of using reason to make faith more intelligible. They believed that truth is unified and therefore that there should be no real conflict between reason and revelation, between science and faith. All knowledge was of God.

The issue that seemed to attract scholastic debate most was the question of *universals*, that is, whether there exist universal prototypes (or ideas, as Plato called them), of which the visual and tangible objects are mere replicas, or whether "universals" are simply names rather than realities. The question touched on the very nature of being and existence. Those who maintained the reality and independent existence of universals were called Realists; they believed all earthly things were patterned after the universal reality that existed in the mind of God. The Nominalists, on the other hand, insisted that only individual objects are real, and that every object is individual and unique. Any common quality they appear to have is derived only through their common name (hence, the term *nominalism*).

Most medieval scholastics were Realists (universalists) because that seemed to be more compatible with church dogma, yet consistent with philosophy. Saint Anselm, abbot of Bec in Normandy and later archbishop of Canterbury, one of the premier theologians of the medieval church, sought to analyze and prove the reality of God and the truths of faith by reason. In the meantime, Peter Abelard, a teacher of philosophy and theology at the University of Paris (and famous for his unhappy love affair with Heloise), disturbed the scholastic community with his questioning mind and willingness to look at both sides of any doctrine. His greatest work was *Sic et Non* (Yes and No), in which he posed a series of questions about theological issues that he then answered from the church fathers, showing how they disagreed and contradicted one another. Only with Peter Lombard's later *Sentences* was Abelard's writing neutralized and the fathers finally reconciled. *Sentences* soon became the standard textbook of scholastic theology.

The height of medieval scholasticism was reached in the thirteenth century with the great Dominicans Albertus Magnus and Saint Thomas Aquinas. With the introduction of the major works of Aristotle into Christian Europe in the twelfth century, a real danger confronted the church and its scholastic defenders. How long could their convenient marriage of Neo-Platonic philosophy and theology last under the onslaught of competing Aristotelian thought, especially since the latter came to them via Arabic translations, accompanied by the commentaries of Averroës (1126–98) and other prominent Moslem philosophers? Averroës, the "Arabic Aristotle," seemed to contradict important Christian doctrines—immortality, for instance, and the Christian doctrine of creation—and it became the life work of Albertus Magnus and his even more illustrious pupil Thomas Aquinas to prove that even Aristotle could be cast in a Christian mold. Saint Thomas's *Summa Theologica* (Theological Summation) is a tour de force of scholastic reasoning in which the many sharp angles of apparent conflict between natural and revealed thought were removed and a harmonious philosophy emerged.

Despite its later acceptance in the church, however, Thomism did not go unchallenged, either during Aquinas's lifetime or after. Its leading opponents were the Franciscan schoolmen John Duns Scotus and William of Occam. To Duns Scotus, faith and reason were not part of the same order. Many church dogmas, he insisted, could not be proved by reason. They were to be accepted solely on faith and the authority of the church. William of Occam carried the Franciscan fight against Thomism even further, maintaining that philosophy and reason are entirely separated from theology. Reason is unable to demonstrate the validity of many basic doctrines of the church, including the existence of God. According to Occamism, faith does not depend on reason, and science does not rely on religion; they are separate realms with independent methods. Yet both positions, the *via antiqua* of Aquinas and the *via moderna* of Occam, remained within the bounds of Catholic theology, at least until the sixteenth century.

Literature and Art

The most vivid expression of medieval thought and attitudes can be found in the literature, art, and architecture of the late Middle Ages. Above all, the cultural manifestations were a reflection of the powerful influence exerted by the church in daily life and thought. This is not to deny the secular, humanistic, and even pagan strains in medieval culture, but these were generally embodied within the framework of institutionalized Christianity.

Literature

The literature of the Middle Ages discloses the variety of interests represented by medieval culture, expressing itself in diverse forms from Latin devotional books and lives of the saints, morality plays, and chronicles, to secular poetry and satire. The earliest types of vernacular literature to appear in Europe were epic poems, first the Anglo-Saxon *Beowulf*, later the Germanic *Hilderbrandslied* and *Nibelungenlied* (songs of Hilderbrand and the Nibelungen), and the Norse sagas. In the twelfth century, the northern French *chansons de geste* (songs of great deeds), long epic poems portraying the heroic deeds of the nobility in the time of Charlemagne, were composed for the entertainment of the feudal courts. The most famous of these is the *Song of Roland*, recounting the last battle and death of Charlemagne's valiant nephew. Similar to the *chansons de geste* were other poems idealizing chivalric ideals and telling the exploits of people like El Cid, the Spanish warrior-hero, the stories of Tristan and Isolde, Percival and the Holy Grail, and King

WALTHER VON DER VOGEL-WEIDE. *The celebrated poet was born in the Tyrol and spent much time wandering from court to court. Inspired by the first line of one of his poems ("I sat me down upon a stone"), this woodcut shows him deep in contemplation over the meaning of life. (Bild-Archiv der Österreich-ischen Nationalbibliothek, Vienna)*

Arthur and his Knights of the Round Table. The Arthurian stories, drawn mostly from earlier Celtic legends, emphasized heroic deeds and tragic love, and were filled with magic and sorcery.

A more lyrical and sentimental poetry was born in the Provençal civilization of southern France, where the troubadours expressed the ideals of courtly love and composed songs of intimacy and emotion. Provençal was closely related to Catalan, the language of northeastern Spain, and the major literary link between them was the poetry of Raymond Lull, the greatest of the medieval Catalan writers. Lull's finest poems, the *Cant de Ramon* (The Song of Raymond) and the *Desconhout* (Comfortlessness), are both soul-searching, autobiographical troubadour-type songs. In Germany the *Minnesänger* (musical entertainers at court) combined the lyric style of the troubadours and the themes of Celtic romances to produce a variety of love poetry that reached its prime in the beautiful verses of Walther von der Vogelweide. In the meantime, secular allegory was exhaustingly represented in the *Romance of the Rose*, a long poem begun in the thirteenth century by Guillaume de Lorris and subsequently expanded by Jean de Meung. It contained both courtly love themes and the idealization of chivalry but scornfully attacked all forms of intellectual and religious shallowness.

Surpassing all other expressions of medieval literature in profundity and grace is a work of Tuscan poetry written by a Florentine politician in exile. Dante's *Divine Comedy*, a lengthy allegorical poem on human destiny, is the literary masterpiece of the Middle Ages. In his tender, idealized love poems to Beatrice, Dante had revealed a sensitivity and artistry scarcely surpassed by the best lyric poets, and in his political testament *On Monarchy*, he disclosed a sharply perceptive mind. But only in the *Divine Comedy* was his full genius manifested. The vision of Dante's descent into the ever-deepening circles of Hell, guided by the Roman poet Virgil, is among the most descriptive poetry ever written. After seeing the progressively worsening tortures meted out to the unbaptized, the pagans, the lustful and avaricious, heretics, tyrants, blasphemers, usurers, flatterers, hypocrites, deceivers, traitors, and finally to Judas and Brutus, Dante mounts the vales of Hell, enters Purgatory, and eventually is lifted upward to Paradise by the divine Beatrice. Not only are Dante's theological categorizations revealing in terms of medieval doctrine, but his cosmological observations also summarize medieval scientific knowledge. However, the personalization of his allegory makes Dante's *Divine Comedy* something more than the summation of medieval thought. It is one of the true masterpieces of world literature.

In a different category, yet also representing something of a superlative in late-medieval literature, is Geoffrey Chaucer's *Canterbury Tales*. No better illustration could be given of the conjunction of medieval otherworldliness and the mundane existence of daily life. Using the journey of a group of pilgrims to the shrine of Saint Thomas à Becket in

Canterbury as a device to portray the various types of human character, Chaucer went beyond the usual literary characterizations. He satirized his types boldly in order to depict and chastise the society of fourteenth-century England.

Art

Medieval art and architecture, no less than literature, reveal the attitudes and hopes of an age committed to an aesthetic ideal based on the ideology of the Catholic church. As Dante expressed it, "Art is the grandchild of God," a visual glorification of the divine Creator. Fresco artists told the story of Jesus, the Old Testament prophets, and the acts of the apostles on the walls, ceilings, and altars of churches and monasteries. They also showed how medieval people lived and worked as well as worshiped. Most delightful and colorful was the work of the miniaturists, who painted tiny scenes, rich in allegory and symbolism, on vellum and other surfaces. This art form was particularly well developed in beautiful and elaborate manuscript illuminations.

Romanesque architecture developed in the tenth to twelfth centuries out of lingering forms of the Roman basilica. Romanesque was predominantly a religious style used chiefly in building cathedrals, churches, and monasteries. Its principal features are massive stone walls with rounded arches supporting a heavy barrel-vault ceiling, huge piers, and consequently, dimly lit interiors. The exteriors of Romanesque cathedrals feature tall towers and many gracefully arched arcades.

NOTRE DAME DE PARIS. *This view from the south side shows the rose window of the transept, the delicate spire over the intersection of transept and nave, and the graceful flying buttresses. (Courtesy of the French Government Tourist Office)*

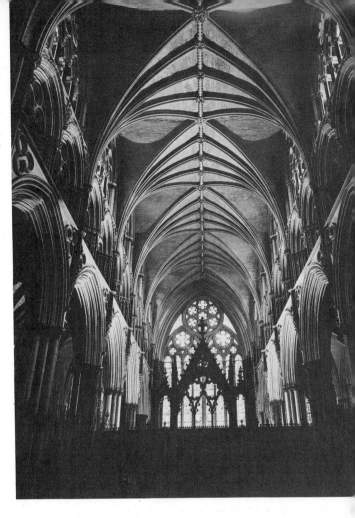

INTERIOR OF LINCOLN CATHEDRAL. *Here can be seen the soaring lines of the pillars and pointed arches along the nave, and the high, rib-vaulted ceiling formed by other intersecting pointed arches. (Courtesy of the British Tourist Authority)*

The full flowering of the high Middle Ages gave birth in the twelfth century to Gothic architecture with its distinctive vertical lines, pointed spires, intricately carved façades, and colorful, light-filled interiors. Abbot Suger of Saint-Denis, just north of Paris, was responsible for introducing the Gothic style in his rebuilding of the royal abbey church of Saint-Denis. From there, the Gothic style spread rapidly throughout northern France and into the rest of Europe. Through the development of ribbed vaulting and the external flying buttress, the medieval builder was able to increase the height of the ceiling and at the same time reduce the width and thickness of the supporting walls, thus giving opportunity for increased lighting through large, beautiful, stained-glass windows. Gothic architecture was not only the most popular building style for cathedrals from the late twelfth to sixteenth centuries, it was also used in many secular structures, such as city halls, parliament buildings, and even private mansions.

Statuary played a prominent role in the Gothic cathedral as a direct or allegorical representation of religious concepts. Seldom, if ever, was its

FAÇADE OF THE COLOGNE CATHEDRAL. *The heavenward thrust of these majestic towers, with their tall, pointed arches and slender statues, reveals the grandeur of late-Gothic architecture. (Courtesy of the German Information Center)*

function purely aesthetic, and it therefore tended to become stereotyped and lifeless in comparison with later Renaissance sculpture; however, there was a noticeable evolution in the realism of Gothic statues in the thirteenth and fourteenth centuries. Above all, Gothic art as revealed in the great cathedrals was an integrated art reflecting the conception of a closed society and universe. Blank walls were abhorred in medieval buildings, so lines, figures, or designs cover every surface. But the lines are not placed randomly or the figures detached. All of the parts form an integrated whole: statues, woodwork, windows, paintings, and music are combined in a single, harmonious composition. All this explains why the Gothic cathedral is the most graphic and majestic expression of medieval art. The upward sweep of the vaults and towers suggest the human struggle to find God; the crowded statuary of saints, angels, and gargoyles depict the spirit world in allegory; and stained-glass windows provide an inspiring display of Bible stories. Even the temporal side of medieval life, with its growing urbanization and intellectual activity, is subtly suggested in many of the pictorial windows and in the graceful flying buttresses. Yet above all, the medieval cathedral was a form of awe-inspiring visual poetry that lifted people's eyes and souls upward toward God. It was a tangible summation of medieval theology as well as art, a Bible in stone and glass.

Science and Technology

The Middle Ages have traditionally been viewed as a period of superstition and ignorance during which no interest was taken nor advancement made in science. That picture is untrue, because far from ignoring nature, many medieval scientists devoted themselves to discovering and understanding the physical world. In the early medieval period, from the sixth to the twelfth centuries, there was little scientific achievement except in the Iberian peninsula, where Arab and Jewish scholars continued to study and comment on natural science. With the increasing intercourse between Islam and the West after the eleventh century, more Arab knowledge and methods were adopted by European culture, along with a recovery of some of the achievements of Greek and Hellenistic science. The introduction of Aristotle into Western thought had as profound an effect on scientific attitudes as it did on theology, for in everyone's mind Aristotle was *the* scientist of the ancient world.

During the thirteenth and fourteenth centuries, several scholars and clerics made significant contributions to scientific thought. One of these was the Oxford theologian, physician, lawyer, and bishop Robert Grosseteste (ca. 1175–1253), whose encyclopedic mind eagerly grappled with physical questions unnoticed by others. He was a strong advocate of experimentation as a proper method of arriving at natural truth, and he believed in scientific investigations. Another Oxford Franciscan was Roger Bacon (1214–94), whose intense interest in all fields of knowledge and bold writings on natural science earned him the jealousy and suspicion of some of his contemporaries. But, with the pope's blessings, he paid little attention to the criticisms of others. His chief contributions were in the fields of optics and methodology.

The most original applications of mathematics to the understanding of physical phenomena were made at the University of Paris by Jean Buridan (ca. 1297–1358) and Nicole Oresme (ca. 1330–82). From their calculations on the phenomenon of falling bodies, Buridan and Oresme contradicted the Aristotelian conception of motion requiring a continuous mover and substituted their own theory of "impetus." Impetus was a characteristic acquired by a body in motion completely independent of the medium through which it traveled or from an outside mover. The theory is not without problems, but the important fact is that people were thinking about physical phenomena and were not always content with the explanations of them given by Aristotle or other authorities. Buridan and Oresme also hypothesized that the earth revolves on its own axis once every twenty-four hours as the Greeks had said, and Oresme put his arguments into writing more than a century and a half before Copernicus did.

The Middle Ages also made great advances in technology. It was, in fact, an age of machines. The most compelling motive for this was probably the relative shortage of manpower, which made the improvement of each person's mechanical advantage a necessity. The masses of human slaves used by the Romans were not available to medieval builders, who were forced to make more efficient use of their limited labor. Hence, the simple wheelbarrow reduced by at least one-half the number of people required to transport building materials for the great cathedrals. Similarly, the use of the screw, especially in conjunction with notched bearings and gears, added a great mechanical advantage to the power of an individual worker. The simple and extremely important crank and cam, which also seem to have been discoveries of the Middle Ages, were quickly adapted to many different applications, from fulling mills (where woolen cloth was shrunk and thickened by moistening, heating, and beating) to papermaking. And the development of the mechanical clock ranks with gunpowder and printing as one of the chief agents in shaping the modern world.

Medieval technological advances in agriculture and transportation were among the most important developments of the era. The adoption of nailed horseshoes and the invention of the horsecollar and tandem harness increased the efficiency and power of the horse, making it the most useful animal of medieval and modern times. The wheeled plow, known in the Roman world but rarely used until it was equipped with an iron-tipped moldboard (for turning the soil rather than merely breaking it), undoubtedly contributed to the development of medieval strip plowing. Improved road-building techniques and the use of lock gates for canals were likewise important in the late-medieval revival of trade. The windmill, known in China, was adopted in medieval

Europe, placed on a more efficient horizontal axis, and used widely for grinding cereal grains. Waterpower was harnessed for operating a multitude of machines.

Many other improvements and adaptations of techniques and products of the Near and Far East were made during the Middle Ages for more efficiently harnessing nature and defeating their enemies. Paper, gunpowder, many medicinal drugs, navigational equipment such as the astrolabe, compass, and sternpost rudder are examples of the rich technological heritage imported from the East and adopted by European civilization during this period.

Eastern Cultures and the Crusades

The transmission of technology is only one indication of the increasing intercourse between Europe and the East in the later Middle Ages. One of the keys to this relationship was the majestic city of Constantinople (formerly Byzantium), capital of the Eastern Roman (Byzantine) Empire, successor to the Roman heritage and to the line of Caesars from the time of Augustus. Here, during the illustrious reign of Justinian in the sixth century, the practices and pronouncements of Roman law were organized and codified, and gradually found their way into western Europe. Byzantine civilization was a composite of Hellenistic Greek culture and language and the oriental Christian religion of Palestine. Byzantium thus became the preserver of important elements of Greek and Latin culture and the intermediary between East and West. In addition to transmitting ancient literary classics, it also added its own distinctive art and technology. Byzantine architecture and mosaic decoration had a particularly great impact on the West, especially on Venice, which had a close commercial relationship with Constantinople. The international Gothic style of painting was likewise strongly influenced by Byzantine art.

Closely connected with the Byzantine Empire were its restless Islamic neighbors to the south and east. From scattered nomadic tribes of the early seventh century, the Arabs had emerged as a powerful and energetic nation, fanatically devoted to the cause of Allah and Mohammed and dedicated to carrying the Islamic religion into all the world. In the course of a hundred years, the entire Middle East, from the Mediterranean to the Indus River, was conquered. The Moslems spread westward, too, overrunning Syria, Palestine, Egypt, and all of North Africa. In A.D. 711 Arabs crossed the Straits of Gibraltar and occupied all but the northern fringe of the Iberian Peninsula. From the Pyrenees to India, Islamic religion and civilization were dominant. Industry, agriculture, and trade were also developed to an unrivaled peak. The silks and glassware of Baghdad were famous for centuries. Damascus and, later, Toledo steel were the finest in the world, expertly tempered and elaborately finished. A Toledo blade was the most coveted possession of the Christian crusaders. Moroccan leather, Persian carpets, tapestries, and brocades, Syrian "damask," and North African drugs were Moslem products eagerly traded on an ever-expanding commercial market.

In science and philosophy, the Arabs had no peers. They made great strides in astronomy, geography, medicine, and mathematics, especially algebra and trigonometry, and adopted the indispensable "Arabic" numerals from India and introduced them to the West. They translated and studied Aristotle and the other Greek philosophers, and made available the commentaries of expert Spanish-Arab scholars. The most renowned of these was the previously discussed Averroës of Córdoba, whose reconciliation of Aristotle and the Koran was only slightly less an accomplishment than Aquinas's harmonization of Aristotle and the Bible. But Averroës, like all Moslem scholars, was less interested in harmonizing science and religion than he was in understanding science itself. To do this, he advocated a "double truth," one for religion and the other for science.

Moslems and Jews found themselves competing and interacting throughout the Middle East and Spain. Since the dispersal of the Palestinian Jews by Rome and the destruction of their temple, Judaism had lost its nationhood and its hereditary priesthood, becoming instead scattered communities led by lay theological scholars (rabbis) who studied their history and Talmudic traditions and encouraged their people to follow the Law and retain their rituals. By the early Middle Ages, Jewish communities were common throughout the Byzantine and Arab empires and had even gone eastward into Persia and beyond. In western Europe, the Jews settled first in Spain, along with the Arabs, and later spread into Italy, then France and Germany (under Charlemagne's protection), and finally into England. They prospered for a time in Europe as leading merchants and bankers.

The greatest flowering of Jewish intellectual life, like that of the Moslems, took place in medieval Spain. Hebrew literature flourished in many Iberian cities, and Jewish contributions to philosophy, medicine, and science were outstanding. One of the leading medieval Talmudic scholars, and the greatest Jewish poet of the Middle Ages, was Judah Halevi of Toledo, a strange combination of mystic, physician, lyric poet, and early Zionist. Then, in the late eleventh and early twelfth centuries, Jewish culture received a setback when two successive invasions by zealous North African Berbers, first the Almoravids and then the Almohads, brought bloodshed and the relentless persecution of Jews (as well as Christians). However, under crown patronage and a good deal of resilience, they were able to weather the storm. By the end of the twelfth century, they had reestablished many of their communities and regained their reputation as the leading scholars, physicians, and financiers in Spain. The commanding figure of Jewish intellectual life in this period was Maimonides (Moses ben Maimon, 1135–1204) of Córdoba. He was not only the greatest Talmudic scholar of the

Middle Ages, he was also skilled in Greek philosophy and science and had a remarkable understanding of Aristotelianism, which he tried hard to reconcile with Judaism. Like Aquinas, Maimonides rejected Averroës's doctrine of double truth, maintaining instead that scientific and religious knowledge were subsumed in a single divine truth.

The Crusades

In the meantime, a change took place in the relationship between Western Christendom and the Islamic East. In the middle of the eleventh century, the Seljuk Turks moved out of the Asiatic steppes into the center of the rich Arabic Empire. Within a few years, they had overrun almost the entire Anatolian peninsula, conquered Syria and Palestine, and taken over much of Egypt. In one respect, however, the conquerors were soon the conquered, for the religion of Mohammed did not retreat. The Turks themselves were converted and became the new champions of Islam in the Levant. Furthermore, the Seljuk masters of the Holy Land had none of the Arab tolerance for Christians and their bothersome pilgrimages to Jerusalem. Soon the Turks began to close down this corridor of encroachment by forbidding Christians from passing through Turkish territory.

The insult to Christendom was obvious. This came at the very time the Cluniac reform movement was heightening Christian devotionalism and religious passion. Throughout the West, especially in France and Lorraine, zealous preachers fanned the embers of piety and "righteous indignation" until the crusading fever burst into flame. Meanwhile, the Turkish victory at Manzikert in 1071 and the subsequent appeal of the Byzantine emperor for aid from the West brought the spirit of crusade to a climax. At the Synod of Clermont in 1095, Pope Urban II called upon Christians to take up the sword against the infidels. His propaganda campaign and the preaching of Peter the Hermit and others stirred thousands of people to action.

The First Crusade was composed of a motley assortment of peasants, villagers, and clerics led by Peter the Hermit and Walter the Penniless. Few of them ever reached the enemy territory, and those who did were almost completely annihilated. The French and Norman knights, totaling some 30,000 under Godfrey of Bouillon, Raymond of Toulouse, and Bohemund of Otranto, fared better, and by the end of 1099, they had succeeded in overrunning most of Syria and Palestine and in capturing Jerusalem. The Latin Kingdom of Jerusalem was established. The victory was hollow, however, for internal troubles had caused the Turks to withdraw most of their western garrisons, leaving only token forces to defend Palestine. When Turkish power revived, especially under Saladin, sultan of Egypt, Palestine was retaken (1187), and the Latin Kingdom of Jerusalem overthrown.

In the meantime, a Second Crusade (1147–49), led by the Holy Roman emperor, Conrad III, and the French king, Louis VII, accomplished little, except to seize a few Greek islands and discredit the movement. But the fall of Jerusalem precipitated a Third Crusade (1189–92), this almost totally secular in motivation and leadership. Sometimes known as the "Kings' Crusade," it was flamboyantly but awkwardly led by three rival rulers: Frederick Barbarossa, Holy Roman emperor; Philip Augustus, king of France; and Richard the Lion-Hearted, king of England. Frederick died en route; Philip returned to France after the capture of Acre; Richard negotiated a truce with the Turks allowing the Christians a coastal strip between Acre and Joppa and access to Jerusalem. During his return to England, Richard was captured and held for a heavy ransom by the Austrians.

Five more major crusades (one of which diverged from its course and sacked Constantinople) and numerous minor ones took place in the next century and a half before the crusading spirit waned in the face of growing domestic troubles and opportunities. Spin-off crusades against the Albigensians of southern France and the Moors in Spain achieved greater military success but increased Christian intolerance of unorthodox views and intensified persecution of non-Christian minorities, especially the Jews.

Out of the crusading movement grew several orders of knighthood. Combining military, chivalric, and religious ideals, some of these orders played important roles in the subsequent political development of Europe: The Knights of the Temple (Templars) were charged with guiding and protecting pilgrims en route to Jerusalem. The Knights of Saint John (or Hospitallers, since they cared for the Hospital of Saint John in Jerusalem) subsequently governed the island of Cyprus, then Rhodes, and finally Malta, where they were known as the Knights of Malta. The Teutonic Knights (Knights of the Hospital of Saint Mary of the Teutons in Jerusalem) later gained the fiefdom of East Prussia, which entangled their history with that of Germany, Poland, and Lithuania. The three Spanish orders of Santiago, Calatrava, and Alcántara were all prominent in the reconquest of Spain from the Moslems.

What other results accrued from these two centuries of crusading activity? Certainly the religious aim was not permanently achieved, although the ruins of crusader castles still dotting the skyline of modern Israel are testimony to the extent of the Christian occupation of the Holy Land. Feudalism did not decline as a result of the Crusades but rather was extended to include, for a short time at least, large parts of Palestine. Yet the Crusades did help accelerate the forces of change that were acting upon European economic and social life. Thousands of Europeans saw for the first time the wealth of the East and used many of the numerous products that appealed to Western eyes and tastes. Perhaps most important of all was the stimulation and advantage given to the commerce and growth of the Italian city-states. Largely as a result of the Crusades, the Byzantine Empire was weakened and practically elimi-

THE CAPTURE OF ANTIOCH. *This painting from the* Chronicle of Jerusalem *was made for Philip the Good of Burgundy in 1467. It depicts the Christian capture of this important stronghold during the First Crusade. (Bild-Archiv der Österreichischen National-bibliothek, Vienna)*

nated as a competitor in the rich Levant trade. Venice became not only "Queen of the Adriatic," but the wealthy mistress of the entire eastern Mediterranean.

The Papacy and the Holy Roman Empire

The launching of the Crusades is only one of many examples of the growing power and prestige of the medieval papacy. For centuries, succeeding popes had claimed universal authority in spiritual and sometimes even temporal matters, but not until late in the Middle Ages were they able to give this claim any degree of continuous credibility. This manifestation fostered chronic rivalry between the papacy and the European princes, especially the Holy Roman emperor, ruler of Germany and central Europe. Princes still made the ecclesiastical appointments in their respective realms, taxed the church when they could, and frequently expropriated church property. These and other points of contact between conflicting political and ecclesiastical jurisdiction made some sort of clash almost inevitable. With the growing strength of papal power and the renewed zeal implanted by periodic reform movements, the impact of the encounter was made more resounding.

The concept of dual jurisdiction of Christendom owes much to the early writings of Saint Augustine, in particular his *City of God*, although the institutionalization of the concept came later. In the tenth century, the ancient idea of a European empire, which had been revived by Charlemagne but collapsed soon after his death in 814, was again renewed by the ambitious German king Otto I (938–73), who had himself crowned Roman Emperor in the West by the pope. This newly formed central European empire (designated "Holy Roman Empire" by Frederick Barbarossa) encompassed most of Germany, the Lowlands, Lotharingia (Lorraine), Switzerland, and Carinthia (southern Austria). By the time of Henry IV (1056–1106), it also included Upper and Lower Burgundy (all the way to the Mediterranean), northern Italy as far south as the Papal States, Austria, Bohemia, and Silesia (the area that is now southwestern Poland). In theory, the emperor and pope wielded the secular and spiritual swords of Christendom, respectively, and conjointly reigned over Europe. But in reality they were contending rivals, each trying to counterbalance and outmaneuver the other with contradicting claims to "universal" authority.

The struggle between the two institutions became bitter when the papacy, under the fiery monk Hildebrand (Pope Gregory VII, 1073–85), launched a vigorous reform program to free the papacy and the church from all lay controls, particularly those imposed by the German emperor. The most dramatic event in the ensuing investiture conflict (the dispute over ecclesiastical versus lay authority in the appointment of church officials) was the famous humiliation at Canossa where, in 1077, Emperor Henry IV stood three days in the snow awaiting the pleasure of the pope to grant him and his kingdom release from the papal interdict that had brought civil war to Germany. Yet Henry's successors were able to restore order and strengthen the empire, which reached something of a zenith under the Hohenstaufen emperors Frederick Babarossa (1152–90) and Frederick II (1220–50).

Nevertheless, by the end of the twelfth century, despite some compromises and frequent political settlements, the problems of lay investiture and other rival claims were still unsolved. Step by step in the early 1200s, the popes ground out victories against the empire until they could boast, not the complete realization of their pretensions, but at least an undisputed triumph in spiritual affairs and in many features of political jurisdiction as well. The thirteenth century has long been recognized as the golden age of the papal monarchy. The pontificate of Innocent III early in the century (1198–1216) marked its zenith. During his rule, Innocent decided between rival candidates for the German crown, dictated terms to warring factions, humbled King John of England, forced Philip Augustus of France to take back a previously divorced wife, and made the crowns of Sicily, Aragon, Portugal, England, Denmark, Hungary, and Poland papal fiefs.

But Innocent's successors were not as fortunate as he, for they found themselves in a power struggle with the most remarkable of all Holy Roman emperors, Frederick II. He was also ruler of Sicily, where he established the most brilliant and enlightened court in Italy. Particularly intrigued by science and mathematics, Frederick founded the University of Naples in 1224. Frederick's despotic but enlightened rule of thirty years in Italy and Germany was the last period of real imperial power for three centuries before the empire was irredeemably shattered by the Protestant Reformation. Although illustrious and active, Frederick's rule failed either to strengthen the empire, enforce imperial control of Italy, or destroy the temporal power of the papacy. When Frederick II died in 1250, an interregnum followed, and the real political strength of the empire never revived. However, neither did that of the papacy. They had each crippled the other. When Pope Boniface VIII (1294–1313) tried to lock horns with the upstart king of France after boldly declaring papal supremacy over all states and rulers, he was humiliated and defeated, and the papacy was removed from Rome.

The Rise of the Feudal Monarchies

One of the distinguishing features of the late Middle Ages was the gradual strengthening of the monarchies of Western Europe. A few common patterns can be distinguished in this process. In most cases, for example, the king was able to gain valuable allies among the middle classes of the rising towns. He could provide them with charters of self-government and exempt them from feudal dues, whereas they in turn could supply him with money in the form of loans and gifts— money that he could then use to hire mercenary soldiers to help control the unruly nobles. Another instrument employed by the feudal monarchs was the representative parliament (called the Estates General in France, the Cortes in Spain). This institution developed out of the king's Great Council, to which members of the lower nobility and representatives of the towns were summoned, along with the grandees (upper nobility), to consult with the king on important matters. This inauguration of broadly representative bodies seems to have begun earliest in Aragon, and its later development in Castile, Burgundy, England, France, and Sicily was highly effective in winning the merchants' support and in reducing the administrative control of the nobles. Moreover, in the long run the monarchs also had time on their side. Except in Germany, feudal custom recognized that fiefs of a vassal dying without legal heirs would *escheat* (revert) to the lord. Thus the royal demesne gradually grew in size during the twelfth to fifteenth centuries as the power of the king increased.

France

The strength of the Capetian monarchs of France grew impressively during the twelfth and thirteenth centuries under the vigorous rule of Philip Augustus (1180–1223), who improved government by establishing a rudimentary civil service; Louis IX (Saint Louis, 1226–70), who

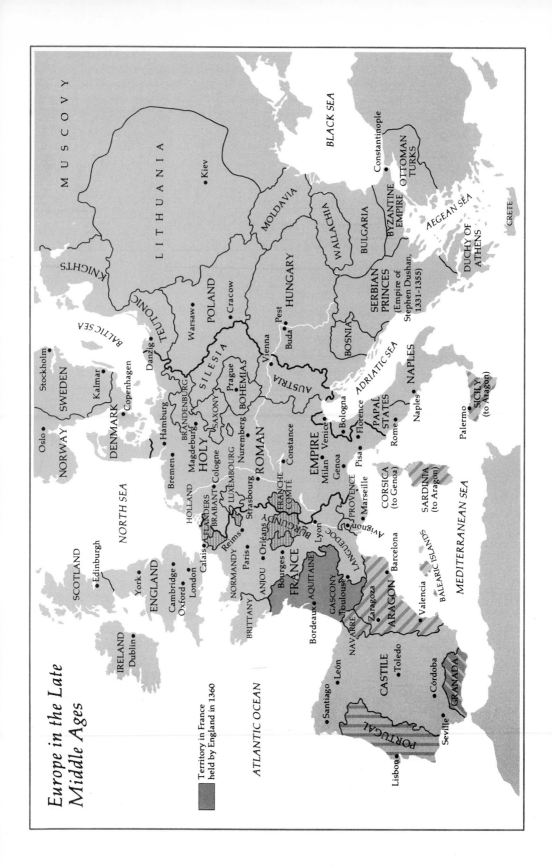

Europe in the Late
Middle Ages

Territory in France
held by England in 1360

MUSCOVY

LITHUANIA

• Kiev

BLACK SEA

Constantinople

OTTOMAN
TURKS

AEGEAN SEA

CRETE

TEUTONIC KNIGHTS

BALTIC SEA

MOLDAVIA

WALLACHIA

BYZANTINE
EMPIRE

Danzig

Warsaw

POLAND

Cracow

HUNGARY

Pest

Buda

Vienna

BOSNIA

BULGARIA

SERBIAN
PRINCES
(Empire of
Stephen Dushan,
1331–1355)

DUCHY OF
ATHENS

Stockholm

SWEDEN

Kalmar

Copenhagen

DENMARK

Hamburg

BRANDENBURG

Magdeburg

SILESIA

Prague

BOHEMIA

SAXONY

AUSTRIA

ADRIATIC SEA

NAPLES

SICILY
(to Aragon)

Oslo

NORWAY

Bremen

HOLLAND

BRABANT

Cologne

LUXEMBOURG

Nuremberg

HOLY

ROMAN

Constance

EMPIRE

Venice

Bologna

Florence

PAPAL
STATES

Rome

Naples

Palermo

NORTH SEA

SCOTLAND

Edinburgh

FLANDERS

Strasbourg

FRANCHE
COMTÉ

BURGUNDY

Milan

Genoa

Pisa

CORSICA
(to Genoa)

SARDINIA
(to Aragon)

MEDITERRANEAN SEA

ENGLAND

York

Cambridge

Oxford

London

Calais

Reims

NORMANDY

Paris

Orléans

Bourges

ANJOU

FRANCE

AQUITAINE

PROVENCE

Marseille

Lyon

LANGUEDOC

Avignon

Barcelona

BALEARIC ISLANDS

IRELAND

Dublin

ATLANTIC OCEAN

BRITTANY

Bordeaux

GASCONY

Toulouse

NAVARRE

Zaragoza

ARAGON

Valencia

CASTILE

León

Toledo

Córdoba

GRANADA

Santiago

PORTUGAL

Lisbon

Seville

extended royal justice and abolished trial by combat; and Philip IV (1285–1314), who greatly expanded royal revenues. By the early fourteenth century, the French crown had realized significant victories over the nobility, the clergy, and even the papacy. Philip IV and his royal agents achieved support from the middle classes after these had been made an active part of the government through representation in the Estates General. The king's success was likewise notable in the subordination of the feudal nobles to royal control and the extension of crown lands to include most of what is now central France.

The success of these rulers in creating a more centralized and efficient administration depended heavily upon the development of more effective legal and financial institutions. The medieval tradition of inherited offices made this a difficult process because so many officials were outside the king's control. Gradually, however, the French crown was able to exercise greater judicial authority, not only in the royal domain but in the outlying counties and duchies as well, as justice slowly became a royal function rather than a private prerogative. This process was aided by the spread of Roman law and the creation of professional judges trained in that law. The apex of the judicial structure was the *Parlement de Paris,* which clarified and extended the royal legal jurisdiction. At the same time, crown income was increased by the establishment of the Chamber of Accounts, and by tightening control of tax collecting—a continuing headache for French rulers. Despite some immediate gains from confiscated wealth, Philip IV's expulsion of the Jews, Italian bankers, and the Knights Templar had very costly long-range results.

England

The development of the English state after the Norman invasion in 1066 paralleled that of France in some respects, but in many others it was unique. The insular position of England and the initial advantage held by the crown following the Norman conquest gave feudalism in England a more centralized structure to begin with than it had on the continent. William the Conqueror (1066–87) was able to exercise greater control over the English lords than could his counterpart over the French nobility. Just as on the continent, however, the growth of government was not a uniform and continuous evolution toward centralization and stronger rule. Under the early Norman-Angevin rulers, royal power was greatly strengthened; however, it was later lost or seriously reduced by weak and incompetent kings. An example of such a setback was the baronial uprising in 1215 that forced King John to sign the Magna Carta. This document was a feudal instrument demanding protection of the medieval customs, freedoms, and rights of the nobles against the encroachments of the king. It was not until centuries later that the Magna Carta was interpreted to include the rights of the common people of England against an overly powerful monarch and aristocratic court. In the Middle Ages, the English commoner usually found the king's rule less oppressive than that of the barons.

The largest steps toward a well-organized and stable government were taken by Henry II (1154–89) and Edward I (1272–1307). As duke of Normandy, count of Anjou (including Maine and Poitou), duke of Brittany, and duke of Aquitaine and Gascony in France, Henry II was already a powerful ruler when he became king of England in 1154. The thirty-five years of his eventful reign saw the increase of royal power through the extension and improvement of royal legal jurisdiction, by the exercise of controls over the church, and through the institution of more efficient organs of government. Especially important were his contributions to English law, particularly the introduction of the jury system into royal justice and the uniform enforcement of the common law. Under his sons Richard and John, however, some of the continental territories of the crown were lost and much of its political strength dissipated. Under Henry III (1216–72), England returned to a state of feudalism, as the barons ignored or tried to control the crown while they engaged in their incessant private wars.

Royal power was once more asserted under the capable rule of Edward I, who brought the Welsh under control, subdued the Scottish lowlands, and regained some of the territories and allegiances lost by his father. Edward's Model Parliament of 1295 had representatives from the middle classes as well as the upper and was summoned to gain the support of these people by making their representatives part of the government. This parliament (as earlier ones of the 1260s and 1270s) had little law-making power, but it did discuss the items put before it by the king, and the members voiced their opinions on many matters of state. In the next two centuries, parliamentary influence and importance grew, especially in the fields of revenue and lawmaking.

The Hundred Years' War

The development of France and England toward unified states was partially arrested in the fourteenth and early fifteenth centuries by the disruptive Hundred Years' War. Beginning in 1337 over the conflicting claims of the two monarchs to the territories of Gascony, Aquitaine, and Flanders, this war—or series of campaigns and encounters stretching over a period of more than a century—brought havoc and dislocation to both countries, especially France. The first phase of the erratic wars saw the French countryside ravaged, because the Valois monarchs (cousins of the direct Capetian line that had come to an end in 1328) were unable to mobilize adequate strength from their feudal estates. In the battle of Crécy (1346) the flower of the French nobility was cut down by the English archers. That disastrous defeat was repeated in 1356 at Poitiers when again the French knights were devastated by the smaller forces of Edward, the Black Prince (illustrious son of the English king). In this encounter the French king himself was captured and four years later signed the Treaty of Brétigny, giving the English complete sovereignty over the provinces of Aquitaine and Gascony and the city of Calais.

During the next two decades, the tide gradually turned as the new French king Charles the Wise (1364–80) rebuilt fallen castles and city walls and created companies of professional soldiers. His ablest commander, Bertrand du Guesclin, carried the attack to the English in the 1370s, and through the employment of "guerilla warfare" recaptured much of the territory previously lost. In 1396 a twenty-year truce was signed. But again France fell on bad times, beginning with the annihilation of a large force of French knights at Nicopolis, in Bulgaria, while on a crusade to free Hungary from the Turks. At home, the raucous

THE HUNDRED YEARS' WAR. *The Battle of Crécy is depicted in this fifteenth-century engraving from Froissart's* Chronicles. *The English archers are represented at lower right. At left the French knights have begun to retreat. (Courtesy of Brigham Young University Special Collections Library)*

rivalries of its most powerful nobles—the dukes of Anjou, Berry, Burgundy, and Orléans—completely undermined the power of the royal government. In the ensuing civil struggles between the Burgundians (the duke of Burgundy, John the Fearless, and his supporters) and the Armagnacs (followers of the duke of Orléans and his vassals) both sides sought foreign allies. The alliance between Burgundy and the English had an important impact on the next phase of the war.

In 1415, Henry V (1413–22) of England crossed the channel at the head of a motley army, to renew the English claim to the throne of France. As he had predicted, he defeated the French army in a decisive battle at Agincourt and moved southward toward the heartland of France. Five years later, most of the territory north of the Loire, plus Gascony in the southwest, was controlled by the English or their Burgundian allies. Charles, the lethargic dauphin of France, known as the "King of Bourges" because of his reluctance to assert his royal claim beyond that city's walls, appeared content to pass his days at court, while the English declared Henry VI (1422–61) king of France. In 1428 they laid siege to Orléans, the gateway to central France.

At that crucial moment, Joan of Arc, a hitherto unknown peasant girl from Domrémy in Lorraine, appeared at the French court announcing that she had spoken with the saints and had been called to deliver France from its enemies. The pseudo-king and most of his courtiers thought she was a hoax, but her persistence and unaccountable acts of clairvoyance persuaded Charles to give her a try. Almost miraculously she helped break the siege of Orléans and turned the tide of the war. In 1429, with the Maid of Orléans at his side, Charles VII was crowned king of France at Rheims. Shortly thereafter, Joan of Arc was captured by Burgundian soldiers who ransomed her to the English. She was subsequently tried and convicted of heresy by a packed ecclesiastical court. Although she recanted her heresy (of speaking with angels), she again relapsed and was burned at the stake in Rouen in 1431. Yet the momentum of her courage carried her comrades to victory. By 1453 the English had been driven from all of France except Calais and two channel islands, and the French monarch was on the road toward achieving sovereign power in an expanded and much more consolidated territorial state.

In England the immediate result of the Hundred Years' War was internal chaos. The confusion caused by the war itself (and particularly by the defeat), the dislocation of commerce with Flanders, and the renewed ambitions of the disrupted nobility, all helped to bring disorder to England. In the interlude known as the Wars of the Roses, petty and ambitious nobles joined with the rival royal families of Lancaster and York to turn central and northern England into a battleground of civil war. Not until the victory of Henry Tudor at Bosworth Field in 1485 did the civil wars end and England resume its progress toward a more orderly rule.

Spain

By the end of the fifteenth century, Spain, like her northern neighbors, was emerging as a strong territorial state. The medieval history of the Iberian peninsula is part of the history of Islam and of the Moslem impact on Latin Christendom. From 711 until 1492, Moslems ruled parts or most of Spain. The height of Arab domination was under the Omayyad dynasty from the mid-eighth to the mid-eleventh centuries and reached its zenith during the caliphate of Abd-al-Rahman III (912–61). Córdoba became the greatest city of Europe with a population of half a million. Contemporaries tell of its beautiful palaces, mosques, libraries, homes, patios, gardens, and fountains. It was also the European center of science and learning. After the Amirid dictatorship (976–1009), the caliphate broke up into petty splinter states (*taifas*), which soon fell before the onslaught of the Almoravids from North Africa in 1086.

Meanwhile, from the mid-eighth to the mid-thirteenth centuries, the Christians carried out intermittent warfare against the Moslems and the excessive penetration of Islamic culture and religion. This *reconquista* was the determining factor in shaping Spanish institutions and attitudes for many centuries. The free-lance Christian warriors gradually pushed south from their tiny saddleback strongholds in Asturias and Navarre, capturing many cities and Arab strongholds. After 1063 the peninsula was declared an area of holy crusade, and the reconquest took on new intensity. Toledo fell to the Christians in 1086, Valencia in 1094, Córdoba in 1236, and Seville in 1248. Earlier temporary fiefs became new, independent kingdoms—Galicia, Asturias, León, Castile, Aragon, and Valencia—which in turn merged into the larger kingdoms of Portugal, Castile, and Aragon. After 1340 all that remained of the once-powerful Arab caliphate was the small and isolated kingdom of Granada.

In 1474 an unpredicted, but not unusual, turn of affairs made the political consolidation of the peninsula a possibility. In that year Enrique IV, king of Castile, died, leaving his daughter, whom he had married to the heir of Portugal, to succeed him. This compact might have led to the consolidation of Castile and Portugal had not Enrique's stepsister Isabel seized the Castilian throne instead, with the support of the Castilian nobles. The importance of this act lay not only in bringing Isabel to the throne but in the sudden conjunction of Castile and Aragon, due to Isabel's previous marriage to Ferdinand, heir to the throne of Aragon. The marital union of the two largest Iberian kingdoms did not bring the immediate creation of a Spanish state, but it did mark the beginning of a union that in the next two centuries had a momentous effect not only upon Spain but upon the history of Europe and the world.

In the meantime, unique political and economic developments in fourteenth- and fifteenth-century Italy combined with a growing intellectual activity there to produce a new cultural awakening of unparalleled proportions, which we will take up in succeeding chapters.

Suggestions for Further Reading

GENERAL

Among the many good general histories of medieval Europe, I prefer Robert S. Hoyt and Stanley Chodorow, *Europe in the Middle Ages*, 3rd ed. (New York, 1976). It is comprehensive, clearly written, and interesting. Other useful surveys are Norman F. Cantor, *Medieval History: The Life and Death of a Civilization* (New York, 1963); Bryce D. Lyon, *The High Middle Ages* (New York, 1964); John H. Mundy, *Europe in the High Middle Ages, 1150–1309* (London and New York, 1973); and Daniel Waley, *Later Medieval Europe: From St. Louis to Luther*, 2nd ed. (London, 1975). Norman Zacour, *An Introduction to Medieval Institutions* (New York, 1969) views the age through its economic, political, religious and educational institutions. Marc Bloch's 2-volume *Feudal Society*, 2nd ed. (Chicago, 1964) is a classic study by the great French social historian. Another, brief classic is Eileen Power, *Medieval Women* (New York, 1976). Morris Bishop, *The Horizon Book of the Middle Ages* (New York, 1968) is both vividly written and extensively illustrated.

ECONOMIC LIFE ON THE MANOR AND IN THE TOWNS

Georges Duby, *Rural Economy and Country Life in the Medieval West*, tr. by Cynthia Postan (Columbia, 1968) contains a wealth of information. M. M. Postan, *Essays on Medieval Agriculture and General Problems of Medieval Economy* (Cambridge, 1973) and *Medieval Trade and Finance* (Cambridge, 1973) are brilliant works by a great expert. Also see Howard Adelson, *Medieval Commerce* (Princeton, 1962); Carlo Cipolla (ed.), *The Fontana Economic History of Europe: Vol. I, The Middle Ages* (London, 1972); and Robert S. Lopez, *The Commercial Revolution in the Middle Ages, 950–1350* (New York, 1976). Fritz Rorig, *The Medieval Town* (London, 1967) is especially informative on German towns, while Harry A. Miskimin, et al. (eds.), *The Medieval City* (New Haven, 1977) is a gold mine of facts and interpretation. J. C. Russell, *Regions and Cities in Late Medieval Europe* (London, 1972) is a fairly reliable demographic guide.

FEUDALISM AND THE MEDIEVAL CHURCH

François L. Ganshof's *Feudalism*, tr. by Philip Grierson, 2nd ed. (New York, 1961) is a brief, basic guide. Joseph Strayer's *Feudalism* (Princeton, 1965) is another short summary, with documents. More detailed is Guy Fourquin, *Lordship and Feudalism in the Middle Ages*, tr. by Iris and A. L. Lytton Sells (New York, 1976). R. W. Southern, *Western Society and the Church in the Middle Ages* (Penguin, 1970) is a good general survey, as is J. B. Russell, *A History of Medieval Christianity* (New York, 1968). These can be supplemented with Roland H. Bainton's short text and documents in *The Medieval Church* (Princeton, 1962) and C.N.L. Brooke, *Medieval Church and Society: Collected Essays* (London, 1971). Stanley Chodorow, *Christian Political Theory and Church Politics in the Mid-Twelfth Century* (Berkeley, 1972) is an important study. See also W. L. Wakefield and A. D. Evans, *Heresies of the High Middle Ages* (New York, 1969).

MEDIEVAL THOUGHT AND LITERATURE

A basic account of medieval thought is Frederick Artz, *The Mind of the Middle Ages*, 3rd ed. (New York, 1962). David Knowles, *The Evolution of Medieval Thought* (New York, 1962) is especially good on religious thought. John B. Morrall, *Political Thought in Medieval Times* (London, 1962), although brief, is remarkably penetrating. Another superb study is John W. Baldwin, *The Scholastic Culture of the Middle Ages* (Lexington, 1971), which briefly shows the relationship between faith and reason. Alan B. Cobban, *The Medieval Universities* (London, 1975) describes the development and organization of the schools.

For an introduction to medieval literature see C. S. Lewis, *The Discarded Image: An Introduction to Medieval and Renaissance Literature* (Cambridge, 1964). Another standard is W.T.H. Jackson, *Medieval Literature: A History and a Guide* (New York, 1966). F. P. Pickering, *Literature and Art in the Middle Ages* (Coral Gables, 1970) is heavy reading but a valuable study showing the interrelations between literature and art. It draws especially from German sources. Roger Boase, *The Troubadour Revival* (London, 1978), focuses on late-medieval Spain.

ART, SCIENCE AND TECHNOLOGY

William R. Lethaby, *Medieval Art, from the Peace of the Church to the Eve of the Renaissance* (New York, 1950, 1969), and Norris K. Smith, *Medieval Art: An Introduction to the Art and Architecture of Europe* (Dubuque, 1967) are good introductions. Also Andrew Martindale, *Gothic Art from the Twelfth to the Fifteenth Century* (London, 1967). The highlight of gothic architecture may be seen in Otto von Simson, *The Gothic Cathedral* (New York, 1964), and the splendid *Horizon Book of Great Cathedrals* (New York, 1968). Sacheverell Sitwell, *Gothic Europe* (New York, 1969) is another richly illustrated study of gothic architecture. In a class by itself is Henry Adams *Mont-Saint-Michel and Chartres* (Many editions since 1913), a vivid and brilliant insight into medieval life as seen through the great cathedrals.

E. Grant, *Physical Science in the Middle Ages* (New York, 1970), and A. C. Crombie, *Robert Grosseteste and the Origins of Experimental Method* (New York, 1963) are important works on medieval science. Lynn White, Jr., *Medieval Technology and Social Change* (Oxford, 1962) convincingly demonstrates that medieval technology was more advanced than is usually recognized. Also see his collected essays in *Medieval Religion and Technology* (Berkeley, 1978). Jean Gimpel goes even further in *The Medieval Machine: The Industrial Revolution of the Middle Ages* (New York, 1976), a provocative interpretation that makes some pretty bold statements. His *The Cathedral Builders* (New York, 1961) is stimulating, too.

EASTERN CULTURES AND THE CRUSADES

A good, brief summary of Byzantine civilization is D. A. Miller, *The Byzantine Tradition* (New York, 1966). Donald M. Nicol, *Church and Society in the Last Centuries of Byzantium* (New York, 1979) examines the contributions of Byzantium in the thirteenth to the fifteenth centuries and discusses its intellectual recovery and reawakening after the devastating Fourth Crusade. David T. Rice, *Art of the Byzantine Era* (New York, 1963) is instructive. On the medieval Arab culture see J. J. Saunders, *A History of Medieval Islam* (London, 1978); W. Montgomery Watt, *The Influence of Islam on Medieval Europe* (New York, 1972); and most recently, Norman Daniel, *The Arabs and Medieval Europe* (London, 1979).

Literature on the Crusades is vast. A compact account is Joshua Prawer, *The World of the Crusades* (London, 1972), with illustrations. More challenging is Hans E. Mayer, *The Crusades,* tr. by John Gillingham (London, 1972). See also Joseph R. Strayer, *The Albigensian Crusade* (New York, 1971); Donald E. Queller, *The Fourth Crusade* (Philadelphia, 1978); and Aziz S. Atiya's classic *Crusade, Commerce and Culture* (New York, 1966). On the most colorful of the kingly crusaders see John Gillingham, *Richard the Lionheart* (London, 1978).

THE PAPAL MONARCHY AND THE HOLY ROMAN EMPIRE

Geoffrey Barraclough, *The Medieval Papacy* (New York, 1968), in the History of European Civilization Library, is a clear and stimulating summary of the growth of papal power. Peter Partner, *The Lands of St. Peter: The Papal State in the Middle Ages and the Early Renaissance* (Berkeley, 1972) is particularly informative on papal government and administration. Geoffrey Barraclough's *Origins of Modern Germany*, 2nd ed. (New York, 1963) is a basic account of the medieval empire. Karl Hampe, *Germany under the Salian and Hohenstaufen Emperors,* tr. by Ralph Bennett (Totowa, 1974), is a German classic. T. C. Van Cleve, *The Emperor Frederick II of Hohenstaufen* (Oxford, 1972) is also impressive.

THE FEUDAL MONARCHIES

The standard study is Charles Petit-Dutaillis, *The Feudal Monarchy in France and England from the Tenth to the Thirteenth Century*, 2nd ed., tr. by E. D. Hunt (New York, 1964). See also Robert Fawtier, *The Capetian Kings of France*, 2nd ed. (London, 1962), and G.W.S. Barrow, *Feudal Britain* (London, 1961). William Woods, *England in the Age of Chaucer* (London, 1976) is short and lucid. On the Hundred Years' War, Edouard Perroy, *The Hundred Years War,* tr. by W. B. Wells (London, 1951) is old but still the best overall guide. Desmond Seward, *The Hundred Years War: The English in France, 1337–1453* (New York, 1978) is a well-written recent introduction intended for the general reader. Alfred H. Burne, *The Agincourt War: A Military History of the Latter Part of the Hundred Years War, from 1369 to 1453* (Westport, 1976) is first rate, and Alan Lloyd, *The Hundred Years War* (London, 1977) has some very good illustrations. Edward Lucie-Smith, *Joan of Arc* (London, 1976) takes a fresh look at the Maid of Orléans. Gabriel Jackson, *The Making of Medieval Spain* (New York, 1972) is brief, clear, and well-illustrated. Angus Mackay, *Spain in the Middle Ages: From Frontier to Empire, 1000–1500* (London, 1977) has extensive notes. The most detailed and scholarly accounts are Joseph F. O'Callaghan, *A History of Medieval Spain* (Ithaca, 1975), and J. N. Hillgarth, *The Spanish Kingdoms, 1250–1516: Vol. I, 1250–1410* (New York, 1976).

CHAPTER TWO

The Italian City-States

HE MEDITERRANEAN LOCATION of the Italian peninsula, with its unique Roman heritage, along with the greater number and size of its cities and the relative weakness and separation of its landed nobility, all helped produce a political experience in Italy that was very different from the feudalism of northern Europe. As Italian cities became the beneficiaries of the growing East-West trade from the thirteenth century on, political power came to be held more and more by successful merchant families who were engaged in commercial activity. This process took place gradually and differed widely in various parts of the peninsula, but it emphasizes the unique position of Italy and the distinct nature of its political development.

The Political Framework of Late-Medieval Italy

Despite its mountainous terrain and relatively poor soil, the southern half of the Italian peninsula is the area with the richest ancient past. The Greeks colonized the shores of southeastern Italy as early as the seventh century B.C., and down to the days of the Roman Emperor Augustus, this region spoke more Greek than Latin. With the exception of Rome itself, the greatest cities, those possessing the highest and most diversified culture, were located in the south. Sicily was the principal granary of the Roman Empire, and the coastal towns of the Italian heel from Bari to Taranto were cosmopolitan commercial centers. In the ninth century, Sicily fell to Islam and its culture took on an Arab flavor, but two hundred years later it had lapsed into political anarchy. Soon, however, both the island and mainland were overrun by the Normans, whose conquest spread as far north as Rome. The Normans overlaid existing institutions with a distinctive Norman feudalism—more centralized than the feudalism of most of Europe—establishing for the first time a viable monarchy capable of bringing law and order to the region. Late in the twelfth century, Sicily fell under the influence of the Hohenstaufens of Germany when Emperor Henry VI married the heiress to the Sicilian throne. Under the benevolent despotism of Frederick II (1215–50), Sicily became highly centralized, trade was regulated and increased, Roman law was applied and enforced, and Palermo became, for the moment, the cultural center of Italy.

But southern Italy still lacked homogeneity, was economically poor, and was exploited by its rulers. After Frederick II's death and during the ensuing Interregnum, most of Italy repudiated its ties to the Holy Roman Empire and rejected the claims of subsequent German emperors to its overlordship. The Kingdom of the Two Sicilies (Naples and Sicily) was seized by Charles of Anjou, third son of the king of France, who ruled recklessly until his bloody overthrow on Easter, 1282, in the so-called Sicilian Vespers. This upheaval not only terminated Charles's rule but also replaced French domination with Aragonese, as first Sicily and then Naples passed to the king of Aragon. During the Renaissance, Naples was in the backwaters of the Italian cultural stream, the capital of a large feudal estate providing an arena for the reckless display of the aristocracy and a burial ground for the destitute peasants who struggled hopelessly against nature and the nobility.

Immediately to the north of Naples lay the Papal States, composed of numerous communities of diverse origins and varied political structures, stretching across the Italian boot from Rome to just north of Pescara and then northward along the eastern slopes of the Apennines to Ravenna and Bologna. The position of Rome was unique in Italian history. Although the effective political control of the Papal States was much smaller than its theoretical dominion, the real power of Rome lay in its international influence as the ecclesiastical seat of Christendom. In the late Middle Ages, La Campagna, to the south of the Tiber River, was largely a malarial marsh, and the rest of the states—with the exception of Ancona and some of the Adriatic coast—were mountainous and uncontrollable. The towns in Umbria and the Romagna were highly civilized but were left predominantly independent of papal control until the end of the fifteenth century. Under the illustrious house of Montefeltro, the duchy of Urbino became the most cultured center of Renaissance life within the Roman sphere. Bologna was another papal fief that, because of its location at the crossroads of northern Italian trade, became a vital key in the political struggles of Renaissance Italy.

In the fifteenth century, papal policy toward its fiefs became increasingly important, and the Roman role in Italian politics grew rapidly under Sixtus IV (1471–84) and his successors. Renaissance popes did not hesitate to use their northeastern territories as pawns in the violent power struggles in Italy, just as their medieval predecessors had done in the chronic rivalry with the empire, employing the neighboring Lombard cities to the north as battering rams against successive German, French, and Venetian enemies.

Adjoining the Papal States on the north and west is Tuscany, cradled between the curving Apennines and the Tyrrhenian Sea. Although hilly, Tuscany is not so rugged that the fertile slopes cannot be cultivated intensively. The topography provided natural frontiers for hundreds of communities and larger cities without preventing easy communication among them. Here the distinctive Renaissance city-state, with its chaotic zeal for self-government and equally energetic rivalry with its neighbors, developed to the fullest. The cities of Tuscany were among the earliest to achieve economic prosperity and some political importance. The leaders here were Pisa, strategically located near the mouth of the Arno; Lucca, important both industrially and politically; Florence, as aggressive in championing Florentine democracy as in gaining wealth; and Siena, proud and independent rival of Florence in the political struggles of the region.

The Ligurian coast, northward from Tuscany, was dominated by the wealthy commercial center and maritime republic of Genoa. Further toward the northwest lay the duchy of Savoy, occupying the rugged Alpine passes into France and the Piedmont regions directly northwest of Genoa. Here, too, was the marquisate of Saluzzo, a territory of almost continual dispute between the dukes of Savoy and the counts of Provence, later inherited by the king of France. The ambitious dukes of Savoy played an important political and military role in the sixteenth century, but Savoy belonged more to Europe than to Italy. Not until three centuries later, as kings of Sardinia-Piedmont, did the Savoyard dynasty occupy center stage as the principal creator of a united Italy.

The richly variegated plains of Lombardy, referred to in modern times as the Po Valley, encompass the northern quarter of Italy from the Apennines to the majestic Alps. Here is the only extensive flatland of the entire peninsula and the richest and deepest soil of southern Europe. The cities of Lombardy are old and numerous, and were among the earliest to assert and win their independence from the Empire and from the landed magnates. They were also the first to lose their political freedoms in the thirteenth and fourteenth centuries, as their very independence gave rise to political tyrants and military adventurers. Here are located the important cities of Milan, the largest city in Italy and second only to Venice in wealth; neighboring Pavia, important as one of the political capitals of the Visconti dukes of Milan; Verona, base of the fierce thirteenth-century tyrant Ezzelino da Romano and later ruled by

Italy in the time of the Medici

D—Duchy   K—Kingdom

M—Marquisate   R—Republic

D. OF SAVOY

D. OF MILAN

R. OF VENICE

Trieste

Turin

Milan

Verona

Padua

Venice

M. OF MANTUA

Adige R.

Pavia

Po R.

M. OF MONTFERRAT

M. OF SALLUZZO

Parma

Genoa

ISTRIA (to Venice)

D. OF FERRARA

D. OF MODENA

Bologna

EMILIA

Ravenna

R. OF GENOA

ROMAGNA

DALMATIA (to Venice)

R. OF LUCCA

Pisa

Arno R.

Florence

R. OF FLORENCE

Urbino

Ancona

Siena

THE MARCHES

ADRIATIC SEA

R. OF SIENA

Perugia

UMBRIA

ELBA

PAPAL STATES

Pescara

CORSICA (to Genoa)

Tiber R.

Rome

Naples

K. OF NAPLES (to Aragon)

Bari

SARDINIA (to Aragon)

Salerno

Taranto

TYRRHENIAN SEA

MEDITERRANEAN SEA

Palermo

K. OF SICILY (to Aragon)

the della Scala family; Mantua, strategically located on the Mincio River draining Lake Garda, becoming, under the benevolent and enlightened rule of the Gonzaga lords, a leader of Renaissance refinement and culture; Ferrara and Modena, squeezed between the Papal States and the expansive powers of Venice and Milan, governed flamboyantly by the Este family; and Padua, precariously close to Venice but able to maintain an independent republic until the fourteenth century when Jacopo di Carrara became its master.

Just off shore, on the Adriatic side of Lombardy, lay the majestic island empire of Venice, unique in almost every way yet as typically Renaissance as any city in Italy. Venetian wealth and glory were the result of her marriage to the sea, as Venetian galleys plied the Adriatic and Mediterranean from Venice to Constantinople and from Alexandria to the Gates of Hercules.

The Rise of the City-States

The effects of two centuries of papal-imperial rivalry cut deeply into Italian political life. The rival parties of *Guelf* (supporters of the pope) and *Ghibelline* (advocates of the emperor) continued to contend fanatically with each other over the slightest provocation long after the invading German armies had retreated across the Alps. By the fourteenth century, the party names had ceased to have any real connection with papal or imperial ideologies or with any particular cause, but their rivalries and wars went on. Many Ghibelline towns were Ghibelline only because their closest rivals were Guelf. Dante spent the last twenty years of his life in exile from his Florentine *patria* (homeland) as a result of such party feuds.

Out of these endless struggles, and in conjunction with the great economic transformations that were taking place, emerged a new form of political association in Italy, the independent secular commune, now more commonly referred to as the *city-state*. As commerce, manufacturing, and banking activities increased in central and northern Italy, so did the size and importance of urban populations and with them the strength of municipal governments. These thriving cities of Tuscany, Umbria, and Lombardy were unlike the commercial towns of France, the Netherlands, and England, which were also growing in number and importance. Nor were they southern replicas of the free imperial cities of Germany, whose political jurisdiction usually extended to the city walls and no further. With their greater strength and sounder economic base, the Italian cities not only consolidated their internal political power but also expanded outward into the country in all directions, competing with neighboring cities for jurisdiction over the outlying lands.

The institutional development and social structure of such Italian communes varied widely, but it is possible to discern some general trends in their evolution. In much of Europe, feudalism gradually gave way to larger territorial states as the feudal kings were able to enlarge and control their royal *demesnes* (domains). But in the Italian peninsula where feudalism was always much weaker (except in the south), it was replaced by the city-states. In this process, the landed nobles lost their political preeminence to the upper middle classes, who dominated the political as well as economic life of the cities. In some cases, quite democratic forms of government emerged at an early date with control of the city being vested in popularly elected councils and law enforcement handled by representatives of the people. In other communes, smaller merchant oligarchies determined the form and policies of government. In only a few instances were the nobles able to maintain their control, although in many Lombard communes they did exercise considerable influence through alliance with the wealthy bourgeoisie (*popolo grosso*, the "fat people"). In cities where there was more democracy, the "little people" (*popolo minuto*), craftsmen, shopkeepers, and the lower middle classes in general also had political input. But even there, the bottom levels of society—rural peasants and urban laborers—had no political rights at all.

Personal and party feuds, bloody war between Guelfs and Ghibellines, and civil strife among the classes of each town eventually brought about a further mutation in the city-state governments of early Renaissance Italy. To bring order out of the civil chaos and maintain a greater degree of governmental stability, a disinterested person from another city was frequently invited to assume temporary power. The authority of this *podestà* was originally carefully circumscribed, but in many instances he was gradually given greater authority over longer periods of time, in some cases eventually becoming ruler for life. In some city-states, influential local lords seized power and ruled until they were overthrown by other leaders. In many cases, the people themselves supported these lords and legitimized their rule through popular consent. All of which emphasizes the fact that Renaissance governments in Italy varied widely in form, effectiveness, and longevity.

The Governments of Florence, Venice, and Milan

Because of their importance during the Renaissance, it will be useful to examine in more detail the distinctive political structures of the three wealthiest and most influential city-states—Florence, Venice, and Milan—each representing a different type of government flourishing at that time.

News of the Sicilian Vespers frightened the wealthy burghers of Florence into making certain constitutional changes in their government that would ensure their supremacy over the restless nobles. The former magistry was superseded by a committee, known as the

Signoria, composed of six *priors* (later eight) chosen from a list compiled from the membership of the seven great guilds of Florence, the *arti maggiori.* These major guilds were the cloth merchants; woolen cloth dealers; silk manufacturers; bankers, judges, and notaries; doctors and apothecaries; and furriers. The six men comprising the *Signoria* were elected to office for terms of two months each, during which time they lived and took their meals in the Palazzo della Signoria. During the next ten years, some of the lesser guilds (*arti minori*), composed of craftsmen and small shopkeepers, were also given the right to share in the operation of government.

In 1293 another step was taken in the development of the Florentine republic with the promulgation of the Ordinances of Justice, aimed specifically at the nobles, who were now required to swear a special oath to the new government and post a bond against public disturbances of the peace. Furthermore, noblemen could not qualify for political office since membership in a guild was not only required but also candidates for office had to practice the profession of the guild to which they belonged. In addition, the *Signoria* was expanded by the addition of another member, known as the standard-bearer of justice (*Gonfaloniere della Giustizia*), who was charged specifically with the enforcement of the ordinances and maintaining order in the city. Various ad hoc committees advised on the daily affairs of government within their respective areas. Throughout the Renaissance, the people of Florence retained the theoretical right to alter the government structure through a commission (*balìa*) chosen by all the citizens who assembled in the great piazza of Florence.

An even tighter merchant oligarchy was represented by the venerable republic of Venice, whose centuries of successful existence without major alterations attest to its stability and functionality. Having at first no landed nobility and relatively fewer interparty rivalries within the city, Venice was able to create a working system controlled entirely by the wealthy merchant families who provided a considerable degree of continuity and political stability.

The highest officer in the Venetian government—at least in splendor, respect, and honor, if not in power—was the *doge,* elected for life by the patrician citizenry. The *doge* symbolized the majesty and grandeur of Venice and was its voice in negotiations with other states. His advisory committees were the Lesser Council, composed of six councilors, and the *Collegio,* or cabinet, made up of twelve ministers selected by the Senate. The chief power, however, lay in the Senate, a body of some 300 persons, half of whom were chosen by a narrow electorate and the other half were *ex officio* members by right of their judicial and administrative offices. Laws were made by the Senate, which also directed the finances of the state, managed foreign affairs, and corresponded with ambassadors. At the base of the political structure was the Great Council, not a functioning political organ as the name might imply but the total

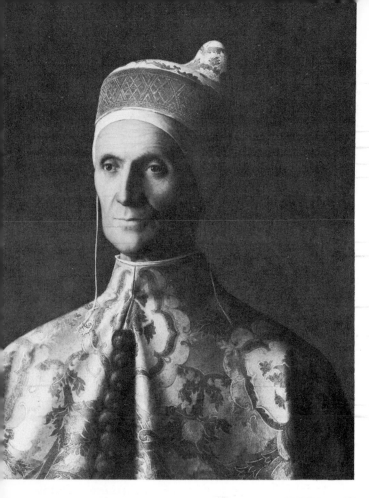

citizenry eligible to vote. It was from and by this body that the administrative officers of the government were chosen.

Another organ, somewhat outside the main lines of authority but with power parallel to the Senate, was the Council of Ten. This was formed in the early fourteenth century from among the more influential and conservative members of the Senate to protect the constitution and uphold the state against internal threat. In time this council became increasingly powerful and tyrannical as its functions overlapped other bureaus and as its tactics of intervention for political "purification" reduced the effectiveness and image of rival groups. Eventually the Ten became the principal judicial organ and through this means greatly influenced life in Venice.

The government of Milan represents a much simpler yet even less democratic form of rule, the type increasingly prevalent in Lombardy in the fourteenth and fifteenth centuries. At one time Milan, too, had been a republic, but the merchant oligarchy was less powerful in Milan than it was in Florence and Venice and less able to oppose the strong arm of a determined despot. In 1258, Martin della Torre, the ambitious leader of the local Guelfs, gained control of the machinery of Milanese government and made himself ruler of the city-state. For two decades, the della Torre family was able to maintain its hold, only to fall before the more ruthless and able Visconti in 1277. For the next 175 years, the Visconti family, claiming Ghibelline affiliation and supported by the landed aristocracy, exercised personal dominion over the Milanese, ruling without constitutional or rival restraints other than occasional attempts by the della Torre family or others to regain power. By conquest, diplomacy, and marriage, the Visconti extended the influence and size of Milan until it eventually included all of Lombardy and even threatened the independence of Tuscany. The Visconti declared Milan a duchy, and in 1311 Matteo Visconti received from the emperor the title of Imperial Vicar, symbolizing both the importance to which the dynasty had risen and the fact that the imperial claim to northern Italy was not entirely dead. Both conditions were to cause internal strife and foreign war for the next two centuries.

Rivalry and War: The Condottieri

The city-states could not supply enough soldiers for the family feuds, party rivalries, and inter-city competition that caused almost continuous fighting during the thirteenth and fourteenth centuries. By then it had become customary to hire mercenary soldiers, mostly from among the impoverished lower classes, led by nobles who had been squeezed out of political power. At first these mercenary troops were employed as the bodyguard of a successful tyrant or as the semi-standing army of a republic. As the leaders of these forces became conscious of their power, they began to form independent armies, sometimes recruiting from as far away as Switzerland and Germany and selling their services to the highest bidder, much like a modern building contractor. Having no national loyalties, these *condottieri* became an increasingly disruptive force in the development of the city-states and their relations with one another.

Warfare in the age of the *condottieri* took on a particular character that distinguishes it from the dynastic and national struggles of a later period and especially from the impassioned religious wars of the sixteenth century. More than ever before, war became a business enterprise with success measured more in ducats and florins than in honor and glory. Of course the *condottieri* fought for victory since to the victor went the spoils, but they had no intention of winning such decisive decisions that the need for their services would end. From this point of view, success depended as much on a continuation of the demand for armies as it did on winning specific campaigns. Thus the wars of the *condottieri* were chronic wars fought over and over again to redress the decisions of previous encounters. They were wars of maneuver and siege, of plunder and ransom.

The *condottieri* themselves came from many countries, bringing followers with them and recruiting additional mercenaries in Italy. The first of these "free companies" to gain success and notoriety was the Great Company of Werner von Urslingen (known in Italy as Guarnieri), a vagabond German baron who ravaged much of Romagna and Tuscany in 1342–43. Ten years later, the Great Company was led by Montréal (Fra Moriale), a renegade French knight of the Hospitallers of Saint John. But the most famous of all the early *condottieri* was Sir John Hawkwood (Giovanni Acuto), an English nobleman who, during a lull in the Hundred Years' War, campaigned throughout Tuscany, usually in the pay of Florence, at the head of his dreaded White Company. By the end of the fourteenth century, the *condottieri* were predominantly Italian, but they knew no more patriotism than did their foreign predecessors. The Company of Saint George, organized in 1379 by Alberico da Barbiano, admitted only Italians to its ranks.

In addition to the nearly continuous *condottieri* wars that kept Italy in a constant state of siege during the fourteenth century, larger conflicts eventually altered the entire political relationship of the peninsula. The first of these duels was the chronic struggle between the maritime rivals Venice and Genoa. Venetian policy was set on maintaining and ex-

tending its trade in the East while adjusting to the changing power relations caused by the decline of the Byzantine Empire and the rise of the Ottoman Turks. Being almost entirely dependent on foreign lands for her food supply and on the flourishing trade routes to the East for her livelihood, the island republic of Saint Mark could not allow an unfriendly power either to control the mainland or to dominate the sea.

For their part, the Genoese, after eliminating the rivalry of Pisa by a successful naval war, dominated the straits to the Black Sea and thus held a virtual monopoly of trade in the Black Sea area. The Genoese port of Kaffa in the Crimea became one of the most flourishing cities in the East. In the western Mediterranean, Genoa dominated the trade with Barcelona and Valencia. Until the middle of the fourteenth century, the balance between the two sea powers was almost equal, except for the greater stability of the Venetian government. During this time, Genoa was one of the most turbulent and factious Italian city-states, paralyzed for long periods by incessant feuds among its noble houses. In 1380, while attempting to crush Venice by blockade, the Genoese fleet was destroyed at Chioggia in a surprise attack by the Venetian captain Carlo Zeno. Genoa's naval power never fully recovered from this disaster.

No sooner had Venice emerged victorious from the wars with Genoa

THE BATTLE OF SAN ROMANO. *Renaissance warfare is portrayed by Paolo Uccello in this panel showing Niccolò da Tolentino leading the Florentines in the opening charge of the 1432 battle between Florence and Siena. (Reproduced by courtesy of the Trustees, The National Gallery, London)*

than a new and even graver danger loomed in Lombardy, a threat not only to Venice but to all of the independent city-states of Italy. A real leviathan had developed in the latter fourteenth century in the formidable power of Milan under its energetic duke Gian Galeazzo Visconti. In the 1380s, through diplomacy, intrigue, and war, Gian Galeazzo came to dominate the entire Lombard plain from the Alps to the Apennines. In 1390 he struck southward into Tuscany and Umbria in a giant, two-pronged invasion. Florence was isolated and Venice was cut off from its mainland supplies. Although John Hawkwood was able to delay the advance temporarily, he could not prevent the encirclement of Florence, as Perugia, Siena, Pisa, and finally Bologna each fell before the determined blows of the Milanese ruler. Suddenly, in June, 1402, when all hope for Florentine survival seemed lost, Gian Galeazzo died and the "kingdom of northern Italy" ended.

The dominions of Gian Galeazzo Visconti were left to his two sons Gian Maria and Filippo Maria, who ruled their empire from Milan and Pavia, respectively. Disorder ensued. *Condottieri* seized many of the cities of Emilia and Romagna. Bologna and Perugia went back to the Papal States in 1403; Siena recovered its republican liberties; Lucca came under control of an independent prince; Pisa overthrew its puppet ruler in 1405 (only to succumb a year later to Florentine aggression after undergoing a crushing twelve-month siege). As Milanese power declined, Venice began creating a mainland dominion to secure its valuable "breadbasket" and to extend its power and prestige. In a few years, the republic had acquired Padua, Verona, and Vicenza, as well as a large share of the Dalmatian coast, which it wrested from the king of Hungary.

Upon the death of his older brother, Filippo Maria emerged as the uncontested ruler of Milan and a worthy successor to his illustrious father. Step by step through diplomacy and war, Filippo Maria began the recovery of the lost Milanese territories, until by 1421 the duchy extended from Piedmont to the River Adige. Once again the threat of a single-power domination of northern and central Italy became a reality. However, with the election of the aggressive Francesco Foscari as *doge* in Venice and growing civic awareness in Florence and neighboring states, opposition to the Visconti advance took on new life. The foundation of this resistance was a comprehensive military alliance negotiated in 1425 between Venice and Florence (joined later by most of the northern Italian city-states).

The next thirty years saw almost continuous warfare, as the mercenary armies of the greatest Italian powers grappled for supremacy. The duke of Milan had in his employ some of the leading *condottieri* of the day: Francesco Bussone, called Carmagnola; Francesco Sforza; Niccolò Piccinino; and Carlo Malatesta. The Florentine forces were commanded by Niccolò da Tolentino (who shares with Hawkwood the distinction of having his equestrian portrait on the wall of the cathedral in Florence).

THE CONDOTTIERE GAT-
TAMELATA. *Donatello's
huge bronze monument, lo-
cated in Padua, reveals the
power and determination of
this famous* condottiere,
*who was employed by
many city-states. He was in
the service of Venice when
he died in 1443.*
(Anderson-Photographie
Giraudon)

Carmagnola switched to Venice in 1425, and the papal *condottiere,*
Erasmo da Narni, known by his nickname, Gattamelata ("Honeyed
Cat"), entered Venetian service in 1434.

From 1431, the year Venice executed Carmagnola for "treason," to
1440, the Milanese forces advanced steadily against the allies and even
laid siege to Rome. So successful, in fact, were the campaigns of Francesco Sforza that he began casting covetous eyes on the newly won
territories of his employer. Sforza hoped to force Filippo Maria's hand
by marrying his daughter and then demanding an independent principality in Lombardy as a dowry. When the duke refused, Sforza turned
against him, joined the Venetian-Florentine alliance, and soundly defeated Piccinino, who was sent to apprehend him. When Filippo Maria
died in 1447, the Visconti dynasty ended. Francesco Sforza was quick to
seize his advantage. After defeating the Venetians at Caravaggio, he
marched on Milan, entering the city in 1450 as its conqueror and new
duke. Next he persuaded Cosimo de' Medici, ruler of Florence, to
withdraw from the Venetian alliance, thereby isolating Venice from
military support in the west. This Milanese-Florentine cooperation finally brought the wars to an end with the Peace of Lodi in 1454.

The settlement of Lodi did more than close a half century of almost
continuous warfare. It also established an alliance system among the
major Italian powers that led to a loose but workable balance of power

within the peninsula. The three original signatories, Milan, Venice, and Florence, agreed to invite other states, including the papacy, to become parties to the pact and form an Italian league that could help create a coordinated but flexible relationship among them. The forty years following the Peace of Lodi were certainly not free from war and political unrest, but the extent and duration of these disturbances were reduced. This in turn produced an atmosphere that was conducive to the flowering of Renaissance art and thought during the second half of the fifteenth century.

Renaissance Diplomacy

The fifteenth-century struggle for supremacy in northern Italy gave birth to a type of diplomatic procedure that became fundamental to the relations among the Italian states during the Renaissance, a system that in the next century was gradually adopted by all the major states of Europe and eventually of the world. The basis of this diplomacy had already been established in earlier times, but its realization did not come until the Renaissance. Permanent diplomacy—distinguished by the assignment of accredited resident ambassadors as contrasted with the ad hoc missions of medieval legates—developed out of the need for continuous contact and exchange of information between parties to a military alliance. Diplomacy was an alternative to war as a means of increasing power and position (although it could also be used to augment the military), and since it was a less expensive alternative, it was favored by the merchant oligarchs who held power.

The first states to establish resident embassies were Mantua and Milan. Gian Galeazzo Visconti employed a rather extensive and sophisticated diplomatic network that enabled him to win many victories without the expense and risk of military operations. Filippo Maria followed his father's footsteps and even expanded the system to encompass some states outside Italy. Francesco Sforza was quick to see the advantages of diplomacy and sent a representative to Florence as soon as he controlled Milan. It was this agent who spearheaded the negotiations for the Peace of Lodi. During the second half of the century, resident embassies became widespread, and the ambassador's duties, responsibilities, and prestige grew accordingly.

The accepted role of the Renaissance ambassador was to win allies through negotiation; counter the designs of enemies; represent his government at ceremonies and public events; and gather and send information to aid in "the preservation and aggrandizement of his own state." Nowhere can these functions be better seen than in the systematic operation of Venetian diplomacy in the late-fifteenth and sixteenth centuries. Ambassadors were carefully selected from among the best-educated patrician families of Venice and sent out on a regular, rotational basis. Their duties and responsibilities were carefully prescribed in regulations established by the Senate and the Lesser Council. While residing at a foreign court, Venetian ambassadors were expected to send weekly dispatches to their government, reporting all matters of direct or remote interest to the Republic. These reports were read by the *doge* to the assembled Senate and then discussed in detail before drawing up written conclusions. Upon return, an ambassador was required to submit a written summary (*relazione*) of his embassy, which was then read before the *doge* and Senate. Responses and instructions from the government to Venetian agents were customarily accompanied by news briefs (*avvisi*) from Venice and other parts of Europe. In this way, Venetian ambassadors became the best-informed representatives of any Renaissance state and consequently provided their government with the most complete information on which to base decisions.

As the role of ambassador increased in importance and extent, the rules, procedures, and ceremonies associated with his functions were also enlarged. The forms and rituals varied at different courts, but the general pattern of activity was similar. Before departing on a mission, the ambassador was provided with several documents: *Credence and Appointment*, which he was required to deliver to his host at the time of his first audience; *Instructions*, given to the ambassador by his own government to guide him in the general conduct of his embassy and outlining the intent and direction of his negotiations; and *Powers*, authorizing him to sign or certify documents in the name of his government. Much attention and significance were given to the ceremonial entry of a newly appointed ambassador. This elaborate procession not only introduced the agent to his host's ministers and functionaries, but by a strict adherence to the hierarchy of precedence and rank, it also reminded everyone of their proper places. When the ambassador came from one of the major states, the formal entry and reception usually ended in a great festival and sumptuous banquet. As part of the ceremony, the ambassador was also presented to the sovereign or his representative, in whose presence he delivered his first formal oration, outlining in his most eloquent Latin the purpose and aspirations of his mission. Later audiences were usually less formal but were still conducted with considerable pomp and the proper deference to precedent.

In the last decade of the fifteenth century, Italian diplomacy spread rapidly. By 1494, when the French invasion of Italy upset the tenuous Italian balance of power, the principal city-states had resident ambassadors in most of the states in Italy and in some courts of northern Europe. The value of continuous diplomatic representation was becoming apparent.

Renaissance Lords and Ladies

During the Renaissance, many city-states fell under the control of powerful ruling families or single despots. Duke Federigo da Montefeltro of

FEDERIGO DA MONTE-
FELTRO, DUKE OF URBINO.
*This successful condottiere
was also one of the most
cultivated princes of the
Renaissance and made his
court at Urbino a model of
refinement and art. He is
shown here, in Pedro Ber-
ruguete's portrait, reading
to his son Guidobaldo.
(Alinari/Editorial Photo-
color Archives)*

Urbino, for example, in addition to being one of the most successful and vigorous warriors of the period, noted for his aggressive generalship as a *condottiere*, was at the same time one of the greatest Renaissance patrons. Duke Federigo made Urbino a cultural and intellectual center during the Renaissance. As benevolent as he was despotic, Montefeltro was notorious for his honesty and good faith, impressing both his contemporaries and later biographers with his high character. The Florentine bookseller and traveler Vespasiano da Bisticci called him the wisest and most just ruler of the age. Castiglione, the noted biographer of Urbino court life, referred to him as "the light of Italy."

All of the credit for making Urbino a cultural jewel should not go to Federigo, however. His wife Battista Sforza, niece of Francesco Sforza of Milan, was a very intelligent and talented woman in her own right and did much to promote letters and art in Urbino. Her contemporaries admired her knowledge of Greek, her polished Latin, and her remarkable memory. Federigo called her "the delight of both my public and my private hours." During her husband's frequent absences, she was left in charge of affairs, and everyone agreed that she governed the state "with firmness and good sense." Their son Guidobaldo da Montefeltro continued to promote culture after he became duke of Urbino in 1482. Even more than in the previous generation, the greatest stimulus to elegance and refinement came from the duchess. This was Elisabetta Gonzaga, Guidobaldo's wife, who set the tone and texture of court life in Urbino for a generation, until her death in 1526. It was she who presided over the circle of illuminaries immortalized in Castiglione's *Book of the Courtier*.

Elisabetta Gonzaga came by her talents naturally. She was the daughter of Federigo Gonzaga, marquis of Mantua, whose court was another important center of art and learning in the Renaissance. The Gonzaga lords attracted some of the leading humanists and artists to Mantua, including Andrea Mantegna, who painted the famous *Sala degli Sposi* (Chamber of the Newlyweds) in the ducal palace for Federigo and his bride. Their son Francesco Gonzaga, like his sister Elisabetta, was brought up in an atmosphere that placed almost as much emphasis on culture as it did on politics and arms. In 1490, he married Isabella d'Este, the illustrious and talented daughter of Ercole I, duke of Ferrara.

Isabella d'Este was renowned for her beauty, good taste, and civility, as well as for her brilliant mind and political wisdom. Many admiring contemporaries called her "the first lady of the world." Growing up in the cultural environment of fifteenth-century Ferrara, Isabella met the foremost scholars and artists of the day and received the best education possible. She was only sixteen when she married Francesco Gonzaga and moved to nearby Mantua. There she became the center of literary and artistic life, taking a lively interest in all branches of learning and attracting people of talent and charm to the court. There, also, she gathered one of the finest libraries in Italy. Her contacts and influence reached far beyond the borders of Mantua as she carried on a lively correspondence with family, friends, princes, and painters all over Europe. Her letters (some 2,000 of which still exist) reveal her personal warmth and brilliance as well as her political judgment and subtle humor. One of her closest friends and correspondents (and her sister-in-law) was Elisabetta Gonzaga, duchess of Urbino, with whom she shared many thoughts and experiences. Another was her dearly loved younger sister Beatrice d'Este, who became the duchess of Milan and the fountainhead of fashion and refinement there by the time Leonardo da Vinci arrived to become her husband's military engineer and court painter.

Both of the d'Este sisters possessed rare political skill and a gift for diplomacy and statecraft. Isabella was especially respected as a shrewd negotiator and for many years was the effective ruler of Mantua, both before and after the death of her husband. She was largely responsible for obtaining the cardinalate for her second son and persuading Emperor Charles V to advance Mantua from a marquisate to a duchy, making her eldest son its first duke. Throughout her life, she followed political events very closely, and at the magnificent papal coronation of Charles V in Bologna, Isabella was placed in rank above everyone else except the emperor and the pope—an indication of the respect and esteem in which she was held. Obviously, the courts of Renaissance Italy were not all dominated by *condottieri* and hardened war lords.

Florence under the Medici

Florence, too, despite its deep-seated republican traditions, succumbed to the dominance of a single ruler. But here was despotism with a difference. The Medici of Florence were not warriors but middle-class citizens who rose to positions of power and wealth through their own industry and skill. The remarkable feature of their rule was the preservation and support it gave to the republican structure of Florence, while excercising political control through influence among the merchant oligarchs and popularity with the people.

On more than one occasion during the chaotic fourteenth century, Florence surrendered its liberties to a single ruler, usually for military expediency and with near-disastrous results in each case. At the end of that century, the Albizzi family grabbed the reigns of government and held them fast for the next two decades. During this time, the Medici first rose to political importance as rivals of the Albizzi oligarchy and friends of the *popolo minuto*. Giovanni de' Medici became an outspoken critic of the regime and a champion of the lesser guilds. The Medici-Albizzi feud reached the highest level of Florentine government when Giovanni was elected to the *Signoria* and then served one two-month term as *Gonfaloniere*. Yet in spite of his criticism of the dominant aristocracy, Giovanni was primarily a merchant and banker, interested more in expanding his financial empire than in acquiring political power. In 1429 he died, leaving to his sons his financial fortunes as well as his feud with the Albizzi.

Cosimo de' Medici was more outspoken in political matters than his father had been. As a result, a confrontation between him and the Albizzi soon developed and Cosimo was sent into exile. But the political winds shifted quickly in Renaissance Italy, and a year later the roles of protagonist and antagonist were reversed. Military defeat by Milan, dissatisfaction with the Albizzi tax policy, and the murmurings of the *popolo minuto* all led to the election of a hostile *Signoria*. A new *balìa* was formed in September, 1434, which in a single stroke recalled the Medici from exile and banished the Albizzi and all their followers. Triumphantly, Cosimo de' Medici returned to his native city. For the next thirty years, his leadership was unchallenged, and for the next 300 years, the words Florence and Medici were synonymous.

In power, Cosimo de' Medici was the businessman and politician par excellence. He employed his wealth and extensive financial connections for political advantage and wielded his political influence to further his economic interests. Serving as *Gonfaloniere* for a total of only six months out of the thirty years of his political ascendency, his power was unofficial, but nonetheless real. A combination of factors explains the apparent discrepancy between his position and power. In the first place, Cosimo saw to it that the pool from which potential priors were chosen would always be acceptable to him. This was accomplished by a single constitutional alteration carried out by the friendly *balìa* that had plucked him from exile. An electoral committee was appointed for the purpose of selecting the priors and *Gonfalonieri* from among the eligible names rather than leaving the selection to chance under the previous system of lots. Thus, by maintaining a Medician electoral committee, Cosimo was assured of a friendly *Signoria* without participating in it himself.

But this does not entirely explain the Medici success. Some of Cosimo's advantage was due to his genuine popularity as a leader. He was far sighted and astute, eliciting loyalty and service from those who administered the laws, and confident support from those who were governed by them. Cosimo was also endowed with a keen political sense. He was aware of the limitations of his power and was careful never to exceed them. Likewise, he understood the difference between the politically possible and the impossible, astutely avoiding enterprises that were unduly risky. To the Florentines, he represented a stable and tranquilizing influence contrasting sharply with the turbulence of preceding years.

As a patron of the arts and letters, Cosimo was also deeply involved in the cultural and intellectual life of Florence. Recent scholarship has revealed that Cosimo may have been credited with more patronage than he actually gave, particularly in the fields of painting and sculpture, but even after making allowances for the exaggerations of contemporaries and for the flattery of those who sought favor, Cosimo is still conspicuous for his active promotion of Renaissance culture in Florence. Either directly or indirectly, he was responsible for scores of buildings, including the sacristy and church of San Lorenzo, the monastery of San Marco, the Medici Palace, and several villas in the country, and he contributed significantly to the development of scholarship and learning. When he died in 1464, he was genuinely mourned by the citizenry of Florence. His tomb in front of the high altar in the church of San Lorenzo bears the single approbatory inscription *Pater Patriae* (Father of His Country). Although untrue, it is symbolic of the esteem in which he was held by his compatriots.

Piero de' Medici, like his father Cosimo, was also a financial wizard and a man of keen political sense. He took over his father's role as the backstage director of Florentine politics and continued his foreign policy and cultural patronage. But Piero's regime was not as stable as the previous one had been, partly because much of the inevitable reaction to Cosimo's rule materialized only after the latter's death, and partly because Piero's poor health prevented him from exercising an overwhelming personal influence, as Cosimo had done. Five years later, Piero's arthritis-ridden body followed his father's to the grave.

Lorenzo the Magnificent

The mantle of leadership now fell upon the shoulders of Piero's twenty-one-year-old son Lorenzo. Young Lorenzo's terse description of the succession reveals a great deal about the nature of Florentine society and government:

> The leading men of the city and state came to my house to condole with me and at the same time to request that I assume charge of the city and state as my father and grandfather had done before me. Owing to my youth, I accepted the responsibility with reluctance and solely in the interest of our friends and their fortunes, since at Florence one lives insecurely without the control of the state.

Lorenzo de' Medici was a complex and gifted man with interests and skills as diverse as the age in which he lived. Educated in the humanistic environment of fifteenth-century Florence, he experienced and reflected the cultural complexity and variety of the Renaissance at its height. He soon came to represent both the virtues and the vices of Renaissance Florence. For his impressively flamboyant leadership of the Florentine state, as well as for his lavish patronage of culture, he was addressed as *"il magnifico."*

Although the Medici succession was accomplished without mishap or serious opposition, foreboding clouds were on the horizon. Two years after Piero's death, Pope Paul II was also laid to rest, and succeeding him was the headstrong and ambitious Franciscan friar Francesco della Rovere, who ascended the papal throne as Pope Sixtus IV.

LORENZO THE MAGNIFICENT. *Andrea Verrocchio's terra cotta bust of Lorenzo de' Medici strongly conveys Lorenzo's hard-nosed practicality but also hints at his appreciation of the "good life." (National Gallery of Art, Washington, D.C., Samuel H. Kress Collection)*

The new pontiff, not particularly impressed with Lorenzo—or perhaps impressed enough to be wary of him—brought about a cooling of relations between the papacy and Florence that had been fundamental to Cosimo's foreign policy. Sixtus was solicitous of many of Lorenzo's bitterest enemies, who flocked to the Roman court in hopes of gaining favor and support against the Medici. Notable among these disenchanted Florentines were Jacopo and Francesco Pazzi, heads of one of the oldest and wealthiest Florentine families and directors of the rival

Pazzi Bank. Sixtus not only encouraged the Pazzi but also lavishly patronized his own nephews Piero and Girolamo Riario and Giuliano della Rovere (later Pope Julius II), who were avowed enemies of Lorenzo de' Medici. He further antagonized Lorenzo by appointing another adversary, Francesco Salviati, to the vacant archbishopric of Pisa, despite violent protests from Florence.

Tensions reached a peak on 26 April 1478 during the celebration of High Mass in the cathedral of Santa Maria del Fiore in Florence. There, with the knowledge and blessing of the pope, a group of conspirators headed by Girolamo Riario, Francesco Pazzi, and Francesco Salviati attempted to assassinate Lorenzo and his younger brother Giuliano and seize the government of Florence. The Pazzi conspiracy succeeded only half way in its initial goal and failed completely in its last. Young Giuliano was brutally stabbed to death, but Lorenzo escaped with only a wound in the shoulder. News of the attack spread quickly throughout Florence, setting the populace in their resolve to defend the regime and awakening their instinct for revenge. If Lorenzo de' Medici's rule was a tyranny as the Pazzi maintained, it was a tyranny condoned and supported by the majority of the people.

From the Pazzi conspiracy and its ensuing war, Lorenzo drew two important conclusions: first, that it was unwise to abandon the foreign policy of his father and grandfather and try to lock horns with the papacy—particularly when this required the assistance of as unreliable a cohort as Venice—and second, that there was much stronger native support for the Medici regime than Lorenzo had dared hope. With these lessons in mind, Lorenzo made some appropriate adjustments in his foreign policy by abandoning his Venetian pact and resuming the alliance with Naples. He also encouraged the cooperation of the major Italian states against the growing threat of a French invasion, while at the same time maintaining close economic ties with France, which was still the chief market for Florentine woolen goods.

At home, while public opinion was still favorable, Lorenzo saw and seized the opportunity to increase his power. He created a new committee, called the Council of Seventy, which thenceforth dominated all facets of Florentine politics. Members of the Seventy were hand picked and served for life, or until their presence seemed prejudicial to the oligarchy. Two permanent committees within the Council of Seventy carried out most of the executive functions of the government. In both of these, the Eight of War and the Twelve of Finance and Commerce, Lorenzo was directly represented, and he sat personally in the Seventy. At last the Medici rule became overt, even though the older institutions continued in name.

In cultural affairs, Lorenzo was an even more illustrious patron than his father and grandfather had been. Because his rule coincided with the zenith of Florentine art and letters and the enthusiastic spread of scholarship sparked by the development of printing, Lorenzo could hardly avoid being associated with the flowering Renaissance. But in addition he was an active promoter of Renaissance culture and a respectable poet in his own right. In varying degrees, Lorenzo had something to do with the development or productivity of the greatest Renaissance artists, many of whom studied or worked at the Medici palace and formed part of the culturally sensitive Medici household.

Yet when Lorenzo died in 1492, the inheritance he passed on to his son Piero was not all golden. Lorenzo had made many enemies, and he had not maintained the diplomatic supports against a possible French intervention that Cosimo had insisted on. When the French did invade and the Medici family was expelled from Florence just two years after Lorenzo's death, it was partly due to Piero's own inabilities but also partly due to the political and diplomatic legacy of Lorenzo the Magnificent. Meanwhile, economic and social factors in the development of the city-states were also having a direct and profound impact on the life and culture of the Renaissance.

Suggestions for Further Reading

GENERAL

In *The Italian City-Republics* (New York, 1969), Daniel Waley shows that the growth of the city-states from the late eleventh century to the early fourteenth was a unique social and political development, especially in the fierce independence of the cities. The violence of that development is emphasized in Lauro Martines (ed.), *Violence and Civil Disorder in Italian Cities, 1200–1500* (Berkeley, 1972), twelve papers from the 1969 UCLA symposium on violence and disorder. The most recent and best overall analysis of the city-states is Lauro Martines, *Power and Imagination: City-States in Renaissance Italy* (New York, 1979). Orville Prescott, *Princes of the Renaissance* (New York, 1969) is a popularization, but a good one, by the former book critic of the *New York Times*. What some contemporaries themselves thought of their governments may be seen in Benjamin Kohl and Ronald Witt (eds.), *The Earthly Republic: Italian Humanists on Government and Society* (Philadelphia, 1978).

FLORENCE

Renaissance Florence has been the focus of a great number of scholarly books. The best of these are Gene A. Brucker's *Renaissance Florence* (New York, 1969), a very successful short account in the Wiley series on Historical Cities; *Florentine Politics and Society, 1343–1378* (Princeton, 1962); and his prize-winning *The Civic World of Early Renaissance Florence* (Princeton, 1977), which describes the period from 1378 to 1434 as the transition from guild politics to elitist rule by professional statesmen. Dale Kent, *The Rise of the Medici: Faction in Florence, 1426–1434* (New York, 1978) is a heavily documented, important work focusing on the problem of patronage during the eight years preceding the Medici ascendance. Marvin R. Becker, *Florence in Transition*, 2 vols. (Baltimore, 1967–68) is a detailed discussion of Florentine politics and society but suffers from being dull reading. Nicolai Rubinstein (ed.), *Florentine Studies: Politics and Society in Renaissance Florence* (Evanston, 1968) is a useful collection of scholarly essays. *Lawyers and Statecraft in Renaissance Florence* (Princeton, 1968) is an interesting study by Lauro Martines of how lawyers were employed in important affairs.

VENICE

The story of the beginning of the Venetian state to the year 1405 is sympathetically told by John J. Norwich in *Venice: The Rise to Power* (London, 1977). D. S. Chambers, *The Imperial Age of Venice, 1380–1580* (New York, 1970) is a volume in the illustrated History of European Civilization Library. Frederic C. Lane is one of the great names in the historiography of Venice. See his *Venice: A Maritime Republic* (Baltimore, 1973), a detailed history from the fifth through the eighteenth century, and *Venice and History* (Baltimore, 1966), a collection of his articles edited by a committee of colleagues and former students. Oliver Logan, *Culture and Society in Venice* (New York, 1972) is a broad-scope synthesis. J. R. Hale (ed.), *Renaissance Venice* (London, 1973) consists of sixteen penetrating essays on Venetian politics, diplomacy, economy, and culture.

MILAN AND OTHER CITY-STATES

E. R. Chamberlin, *The Count of Virtue: Giangaleazzo Visconti* (New York, 1965) is a strong vindication of the Visconti despotism. Other city-states are studied in John K. Hyde, *Padua in the Age of Dante: The Social History of an Italian City-State* (New York, 1966); Werner L. Gundersheimer, *Ferrara: The Style of a Renaissance Despotism* (Princeton, 1973); John Larner, *The Lords of Romagna* (Ithaca, 1965); David Herlihy, *Pisa in the Early Renaissance: A Study of Urban Growth* (New Haven, 1958) and *Medieval and Renaissance Pistoia: The Social History of an Italian Town* (New Haven, 1968); Christine Meek, *Lucca, 1369–1400: Politics and Society in an Early Renaissance State* (Oxford, 1978); Robert Brentano, *Rome before Avignon: A Social History of Thirteenth Century Rome* (London, 1974); and Alan Ryder, *The Kingdom of Naples under Alfonso the Magnanimous: The Making of a Modern State* (Oxford, 1976).

WAR AND DIPLOMACY

Geoffrey Trease, *The Condottieri: Soldiers of Fortune* (New York, 1971) is an illustrated biographical study of the great free-lance generals of the fourteenth and fifteenth centuries. The best analysis of Renaissance warfare is Michael Mallett, *Mercenaries and Their Masters: Warfare in Renaissance Italy* (Totowa, 1974). On diplomacy, see Donald E. Queller, *The Office of Ambassador in the Middle Ages* (Princeton, 1967), which includes the fourteenth and fifteenth centuries; Garrett Mattingly, *Renaissance Diplomacy* (Boston, 1955), a seminal study; and Vincent Ilardi, "The Italian League, Francesco Sforza, and Charles VII (1454–1461)," *Studies in the Renaissance*, 6 (1959), 129–66.

FLORENCE UNDER THE MEDICI

Christopher Hibbert, *The House of Medici: Its Rise and Fall* (New York, 1975) is a popular, general history, not altogether replacing Ferdinand Schevill's brief but insightful, *The Medici*, 2nd ed. (New York, 1960). C. M. Ady, *Lorenzo dei Medici and Renaissance Italy* (New York, 1962), from the Teach Yourself History Library, uses the biography of a great man to describe the entire age. Maurice Rowdon, *Lorenzo the Magnificent* (London, 1974) is a good, recent biography, and H. Ross Williamson's lavishly illustrated *Lorenzo the Magnificent* (London, 1974) provides some additional insights. Nicolai Rubinstein, *The Government of Florence under the Medici, 1434 to 1494* (Oxford, 1966) is a scholarly analysis of Florentine politics and Medici manipulation. The most recent contribution to this subject is J. R. Hale, *Florence and the Medici: The Pattern of Control* (London, 1977), a skillfully written book covering the entire Medici period.

CHAPTER THREE

Economic and Social Change in the Renaissance

NE OF THE DISTINGUISHING features of the Renaissance age was the increase in the amount and fluidity of wealth in western Europe. The main cause of this growth was the commercial activity carried on by the coastal cities of northern Italy. We have already seen how the subsistence economy of the medieval manor was being transformed in the late Middle Ages by the development of trade and urban industry. This trend gained momentum in the thirteenth and early fourteenth centuries, particularly in Italy, and from there it spread gradually into other parts of Europe. This expanding commerce, accompanied by the exchange of ideas, institutions, and technology as well as goods, had a profound impact on Renaissance culture.

The Italian Commercial Revolution

The reasons for Italian predominance and early leadership in international commerce are not hard to find. Because of their favorable geographical location on intersecting trade routes between Europe and the East, the Italian cities were able to capitalize on the lucrative trade that had been gaining momentum since the time of the Crusades. Venetian and Genoese merchants continued to trade with Constantinople and other cities of the Byzantine Empire and in doing so had developed organizations, techniques, and experience that placed them in a favorable position for commercial leadership. The relative freedom from feudal controls enjoyed by the Italian towns also gave them an advantage over their northern neighbors. And the predominant political role played by the merchant class in the city-states greatly stimulated commercial interests.

Many Italian cities participated in the expansion of trade in the thirteenth and early fourteenth centuries. With the growing demand for goods from the Levant and the Far East, vessels from these cities were soon plying the water routes to the eastern Mediterranean, where they purchased valuable wares from Arab tradesmen, returning to their home ports laden with cottons, silks, taffeta, muslin, damask, dyestuffs, medicines, spices, perfume, alum, and pearls. There they had little difficulty marketing their imports to the merchants who anxiously awaited their arrival. Mark ups were great enough to cover the uncertainties of ocean travel and still leave a large margin of profit—most of the time. Peppercorns, for example, which were bought by Arab traders in Calicut on the Malabar coast of India for the equivalent of $2\frac{1}{2}$ to 3 Venetian ducats, were purchased from the traders in Alexandria for 80 ducats and sold in Venice for 180 to 200.

Of all the cities involved in this commercial revolution, Venice stood in the most favorable position and reaped the greatest profits. For centuries, this island city could justly claim the title of Queen of the Adriatic, a role that down to the end of the eighteenth century was symbolically reaffirmed each year on Ascension Day in a great ceremony representing the wedding of Venice to the sea. From the deck of the richly adorned state galley, the Venetian *doge* would cast a golden wedding ring into the Adriatic, dedicating the city to its continued alliance with the words, "Oh sea, we wed thee as a sign of our true and everlasting dominion." After the diverted Fourth Crusade captured rival Zara and sacked Constantinople in 1202–04, there was little doubt that Venice controlled the eastern Mediterranean and through it maintained a virtual monopoly on the valuable Black Sea commerce. Nor did Venice shrink from aspirations in the Far East, as the travels of Marco Polo and others attest. Although completely dependent on imports for food and raw materials, Venice made money profits from her Eastern trade and paid for most of her mainland supplies in cash. The splendor and affluence of Venetian life is attested to by the native chronicler Marino Sanuto who proudly declared in his *Diaries*:

> In this land where nothing grows, you will find an abundance of everything; for all manner of things from every corner and country of the earth which has stuff to send, especially food, are brought to this place; and there are plenty to buy, since everyone has money. The Rialto looks like a garden, such a wealth there is of herbs and vegetables from the places nearby, such an endless variety of fruits and all so cheap, that it is wonderful to see.

Eager to share in the new-found profits, merchants from northern Europe flocked to cosmopolitan Venice, where they established houses

THE ARSENAL AT VENICE. *According to Pero Tafur's 1439 account, the Venetian "assembly line" could fully arm ten war galleys in six hours. This detail from Jacopo de' Barbari's large woodcut of Venice shows the Arsenal during its heyday. (Courtesy of Civici Musei Veneziani d'Arte e di Storia)*

of trade along the banks of the Grand Canal to buy the valuable cargoes brought by the returning fleets. Such an establishment was the famous *Fondaco dei Tedeschi*, "the Warehouse of the Germans," handily located in front of the Rialto Bridge.

From the design and construction of the galleys to the marketing of wares, the Venetian trade was closely regulated by the merchant oligarchy that ruled the city. Shipbuilding was centered mostly in the great Arsenal, the largest contemporary shipbuilding establishment in the world, employing between 2,000 and 3,000 workers. The Arsenal production lines were capable of constructing and completely outfitting a war galley in ninety days. Private shipwrights were also involved in this industry but were closely controlled by the Venetian state. Once built, the ships were let out for commercial use to the highest bidders at public auction or used by the state for military purposes. The merchants assembled their galleys into fleets, which were dispatched at different times of the year to the Levant ports and Egypt, to the Barbary coast of Africa, and to Greece, Constantinople, and the Black Sea. Under this

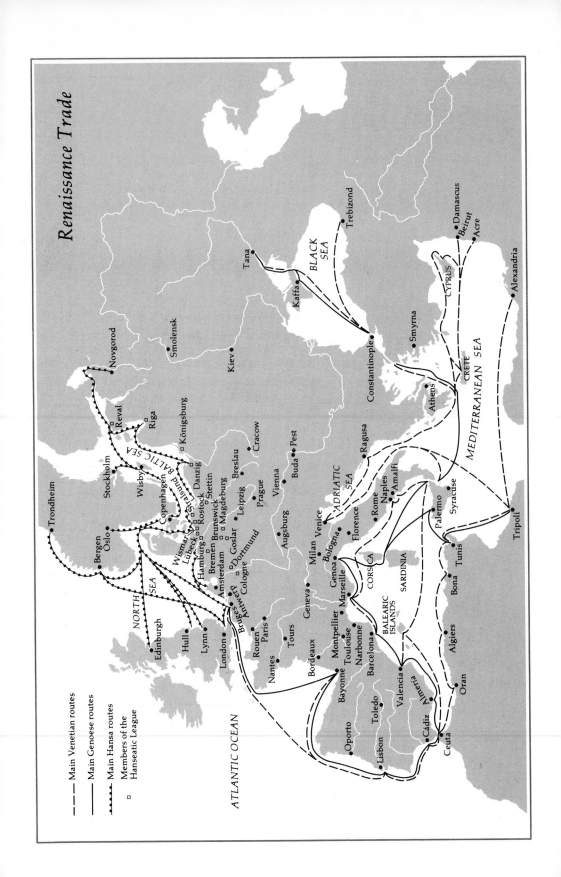

Renaissance Trade

ATLANTIC OCEAN

NORTH SEA

BALTIC SEA

BLACK SEA

MEDITERRANEAN SEA

ADRIATIC SEA

--- Main Venetian routes
— Main Genoese routes
••• Main Hansa routes
☐ Members of the Hanseatic League

Trondheim
Bergen
Oslo
Trebizond
Damascus
Beirut
Acre
Tana
Kaffa
Alexandria
Novgorod
Smolensk
Smyrna
CYPRUS
CRETE
Athens
Constantinople
Kiev
Ragusa
Cracow
Reval
Riga
Königsburg
Breslau
Pest
Buda
Vienna
Prague
Leipzig
Stralsund
Danzig
Stettin
Magdeburg
Rostock
Brunswick
Goslar
Stockholm
Wisby
Copenhagen
Wismar
Lübeck
Hamburg
Bremen
Dortmund
Amsterdam
Cologne
Augsburg
Milan
Venice
Bologna
Genoa
Florence
Rome
Naples
Amalfi
Palermo
Syracuse
Tunis
Bona
Tripoli
Edinburgh
Hull
Lynn
London
Bruges
Antwerp
Rouen
Paris
Tours
Geneva
Bordeaux
Montpellier
Marseille
Toulouse
Narbonne
Nantes
Bayonne
Barcelona
BALEARIC ISLANDS
CORSICA
SARDINIA
Valencia
Almeria
Algiers
Oran
Toledo
Oporto
Lisbon
Cádiz
Ceuta

system, Venice became the principal carrier of Eastern products and the bridge not only between East and West but also between the Middle Ages and the Renaissance.

International Trade in the Early Renaissance

The intensification of commercial exchange increased rivalries among competing states, yet at the same time, by multiplying the frequency and extent of contact between peoples, it also broke down barriers to intercourse that had existed for centuries. By the fourteenth century, ships from all the northern Italian ports were carrying on a flourishing commerce throughout the Mediterranean. The trade between Italy and Egypt was still dominated by the Venetians, but Genoese traders competed at Constantinople and the Black Sea ports of Kaffa and Tana (modern Rostov). Genoese shipping was also active in the western Mediterranean from Sicily to Barcelona and from Tripoli to Ceuta. Ragusa (modern Dubrovnik), on the Dalmatian coast, likewise participated in this Mediterranean trade, as did Marseille, Montpellier, Narbonne, and Barcelona, and even some of the northern cities.

The products of this commerce were diverse and in great demand, composed largely of cloth, foodstuffs, and Eastern luxury goods. The cloth trade was a staple of Renaissance commerce, especially between northern Europe and the Mediterranean. Textiles from England and Flanders were impressive in variety and in great demand throughout Europe. The chief carriers were Italians who purchased the cloth at the Champagne fairs, transported it to Italy (first overland, via the Rhône Valley to the Ligurian coast or over the Alps to Lombardy, and later by sea in the Flanders Fleet), then remarketed it at considerable profit all the way from Valencia to the Levant. As Italian production of fine woolens increased, the cloth merchants found eager markets for them throughout the Mediterranean and in northern Europe.

Commerce in foodstuffs consisted mainly of grain, salt, sugar, fish, and wine. Although grain was grown throughout Europe, many parts of the continent did not produce sufficient quantities for the mounting needs of a gradually increasing population; furthermore, if drought or other unseasonal variations in the weather occurred, local production was totally inadequate. Therefore wheat, rye, and other grain products were carried from Apulia, Sicily, and Egypt all the way to Danzig and beyond. Salt was another necessary commodity that because of its abundant use as a food preservative as well as a savor, occupied a vital place in Renaissance trade. Salt was produced by evaporating sea water in artificial pools near Venice, in the natural lagoons of the Bay of Biscay, in Istria and Sicily, and was mined from the mountains of the Austrian Salzkamergut. Venetians were the chief carriers, but the Salt Fleet from northern Germany was a vital link between the north and south around the Atlantic route. Much of the salt was used in the transportation and preservation of herring caught in the North Sea and sold in many parts of Europe. Sugar was supplied mostly from Crete and Cyprus but also from eastern Spain, and was carried by Venetians, Genoese, and Pisans. Wine, in great demand in all countries, was produced in many varieties and vintages from the sun-bleached Mediterranean shores to the slopes of the Rhineland. Gascony and Guyenne, in southwestern France, exported great quantities of red clarets and Bordeaux white wines, while port from Oporto, Portugal, and sherry from Jerez, near Seville, were highly valued in England and the north.

Olive oil from southern Spain and Italy, cheese from Sardinia and Parma, alum from the Levant, copper ore from Germany, and lumber and other forest products from the north also made up large portions of the cargo of Mediterranean shippers. However, for quick profits, nothing quite compared with the trade of luxury goods from the East. Persian and Chinese silks brought immediate and inflated prices at European fairs, as did Indian cotton cloth, Damascus lace and steel, and blown glass and all varieties of precious stones from India, Burma, and Ceylon. The supply of white and black pepper from the Malabar coast and Sumatra never exceeded the demand, even with the growing popularity of other Eastern spices—cinnamon, nutmeg, mace, cloves.

Soon enterprising merchants and seamen were extending their lines of trade beyond the Mediterranean north along the Atlantic seaboard. Venice developed the great galley—a huge vessel employing three banks of oars plus sails and capable of carrying cargoes of over 200 tons—and used it in her Flanders Fleet to establish a direct sea route from Venice to England and the Netherlands. The Genoese also engaged in direct water communication with the trading centers of northern Europe, but not as regularly and systematically as the Venetians did. For a while in the early fifteenth century, even Florence aspired to

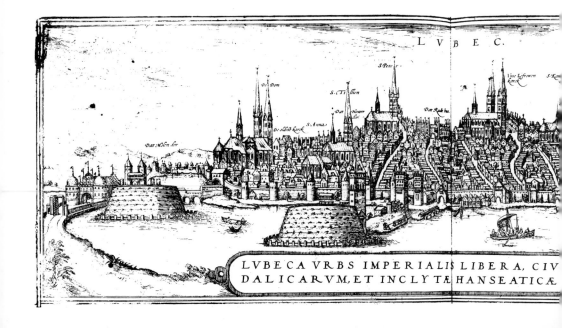

L V B E C.

LVBECA VRBS IMPERIALIS LIBERA, CIV
DALICARVM, ET INCLYTÆ HANSEATICÆ

become a maritime power. Having conquered Pisa and secured an outlet to the sea, the Florentine government launched a program for constructing merchant galleys at the Pisan arsenal and began sending fleets to Alexandria, Constantinople, and even to England and the Flanders coast. But the enterprise failed to achieve the continued success that had been anticipated and was eventually abandoned.

The Hansa

With the extension of Mediterranean commerce into the English Channel and the North Sea, an important link was made with the trading regions of northern Germany. In the early thirteenth century, several north-German coastal towns, including Lübeck, Hamburg, and Bremen, as well as cities on the navigable rivers as far inland as Cologne, had obtained favorable trading rights in some of the Flemish cities. In order to secure their sea lanes from the devastating raids of pirates and the rival shipping of Swedish and Danish merchantmen, these and other northern towns banded together in a commercial and military league known as the Hansa, or Hanseatic League. By mid-fourteenth century, some fifty towns had joined the brotherhood and were engaged in expanding trade from the eastern Baltic to the Atlantic. By the end of the century, over eighty cities were in the League. Together, these cities exercised a controlling role not only in northern commerce but in military and diplomatic affairs as well. The Hansa bought and sold goods, transported and stored them, made treaties and alliances, and on occasion even went to war. By treaty, the Hansa acquired full navigational rights between the Baltic and North seas, exemption from Danish customs duties, and a concession to establish trading "factories" in Danish territories. For nearly two centuries, the Hanseatic League maintained a fruitful monopoly on the northern-

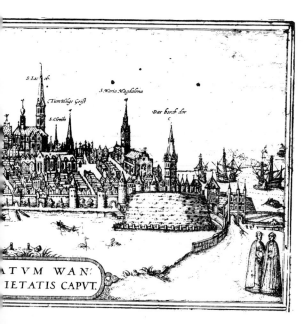

THE HANSEATIC CITY OF LÜBECK. *One of the original members of the Hansa, Lübeck continued to exercise a dominant role in the league throughout the fourteenth and fifteenth centuries. This woodcut shows the port about 1572. (New York Public Library)*

European trade in timber, fish, grain, furs, copper, tin, iron, leather, tallow, hemp, wax, honey, and wines.

The Hanseatic trade moved both northward and southward from Norway to Flanders, and east-west from Novgorod, in Russia, to London. An important feature of this trade was the establishment of settlements and commercial bases such as the ones at Bruges, Bergen, Novgorod, and the "Steelyard" in London. These factories bought, sold, and stored the products of their trade. By the fourteenth century, Bruges, the Hansa's southern terminus in Flanders, had become the economic crossroads of Europe and the point of contact between the merchants of the Hansa and the Flanders Fleet from Venice. For that reason, Bruges also became something of a melting pot of European cultures. Throughout the year, it was a city teeming with activity and excitement as merchants from all over Europe displayed and sold their wares, purchased products for resale abroad, floated loans, exchanged coins, and told endless tales of their travels to faraway cities.

The Techniques of Capitalism

The commercial revolution of the twelfth, thirteenth, and early fourteenth centuries gave rise to large capital accumulations, especially in Italy, and this capital was in turn employed to promote further trade, increase industrial development, and even expand mining and agriculture. All of these activities returned additional income to the entrepreneurs, thus giving birth to a full-scale system of capitalism—that is, the private accumulation and employment of liquid wealth for the purpose of making further financial profits. Broadening the European market was both a cause and an effect in this process and promoted an increase in large-scale enterprises of all types. The rise of capitalism gradually contributed to many changes in European economic and social life. The change to a predominantly money economy caused a decisive alteration in the manorial system, for example, as feudal obligations were commuted from services into cash payments and dues. With the increased demand for money came more intensive mining operations and a remarkable increase in minting and circulating coins. This in turn gave rise first to the ubiquitous money changer, then to banks, and finally to improvements in financial techniques and the development of credit.

Investment in commercial enterprises took many forms in this period and allowed a great variety of opportunity, and risk, to the investor. One common form of investment was the *sea loan*, involving an investor who advanced money to a trader or ship's captain at the outset of a commercial voyage. If the venture was successful, the investor received a predetermined percentage of the profit. If it failed, the money was lost. From this simple form of transaction grew many related techniques of investment, underwriting, and insurance. Also common were several types of commercial partnerships, with variations in the percentage of investment and degree of liability. The most popular of these was the *commenda*, which provided a wide range of participation, making it possible for people of modest means to engage in profitable investment. The *commenda* was a sharing arrangement by which one partner contributed capital and the other contributed time and labor, with the profits usually shared on a ¾/¼ basis. Many times, long-range commercial partnerships were formed by selling shares in an enterprise to an entire group of people who then shared in both profits and losses according to the amount of their investment. This type of joint stock company became customary in the development of the handicraft industry and banking.

To facilitate these business transactions, many techniques of money transfer were also developed, such as bills of exchange (promises of a purchaser to pay a seller at a certain time and place), drafts (bills of exchange involving three or more parties), acceptances (agreements by a drawee to pay money as directed by the drawer), *lettres de foire* (promissory notes usually negotiated with a moneylender at a fair), and many others. Of particular importance in the growth of these facilities and in keeping accurate and conveniently readable financial accounts was the development of double-entry bookkeeping. This efficient debit and credit accounting was first used in northern Italy in the fourteenth century and from there spread to the rest of Europe.

The growing need for more rapid and convenient exchange and conversion of coins caused an expansion of the functions of money changers, who were soon holding and guarding large sums of money, effecting the transfer of funds between debtors and creditors, and extending time loans to merchants and other bankers. Because they were excluded from landowning and other "acceptable" forms of economic endeavor, and because the medieval Catholic church took a very dim view of financiers, these money changers were usually Jews. Indeed, until their expulsion from most western-European countries (and even afterward), the Jewish involvement in trade and business enterprise was prominent. Their earliest activity was pawnbroking, that is, granting high-interest loans on valuable security such as jewels and silverware. But as the demand for their services increased, they diversified their activities and extended their forms of credit. Granting loans and using the money entrusted to them by depositors soon became a common financial activity, and they carried on many of the deposit, credit, and transfer functions of modern banks.

However, there were still obstacles to the natural expansion of financial capitalism in the early Renaissance, among them the opposition and restrictions of the church. Interest charged for the loan and use of money was considered usury by the medieval church because "money is sterile" and therefore cannot increase. This static conception of money continued into modern times, even while the merchants and bankers were proving it false. According to medieval interpretation, if people needed money, it should be loaned to them without charge. Any extension of credit for the purpose of gaining a profit was condemned as usury. Nevertheless, as investments expanded and fluid wealth became more necessary, ways were found to circumvent the regulations of the church against usury. In fact, the papacy itself was one of the first to insist that moderate interest paid on money invested *at a risk* to the creditor should not be considered usury. Furthermore, it was not usury when a charge was made for loans repaid after the promised date for repayment, or when the credit was in land instead of money. Although the church continued to condemn the exorbitant rates of interest frequently charged for the use of money, the practice of interest taking continued and expanded as an integral part of the rise of capitalism. The church contributed to this development in its organization for collecting ecclesiastical revenues.

By the end of the thirteenth century, Florence had become the recognized banking center of Europe. Capital was employed by increasing numbers of family firms for the purpose of financial investment and the stimulation of further commercial and industrial development. In the last decade of that century, the Bardi and Peruzzi families established banks in England; thirty years later they completely dominated the financial activities of that country. Confident in the Florentine banks, the papacy turned most of its business to them. By 1338 some eighty banking houses were operating in Florence, with exchanges in every part of Europe.

The banking activities of the Renaissance were diverse and elaborate. In addition to the family organizations prevalent in all of northern Italy,

MERCHANTS AT WORK. *This fifteenth-century miniature shows merchants busy changing money and selling shoes and pewterware. (Bibliothèque Municipale de Rouen)*

there were other privately owned banks of varying size and influence, as well as a number of government-chartered and at least partially government-owned banks. In 1401 the city of Barcelona founded a municipal bank, known as the *Taula,* and a few years later a similar establishment was created in Valencia. One of the most successful banks over the longest period of time was the famous Bank of Saint George in Genoa, founded in 1407 by state creditors and supported and directed by a board of directors who determined company policy and managed the bank's resources. The importance of credit banking increased during the fifteenth and sixteenth centuries as the European rulers required greater sums to finance their costly wars. Such loans to monarchs were profitable transactions, since rulers were frequently willing to pay enormous rates of interest, sometimes as high as 45 to 60 percent. But this was also a risky business, and most bank failures of the Renaissance period were due to overextended loans to rulers who failed to pay their debts.

(similar to today)

Industrial Development

The economic boom of late-medieval Italy was not confined to commercial and financial activities. Manufacturing flourished in Tuscany and in most of the northern city-states as it never had before. Industry thrived on trade, and trade stimulated further industrial development. Some of the industries were new, activated by the growing demand for wares formerly produced in the East and distributed in increasing amounts by Arab and Venetian merchants. In this way were developed the fine-glass–making craft in Venice (as well as lace, silks, brocades, and velvet), lace and silk production in Lucca, and steel manufacturing in Milan. Other industries, such as building ships, producing armor, weapons, and tools, and processing foodstuffs (particularly salted fish) were centuries old but experienced new vigor during the Renaissance.

The greatest volume industry of the thirteenth century, however, was cloth. Florence had been involved in the textile industry for a long time, primarily as a buyer of coarse cloth from the fairs in Flanders and Champagne, then dyeing, dressing, finishing, and marketing it throughout Europe and the Mediterranean basin. Due to the Florentine expertise in dyeing, that city held a monopoly on the manufacture of rich ecclesiastical vestments. This industry was controlled at all stages by the powerful guild of cloth finishers and merchants called the *Arte di Calimala.* The *Calimala* was an organization of merchants and industrialists closely linked in the cloth business, including many related enterprises, from shipwrights to bankers.

In the fourteenth century, the preeminence in Florence shifted from the *Calimala* to the *Arte della Lana,* specialists in the manufacture of woolen cloth. The wool guild imported raw wool primarily from Spain (and, beginning in the early fourteenth century, from England) and had

WOOLEN CLOTH MANUFAC-TURE. *Although, as a Spanish slogan goes, "La lana no se hace, nace" (Wool is not made, it is born), it must still go through many steps of processing before it becomes a finished product. Here, in Mirabello Cavalori's 1572 painting, wool is being washed and dried. (Editorial Photocolor Archives)*

it turned into woolen cloth for export abroad. Wool spinning and weaving had been a basic industry of the medieval towns for centuries, but in the hands of the Florentine *Lana* it now became a truly capitalistic enterprise. Raw wool was distributed by the *Lana* merchants in a "putting-out" or domestic system to many shops and homes for processing through its various stages: washing, beating, combing, carding, spinning, weaving, cleaning, fulling, tentering (stretching), raising, shearing, dressing, dyeing, stretching again, and cutting. During the manufacturing process, ownership of the material was retained by the original merchant-industrialist who paid for the labor by the piece and then, after the cloth was finished, sold it through outlets in Italy and elsewhere.

By the middle of the fourteenth century, the Florentine wool industry had not only brought great wealth to the members of the guild, but, it has been estimated, it also provided the principal or sole livelihood for some 30,000 people in and around Florence. It is not surprising, then, that the *Calimala* and the *Lana* also dominated Florentine politics during that time. By the middle of the fifteenth century, their preeminence was shared by the silk manufacturers of the *Arte della Seta*. Silk production never involved as many people in Florence as did wool and required less division of labor, but it did bring enormous wealth to those who controlled it.

Another, perhaps even more important, manufacturing area for woolen textiles was the southern Netherlands: Brabant, Hainaut, Artois, and, above all, Flanders. Not only were the active Flemish towns of Ypres, Ghent, Bruges, Arras, Saint Omer, Douai, Lille, and Tournai the greatest producers of all grades and types of woolen cloth, but almost every town in Flanders made and marketed cloth by the end of the thirteenth century. This alone made Flanders one of the wealthiest economic regions of Europe. Some raw wool for the Flemish looms came from local producers, but most of it was imported from England, mostly from Lincolnshire and the Cotswolds. After the mid-thirteenth century, long-staple merino wool was also imported from Spain. The vital economic connection between England and Flanders remained close even after the rise of a sizable English cloth-manufacturing industry in the fifteenth century absorbed an increasing share of the English wool production, and gradually changed England from a wool- to a cloth-exporting country. Flemish buyers and merchants, organized in the Flemish League of London, remained in constant touch with the English growers and with the merchants of the English Company of Merchant Staplers, who marketed their valuable product. The finished broadcloths were traded at the Champagne fairs, sold in bulk to the traders of the Hanseatic League and to the Venetian, Genoese, and Florentine merchants for distribution throughout the Mediterranean.

Economic Collapse and Recovery

Unfortunately, the story of economic prosperity and expansion is not a continuous one. At one time, scholars equated the commercial revolution and the vigorous early period of Italian financial and industrial activity with the cultural flowering of the Renaissance, but such a direct equation is no longer possible. It is untenable because the evidence of widespread economic depression, beginning in the early decades of the fourteenth century with the devastating famine of 1315–17, is undeniable. Droughts, bad harvests, and pestilences were not new to Europe, but seldom had they been so frequent and so disastrous. A crop failure that two centuries earlier might have caused only local famine now could upset the economy over a wide area. Furthermore, these calamities, triggered by a remarkable climatic change that lowered the average temperature several degrees and produced torrential and continuous rains, were accompanied by many human disasters that added to the seriousness and extent of the economic collapse. The outbreak of the Hundred Years' War, corresponding in time with the great increase in chaotic mercenary warfare in Italy, not only brought havoc and devastation to large areas but also disturbed and in some cases severed the vital lines of commercial communication that were gradually making Europe more interdependent. The collapse of the Mongol Empire in Asia and the rise of the hostile Ottoman Turks in the Middle East likewise imposed new constrictions on the Eastern trade routes and impeded all forms of transportation.

Then, in 1348 and 1349, Europe was swept by the Black Death, a pestilential epidemic of the dreaded bubonic plague (accompanied, it is now believed, by the more infectious pneumonic plague), leaving death, misery, and destruction in its wake. The population dropped sharply, especially in the crowded cities, where the plague raged uncontrollably. Florence, for example, declined from a city of nearly 100,000 inhabitants in 1338 to less than 50,000 in 1351. Thousands of European villages completely disappeared. Death and misery were accompanied by financial collapse. Markets shrank, industry declined, businesses went bankrupt, and banks failed. In 1345 and 1346, the English king, pressed by the exigencies of the war in France, repudiated his debts to the Bardi and Peruzzi bankers. Many firms had already fallen during the costly war between Florence and Lucca, and others followed the Bardi and Peruzzi crash. Soon the entire financial network of Europe was in shambles.

Recovery from these catastrophes was sporadic and slow. The plague continued intermittently to devastate urban areas throughout the rest of the century and remained a recurring threat for the next 300 years. The economic disorders of the period were accompanied by serious social upheavals and mass rebellions. In 1347 a mob of frenzied Romans, agitated and led by the visionary Cola di Rienzo, seized the government

of Rome and for seven months defied both the nobles and the pope (who resided now at Avignon but still considered Rome his possession). Six years later, the Roman populace again asserted its strength, took control of the city, and recalled their leader from exile. But in less than a year, Rienzo was murdered by the same people who had raised him to power. At the same time, France was shaken by a more widespread and devastating upheaval known as the *Jacquerie*. This was primarily a rural revolt but was accompanied by a Parisian uprising in 1358 instigated by Etienne Marcel. At the height of his crusade against the power of the aristocracy, Marcel, like Rienzo, was struck down by assassins.

Nowhere were the class antagonisms and struggles more bitter than in Florence where cloth workers (*ciompi*) and propertyless piece-laborers struggled for civil and economic rights. Widespread cutbacks in the labor force, due to the economic decline, added unemployment to the growing list of labor hazards. In 1378 the *ciompi* rose in revolt against the merchant oligarchy and the powerful guilds who ruled Florence. For a while, it looked like they would attain some of their goals, but the revolution was suppressed and they were forced back into their prior role.

The 1381 insurrection in England, known as the Peasants' Revolt, was another example of the social unrest resulting from the economic upheavals of the period and the decay of medieval institutions and patterns that had been undermined and rendered obsolete by the rise of a money economy and international trade. These mass uprisings were not only examples of the oppressed classes trying to alter the conditions of their life but also the protests of disillusioned and frightened people against the changes that were enveloping them and threatening their security.

Although economic historians continue to dispute the extent and duration of the early Renaissance depression, and especially the degree of recovery achieved during the fifteenth century, some valid generalizations can be made. In the first place, Europe as a whole did not again experience the overall economic boom that she had enjoyed in the thirteenth and early fourteenth centuries. The wealth of the fifteenth century was very unevenly distributed and reflected only sporadic and limited prosperity. Nevertheless, recovery did take place and seems to have begun earlier in many of the northern Italian cities than in the rest of Europe, which remained in economic doldrums until the early sixteenth century. Early in the fifteenth century, Florentine wool output

BURYING VICTIMS OF THE PLAGUE. *The devastation and depopulation caused by the Black Death were so great that burial of the dead became a twenty-four-hour routine for the living, as shown in this fourteenth-century manuscript drawing. (© Bibliothèque royale Albert Ier, Brussels)*

began to climb, and although it never reached the peak production of 1,200,000 florins of 1338, it did recapture many of the markets lost in the previous decades.

Much of the Florentine recovery came about because of the development and expansion of certain luxury industries—especially lace and silk manufacturing—and the recovery of preeminence in banking. Throughout the fifteenth century, as the demand for brocades, damasks, and luxury dress increased, the silk industry prospered in Florence and Lucca and was accompanied by an increased production of lace, embroidery, ceramics, glassware, and handiworked items in wood, metal, and precious stones. These industries did not employ as many people as the woolen industry and therefore contributed less to overall prosperity, but they did help make some groups fabulously rich and in this way added to the economic, social, and cultural characteristics of the Renaissance. It was, after all, concentrated wealth, not evenly distributed prosperity, that built the great Renaissance palaces and patronized the painters and sculptors. It may also be true, as Robert Sabatino Lopez suggests, that with fewer economic opportunities for the investment of capital than existed in the thirteenth century, fifteenth-century entrepreneurs and wealthy patrons invested more of their money in culture than ever before.

Renaissance Businessmen

If the fifteenth century was not a period of total prosperity, it was at least an age of successfully renewed business enterprises and of great financial fortunes won and lost. One example of these successful businessmen of the last decades of the fourteenth century and the early fifteenth was Francesco Datini from Prato, near Florence. At the age of fifteen, Datini set off for Avignon to seek his fortune at the papal court. There, amid the luxury and squalor of this crowded city, he became a prosperous merchant, dealing chiefly in arms and armor, which he sold to all buyers, and later in salt, silverware, artwork, and money changing. He also traded in precious stones, French enamels, Genoese linens, Cremonan fustians (coarse cloth), fine Florentine woolens, and reaped great profits from the sale of decorated travel coffers and jewel cases, embroidered luxury clothes, clerical vestments, and religious pictures. After returning to Prato, he grew from a prosperous local merchant to a hard-headed international businessman of the first rank, with agents in Florence, Pisa, Genoa, Majorca, Montpellier, Avignon, Valencia, Barcelona, Bruges, and London. The watchword of Datini's success is expressed by the caption on his account books: "In the name of God and profit!"

The financial activities of the Venetian merchant Andrea Barbarigo provide another interesting example of the successful entrepreneur of Renaissance Italy. Barbarigo came from a family of merchant nobles whose livelihood and position had depended on the sea. His apprenticeship on the Venetian galleys was begun at the age of nineteen as a "bowman of the quarterdeck," where he not only learned about ships and the sea but also about money, trade, and markets. Andrea Barbarigo began his commercial career with 200 ducats, and from that beginning, he eventually became one of the wealthiest and most successful men in Renaissance Venice. Through his business ledgers, beginning in 1431, we can follow much of Barbarigo's career and see many of his mercantile enterprises. Like other successful merchants of his day, Barbarigo diversified his financial interests, being careful not to put all of his ducats in one galley. At the height of his mercantile activity, he traded in every conceivable product and service but derived his most profitable returns from Eastern cottons, silk, and pepper; woolen cloth, pewter, and tin from northern Europe; and olive oil, Brazilwood, leather, cloth, and gold thread from Italy and Spain. Aided by the regularity and reliability of the Venetian fleets and the favor of the government, Andrea Barbarigo succeeded handsomely in an age of economic revival and expansion.

Successful businessmen of the fifteenth century were not all from Italy, of course. One of the most remarkable was Jacques Coeur of Bourges, in central France. From his first voyage to the Levant in 1427 until the dazzling climax of his career in 1449, Jacques Coeur displayed a "Midas touch" in every venture. From his home base at Montpellier, he extended his lines of trade throughout the Mediterranean and Europe, with principal factors in Marseille, Avignon, Lyon, Limoges, Paris, Rouen, and Bruges, engaging in the lucrative East-West traffic in spices, silks, furs, carpets, armor, jewels, cloth, and slaves. Soon he owned a fleet of merchant galleys, which not only added to his wealth but also involved him in political and diplomatic affairs. He coined money for the French crown, negotiated a treaty with the Moslems of Egypt and Syria, opened diplomatic relations between France and the sultan, and served as French ambassador to Rome. By mid-century, Jacques Coeur was the wealthiest citizen of France, and his businesses were located throughout Europe. He operated a silk factory in Florence, paper and cloth mills in Provence, and salt, copper, silver, and lead mines near Lyon. He became the royal banker and paymaster of the king, as well as a member of the king's council.

The fall of Jacques Coeur was even more sudden than his rise. In addition to wealth and prestige, his success also brought him jealousy and intrigue. In 1451 he was accused of murdering the king's mistress, then arrested and charged with kidnapping French sailors for his galleys, negotiating with the infidels, and many other offenses. His property was confiscated, he was heavily fined, sentenced to banishment and prison, and tortured on the rack before he died in 1456 on the island of Chios. All of which illustrates how capricious a mistress was fortune and fame in the Renaissance. Yet it is also true that Jacques

Coeur was a less cautious businessman than Barbarigo and, unlike Datini, spent too much of his wealth and time on the affairs of princes.

The Medici Enterprises

Of all the examples of Renaissance economic success, none was quite so extensive or politically significant as that of the Medici family of Florence. What is usually referred to as the Medici bank was in fact an extensive complex of interlinking partnerships, resembling a modern holding company, engaged in a variety of banking, commercial, and industrial activities. The many branches and partnerships were independent of each other, and their managers enjoyed the right to make many decisions on the operation of their branches. Overall policy, of course, was set by the Medici patriarch in Florence, whose ultimate domination of all subsidiaries was maintained by having control of at least 50 percent of the companies' stock. The partnership agreements between the Medici and their subsidiaries specified in detail the extent and nature of their relationship and the duties, responsibilities, and prerogatives of each.

The foundations of the Medici enterprises were laid by Giovanni de' Medici in 1397 with the creation of a banking house for trade in foreign bills of exchange and in commodities of all kinds. By the time of Giovanni's death in 1429, the Medici firm had branches in Rome, Venice, Geneva, and, for a while, in Naples, with extensive operations in the international cloth trade and all forms of banking activity. Under the skillful supervision of Giovanni's son Cosimo, the Medici firm became one of the most active and prosperous commercial organizations in Italy and the greatest banking house in Europe. Cosimo established branches in Pisa, Milan, Avignon, Bruges, and London, with scores of factors and agents in other cities as well. Besides the bank, he also controlled three cloth-manufacturing complexes in Florence.

Through their branch in Rome, the Medici were the official bankers and fiscal agents of the papacy (except for the period between 1476 and 1481 when Pope Sixtus IV changed to the rival Pazzi bank), and after 1466 they gained a controlling interest in the *Societas Aluminum*, which exploited the papal alum mines at Tolfa, in northeastern Italy. The extensive use of alum in the textile-dyeing process made it a valuable product of European trade, and since most of the alum had previously been imported from the Turkish-controlled Levant at excessive prices, the potential market for the Tolfa product was almost unlimited. For a time, the Medici were able to corner the alum market through a cartel with the papacy.

More important, however, than their industrial and mining operations were the Medici financial functions. Throughout the fifteenth century, the Medici bank dealt in all forms of credit and loans, and was a leading trader in foreign bills of exchange. It also accepted money for deposit, which it in turn invested at profitable rates in a variety of enterprises. In these operations, which brought not only financial profits but also great political influence, the Medici made use of their connections to facilitate further transactions and surpass their competitors.

The "Medici magic" did not continue indefinitely, however. Many factors combined to cause the decline and eventual demise of the Medici bank. The greatest of the Medici politicians and patrons of art, Lorenzo the Magnificent, was not the financial manager his grandfather Cosimo had been. Lorenzo lacked Cosimo's business ability and was less interested in the activities of the bank. He therefore delegated more authority to junior partners and branch managers. This need not have caused difficulty, but many of these managers were less skillful and some were extremely imprudent in their use of funds for risky loans. Perhaps even more disastrous was the increasing tendency under Lorenzo's administration to expend great sums for household expenses and costly luxury and pomp instead of reinvesting it in the business. Large amounts of money were also tied up in dangerous loans to princes, several of which, like the loan to Charles the Bold, Duke of Burgundy, were never repaid. Matters outside Medici control also contributed to the decline. For example, the price differential between gold and silver increased drastically between 1475 and 1495, causing serious payment problems with the gold florin, which was the basic unit of Medici banking and trade. Much of their income was in low-value silver from France, Flanders, and England, while their debts were in high-value gold florins.

Ultimately, however, the collapse of the Medici enterprises came not so much from economic as from political causes. Although several branch operations were suspended before 1494, the French invasion of Italy in that year, with its accompanying revolution in Florence and the expulsion of the Medici family and confiscation of their remaining assets, brought an end to the organization that was the largest and most influential banking complex of the fifteenth century.

Urban Life in the Renaissance

Commercial capitalism had spawned a race of merchants and businessmen who came to play a dominant role in the political, economic, social, and cultural life of the time. We have looked at some of the activities and accomplishments of this prosperous class. But we should not assume that the merchant-nobles alone molded Renaissance society, even though they did play a predominant role in it. Like the varieties and contrasts of an Italian landscape, urban life in Renaissance Italy was ever changing, as the cities became the melting pots of every ingredient of human society, rural as well as urban. In every Italian city, the stone battlements guarded only against military attack, not, as had the high towers of the medieval castle, against the cultural and economic influences from beyond its walls.

Most Renaissance cities had grown from medieval or ancient nuclei outward in all directions like the rings of a tree, with concentric circles of protective walls marking the stages of growth. Cobblestoned streets were narrow and crooked, terminating either at the city walls or winding back and forth in meaningless labyrinths. Only after the recovery of Vitruvius's ancient work on architecture late in the fifteenth century did builders begin to apply rules of art and order to city planning. The Vitruvian concept of a city as a functional unit, designed with each part—streets, squares, sewage and water systems, public buildings and homes—contributing rationally to the whole was greatly popularized by the Florentine Leon Battista Alberti. But even then, necessity and tradition still dictated the direction of urban growth, and only in such rare cases as Palma Nova, near Venice, where a completely new city was built, could this ancient-Renaissance conception of city planning be fully realized. Yet despite the hodgepodge growth of the Italian cities, they presented, in their large civic buildings, ample squares, elegant churches, and towering patrician houses, a favorable contrast to the squalid towns and cities of the rest of Europe. Citizens of these Italian communes took great pride in their churches and public buildings, and contributed both time and money to the upkeep of the city walls. The guilds of Florence and other cities sponsored ambitious projects of beautification and expansion, and contributed much to artistic growth through their patronage of artists and builders.

In many ways, life in these cities was much like that in the country, lived outdoors and in community. Signs of the *contado* (the rural area outside a city) were present everywhere. Vegetables grew in small plots between the buildings and along the city walls. Goats, pigs, chickens, and cows wandered almost as freely in the streets as they did in the fields. Daily, fishermen brought their catch into the city for sale in the fish markets, just as peasants poured through the gates bringing fruit, vegetables, and fowls, and the country miller distributed wheat and barley flour to the city bakers. At harvest time, the smell of grapes and olive oil filled the air, and a little later, the pungence of fermentation told how bounteous the vintage had been. The activities of the tailor, cobbler, weaver, and goldsmith were carried on in the open in hundreds of tiny shops fronting on the streets, with an upper story or a back room or two where the family ate and slept.

People gathered in the public square not only to hear announcements and orders from the government, but also occasionally to participate in that government and to witness the daily execution of punishment for the violation of public laws. The spectacle of a naked prostitute being whipped through the streets, of a thief having his hand chopped off, of a tax violator chained to the pillory being baited by dogs, of a dishonest saddler or potter being flogged, of a heretic being dragged behind

horses to the square to be burned alive, were events eagerly attended by all classes of society. Happier participation was afforded by the celebrations of frequent holy days, when public feasts, games, and religious processions were the order of the day. Nothing was spared to make these holidays spectacular in every way. In addition to the religious festivals, many secular celebrations were also held, commemorating the memory of great heroes and events of the past or the changing of the seasons. Elaborate masquerades, displays, and splendid processions accompanied these celebrations. Especially impressive were the Venetian carnivals that sometimes lasted for many days.

Even on ordinary work days, apparel was becoming colorful and elaborate. For those who could afford it, brocades, velvets, silks, and gold embroidery with precious stones were the signs of affluence by which both men and women hoped to impress each other and dispel their own nagging fears of death. Ladies' fashion as set by the women of the Italian courts reached its most elegant and bizarre extremes in fifteenth- and sixteenth-century Venice, where color and ornamentation knew no limits. Venetian women, with their exposed bosoms, painted faces, and elaborately laced and scented silks, were the talk of travelers and courtiers from far around—although Montaigne, in 1581, found them to be rather disappointing. Perhaps the stories had caused him to expect too much. Men's fashions were even more colorful and elaborate, with multicolored doublet and hose, slashed and detachable sleeves, and velvet cape making up the costume of the well-dressed gentleman.

Less concerned over this affectation for dress and display were the forgotten people of the Renaissance: the rural peasants, propertyless laborers, and jobless vagabonds. Peasant life in the Renaissance was not markedly different from the Middle Ages, nor was there much to distinguish between the conditions of rural life in Italy and in many other countries of Europe. The legal status of peasants had generally changed from that of bonded serfs to free peasants, but that emancipation was still far from complete and was fraught with many hardships. The feudal tenure of land had long since broken up in Lombardy and Tuscany, yet in Naples, vestiges of serfdom continued to exist into modern times, and new forms of vassalage emerged throughout Italy. Sharecropping became common in the fourteenth and fifteenth centuries, with the peasants living on and working the land for a percentage of the harvest (seldom more than enough to pay their rent and expenses) and the owner, who lived in the city or a nearby villa, receiving the rest. The relationship between landowner and tenant in this situation was usually strained. Quarrels over the ownership of property, tools, goods, and even livestock, were frequent—and almost always settled in the landlord's favor. Peasants were frequently so far in debt to their landlord and other creditors that to call them freemen is a travesty of words. Some peasants were better off than this, however, with more favorable lease-holding arrangements and higher-yield farms. Peasant ownership of land was also growing slowly in some areas and producing a new class of semiprosperous yeoman farmers.

The dregs of society were the propertyless pieceworkers and those with no job at all. Social ossification deprived many otherwise willing workers of any hope even for simple security, much less for advancement. Of course the vagabond ranks were also swollen with many "sturdy beggars" who would not have worked even if they had had the opportunity. But Renaissance society had little patience and no compassion for either of these groups, making no distinction between the poor and the idlers. They were both considered and treated like criminals. "Those that are lazy and indolent in a way that does harm to the city, and who can offer no just reason for their condition, should either be forced to work or expelled from the Commune," wrote Matteo Palmieri, a rich merchant of Florence. "The city would thus rid itself of that most harmful part of the poorest class. . . . If the lowest order of society earn enough food to keep them going from day to day, then they have enough." Indeed, for them, staying alive was the supreme achievement. These were some of the people passed up by the flowering Renaissance, for although the fifteenth century was an age of refinement and culture, it could be fully enjoyed only by the wealthy or the noble. Lorenzo the Magnificent reflected the attitude of the time when he wrote, "Only men of noble birth can obtain perfection. The poor, who work with their hands and have no time to cultivate their minds, are incapable of it." During the course of the Italian Renaissance, many social barriers to the lower classes were removed or bypassed, but this was not yet a time of emancipation for the masses.

Nevertheless, strong forces of amalgamation were at work. Not the least of these were the leveling effects of disease and plague, which did not discriminate between rich and poor, good and bad, old and young. Periodic outbreaks of the plague devastated Europe during most of the period from the mid-fourteenth to the mid-seventeenth century. It struck with greatest fury during the late summer months, without warning and without a predictable pattern. In some cities, half or three-quarters of the population might be annihilated in a single epidemic; in many areas, there were not enough living to bury the dead. Highly contagious and apparently uncontrollable, the plague was attributed to the ravaging of the Devil or the chastisement of God. Every known method of prevention was employed to combat the disease, from ringing bells, shooting firearms, and playing loud music, to burning goat horns, absorbing the poisons with live birds and spiders, and wearing strange amulets made of "unicorn horn" or exotic stones, or hazelnut shells filled with mercury, or the head of a toad held next to the body. The omnipresence of this dreaded pestilence brought an awareness of death to Renaissance life and provided a grim paradox to the age of "rebirth."

Domestic Life

The Role of Women

Family life in the Renaissance centered around the woman, whose chief function, as in the Middle Ages, was to bear and rear children. Nevertheless, notable changes were taking place in attitudes toward the role of women in Italian society. In the first place, the wide discrepancy between the idealization and the treatment of women as practiced in the age of chivalry was gradually narrowing. In general, they were romanticized less but treated better. In the fifteenth century, it was becoming more common to consider women as individual personalities of considerable merit, intellectually, at least, almost equal to men. For this reason, greater stress was given to the education of young girls, to train their minds and better prepare them to teach their own children the rudiments of knowledge. The literacy level of women in the Italian cities was remarkably higher than it had ever been; many women had not merely an elementary knowledge of reading and writing but had mastered Latin grammar, studied the church fathers, and even read the classical literature that was becoming such a rage. Many women took an active part in the art, literature, and music of the time, and the list of very gifted women who developed their talents and trained their intellects is impressive. Some of them, such as the brilliant Isabella d'Este, Veronica de Gambara, Battista Sforza, Elisabetta Gonzaga, and Vittoria Colonna, also became noteworthy patronesses of the arts themselves.

Of course, these and many others like them were remarkable individuals whose noble birth or high position gave them unusual advantages. All Renaissance women were not so fortunate. The condition of those in the lower orders of society was difficult and depressing. A Florentine bookseller reflected a widespread attitude when he enumerated the following behavioral responsibilities of women. "One: to bring up their children piously, and two: to be quiet in church, to which I myself would like to add: to be quiet everywhere else also." Even Castiglione, who wrote the most favorable and widely circulated assessment of women, confessed that he was speaking of the court lady, not of women in general. Female education was definitely aimed at preparing a girl for one of two careers, either the convent or marriage.

THE RENAISSANCE LADY. *Beatrice d'Este, duchess of Milan and sister of the renowned Isabella d'Este, was one of the most accomplished women in Italy. Married to Ludovico Sforza, she brought refinement to the court of Milan. This portrait is attributed to Ambrogio de Predis, Leonardo da Vinci's business partner and pupil. Leonardo himself may have put finishing touches on it. (Alinari/ Editorial Photocolor Archives)*

Girls married young, usually before they reached twenty, and began a life of subservience to their husbands. In rural Italy, men were customarily seven or eight years older than the woman they married. In the cities, they were thirty to thirty-five years old, and frequently as much as forty, accounting for the high ratio of single adult males in most cities and explaining the commensurately large number of courtesans and prostitutes. This age differential further emphasized the wife's subordinate role, but worked to her advantage when the husband died, leaving her, a fairly young widow, with full legal possession of all his money and property. Betrothals were always arranged by the parents. The contract was usually in writing and specified the nature and size of the dowry as well as the living facilities and clothes the bridegroom promised to provide his wife.

Depending on wealth and status, the household duties of women varied greatly from toiling continuously at every task (including work in the fields or laboring in the artisan shops) to supervising and managing a houseful of servants. During their fertile years, women spent much of their time bearing children. Eight, ten, or even fifteen births were not unusual; but with the high rate of infant mortality, seldom more than four or five survived infancy. The care and education of these children was the mother's task. Family size generally increased in the fifteenth century as the plague slowly lost its virulence, but the vicissitudes of war, famine, and disease still threatened whole families as well as individuals.

The Family

Family ties and traditions were very strong in Renaissance Italy. This intense concern for maintaining the continuity and strength of the family is witnessed in many facets of Renaissance life. There was active interest in genealogy and family roots, in tracing family lineage back to earlier times and discovering relationships to important people. Happily for the historian, this produced a flurry of family chronicles, personal histories, and books of family counsel. Heads of families were concerned not only about their roots but also their values, present prosperity, and future outlook. For this purpose, Leon Battista Alberti wrote his celebrated *Della famiglia* (On the Family) in 1443. He advised the family to be united and stay close together, expand the family circle and strengthen its ties by having many male children, and promote the family's good name.

Alberti's was a typical family unit of the Renaissance, an extended household of considerable size including father, mother, brothers, children, possibly grandparents and other blood relatives, as well as servants, all bearing the same family name, wearing the same family insignia, and eating under one roof. Such families were legal units, with each member enjoying the same rights, prerogatives, and respon-

A NOBLE'S WEDDING. *The elegance of aristocratic life is revealed in a contemporary illustration of the nuptials of Renaud de Montauban and the daughter of the ruler of Gascony. The wedding procession is shown at left; beyond the doorway the newlyweds reach their bed chamber. (Bibliothèque Nationale, Paris)*

sibilities as the whole. If the family name was entitled to a tax exemption, each individual benefited personally. By the same token, liability for a crime committed by any member fell on the entire family. Consequently, whenever a member of one family insulted or harmed a member of another, a *vendetta* might follow that could involve seventy-five or a hundred people. The classic dramatization of such an occurrence is Shakespeare's *Romeo and Juliet.* It is small wonder, then, that the social life of Renaissance Italy was marked by violence and disorder as well as prosperity and progress.

The Home

The home life of most Renaissance families—except for the very highest and lowest classes—was both simple and reasonably comfortable. Middle-class houses in the city-states were usually one- or two-story structures made of wood and stucco. Window glass was seldom used in Italian homes, although it was gaining popularity with those who could afford it in the colder countries of the north. Instead, windows were covered with wooden shutters that in the warmer climate of Italy could be opened to both light and air during the day. In wintertime, they had to remain closed to conserve heat. The Renaissance invention of the enclosed stove (first used in Germany), with its greater efficiency than an open fireplace, helped make life more comfortable.

Rooms were intended to be more functional than private, and therefore served multiple purposes: bedrooms were also sitting rooms and kitchens served also as dining rooms. Rooms opened directly into each other because halls obviously wasted space. A minimum of bedtime privacy was provided by surrounding the bed with a hanging curtain. Wooden bathtubs appeared in some middle-class homes of the Renaissance because public baths, so popular in the Middle Ages, had almost gone out of existence since the Black Death. Moreover, the expense of firewood for heating the water in the cities and the fear that bathing was connected with the plague caused the bath itself to become very rare, especially in winter. Understandably, the demand for aromatic colognes and perfumes increased.

Common household furnishings included wooden tables, chairs, cupboards, and large chests, or trunks, that held many of the householder's belongings. A well-stocked *cassone* (dowry chest) was the prized possession of a new bride when she began married life. Tapestries, vases, porcelain, glassware, and other objects of art, as well as pictures and books, especially after the development of printing, became increasingly important to domestic life, as people were able to afford them.

In most households, eating utensils were simple and limited, consisting primarily of plates (wooden or earthenware), knives, spoons, and drinking mugs, which were usually made of metal, although sometimes they were of ceramic or glass in the more affluent homes. The fork was invented in Renaissance Italy but only slowly came into use in the other countries. As late as 1611, the English traveler Thomas Coryat noted the unique Italian practice of eating meat with a fork. "The reason of this curious custom," he wrote, "is because the Italian cannot by any means endure to have his dish touched with fingers, seeing all men's fingers are not alike cleane." Many features of table etiquette originated in the Renaissance when Italy set the standard of manners and style. Catherine de' Medici, Lorenzo's great granddaughter, who became queen of France, is credited with introducing urban Italian table manners into France.

The cultured courts of Umbria, Tuscany, Emilia-Romagna, and Lombardy set the tone of refined eating, with elegant banquets complete with music, ingenious and sometimes animated arrangements of food, and an endless variety of savory dishes. Even the meals of the average citizen were tastefully prepared and eaten with an elegance incomprehensible beyond the Alps. Pasta, prepared and flavored in many ways depending on the region and personal taste, was already the basis of the Italian diet. Salads were also popular, as were melons, light soups, mushrooms (especially the delicate little *prugnoli*), pigeon, chicken, and veal. A famous Florentine delicacy was pork-liver sausage, known as *fegatelli*. Renaissance tables also knew many varieties of cheese, fruit, and, of course, wine.

Bread was the staple in peasant households, usually made from barley flour ground locally at the community mill and baked at home in large earthen ovens. Most urban housewives sent their dough to the town bakeries where it was baked for them by guild bakers. Officials regularly inspected the bakeries to ensure high quality and honesty. Taking dough to the baker and picking up the baked loaves was only one of the many jobs assigned to household servants hired to help with menial labors.

Domestic slaves also became common in the fifteenth century with the beginning of the Portuguese black slave trade in West Africa. Likewise, captured Tartars and Turks from the Levant were sold at the slave markets of Venice, Ancona, Pisa, and Genoa, and took their place in the domestic life of the Renaissance. The rising cost of imported slaves, however, along with a growing Turkish domination of the slave markets, sharply reduced the supply of domestic slaves in Italy in the sixteenth century, except in the Mediterranean galleys. In the meantime, the wholesale transplanting of African slaves into the New World colonies began another era of social discrimination and oppression.

Suggestions for Further Reading

ECONOMY, TRADE, AND INDUSTRY

The best short studies of Renaissance economic affairs are Harry A. Miskimin, *The Economy of Early Renaissance Europe, 1300–1460* (New York, 1975) and *The Economy of Later Renaissance Europe, 1460–1600* (New York, 1978). Anthony Molho, *Social and Economic Foundations of the Italian Renaissance* (New York, 1969) is an important collection of scholarly essays. Gino Luzzato, *An Economic History of Italy from the Fall of Rome to the Beginning of the Sixteenth Century*, tr. by Philip Jones (New York, 1961) is a basic general account. On trade, see Armando Sapori, *The Italian Merchant in the Middle Ages*, tr. by Patricia Ann Kennen (New York, 1970); Michael Mallet, *Florentine Galleys in the Fifteenth Century* (Oxford, 1967), describing the brief Florentine attempt to become a sea power; Wendy R. Childs, *Anglo-Castilian Trade in the Late Middle Ages* (Totowa, 1978), a scholarly study of the fourteenth and fifteenth centuries; John H. A. Munro, *Wool, Cloth and Gold: The Struggle for Bullion in the Anglo-Burgundian Trade, 1340–1478* (Toronto, 1972); and Philippe Dollinger, *The German Hansa*, tr. by D. S. Ault and S. H. Steinberg (Stanford, 1970).

ECONOMIC COLLAPSE AND RECOVERY

The "depression" thesis is best presented in Robert S. Lopez and Harry A. Miskimin, "The Economic Depression of the Renaissance," *Economic History Review*, 14 (1962), 408–26. Carlo Cipolla, "The Economic Depression of the Renaissance?" *Ibid.*, 16 (1964), 519–24, is a careful critique of Lopez and Miskimin. Robert S. Lopez, "Hard Times and Investment in Culture," *The Renaissance: Six Essays* (New York, 1962), accounts for the flowering of Renaissance culture by the decline of capital investment in economic enterprises. Other expressions of trouble are seen in Benjamin Kedar, *Merchants in Crisis: Genoese and Venetian Men of Affairs and the Fourteenth-Century Depression* (New Haven, 1976); Michael Mollet and Philippe Wolff, *The Popular Revolution of the Late Middle Ages* (London, 1973). Philip Ziegler, *The Black Death* (New York, 1969) focuses on England. A vivid and dismal picture of the age is drawn by Barbara W. Tuchman in *A Distant Mirror: The Calamitous Fourteenth Century* (New York, 1978).

Remarkable recovery is evidenced in Iris Origo, *The Merchant of Prato: Francesco di Marco Datini* (London, 1963); Frederic C. Lane, *Andrea Barbarigo, Merchant of Venice, 1418–1449*, 2nd ed. (New York, 1967); and Robert A. Goldthwaite, *Private Wealth in Renaissance Florence: A Study of Four Families* (Princeton, 1968), which depicts family households as reflected in the account books of the Strozzi, Guicciardini, Gondi, and Capponi families Anthony Molho, *Florentine Public Finances in the Early Renaissance, 1400–1433* (Cambridge, Mass., 1971), examines the fiscal crisis that brought the Medici to power. Raymond de Roover, *The Rise and Decline of the Medici Bank, 1397–1494* (New York, 1966) is the definitive work on the Medici enterprises.

LIFE IN THE RENAISSANCE

The most complete and authoritative look at what it might have been like to live during the Renaissance is J. R. Hale, *Renaissance Europe: The Individual and Society, 1480–1520* (London and New York, 1971), in the History of Europe series, edited by J. H. Plumb. Other examinations of daily life include J. Lucas-Dubreton, *Daily Life in Florence in the Time of the Medici*, tr. by A. Lytton Sells (London, 1960); E. R. Chamberlin, *Everyday Life in Renaissance Times* (London, 1965); and John Gage, *Life in Italy at the Time of the Medici* (New York, 1968); the latter two are short works with many woodcuts and drawings. Brian Pullan, *Rich and Poor in Renaissance Venice* (Cambridge, Mass., 1971), is a penetrating analysis. See also John H. Langbein, *Prosecuting Crime in the Renaissance* (Cambridge, Mass., 1974). Gene Brucker (ed.), *The Society of Renaissance Florence* (New York, 1971) is an interesting documentary collection revealing aspects of Renaissance life.

WOMEN AND THE FAMILY

David Herlihy, *The Family in Renaissance Italy* (St. Louis, 1974) is a brief but very insightful summary. Francis M. Kent, *Household and Lineage in Renaissance Florence: The Family Life of the Capponi, Ginori, and Rucellai* (Princeton, 1977) is both revealing and significant. Recent and thought-provoking works on Renaissance women are Ruth Kelso, *Doctrine of the Lady of the Renaissance*, 2nd ed. (Urbana, 1978); S. Chojnacki, "Patrician Women in Early Renaissance Venice," *Studies in the Renaissance*, 21 (1974), 176–203; and Lauro Martines, "A Way of Looking at Women in Renaissance Florence," *Journal of Medieval and Renaissance Studies*, 4 (1974), 15–28. Hannelore Sachs, *The Renaissance Woman*, tr. by Marianne Herzfeld (New York, 1971) is a brief text with many illustrations.

CHAPTER FOUR

Thought and Literature in Renaissance Italy

HE INTELLECTUAL LIFE of the Renaissance was varied and active. Italy had reached a crossroads not only in political and economic development but in culture as well. It was a time of intense interest in ideas—new and old—and of clothing those ideas in words worthy of the greatest writers of antiquity. Eloquence was not accidental; it was sought and cultivated by every Renaissance writer regardless of the genre or subject of the writing. The scope of this intellectual and artistic activity was broad, causing us to identify "Renaissance man" with versatility, universality, and completeness. These and other characteristics might best be understood as manifestations of the conscious effort to recover the thought and style of past cultures and reconcile them with the present. Such harmonization was an implicit part of Renaissance humanism.

The Meaning and Rise of Humanism

Renaissance humanism was both an outlook and a method. It has been described as "man's discovery of himself and the world." Certainly there was something of this self-awareness and pride in the humanism of Renaissance Italy. There was also an implied acceptance of the worth of earthly existence for its own sake and a deep-rooted revolt against the "other-worldliness" associated with medieval Christianity. In this sense, the humanists challenged the interpretations of the scholastics and theologians in regard to mundane life, affirming that it had intrinsic value and meaning and that the promotion of worldly pursuits was not only justifiable but meritorious. Closely allied with this was a remarkable devotion to nature and earthly beauties, not in place of but as part of a broadened religious outlook.

Yet to be properly understood and appreciated, humanism must be viewed from still another point of view. Humanists of the fourteenth and early fifteenth centuries were those who devoted themselves to the *studia humanitatis,* or as we would call it today, the liberal arts. To the early Renaissance, this meant a specific and dedicated commitment to such intellectual and literary pursuits as history, literary criticism, grammar, poetry, philology, and especially rhetoric. It also meant looking back to classical Greece and Rome for guides to understanding human nature and for the best literary expressions of the most relevant ideas. Although knowledge of Greek eventually became the most prestigious possession of many humanists, their primary interest was in classical Latin and the literature of Augustan Rome.

Although Renaissance humanists added little (at least during the fourteenth and early fifteenth centuries) to systematic philosophy, theology, or science, they did make lasting contributions to the fields of literature, history, education, moral thought, and, above all, classical philology and literary criticism. As compulsive collectors of ancient manuscripts, they made known and available for the first time almost the entire body of extant classical Latin literature. They read, compared, copied, and plagiarized their prized discoveries, and tried to revive and purify the use of classical Latin. The excitement with which these amateur archaeologists ransacked ruins, monasteries, castles, and private houses in search of precious Latin manuscripts almost reached the point of frenzy. They then studied these ancient writings as models for reviving the language and broadening the content and horizons of literature. In the writings of Cicero and others, they found the same breadth of outlook that they esteemed in their own interpretation of life, which helped them justify their belief in human dignity, the universality of truth, and the beauty of earthly things.

The humanists' devotion to grammar and rhetoric was related to another feature of their activity—their desire to communicate their ideals to a broader audience. They were absorbed by the problems and the artistry of communication, oral as well as written, and took a great interest in the ancients' solutions to these problems. Clarity as well as eloquence was cultivated by Renaissance humanists and was one of their greatest legacies to succeeding generations. Grammar was an important tool in achieving this clarity, as were precise translations and careful historical analyses. Closely related to literary style was the cultivation of the art of speaking. The humanists engaged in public orations of many kinds, from academic addresses and political speeches to wedding and funeral orations. In developing these rhetorical skills, they emphasized eloquence and beauty of expression. Indeed, eloquence was most highly esteemed by the humanists, who thought of it as the supreme balance of wisdom and style.

The roots of Italian humanism go far back into the Middle Ages. Elements of their rhetorical bent can be seen in the early teaching techniques for papal and governmental secretaries. Latin grammar was also studied in the medieval cathedral schools, where it was frequently joined with the reading of classical authors and the church fathers. But there was a difference between the classicism of the twelfth century and that of the fifteenth. In the earlier period, it was primarily an accessory to Christian doctrine; in the Renaissance, it became a system of belief itself, as well as a source of enjoyment. To better understand its meaning and effects, we must look more closely at some of the men who illustrate its variety and scope.

The Age of Petrarch

Francesco Petrarch (Petrarca, or Petracco, 1304–74) has been called the father of humanism. It is not always clear just what this means, but usually it at least implies that Petrarch was the first of the great Italian writers to abandon the methods and objectives of medieval thought in favor of the Latin classics, and in them to find the motivation and outlook that made him aware of the values of life, especially the life of literature and scholarship. There is truth in this judgment, but it is incomplete.

Petrarch was born in Arezzo, fifty miles from Florence, of industrious but poor middle-class Florentine parents. For eight years after Petrarch's birth, the family wandered about central and northern Italy, political exiles from their native Florence. In 1312 they moved to southern France where they settled near Avignon—seat of the papacy since 1305—and there Petrarch grew up. In grammar school he studied Latin and discovered Cicero. He confessed,

> From my early youth, when the other boys were studying only in Prosper and in Aesop, I gave myself wholly to Cicero. . . . At that age I was incapable of understanding what I read, but I took so much delight in the harmonious disposition of the words that any other book I read or heard read seemed to me to give off a graceless, discordant sound. . . . That love for Cicero increased day by day, and my father, amazed, encouraged my immature propensity through paternal affection. And I, dodging no labor that might aid my purpose, breaking the rind, began to savor the taste of the fruit, and couldn't be restrained from my study.

At the age of twelve, Petrarch was sent by his father to the University of Montpellier to study law. For the next ten years, first at Montpellier, then at Bologna, he was immersed in the civil law, but to no avail. He felt nothing but contempt for the lawyers and their "trade." When his parents died leaving him free to choose his own calling, he abandoned the legal profession entirely and turned to letters, poetry, and a carefree life at Avignon. Eventually he took religious vows and held the succeeding benefices of chaplain, canon, and archdeacon. But Petrarch was still a young and restless man-about-town, hopelessly and passionately in love with the mysterious Laura, when he began his years of wandering—to Lombes and Toulouse, Paris, Ghent, Liège, Cologne, England, and then to Rome. Finally in 1337, at the age of thirty-three, he retired to the serene and secluded valley of Vaucluse, some fifteen miles east of Avignon. Here amid the remarkable handiworks of nature, Petrarch devoted himself to poetry and thought. During his travels, he had continued to write (songs to the beauty of nature, poems to the wisdom of the ancients, and sonnets to Laura), but at Vaucluse his greatest literary energy burst forth.

In 1341 Petrarch was crowned in Rome with the highest honor bestowed upon poets, the laurel wreath. He remained in Italy for many years, living at Parma, Bologna, Venice, and Verona, with occasional journeys back to Avignon and Vaucluse. Now his interest and affection for the classic authors of ancient Rome increased. He devoted more of his time to the search for Latin manuscripts and to the transcription and study of ancient lore. Scholarship pushed poetry to the side as he set himself to the recovery of ancient knowledge and style, and to teaching the arts of good living. Notable among his creations of this period are the *Africa,* a Latin epic poem celebrating the life of the Roman general Scipio Africanus; and *Lives of Illustrious Men,* a series of narrative biographies of famous Romans.

Yet despite his devotion to books, the ancient classics especially, to Cicero, and to the moral and life-giving value of literature, Petrarch was torn by the contradictions of life and the attractions of two worlds, by the struggles of flesh and spirit, mind and heart, that constantly tortured his soul. He was as much a paragon of the Middle Ages as the father of Renaissance humanism. Standing at one of the great crossroads of history, Petrarch remained forever undecided as to which route he should follow. He felt the dilemma in language when he exalted the Latin tongue as the goddess of expression and hoped to ennoble it even further in his own letters, dialogues, and epics. Yet he was impelled to compose his love sonnets, *canzoni,* and Triumphs in vernacular Tuscan. The continually gnawing conflict between his passions and ideals, between his love of life and fear of death, his yearning for knowledge and his struggle for faith, marked his later years. "I will pull myself together and collect my scattered wits, and make a great endeavour to possess my soul in patience," he promised in his imaginary dialogue with Augustine. "But even while we speak, a crowd of important affairs, though only of the world, is awaiting my attention."

In spite of his admitted sensual desires, Petrarch was a religious man, split between a life of secular learning and loyal devotion to the church. Like his countryman Dante, he was strongly attached to medieval Christianity, and the inward struggle he described in the "Ascent of Mont Ventoux" shows his ultimate commitment to the church. Here

Petrarch describes in vivid detail the beauties of nature and his exaltation upon reaching the summit of the mountain, when he is suddenly reminded of the futility and vanity of all else but the soul.

One of Petrarch's greatest contributions to humanism was the stimulation he gave to his admirers to continue and expand the study of classical literature. His example soon gave rise to a veritable "revival of learning," learning, that is, of the ancients. Among his many friends, Giovanni Boccaccio (1313–75) became his most illustrious successor. Like Petrarch, Boccaccio admired the classics and appreciated the style and message of Roman writers, especially Tacitus and Livy. He was a fond collector of ancient manuscripts and is credited with finding Tacitus's *Histories* and part of his *Annales*. He credits himself with being the one who introduced Greek poetry to Italy. Shortly after his first meeting with Petrarch in 1350, he wrote *On the Genealogy of the Gods*, a very uneven Latin encyclopedia of Greek and Roman mythology, and two biographical dictionaries—after the fashion of Petrarch's *Lives of Illustrious Men*—called *On the Fortunes of Great Men* and *On Famous Women*, the latter reflecting a different attitude toward women than was found in the medieval songs of courtly love. But Boccaccio's principal claim to greatness, like Petrarch's, was his vernacular poems and tales, particularly the *Decameron*, which will be discussed later in this chapter. He was the most important follower and popularizer of Petrarch and contributed much to the growth and eventual flowering of humanism during the next generation.

Boccaccio was not Petrarch's only disciple. From the middle of the fourteenth century on, Petrarch's circle of friends and admirers grew steadily, and with them an increasing interest in classical letters. By the time of Petrarch's death in 1374, several active groups of men, meeting in the homes of enthusiastic patrons, where they shared ideas and exchanged views on a wide variety of subjects in an environment of mutual stimulation, were cultivating the seeds planted by their mentor. (By a century later, some of these groups included women.) Petrarch's century of humanism reached its zenith with two of his illustrious followers. Giovanni Conversini (1347–1406), a teacher of rhetoric at the University of Padua and later its rector, introduced and promoted classical studies at that renowned center of Aristotelianism. Conversini stimulated many later humanists with his attention to classical letters and especially with his devotion to the writings and thought of Cicero.

Even more influential in the spread of the classical cult was the Florentine scholar, lawyer, and political functionary, Coluccio Salutati (1330–1406). Salutati was not only an admirer of Petrarch (and naturally of Cicero) but also a great Latin stylist in his own right. For thirty years, Salutati served as chancellor (principal secretary) of the Florentine *Signoria*. During that time, Florence became the undisputed center of classical studies and the Italian leader in the cultivation of the liberal arts. The effect of this conjunction of politics and culture was a rapid growth of humanism among the wealthy and powerful. In addition to befriending and encouraging other humanists, Salutati was one of the greatest discoverers and collectors of Latin manuscripts, including the influential *Familiar Letters* of Cicero. It was through Salutati's influence that a new phase in the history of humanism was initiated when he brought the leading Greek scholar of the Eastern Empire, Manuel Chrysoloras, to teach at Florence.

Scholarship and Civic Humanism in the Quattrocento

It is obvious that humanism had become an important and influential movement throughout Italy by the first years of the fifteenth century. It was also undergoing changes. The distinctions between the humanism of the Age of Petrarch and that of the early Quattrocento (literally "400," meaning the 1400s, or the fifteenth century) were most apparent in three areas: the spread of Greek language and thought, the politicization of humanism, and the intensification of literary and linguistic scholarship.

Manuel Chrysoloras' introduction of Greek study into the curriculum at Florence in 1397 had an immediate and profound effect on the

MANUEL CHRYSOLORAS. *The great Byzantine scholar taught Greek to a generation of Italian humanists between 1397 and 1403. The revival of Greek studies had a great impact on fifteenth-century thought in Italy. (Musée Louvre, Cliché des Musées Nationaux-Paris)*

outlook of Italian humanists. Few of them mastered the intricacies of the language, but they did become aware of the Greek heritage and of its importance to the culture of classical Rome. Henceforth, humanists did not consider their education complete unless it included a liberal portion of Greek culture and an honest struggle with the language. This emphasis on Greek literature and philosophy was to have its greatest impact during the final phase of humanism in the second half of the fifteenth century. In the meantime, the introduction of Greek into Italian thought was symptomatic of a general broadening and deepening of humanism in the early Quattrocento. Whereas Petrarch's age had been a period of exuberant discovery of the classical past, the fifteenth century was a time of fuller recovery, analysis, exploration, and cultivation of that literature and thought, and the application of its various lessons.

This broadening of humanism can be seen in the works and activities of any number of Quattrocento humanists, most of whom studied Greek under Chrysoloras, and made significant contributions to the expansion of Greek culture in Italy. Along with Salutati, Niccolò Niccoli (1364–1437) was influential in bringing Greek scholarship to Florence, and for three decades, while collecting and making available for others one of the finest classical libraries in Italy, was one of the leading forces behind the spread of Greek and Latin thought. Niccoli was also an avid collector of ancient artifacts. Ambrogio Traversari (1386–1439), a Camaldolese monk, went beyond most of his associates in the cultivation of Greek—and Hebrew as well. Traversari mastered Greek very early and dedicated himself to making the best Greek literature available in the West.

A second feature of early fifteenth-century humanism, particularly as it was expressed in Florence, was the new awareness and participation of the humanists in political life. The former exaltation of the contemplative life was giving way to a promotion of civic and political activity. This "civic humanism," as it has been styled, not only meant an advocacy of the active life but also reflected a new emphasis and interpretation of the classics as guides to that life. The ancient Roman Republic, rather than the later Empire, was seen by Leonardo Bruni and others as the model state. Cicero's political activity and civic spirit were acclaimed by Salutati and loudly praised by Bruni. This civic orientation was further intensified by the political and military crisis resulting from Gian Galeazzo Visconti's expansion over northern Italy, which threatened to exterminate Florentine liberties. Hans Baron believes that it was this conjunction of political and intellectual developments that gave vitality and direction to the Florentine Renaissance. In other words, humanism was losing some of its earlier narrow devotion to antiquity and was broadening into a movement of awareness, concern, and participation in the vital issues of the day. It was becoming relevant politically as well as intellectually.

The humanists' involvement in civic affairs is readily seen in the great scholars of the early fifteenth century, who were predominantly wealthy people from the upper classes and thus actively engaged in the political life of their city-states. We have already noted that Salutati was Florentine chancellor for some thirty years. He was followed in that office by another even more renowned humanist, Leonardo Bruni (1374–1444), who had been one of Chrysoloras' most gifted students. Soon Bruni was a tutor in the house of Medici and from there entered the world of affairs as secretary to Pope Innocent VII. In 1410, six years after Salutati's death, Bruni returned to Florence to become chancellor, followed by several diplomatic missions and election to the Ten of War and the *Signoria*. Three more popes employed him in different secretarial and scholarly capacities before he again accepted the chancellorship of Florence in 1427. In spite of his active political life, Bruni's scholarly and literary output was truly impressive, both in quantity and quality. He wrote commentaries on the classical authors and translated much of Plato, Aristotle, and Plutarch into Latin. More than anything else, his interpretation of history as the pursuit of liberty (seen particularly in his *History of the Florentine People*) reflects the civic humanism of the early Quattrocento.

Bruni was succeeded as chancellor in Florence by Carlo Marsuppini (1399–1453) who, although not as prolific a writer as Bruni, was an influential teacher of Greek, Latin, ethics, poetry, and rhetoric at the University of Florence. For his civic and literary prominence, he was also appointed honorary papal secretary. Another Florentine chancellor, who likewise began the study of Greek under Chrysoloras, and who served as papal secretary, was the distinguished and renowned humanist scholar Poggio Bracciolini (1380–1459). During his many years in the employ of the Roman curia, Poggio had a great humanizing influence on that body and contributed significantly to the raw materials of humanism by discovering and collecting many classic manuscripts from the various monasteries and ruins of Rome. Among his important discoveries were the full text of Vitruvius's *On Architecture*, several of Cicero's orations, some of the poems of Lucretius, and the first complete copy of Quintilian's *Institutes of Oratory*.

A final example of the activities of early Quattrocento humanists may be seen in the work of Lorenzo Valla (1407–57). Valla received his early humanist education from Leonardo Bruni and the Greek scholar and collector Giovanni Aurispa. While in Rome, Valla was an associate of Poggio and Marsuppini, and through years of travel throughout the peninsula, he became acquainted with most of the other humanists in Italy. As secretary to King Alfonso of Naples, Valla became the royal master of the classics and advisor to the king on cultural matters. More than any of the other humanists, he exemplifies the triumph of grammar, philology, and literary criticism in the interests of humanistic scholarship. Even when employed by the church, his methods and aims were secular. By applying his critical intellect to an examination of some of the venerated documents of the church, Valla disclosed some amazing fallacies. He denied the authenticity of the Apostles' Creed and condemned the translation and style of the Vulgate Bible. At the same time, in his *Elegancies of the Latin Tongue* (1444), he attempted to improve the level of Latin composition both within and outside the church. For its day, this book was a model of critical method and served as the foundation for good Latin style for many generations.

Valla's most famous critical work was an exposé of the "Donation of Constantine," the alleged grant of secular authority from the Emperor Constantine to the Roman pope. By careful application of internal textual criticism, Valla demonstrated that the famous document could not have been written earlier than a century or more *after* Constantine's death and was therefore a flagrant forgery. Of course, this raised some ripples in ecclesiastical circles, but not as great as one might think; after all, the papacy had long since passed the time when it needed the crutch of an imperial donation in order to assert its authority. Seven years later, Lorenzo Valla became apostolic secretary to Pope Nicholas V.

Humanism and Education

Along with their intense interest in grammar, philology, and classical studies, the fifteenth-century humanists were deeply concerned with education. Into the structure and curriculum of the elementary and grammar schools, the humanists now introduced new attitudes and methods. They placed greater emphasis on classical letters, Latin grammar, and moral development, and they advocated a more complete education of the student—physical, aesthetic, intellectual, and moral—than was provided by the medieval parish, town, and cathedral schools.

Perhaps the first to give clear expression to these ideals was Pietro Paolo Vergerio (1349–1420). His treatise *On the Manners of a Gentleman and on Liberal Studies* (ca. 1393) was intended as a practical guide for the education of the son of his patron, the lord of Padua. Vergerio emphasized the value of a broad, well-rounded education, and the necessity of adapting subject matter and scope to the age of the student. He stressed training in manners and behavior as well as academic subjects, and advocated teaching Latin literature as an integral part of education. Vergerio's definition of a liberal education has become a classic expression:

> We call those studies liberal which are worthy of a free man; those studies by which we attain and practice virtue and wisdom; that education which calls forth, trains, and develops those highest gifts of body and mind which ennoble men and which are rightly judged to rank next in dignity to virtue only, for to a vulgar temper, gain and pleasure are the one aim of existence, to a lofty nature, moral worth and fame.

Poggio's discovery of Quintilian's *Institutes of Oratory* in 1416, which Vergerio published, also had a profound effect on Renaissance education, for it made available the educational wisdom of one of the great minds and teachers of ancient Rome. Vergerio's and Quintilian's treatises, along with the subsequent unearthing of Cicero's *The Orator*, and the publication of Plutarch's *On the Education of Children*, became the theoretical foundations of humanist educational ideas. Others soon added to the growing body of educational literature: Leonardo Bruni wrote his tract *On Studies and Letters*, in which he affirmed that "the foundation of all true learning must be laid in the sound and thorough knowledge of Latin: which implies study marked by a broad spirit, accurate scholarship, and careful attention to details"; Aeneas Sylvius Piccolomini (later Pope Pius II) wrote *On the Education of Children*, emphasizing, like Vergerio, the primacy of morals and the development of character as the ultimate goal of education; and the Augustinian monk Mapheus Vegius added *On the Education of Boys and Their Moral Culture*.

Many humanists of the period were teachers themselves, giving classes both inside and outside the existing schools. None of these educators was more devoted to this calling or more influential over a long period of time than was Guarino da Verona (1370–1460). From his native Verona, where he taught children in his home, in the fields, or wherever they met on the streets, Guarino moved to Ferrara where Niccolò d'Este had invited him to tutor his son. From that time on, Guarino remained a recipient of d'Este patronage and a spokesman and practitioner of humanist education based on the complete training of body, mind, and character.

Guarino's most gifted student, and the person generally recognized as the greatest educator of the Renaissance, was Vittorino da Feltre (1378–1446). After many years teaching grammar, rhetoric, and mathematics in Padua, Vittorino opened a school of his own in Venice before accepting the invitation of Gian Francesco Gonzaga, ruler of Mantua, to undertake the education of his family. Devoted both to his subject and his pupils, Vittorino introduced classical and humanistic ideals into his school curriculum and made his Mantuan "Happy Home" (*La Giocosa*), under willing Gonzaga patronage, the foremost grammar school of Italy. For twenty-two years, he conducted this school, teaching first the sons and daughters of his patron, and those of other noble families, and eventually many other promising young people from all over Italy. Vittorino translated the educational theories of his contemporaries and the ancients into a practical program intended to combine the mental disciplines of the medieval *trivium* and *quadrivium* with classical studies and the development of body, spirit, and character, thus harmonizing humanistic learning with traditional Christian values.

The impact of humanism on education was also felt in the universities, although not as soon nor as completely as in the grammar schools. In many cases, the universities remained the strongholds of scholastic method throughout the Renaissance; but they also experienced a gradual shift in emphasis from logic to language, from dialectic to rhetoric, and from natural science to Latin literature. Furthermore, university education gradually developed a conception—in some circles, at least, and in some universities more than others—that was intended to produce good citizens as well as learned minds. This mood was reflected first in the areas of the university where humanists were most likely to be found—in the arts faculty. In theology, medicine, and law, medieval methods continued without major alterations until the sixteenth century.

Renaissance Philosophy

A final phase of Italian humanism may be discerned in the second half of the fifteenth century. With the decline of active and relatively democratic participation in Florentine politics, associated with the rise and consolidation of Medici power, also came a comparable decline in civic humanism. This is reflected not only in the noticeable reduction of humanists and literati in important political offices as the opportunities for participation became constricted, but also in the gradually changing attitude of the humanists toward politics and government. The late fifteenth-century humanists came more and more to praise the contemplative life over the active, as Petrarch had done a century earlier, and to admire things of the mind and spirit above those of the world. It would be an exaggeration to say that after 1450 the humanists rejected the world in favor of spiritual or religious meditation, but it is evident that many of them, particularly in Florence, became increasingly concerned with philosophical matters as their own active involvement in government decreased. The fall of Constantinople in 1453 may have helped promote this change by cutting off the steady supply of Greek manuscripts entering the West and thereby forcing humanists to turn to philosophizing. The development of printing probably had a greater effect by reducing the necessity for the humanist's hand-done copywork.

Whatever its cause, this new concern for philosophy and metaphysics might be regarded as a further expansion and maturing of humanism rather than its coagulation or decline, for in the process of broadening and accommodating, humanism became a more effective instrument of enlightenment and correction to the church. It was only in this phase that Italian humanism had something to offer northern Europeans and became the catalyst for the religious and intellectual changes of the next century. The decline of civic consciousness was a regrettable loss, but it was neither universal nor lasting. In many parts of Italy, political participation had not existed for most of the people anyway, while in other cities, it was as active in the late Quattrocento as it was in the earlier.

Furthermore, the permanent ingredients added to humanism, through its new awareness and involvement in philosophy, amply compensated for the temporary loss of some of its civic features.

Platonism

The principal factor in the development of a humanist philosophy was the reintroduction of Plato into Italy. Of course Plato was not unknown there before the fifteenth century. Neo-Platonism had played a large role in the church since the fourth century. But translations of hitherto unknown (or at least unused) Platonic writings and commentaries on them, which were produced in the early Quattrocento, revealed a new and different Plato from the universalist philosopher known to the medieval churchmen. In the new Latin translations of Plato's *Laws*, the *Gorgias*, parts of *Phaedrus*, and even the *Republic*, a Plato emerged who was new to the minds of most Western thinkers, and who stimulated or reinforced attitudes and ideas that had only been vaguely expressed before.

This revived or renewed Platonism meant a number of things to its fifteenth-century advocates. First, it meant a greater emphasis on soul and spirit, that is, the continuation and extension of the essence of life beyond death. This stress on the value and immortality of the human soul gave rise to another characteristic of Renaissance Platonism—the role and primacy of contemplation. Through contemplation, the soul transcends the mortal body and the material world to become attuned with the Divine, thus not only assuring one of God's existence but also fortifying him against the adversities of life. A related concept of great interest to the humanists was the theory of Platonic love, which was interpreted as a spiritual and intellectual bond between persons participating in the contemplative life. Other Platonic concepts that greatly influenced Renaissance thought during the second half of the fifteenth century were the belief in the existence of truth outside and above the institutionalized church, a great respect for numbers and mathematics in the process of acquiring knowledge, the idea of the essential unity of the world, and its important corollary, belief in individual worth.

The greatest stimulant to the study of Plato came with the establishment of the Platonic Academy of Florence by Cosimo de' Medici. The academy was not a formal institution of learning but rather a circle of people interested in studying and discussing Platonic thought under the guidance of the most capable and active Platonist of the period, Marsilio Ficino. The activities of the Academy consisted mostly of informal conversations and discussions, occasional speeches delivered on special celebration days, public studies given by Ficino in the church of Santa Maria degli Angeli, and private tutoring based on the reading of Plato and his commentators, given at Ficino's villa of Careggi outside of Florence.

Marsilio Ficino (1433–99) was a remarkable person in an age of outstanding individuals. Son of a physician, he received early training in Latin grammar and rhetoric at the University of Florence, as well as Aristotelian physics and medicine. From his earliest written works, it is apparent that his interests were broad and his abilities were equal to his interests. He was familiar with music and music theory, was a knowledgeable and practicing poet, and had a thorough knowledge of Greek. While still a very young man, he became intimately acquainted with Plato's works and began his lifelong work of translation, commentary, and teaching. He translated all of Plato's *Dialogues*, wrote an influential philosophical study on Platonic theology, and, under Medici patronage, devoted his talents to teaching Plato. Ficino's interpretations provided a needed reconciliation between medieval mysticism, earlier Italian humanism, and Thomist scholasticism. His synthesis, with its emphasis on Platonic love, the dignity of man, freedom of the human will, and the immortality of the soul, provided humanism with a philosophy that could carry it beyond the relatively sophisticated circle of urban Italian enthusiasts to the schoolrooms, cloisters, and palaces of the rest of Europe. With Marsilio Ficino, reason and fact were not ends in themselves but means of attaining "universal truth and goodness."

Pico della Mirandola and the Broadening of Humanist Thought

The most illustrious and influential product of the Platonic Academy was Giovanni Pico della Mirandola. Pico was a wealthy and gifted son of the prince of Mirandola, a small principality in the Po Valley. His noble birth, abundant wealth, and alert mind gave him an early advantage that he augmented with enormous energy and an insatiable thirst for learning.

GIOVANNI PICO DELLA MIRANDOLA. *The brilliant young prince of Mirandola was one of the most precocious and active thinkers of the Renaissance, and his influence reached to all parts of Europe. He is shown here in a contemporary medallion. (Photographie Giraudon)*

He began the study of canon law at Bologna while he was still in his mid-teens; then at Padua and later Paris, he immersed himself in scholastic philosophy. While at the Sorbonne, the citadel of scholasticism, he conceived his ideas about the unity of all things, and in that context tried hard to harmonize the philosophical systems of Plato and Aristotle. At the age of twenty-one, he returned to Italy and, in Florence, joined the circle of Platonic enthusiasts studying with Ficino. In 1486, at the age of twenty-four, Pico went to Rome where he compiled a list of 900 theses on philosophical and theological matters drawn from the lore of all ages and places and offered to debate them with any and all scholars. His most influential book, *Oration on the Dignity of Man*, was intended as an introduction to these theses. However, the ecclesiastical powers in Rome were not so impressed with Pico's erudition, and an investigation of his theses found several of them to be heretical. He wrote a hasty apology, which got him into more trouble, and was forced to flee to France for safety. Through the instigation of the papal legate, he was eventually arrested and imprisoned at Vincennes castle, but influential friends arranged his escape and he returned once more to Florence. There, in the early 1490s, he came under the bewitching spell of the zealous monk Savonarola. He also became deeply interested in Hebrew studies, especially in mystical Cabalism. But in the year Savonarola's reforming zeal brought him into political power in Florence, Pico suddenly died of the plague, at the age of thirty-two.

The breadth of Pico's thought was a challenge and stimulation to future generations. He strongly defended the truth and beauty of all ages and searched diligently in the teachings of Jesus, Zoroaster, Pythagoras, Mohammed, Saint Thomas, Plato, and Cicero for the "precious nuggets of universal truth," that he believed were all a part of God's revelation to humanity. "And surely it is the part of a narrow mind to have confined itself within a single Porch or Academy," Pico declared, "Nor can one rightly choose what suits one's self from all of them who has not first come to be familiar with them all."

On the Platonic theme of individual worth, Pico had some of the boldest things to say. Man is the most blessed of all living creatures, he affirms:

> To him it is granted to have whatever he chooses, to be whatever he wills. Beasts as soon as they are born (so says Lucilius) bring with them from their mother's womb all they will ever possess. Spiritual beings, either from the beginning or soon thereafter, become what they are to be for ever and ever. On man when he came into life the Father conferred the seeds of all kinds and the germs of every way of life. Whatever seeds each man cultivates will grow to maturity and bear in him their own fruit. If they be vegetative, he will be like a plant. If sensitive, he will become brutish. If rational, he will grow into a heavenly being. If intellectual, he will be an angel and the son of God.

FOUR FIFTEENTH-CENTURY HUMANISTS. *The figures in this detail from Ghirlandaio's* Zacharias in the Temple *have tentatively been identified as Marcilio Ficino, Cristoforo Landino, Angelo Poliziano, and the noted Greek teacher Demetrius Chalcondilas. (Editorial Photocolor Archives)*

The broadening effect of Platonic studies on Italian humanism in the second half of the Quattrocento can be illustrated in two other noted scholars of that period who were also members of the Platonic Academy; they are Cristoforo Landino (1424–92) and Angelo Poliziano (1454–94). As professor of rhetoric and poetry at Florence, Landino was the respected dean of Florentine scholars during the late fifteenth century, and as a translator and author, he was among the most gifted. His *Disputationum Camaldulensium* (Discussions in a Camaldolese monastery) tells a great deal about the discussions of Plato in the Ficino circle and about Landino's own role as a teacher of Lorenzo de' Medici. Poliziano was a more flamboyant, if less learned, scholar than Landino, and a more accomplished poet. He belonged to Lorenzo de' Medici's inner circle of friends, and as a result, had many opportunities to influence and direct the course of late Quattrocento culture. It was largely due to Poliziano that humanism became less exclusively Ciceronian in favor of a broader modeling of Greek and other authors.

Aristotelianism

Simultaneously with the revival of Platonism in Florence, there began, particularly in the university at Padua, a reevaluation of Aristotle and the development of what might be called an Aristotelian humanism. Italian Aristotelianism had long been associated with the study of logic, natural philosophy (physics), and medicine, and thus developed independently from humanism. This Aristotelian tradition, based on the interpretations and commentaries of the great Spanish-Arab philosopher Averroës, continued to thrive during the Renaissance wherever faculties were pursuing studies in natural philosophy, especially at the universities of Padua, Salerno, Naples, and Bologna. Another type of Aristotelianism, associated with the medieval church and providing the greatest strength to Scholasticism, had developed in the great universities of northern Europe, although this was less significant in Italy. A third form of Aristotelianism now arose in Renaissance Italy and created an Aristotelian humanism different from, though still resembling, the Platonic humanism of fifteenth-century Florence. This development was especially strong in Padua, where Aristotle and the university had been almost synonymous for centuries. The Paduans responded to the challenge of Ficino's Platonism, observes John Herman Randall, "by proving that Aristotle as well as Plato spoke Greek." They replied to Ficino's attack on their Averroist naturalism by reorienting their own thought toward a more humanistic conception of people and their destiny. Thus these Aristotelians arrived at many of the same conclusions as had the Platonists about human dignity, immortality of the soul, and freedom of the will; but they did it through the naturalism of Aristotle rather than through the idealism of Plato.

The greatest of the Renaissance Aristotelians was Pietro Pomponazzi (1462–1524), who personalized the usual view of human nature and made his philosophy a living thing rather than a mental exercise. Pomponazzi was born in Mantua and received his early Thomist training in Padua under Francesco di Nardò. He distinguished himself at the university and soon won the distinguished post of *lector extraordinarius* (Special Reader), before moving to Bologna, where he remained for the last twelve years of his life. The striking thing about Pomponazzi's interpretation of Aristotle is that it combined all three Aristotelian traditions just mentioned. As with Ficino, Pico, and other humanists of the late Renaissance, the key words for Pomponazzi were recovery and reconciliation.

Vernacular Italian Literature

The rise and development of vernacular literature in Italy began before the advent of humanism and continued in conjunction (although at times in competition) with it. In Chapter One we briefly discussed

Dante's great epic poem the *Divine Comedy*, and in this chapter, we mentioned some of Petrarch's important contributions to vernacular literature. Of particular significance is Petrarch's *Canzioniere* (Songbook), a collection of some 366 vernacular poems and songs on every subject, but mostly love sonnets to his beloved Laura, written in the lusty and expressive language of his native Tuscany. The beauty and feeling of these poems have scarcely been equaled since. The following lament on the rapid passage of life, stimulated by the plaintive song of a bird, illustrates Petrarch's power to put thoughts into words. Even in English translation, its beauty and pathos are clear:

> O lovely little bird, I watch you fly,
> and grieving for the past I hear you sing,
> seeing the night and winter hastening,
> seeing the day and happy summer die.
> If you could hear my heart in answer cry
> its pain to your sad song, you'd swiftly wing
> into my bosom, comfort you would bring,
> and we would weep together, you and I.*

Boccaccio, too, wrote stories, poems, and romances in the Tuscan vernacular, among them *Il Filocolo* (Love's Labor), a long prose romance of French origin, relating the adventurous search by the young prince, Florio, for Biancofiore; *Filostrato* (meaning, says Boccaccio, "a man overcome and vanquished by love"), the first octave rhyming narrative poem, which tells the story of Troilus and Cressida set in the time of the Trojan War; *Teseida*, an epic poem after the fashion of Virgil's *Aeneid*; and *L'amorosa Fiammetta*, a psychological romance concerning his own love affair with the beautiful Fiammetta. Boccaccio's greatest literary skill was revealed in his short and witty tales about contemporary life and mores. Hist best book was the *Decameron*, a collection of 100 such stories told over a period of ten days by a group of ten young people who had fled from Florence at the time of the Black Death. Lucid, colorful, and irreverent—when not outright bawdy—these tales are told with such artistic finesse that to the present day they have remained the most popular writings to come from the Renaissance.

In spite of the overwhelming emphasis placed on Latin by the early humanists, vernacular literature continued to flourish in the fifteenth century alongside the Latin revival, and in some cases it was promoted by the humanists themselves. Leon Battista Alberti defended the Italian tongue against the derogatory attacks of some of his fellow humanists, and Poliziano was as versatile in one as in the other. Indeed, the relationship between the two was vital to the eventual triumph of

Source: Extracted from *Petrarch and His World* by Morris Bishop. Copyright © 1963 by Indiana University Press. Reprinted by permission of the publisher.

meaningful and artistic vernacular prose and poetry, for the vernaculars of the fourteenth century could never have become the literary language of Italy without undergoing some major changes, changes brought about by the influence of classical Latin. From the Latin classics and the lessons in grammar and composition taught by the humanists, vernacular writers learned much-needed lessons about form, structure, lucidity, precision, and style. Now they learned how to make epigrams crisp, sonnets rhythmic, dramas clear cut, dialogues distinct, and epics unified. In this transformation, as in most others of the time, Italy led the way. By the end of the fifteenth century, Italy's vernacular literature was the admiration of all Europe.

The Italian influence on European literature was particularly strong in the sonnet and to a lesser degree in lyrical poems, but it was also important in short stories, novels, and comedic satire. In addition to these, Italians contributed two new forms that were to have many imitators in the following years: the pastoral romance and the romantic epic. The former is best represented by Boccaccio's *Ameto,* in which seven woodland nymphs tell stories of their loves to the hunter Ameto, and Jacopo Sannazaro's *Arcadia.* The *Arcadia* is an interesting combination of prose and poetry describing the unrequited love of a Neapolitan shepherd who fled to the Arcadian countryside in Greece, where he hoped to find solace and relief from his emotional distress. Alarmed by a dream, he quickly returned to Naples only to find his loved one was dead. The theme of this poem was later employed by many European writers, including Sir Philip Sidney, Jorge de Montemayor, Lope de Vega, and Cervantes.

Italian poetry reached its zenith with the romantic epic, which combined the classical epic with medieval romance to create an emotional entertainment complete with irony, pathos, and moving narrative, and in such a way as to produce a literary genre than became influential throughout Europe. Three writers excelled in this new medium—new in its structure and style, though not in subject matter, which was drawn mostly from medieval chivalric romance—these were Luigi Pulci (1432–84), Matteo Boiardo (1434–94), and Ludovico Ariosto (1474–1533). Pulci's *Morgante* is a poem of adventure and knight-errantry. Based on a recasting of the story of Roland and other tales, the poem is entertaining and mildly satirical with witty humor provided by the crude but likeable giant Morgante. The author was a favorite friend of Lorenzo de' Medici, who frequently invited him to share his storytelling ability at the banquet table. Matteo Boiardo was an employee of the d'Este dukes of Ferrara and a humanist of some repute. His epic *Orlando Innamorato* (Roland Enamored), however, possesses little in common with humanistic literature. It is a chivalrous romance reminiscent of the earlier *chansons de geste* and concerned with the Christian-Saracen struggles, but written with a depth of feeling and sentimentality that distinguishes it from its medieval counterparts.

Ludovico Ariosto was also associated with the ruling house of d'Este. After being freed from several years of law study at Ferrara, he turned his abilities to literature. His *Orlando Furioso* (Roland Enraged) was intended as a continuation of Boiardo's poem, and in its general subject matter—the legends of Charlemagne and Roland (Orlando) and their wars with the infidels—it is in the same tradition. But it contains many characteristics and attributes not possessed by the *Orlando Innamorato*. For one thing, Ariosto is more satirical than his predecessor and seems to take his chivalry less seriously. The octave rhyming poem remains high spirited and adventurous, but before it is finished, Ariosto has given us food for thought as well as for entertainment, and it is a storehouse of insights into the circumstances and conditions of his time.

Another kind of poetic literature that was popular and widespread in the Renaissance—as it had been earlier—is religious poetry. Its expression took many forms and varieties, one of which is represented in the devotional sonnets of Vittoria Colonna (1490–1547). Although not considered one of the great poets of the Renaissance, she was certainly an important and influential voice in the first half of the sixteenth century. Best known for her inspiration to Michelangelo, she was a respected humanist and literary artist in her own right. She was deeply religious and inclined toward an Augustinian view of justification by faith, yet she unquestioningly accepted the church hierarchy (but not clerical corruption) and was loyal to the pope (although she did not always agree with him). Most of all she was devoted to what might be called evangelical Catholicism—that is, the expression of piety and spiritual devotionalism without any departure from the traditional standards of orthodoxy. Her devotional poetry was Christ-centered but also reflected the influence of Plato, and it emphasized the hope for the harmonization of the two world views. Her sonnets "Our Lady," "The Annunciation," "The Star," and "The Cross," among others, illustrate both a transcendent, almost mystical, piety and a down-to-earth concern for human kindness.

Castiglione

One of the best examples of Italian prose literature of the Renaissance, and the fullest look into the sophisticated court society of the late fifteenth and early sixteenth centuries, is Baldassare Castiglione's *Book of the Courtier* (*Il Cortegiano*). Born of a noble family near Mantua and related to the Gonzaga lords, Castiglione (1478–1529) enjoyed the advantages of the best education Renaissance Italy could provide. He was taught Latin and Greek by the best teachers of the day and rounded out his training at the courts of Milan, Mantua, and Urbino. He served longest under Duke Guidobaldo Montefeltro of Urbino and his talented wife, the Duchess Elisabetta Gonzaga, during the time that court was

BALDASSARE CASTIGLIONE. *This famous portrait by Raphael shows the accomplished courtier, diplomat, and writer at the height of his career, around 1515. It exemplifies the poise, sobriety, restraint, and inner calm of the perfect courtier. (Musée Louvre, Cliché des Musées Nationaux-Paris)*

among the most cultured in Italy. For many years, numerous leading scholars, poets, churchmen, and rulers met here to discuss the subjects that interested them most.

The Courtier is an account of such a gathering debating the current issues of art, ethics, literature, women, religion, sports, language, love, psychology, politics, and, above all, the characteristics and qualifications of the ideal courtier, the Renaissance gentleman. The type of man created in these discussions never existed in real life, but it is instructive to see the attributes they felt he should possess. He should be loyal to his prince as well as an honest and wise counselor; robust and athletic of body, but not excessively active; skilled in games, though not a gambler; a graceful dancer; accomplished with the sword, yet not rash in using it. He should be conversant in Latin and Greek and learned enough to be familiar with the poets and historians of the past as well as the present. He should write well, especially in the vernacular, and his conversation should be pleasant and, when need be, profound. Music should be easy for him and he should be able to draw and paint, not like the masters, but with ease and assurance. He should be both well traveled and well read. His character should be above reproach; he should be tactful, well mannered, and urbane, yet should avoid all signs of affectation and arrogance. In short, he should be the "universal man" of the Renaissance.

The court lady should be equally perfect: graceful, beautiful, circumspect, prudent, magnanimous, kind, affable, vivacious yet reserved, pure without being prudish, revealing "a certain gravity, tempered with wisdom and goodness, [which] is like a shield against the insolence and brutishness of presumptuous men." Going further than merely speculating on the qualities of the ideal woman, however, Castiglione affirms, through the mouth of Giuliano de' Medici, that virtues of the mind are as necessary and as evident in women as in men, and he rebukes the latter for arrogating to themselves the right to rule over women. In countless ways, women are equal or superior to men in ability, wisdom, and virtue, he declares, yet they should not and cannot be alike in every way. They are distinct, complementary, and incomplete without one another. "I think," he continues, "that in her ways, manners, words, gestures, and bearing, a woman ought to be very unlike a man; for just as he must show a certain solid and sturdy manliness, so it is seemly for a woman to have a soft and delicate tenderness, with an air of womanly sweetness in her every movement, which, in her going and staying, and in whatever she says, shall always make her appear the woman without any resemblance to a man."

Perhaps the greatest importance of Castiglione's *Courtier* lies in its long-range effects on educational thought, as it reinforced the humanist ideal of educating "the whole person," and its scintillating treatment of so many timeless and universal themes. Its relevance to our own time is obvious in such topics as the role (fate, opportunity, responsibility) of the individual in society; the nature and substance of freedom; the distinction and relationship between good and evil, truth and tact, humility and pride, reality and appearance, beauty and goodness; and the content of love.

Machiavelli

Whereas Castiglione's courtier shows us the aristocratic and idealistic side of Renaissance cultural life, his Florentine contemporary Niccolò Machiavelli (1469–1527) lays before us the popular, realistic, vulgar side, and introduces us to the not-so-gentlemanly and not-so-ladylike types. We will discuss Machiavelli's histories and his political writings later, but he was also one of the great literati of his day and contributed significantly to Italian poetry, drama, and especially comedic satire. In *Clizia* he humorously portrays Florentine family life in the early sixteenth century. *Belfagor* is a delightful parody on marriage—or more precisely, on domineering wives. *The Golden Ass* is a slightly more subtle satire on political mores. But Machiavelli's best comedy drama is the *Mandragola* (the Mandrake), a frank and sometimes crude burlesque of Florentine life, particularly the seamier side of it, in his day. But it is not the facetious plot that attracts one to the *Mandragola*, although Machiavelli's feeling for plot is among the best in Renaissance literature; it is the skill and sureness with which he unfolds the plot, without its ever becoming burdensome or slow, coupled with an unusual sense of dramatic timing and clever use of dialogue, that makes this one of the outstanding comedies of the Renaissance. One is never certain whether the author is laughing more at the ridiculous characters in the play or the tidy complacency of the reader.

Aretino

The strangest and most colorful literary personality of the High Renaissance was the sensuous and unscrupulous Pietro Aretino (1492–1556). Born at Arezzo in the year of Lorenzo de' Medici's death, Aretino had little education and lived as a waif during much of his boyhood. He eventually found his niche in Renaissance society as a satirical "journalist." For a time in Rome he received the protection of the banker Agostino Chigi and Pope Leo X, but a number of obscene sonnets and other mordantly witty verses cost him his patronage. For years he wandered about Italy and France as an adventurer and sycophant, writing licentious dialogues and libelous pasquinades against rulers, princes, and men of affairs. His defamation of other candidates was considered a factor in Giulio de Medici's successful bid for the papacy in 1523. Four years later, he settled in Venice and lived there like a king on the blackmail money received from those who feared his caustic pen.

Aretino's writing was a pungent mixture of vitality, venality, and

PIETRO ARETINO. *The notorious writer is depicted as a Renaissance patrician in a famous portrait by Titian. Aretino called this picture* una terribile maraviglia, *"a terrible marvel." (Copyright The Frick Collection, New York)*

validity, which brought him the cognomen "Scourge of Princes." In addition to his extortionary libels, however, he wrote a number of amusing comedy satires and one good tragedy, the *Orazia* (Horatius), based on Livy's familiar story of the combat between the Horatii and the Curiatii, where love and happiness are sacrificed to honor and patriotism. Critics consider this to be the best Italian tragedy of the sixteenth century.

Renaissance Views of the Past

No literary form changed more dramatically in the Renaissance than did the writing of history. To the Middle Ages, history was simply the manifestation of Divine will in the lives of people. Medieval church writers usually divided their histories and chronologies into theological periods (that is, six years for the six days of creation, or four monarchies after the prophecy of Daniel, and so forth) having nothing to do with historical causation or cultural unity, and then wrote their accounts as though people were only a passive ingredient in the unfolding of God's will. The secular chroniclers, who were usually employees of the princes, focused their attention on the heroic deeds and military successes of their patrons, without forgetting, of course, ample references and evidences of Divine sanction and intervention. Legends, myths, and hearsay were uncritically employed as though they were established truths. There was little attempt to explain or evaluate the events or movements of history, much less the sources from which it was drawn. Although they wrote descriptively, even the best medieval chroniclers, Dino Compagni, Giovanni Villani, and Jean Froissart, were uncritical in their use of sources—when they used them at all—and lacked any meaningful awareness of historical perspective.

The understanding and full utilization of the time dimension of history seems to have been a Renaissance contribution to historiography. Italian humanists became conscious of the time separating themselves from the age of Cicero and of the vast intervening "dark ages." In Petrarch we can see the transition from the medieval chroniclers to the Renaissance historians. His *History of Rome* used sources much more judiciously and reflected an awareness of the passage of time, but still lacked a true critical approach and comprehension of what that thousand years had meant in the evolution of mankind. Boccaccio's *Life of Dante* was better history, if only because it was easier to "recreate" the setting of thirteenth-century Florence than it was of first-century Rome. Gradually, the humanists developed an outlook toward the nature and function of history that was unlike that of any previous writers since the time of Tacitus. To them, history was a choice form of literary expression, highly regarded by the classical writers, that demanded technical accuracy and factual completeness. In turn it provided practical lessons in politics, ethics, and law that could not be learned elsewhere. History was considered so valuable as a teaching tool that all too frequently Renaissance historians consciously and unconsciously distorted facts to make them fit what they thought were the needs of the time. Their attraction to ancient Rome was so great that they used Roman history as the principal treasury of examples, forcing them to fit modern questions whether they did or not.

The first important humanist historian was Leonardo Bruni, whose *Florentine History* and later *Commentaries* best reflected the ideals and methods of Quattrocento historiography. Bruni's purpose was to write political and military history eloquently, dramatically, and accurately, as Titus Livy had done fourteen centuries earlier. Although keenly aware of the perspective of time, Bruni nevertheless believed the methods and lessons of antiquity had relevance to his own day and could be employed to improve Florentine life. His philosophy is stated in the opening lines of his *Commentaries*: "I sense an obligation to this my age, to give some notice of it to posterity in whatever light it may appear to the future. If only those who lived before us, who had some literary ability, had done this, we would not today find ourselves in such a state of darkness and ignorance."

Following closely in Bruni's footsteps, Poggio Bracciolini was another respected historian of the early fifteenth century. His contemporaries rated him higher than Bruni, though subsequent generations have reversed this opinion. Poggio was perhaps a better Latin stylist than Bruni but his *History of the People of Florence*, covering the century of Florentine-Milanese wars, 1352–1455, followed the classical models too closely and resulted in a less frank appraisal of Florentine politics. He did have great respect for sources, however, and on the whole used them critically.

The greatest Quattrocento historian was Flavio Biondo (1388–1463). Like many Italian humanists, Biondo dedicated his life to the retrieval and study of ancient manuscripts, but unlike most of them, he continued to maintain interest in the ten centuries or so following the fall of Rome. His *Decades of History since the Decline of the Roman Empire, 412–1440*, was the most important contribution to medieval history written during the entire Renaissance. He wrote many other works also, including *Rome Established* and *Rome Triumphant, History of the Decades of the Roman Empire*, and *History of Italy*. Biondo was less a stylist than most of the other humanists, but he was a much better historian, interested more in the facts and content of history than in its form.

A younger contemporary of Biondo, who merits more space than a quick survey of Renaissance historiography can afford him, was Aeneas Sylvius Piccolomini (1405–64). Aeneas, one of the most remarkable men of the century even before he became Pope Pius II, wrote many historical works that, though inferior as history to those of Biondo, Poggio, and Bruni, were significant contributions by a person who, like Winston Churchill, spent his life making history while he was writing it. Among his many writings are a *History of Bohemia, History of Frederick III, History of Europe, Universal History*, and *Commentaries*, the latter a dramatically written autobiography.

Machiavelli and Guicciardini

The zenith of Renaissance historiography was reached in the early sixteenth century with the works of two prominent Florentines, Niccolò Machiavelli (1469–1527) and Francesco Guicciardini (1483–1540). We have already noted that Machiavelli was more than a civil service employee of the Florentine government. Not only were his literary skills impressive and his insight as a political observer unequaled, but he was also a highly respected historian—perhaps more respected than he deserved. Machiavelli's approach to history in his *History of Florence*, as well as in many of his other political writings, was entirely utilitarian; that is, he used history as a storehouse of examples to support and defend his political assumptions. He believed in cyclical recurrence in history and held that human nature is unchanging. Thus historical situations as well as events repeat themselves within a limited set of circumstances and combinations, making political prediction possible. Based largely on Bruni and Biondo, Machiavelli's *History of Florence* is superior to these in some respects, particularly in its greater unity and cohesion, with its many episodes woven around the thread of civil discords as the cause of domestic troubles. Characters in the *History of Florence* are more convincing than those of earlier histories. But like many of the humanists, Machiavelli was so blinded by the glory of Rome that everything else was seen as an afterimage. Believing in the *fortuna* of historical recurrence, he thought the golden age would return if he could convince his countrymen of their follies and get them to imitate the thoughts and actions of the ancient Romans. Insensitive to cultural change and without much respect for sources, Machiavelli used history primarily for answers to current political problems. But he wrote it unusually well.

Although Guicciardini, like Machiavelli, had great respect for ancient Rome, he could not put the same trust in Roman examples that Machiavelli did. In fact, he was skeptical about any historical generalization because he was more aware of the infinite variety and changeability of history. He did not reject the idea that history taught lessons, but he did not believe the lessons were as obvious or as simple as they seemed to Machiavelli. History is complex and cannot simply be reduced to a number of maxims and aphorisms to explain human behavior. Besides, Guicciardini was not at all sure that people were the same in Roman days as they were in his own. With his sharper critical powers, Guicciardini was able to recreate the actuality of historical occurrences and situations more accurately and truthfully than his predecessors had. His works are crisp and balanced, and reflect his respect for reliable sources. Furthermore, with the abundant experience he had accumulated in government and diplomatic affairs, and with his ability to observe and analyze political situations, Guicciardini was better able to recognize and evaluate people's motives.

A member of one of Florence's wealthiest and most important families, Guicciardini was educated in the civil law, which he practiced for seven years after receiving the doctorate at the age of twenty-two. In 1511 he was sent on a diplomatic mission to the court of Ferdinand of Aragon, and from that time until his death in 1540, he was always in some form of government service, including numerous embassies, governor of the Romagna under Pope Clement VII, papal lieutenant-general at the negotiations of the League of Cognac (1526–27), legal and political advisor to Dukes Alessandro and Cosimo de' Medici. During and between some of his early diplomatic assignments, Guicciardini wrote his *Florentine History*, covering the period 1378–1509. This history was at once original and alive, with none of the empty rhetoric of many humanist histories and with few of the usual digressions and irrelevant trivialities. Above all, it was a moving political narrative clearly describing the essential facts and candidly evaluating the men and women involved. Here, in spite of the author's youth, was analytical history at its Renaissance best, written in the descriptive Tuscan vernacular that Machiavelli also used in his works.

Even more significant in terms of historical approach and scope, but less original in method and style, was his *History of Italy*, written thirty years later from the perspective of a full and active lifetime of participation in Italian politics. This larger work, intended perhaps as his magnum opus, considered the entire range of Italian history during his own time, the period from the death of Lorenzo de' Medici in 1492 to that of Pope Clement VII in 1534. Guicciardini relied heavily on documentary sources as well as personal experiences to write this monumental work, and although he compromised his style with the more "acceptable" humanist practice of including direct (usually fabricated) discourse and many speeches, along with detailed descriptions of battles, he nevertheless produced a history of late-Renaissance Italy that was both readable and reliable. In some respects, it has not been superseded yet.

Suggestions for Further Reading

RENAISSANCE HUMANISM

There are many stimulating, brief discussions of Renaissance humanism, beginning with Frederick B. Artz, *Renaissance Humanism, 1300–1550* (Oberlin, 1966); Eugenio Garin, *Italian Humanism: Philosophy and Civil Life in the Renaissance*, tr. by Peter Munz (New York, 1965); and Jerrold E. Seigel, *Rhetoric and Philosophy in Renaissance Humanism: The Union of Eloquence and Wisdom, Petrarch to Valla* (Princeton, 1968). The leading authority on Renaissance humanism is Paul Oskar Kristeller. See his *Renaissance Thought: The Classic, Scholastic and Humanist Strains* (New York, 1961), a revised and enlarged version of his earlier *The Classics and Renaissance Thought*, a collection of brilliant lectures; *Renaissance Thought II: Papers on Humanism and the Arts* (New York, 1965); and another volume of lectures entitled *Renaissance Concepts of Man, and Other Essays* (New York, 1972). S. Dresden, *Humanism in the Renaissance*, tr. by Margaret King (New York, 1968) approaches the period directly through the key works of the humanists.

THE AGE OF PETRARCH

The most exciting introduction to Petrarch is Morris Bishop's *Petrarch and His World* (Bloomington, 1963), which is largely told in Petrarch's own words. Another excellent and scholarly biography is Ernest H. Wilkins, *The Life of Petrarch* (Chicago, 1961). The papers of a 1974 Petrarch symposium are published in Aldo Scaglione (ed.), *Francis Petrarch, Six Centuries Later* (Chicago, 1975), and the assessments of the humanists themselves in David Thompson and Alan Nagel (eds.), *The Three Crowns of Florence: Humanist Assessments of Dante, Petrarca, and Boccaccio* (New York, 1972). For Petrarch's immediate followers, see Thomas C. Chubb, *The Life of Giovanni Boccaccio* (Port

Washington, 1930, 1969); B. L. Ullman, *The Humanism of Coluccio Salutati* (Padua, 1963); and Ronald G. Witt, *Coluccio Salutati and His Public Letters* (Geneva, 1976).

HUMANISM IN THE FIFTEENTH CENTURY

The most provocative and important interpretations of fifteenth-century humanism are Hans Baron, *The Crisis of the Early Italian Renaissance: Civic Humanism and Republican Liberty in an Age of Classicism and Tyranny*, 2nd ed. (Princeton, 1966); Hanna H. Gray, "Renaissance Humanism: The Pursuit of Eloquence," *Journal of the History of Ideas*, 24 (1963), 497–514; Jerrold E. Seigel (cited previously); and Charles Trinkaus, *In Our Image and Likeness: Humanity and Divinity in Italian Humanist Thought*, 2 vols. (Chicago, 1970). Other stimulating studies include Lauro Martines, *The Social World of the Florentine Humanists, 1390–1460* (Princeton, 1963), which looks at the humanists' wealth and civic activities; George Holmes, *The Florentine Enlightenment, 1400–1450* (New York, 1969); Walter Ullman, *Medieval Foundations of Renaissance Humanism* (Ithaca, 1977), a very revisionist interpretation of humanism; Charles L. Stinger, *Humanism and the Church Fathers* (Albany, 1977), about Ambrogio Traversari and the study of Christian antiquity; and Alison Brown, *Bartolomeo Scala, 1430–1497, Chancellor of Florence: The Humanist as Bureaucrat* (Princeton, 1979).

EDUCATION AND RENAISSANCE PHILOSOPHY

W. H. Woodward, *Vittorino da Feltre and Other Humanist Educators*, 2nd ed. (New York, 1963) is a classic, first published in 1897. For the Greek contributions, see Deno Geanakoplos, *Byzantium and the Renaissance* (Hamden, 1973), a reissue of his *Greek Scholars in Venice*. Earlier influences are explored in Paul O. Kristeller, *Medieval Aspects of Renaissance Learning* (Durham, 1974). Ernst Cassirer, *The Individual and the Cosmos in Renaissance Philosophy*, tr. by Mario Domandi (New York, 1963) is a fundamental interpretation of Renaissance thought, originally published in Germany in 1927. Paul O. Kristeller, *Renaissance Philosophy and the Medieval Tradition* (Latrobe, 1966), like all of Kristeller's works, is of great importance. The newest study of Ficino's Platonism is Ardis B. Collins, *The Secular is Sacred: Platonism and Thomism in Marsilio Ficino's Platonic Theology* (The Hague, 1974). A superb new look at Renaissance thought and aesthetics is Dorothy Koenigsberger, *Renaissance Man and Creative Thinking: A History of Concepts of Harmony, 1400–1700* (Hassocks, 1979).

ITALIAN LITERATURE

J. H. Whitfield, *A Short History of Italian Literature* (London, 1960) is a satisfactory introduction. More detailed is Jefferson B. Fletcher, *Literature of the Italian Renaissance*, 2nd ed. (New York, 1964), and the first half of Ernest H. Wilkins, *A History of Italian Literature*, rev. ed. (Cambridge, Mass., 1974). O. B. Hardison, "The Orator and the Poet: The Dilemma of Humanist Literature," *Journal of Medieval and Renaissance Studies*, 1 (1971), 33–44, is short but very interesting. Hans Baron, *From Petrarch to Leonardo Bruni: Studies in Humanistic and Political Literature* (Chicago, 1968), is indispensable. Also the appropriate articles in B. L. Ullman, *Studies in the Italian Renaissance* (Rome, 1973).

The most pertinent examination is Donald J. Wilcox, *The Development of Florentine Humanist Historiography in the Fifteenth Century* (Cambridge, Mass., 1969), which focuses on Bruni, Poggio, and Bartolommeo della Scala. Other insightful studies are Robert Weiss, *The Renaissance Discovery of Classical Antiquity* (Oxford, 1969); Myron P. Gilmore, *Humanists and Jurists: Six Studies in the Renaissance* (Cambridge, Mass., 1963); and Peter Burke (ed.), *The Renaissance Sense of the Past* (New York, 1969), documents and interpretation. Peter E. Bondanella, *Machiavelli and the Art of Renaissance History* (Detroit, 1973) focuses on Machiavelli's interest in the important figures of history and on his vivid literary style. Bondanella, *Francesco Guicciardini* (Boston, 1976), and Mark Phillips, *Francesco Guicciardini: The Historian's Craft* (Toronto, 1977), assess this Renaissance historian.

CHAPTER FIVE

Renaissance Art

IN ART, NO LESS THAN in politics, economics, and learning, the early fifteenth century marked the beginning of a new course in Renaissance Italy. With the generation maturing in the first quarter of the Quattrocento, a new technique of art was developing that expressed the creative orientation of the upper bourgeoisie, especially in Florence, at a time when the city-state was entering a new phase after the depression- and plague-ridden fourteenth century. The artistic style emerging from the declining Gothic during this transitional period reflected new confidence in the world and an optimisitic belief in a rational, focused, harmonious universe. Renaissance artists, like the humanists, were individuals, but they functioned in a tightly organized society that made many demands and expected certain patterns of response in return. Thus we see a great variety in artistic styles and methods, but all within the same general framework of motivation and purpose. Keeping in mind the many variations and moods of individual artists, we can better comprehend and understand Renaissance art if we outline some of its basic assumptions and common characteristics. These traits will be described under the five general headings of naturalism; grace, elegance, and beauty; classicism and secularism; unity and rationalism; and creativity.

The Nature and Assumptions of Renaissance Art

Naturalism (not in its nineteenth-century stylistic meaning, but rather signifying the observation and reproduction of nature) was certainly not a new thing in art. It goes back as far as early Egypt and beyond. But the conscientious study and meticulous copying of nature as an end in itself became common only in the Renaissance. Artists of the Middle Ages appreciated and used nature in their artistic representations, but they employed it as a tool, a means to heighten or emphasize the courtly or ecclesiastical lesson being taught, rather than as an end in itself or as the inspiration for artistic expression. To the artist of the Renaissance, reproducing nature became one of the cornerstones of artistic truth. This tendency to view art as a study of nature explains the Renaissance artist's attention to the problems of perspective, light and shadow, proportion, texture, and form. More successfully than any of their predecessors—because they consciously applied themselves to it—the Renaissance artists solved most of the problems of technique in reproducing on a two-dimensional surface the illusion of three-dimensional objects possessing the same texture, form, and mass as the original subject.

Characteristically, the Renaissance placed a high premium on elegance and beauty—perhaps not so inclusively as Burckhardt would have us believe when he described everything of the period (even the Renaissance state) as a conscious work of art; but Renaissance artists *were* creators of beauty even more than they were teachers of moral or spirtual lessons. Beauty, like naturalism, was a goal rather than a by-product of Renaissance art. "Medieval art aimed at interpreting life and elevating man," observed Arnold Hauser, the well-known art historian, "Renaissance art at enriching life and delighting man." One of the favorite artistic themes for thus delighting man was the human figure, which many fifteenth-century artists considered to be the most graceful and most perfect form in nature. Furthermore, according to Bernard Berenson, Renaissance paintings possess "tactile value," that is, intrinsic qualities of visual attraction apart from the message portrayed. In other words, they appeal to the senses.

The greatest stylistic innovations of the Renaissance resulted from the influence and imitation of classical Greek and Roman art. This influence varied greatly and was not as pronounced in painting as in sculpture and architecture, but it was one of the principal characteristics of Renaissance art. Not only was subject matter frequently chosen from classical themes, but execution also conformed to classical style. Thus the classical ideals of harmony, balance, proportion, symmetry, and moderation gradually became the hallmarks of Renaissance style. Mythological themes from classical times were among the most popular in the fifteenth and early sixteenth centuries.

More difficult to distinguish and define than classicism, yet closely related to it, is secularism. By secularism, we cannot mean the absence of religious themes, for in fact the output of religious art in the Renaissance far exceeded that of any other type and was even greater than during the Middle Ages. What secularism in Renaissance art means is a great increase in the number of nonreligious themes, including the classics, mythology, landscapes, courtly art, and so forth, and less-symbolical and pedagogical interpretations of the religious themes themselves. The increasingly worldly rendition of religious paintings and sculpture is one of the chief characteristics of fifteenth-century Italian art. This is why a Quattrocento Madonna and child is much more likely to be a study in artistic composition, with realistic mass and texture, and even recognizable contemporary attire, than anything produced by medieval artists, although a great deal of symbolism and allegory still remained in Renaissance art. Associated with secularism was the great increase in portraiture during the fifteenth century. This feature reflects the growing interest of wealthy patrons—lay and ecclesiastical—in art and in preserving their own likenesses for posterity. Portrait painting, which originated in northern Europe, especially in France in the late 1300s, flourished in Italy in the second half of the Quattrocento and in the High Renaissance. Even Biblical scenes contained many portraits of contemporaneous patrons and important people.

The unity and rationalism of Renaissance art are harder to describe. Nevertheless, reflections of the artist's optimistic confidence in a closed, unified, and rational universe can be seen in many Renaissance works. The orderly, self-enclosed unity of Renaissance paintings, for example, and their autonomous "inner repose," have the effect of telling a complete and harmonious story. This impression of unity, or at least reconciliation of the various parts within the composition, reflects the yearning of the time for a reconciliation of the spiritual and mundane worlds. To people of the Renaissance, these two worlds were not so much in conflict as they were to the Middle Ages. Medieval artists avoided the too-close association of mortal and divine; Renaissance artists gloried in depicting God in the image of man.

A final generalization about Renaissance art is its growing tendency to become individualized and unique—sometimes even eccentric. Obviously, all artists are unique in some way, whether they worked in the Middle Ages or in ancient Greece, but this uniqueness was played down in medieval art. The Renaissance artist, on the other hand, was above all an individual and a creator; by the early sixteenth century, some of them (Michelangelo being the best example) were esteemed by their contemporaries as not only gifted but almost superhuman.

Sculpture and Architecture

Gothic architecture and its distinctively related sculpture predominated in northern Europe until into the sixteenth century. However, in Italy, where it had never entirely replaced Italic-Romanesque except for the

PANORAMA OF FLORENCE. *In the distance at left is the Ponte Vecchio, spanning the Arno River. Rising above the other buildings are the tower of the Palazzo Vecchio, the cathedral with Giotto's campanile, and Brunelleschi's magnificent dome. At right stands the church of the Santa Croce. (Alinari/Editorial Photocolor Archives)*

general adoption of rib-vaulted ceilings and occasionally spired façades (Milan Cathedral), the early fifteenth century saw a veritable architectural revolution. Geographical and spiritual nearness to Rome, and the almost constant physical reminders of past Roman grandeur and strength, caused Italian builders to turn to Rome for architectural guidance and inspiration, just as the humanists did for intellectual and literary stimulation. The architectural revival of early-fifteenth-century Italy was led by three Florentines whose energy and genius literally rebuilt Renaissance Florence: Filippo Brunelleschi (1377–1446), Bartolommeo di Michelozzo Michelozzi (1396–1472), and Leon Battista Alberti (1405–72).

The cathedral of Santa Maria del Fiore in Florence was begun in 1296, but work on it essentially stopped about 1350. For over seventy years nothing further was done; finally, in 1420 Brunelleschi, a gifted Florentine sculptor and architect-engineer, was commissioned to complete it. Sixteen years later it stood majestically above all other edifices in Florence, as it does today, like a colossus, symbolizing the birth of Renaissance architecture in the heart of Florence. Remarkably harmonious beside Giotto's Campanile (bell tower) built a century earlier, Brunelleschi's white-marble structure, with its alternating stripes of red and green marble culminating in the gigantic red-tiled Byzantine dome, is a vivid reminder of the Renaissance disposition for harmony and balance, for the euphony of space, light, and mass. The wide arches, sturdy square columns, spacious dome (spanning 140 feet at its base), and classical statuary of Santa Maria del Fiore make it the embodiment of the Renaissance revolution in architecture.

But innovation and adaptation did not end with the first structure. Brunelleschi erected many other buildings in Florence: a foundling hospital commissioned by the silk-merchants' guild, the churches of

INTERIOR OF SAN LORENZO. *The architecture of this Renaissance church, with its spacious interior, classical columns, and extended Corinthian capitals, rounded arches, and coffered ceiling, contrasts sharply with the Gothic style of the north. (Alinari/Editorial Photocolor Archives)*

Santo Spirito and San Lorenzo with their graceful arches and coffered ceilings, and the Pazzi chapel in the church of Santa Croce. All of these reveal his active feeling for space, harmony, and balance, and his intense concern for accurate mathematical proportions.

Michelozzo was Brunelleschi's successor as the leading builder in Florence, and although he constructed nothing on the scale of the cathedral, he did build many of the graceful palaces and homes of the wealthy Florentine patrons, including the Medici Palace, the courtyard of the Palazzo Vecchio, and the monastery of San Marco. Michelozzo's

THE PALAZZO MEDICI-RICCARDI IN FLORENCE. *Michelozzo Michelozzi's plan for the Medici Palace features the three-level rusticated stonework and arched window design that became characteristic of Florentine domestic architecture. (Alinari/Editorial Photocolor Archives)*

domestic architecture followed a distinctive pattern that makes it easy to recognize: a ground story built of huge, unfinished stones above which rise two more stories, one of finished stone with beveled edges and the top of polished stone. The symmetrical windows of the upper two stories are separated by columns supporting individual arches over each half-window.

One of the great "universal men" of the Renaissance was Leon Battista Alberti. A talented painter, sculptor, writer, mathematician, lawyer, and musician, as well as a renowned architect, Alberti had one of the most original and creative minds of the time. His ideas on architecture were in large part formed and greatly influenced by the recently discovered writings of Vitruvius on Roman architecture. Using Vitruvius as his text, Alberti set out to reform contemporary notions about building. He thought of architecture as a civic activity and designed his structures to fit into an overall harmony. At the same time, believing that buildings are made for people and not vice versa, he was uniquely conscious of the functions of space, even though he made much use of columns and pilasters for strictly artistic purposes. Alberti insisted that his works be not only externally harmonious but also intellectually and scientifically true because, he maintained, beauty is not a subjective or capricious thing. It is truth and is therefore recognized by a rational faculty of artistic judgment, not by mere "taste." This opinion is the reason Alberti placed so much emphasis on mathematics and mathematical laws in his writings on architecture and painting, and why he was so devoted to the principles of perspective. Among his most representative edifices are the Rucellai Palace in Florence, the façade of the church of Santa Maria Novella, the façade of Sant' Andrea in Mantua, and the uncompleted San Francesco church in Rimini. At the invitation of Pope Nicholas V, he also made the first plans for rebuilding Saint Peter's in Rome, to which Bramante, Raphael, and later Michelangelo added and built. For half a century, Alberti's treatise *On Architecture* was the best guide to Renaissance building in Italy.

Closely associated with architecture since ancient times was its nearest relative, sculpture. In the medieval Gothic cathedrals, the two arts were almost inseparable. Brunelleschi's most illustrious, and cantankerous, contemporary in sculpture was Lorenzo Ghiberti (1378–1455) who, after winning the competition in 1401 for models for the north doors of the baptistry in Florence, spent the next twenty-one years designing, modeling, and building these bronze doors, and another twenty-seven years producing the more famous east doors. Ghiberti was not the first sculptor of the Renaissance. He built on the tradition of Jacopo della Quercia of Siena and the three Pisanos—Niccolò, Giovanni, and Andrea—who in the previous century and a half had produced some great works of art, among them the pulpits in the baptistry and cathedral at Pisa, the pulpit in the cathedral of Siena, and the south doors to the baptistry in Florence. But Ghiberti's work breathed a new spirit and style. Here, according to no less an authority

GHIBERTI'S "GATES OF PARADISE." *The east portal of the Florentine baptistry contains Lorenzo Ghiberti's immense (eighteen and a half feet tall) gilt-bronze doors, brilliantly depicting in bas relief ten episodes from the Old Testament. (Alinari/Editorial Photocolor Archives)*

than Michelangelo, is the finest example of the goldsmith's craft applied to the broader field of Renaissance sculpture, conceived with almost divine insight and executed with consummate skill and beauty. Almost a century after they were made, Michelangelo pronounced Ghiberti's east doors worthy to be the gates of paradise. Since that time, they have been known as the "Gates of Paradise." These bas-relief panels, five on each of the two doors, depict in vivid detail and delicacy scenes from the Old Testament. Ghiberti's attention to the problems of linear perspective, the harmonious balance of space and mass, and the focused effect of each panel, along with the unity of the total, makes this an impressive example of Renaissance art at its best.

The greatest Quattrocento sculptor was Brunelleschi's and Ghiberti's younger contemporary, Donatello (1386–1466). In his early years, Donatello was associated with the Ghiberti workshop, where he learned the techniques and skills he later used in a whole galaxy of creations, from tiny medallions to the great bronze equestrian statue of the *condottiere* Gattamelata. He was a close and life-long friend of Brunelleschi. Donatello's conception of art was vast, and he restricted himself to no single form or single medium of expression. Yet in all his work can be seen the same attention to harmony, action, and idea, and

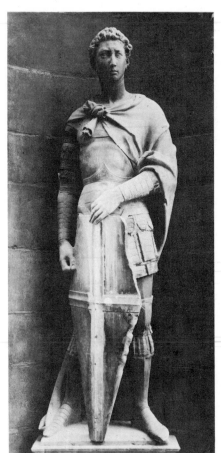

DONATELLO'S MARBLE "SAINT GEORGE." *The simplicity and strength of Donatello's youthful figure reveal the sculptor's artistic skill and his ability to depict both character and form.* (Alinari/Editorial Photocolor Archives)

the depiction of mood and temperament. By Donatello's time, sculpture had achieved a high degree of naturalism, but little of it had attained such a grasp of character. No other Renaissance sculptor save Michelangelo was able to depict such power and majesty in his figures, yet Donatello did it with such simplicity and economy of detail that his works can be enjoyed today almost as much as they were in his own time. The best examples of his depiction of physical and moral strength can be seen in his great statues of the prophets *Jeremiah, Hosea, Job,* and *Habakuk,* intended for the front of the campanile in Florence but now located in the Cathedral Museum. His most popular are the *David* and *Saint George,* while the most striking is his *Gattamelata,* the first bronze equestrian statue to be cast since Roman times, located on the Piazza di Sant' Antonio in Padua.

After Donatello's death, the leading Florentine sculptor was Andrea del Verrocchio (1435–88), a distinguished goldsmith, painter, and engineer, as well as sculptor. Verrocchio emphasized movement and grace, especially in his bronze *David* and the small bronze *Boy with a Dolphin,* located in the courtyard of the Palazzo Vecchio in Florence. A completely different mood is revealed in his powerful equestrian statue of the *condottiere* Bartolomeo Colleoni, standing today in the Campo dei SS. Giovanni e Paolo in Venice.

Italian Painting in the Quattrocento

Guidebooks on Renaissance art usually begin with Cimabue, Duccio, and especially Giotto (1266–1337). A contemporary and close friend of Dante, Giotto displayed in his frescoes adorning the walls of several churches in Florence, Padua, Assisi, Naples, and even Avignon, a great feeling for nature and for realistic reproduction; however, like Dante's own *Divine Comedy,* the method and motives of his works seem to represent more the culmination of medieval art and thought than they do Renaissance style. At any rate, whatever Renaissance elements are contained in his works, these were not picked up by his immediate disciples who continued in the international Gothic tradition of the time. We must jump 100 years, to the early fifteenth century, before we see a full-scale and continuous development of Renaissance painting.

The first, and in many ways the greatest, of the true Renaissance painters was the Florentine, Masaccio (1401–28). A younger contemporary of Masolino, his teacher, and Fra Angelico, Masaccio surpassed them both in just about every feature of Renaissance art. According to the testimony of Vasari, it was Masaccio "who first clearly perceived that painting must be founded on nature both in form and in color." Masaccio possessed the unrivaled ability to visualize and create on a surface the illusion of live human beings, not symbols or allegories, but real people. Furthermore, his figures have individuality and personality as well as form and mass. The faces of the Apostles in his *Tribute Money,* for example, reveal much about the character of these men, as well as

MASACCIO'S "TRIBUTE MONEY." *This realistic fresco panel in the Brancacci Chapel is a landmark of early Renaissance painting. Here the young Masaccio vividly illustrates the episode described in Matthew 17:24–27. (Alinari/ Editorial Photocolor Archives)*

their feelings and reactions to the situation depicted. Finally, Masaccio's awareness and use of a single light source with a linear vanishing point for accurate perspective set him apart from thirteenth- and fourteenth-century artists. He even seems to have been conscious of the physical quality of atmosphere, giving it content as well as depth. In their realism, simplicity, and narrative impact, his famous frescoes on the walls of the Brancacci Chapel of Santa Maria del Carmine in Florence established a new standard and direction for Florentine painting. For the next seventy-five years, these frescoes were admired and religiously studied by all aspiring young artists. Masaccio's genius becomes even more striking when we recall that he was only twenty-eight when he died.

The important painters of the Quattrocento are far too numerous to mention more than a few who will be singled out to illustrate some of the characteristics of Renaissance art. Influenced by Brunelleschi's and Alberti's work on perspective and by association with like-minded artists in Ghiberti's workshop, Paolo Uccello (1397–1475) became obsessed with the problems and possibilities of perspective; in fact, all of his paintings can be seen as studies in the solution and perfection of linear perspective. Vasari charged that "Uccello might have been the most original and inventive genius in the art of painting since Giotto's day, if he had but spent half the time on drawing men and animals that he threw away in the fine points of perspective." For his part, Domenico Veneziano (ca. 1405–61) experimented widely with pigments, techniques, and subjects to create the realistic effects he desired in his paintings. He was particularly interested in the mutation of color when it is exposed to various sources and kinds of light. Another outstanding artist, Fra Filippo Lippi (ca. 1406–69), was an orphan at the

Convent of the Carmine when Masaccio painted his frescoes there. Masaccio's influence is recognized in the realism and character of Filippo Lippi's works, although they tend to be more dramatic than his mentor's and reveal a softer tenderness and beauty. Andrea del Castagno (1421–57), on the other hand, emphasized form and movement, particularly as they could be applied to the portrayal of powerful masculine physical energy.

Veneziano's most gifted pupil was Piero della Francesca (ca. 1416–92), whose many frescoes and temperas reflect the influence of Alberti's notions of mathematical perspective and form. So interested was Piero in the science of perspective that he wrote a treatise on its practical application to painting. He was also excited by the problems of space, air, and light. The familiar silvery tones added to the backgrounds of his portraits and Madonnas were attempts to meet these challenges. Motion, on the other hand, did not interest Piero. He was content to leave his figures serene and immobile if he could balance color, light, and form to give the composition depth, naturalism, and a sense of focus. His series of remarkable frescoes in the choir of the church of San Francesco in Arezzo, depicting the legend of the True Cross, reveal his forceful yet delicate handling of both form and color.

In the second half of the fifteenth century, Florentine artists paid increasing attention to aspects of their craft that had not been emphasized by earlier artists. For example, many of them stressed the emotional nature of their subject and tried to convey the feelings and pathos of a scene to the viewer. Others accentuated linear elegance and grace, while some concentrated on movement or harmony of colors.

Antonio Pallaiuolo (ca. 1432–98) is noted for his expressive studies of the human figure in motion and for his many graceful portraits. Andrea del Verrocchio, Leonardo da Vinci's teacher, tried in his own way to solve the problems of space and atmosphere. By a sensitive blending of blues and purples in his landscapes, Verrocchio was able to achieve a new level of ethereal "reality." His busy workshop's attention to problems of atmospheric space came to fruition in his illustrious pupil. In the meantime, another Florentine workshop vied with Verrocchio's both in the output of artwork and of skilled artists. Domenico Ghirlandaio (1449–94) was a devoted naturalist and something of a technical perfectionist. His greatest fame came from his fresco scenes from the *Life of the Virgin* and the *Life of John the Baptist* in the choir of Santa Maria Novella, and his giant fresco of the *Calling of the First Apostles* on the wall of the Sistine Chapel in Rome. A popular painter of Florentine life, Ghirlandaio had a greater feeling for movement than did most of his predecessors, as well as a deep appreciation of accurate form and vivid color. Perhaps some of these traits rubbed off on his most renowned pupil, Michelangelo.

Almost in a category of his own, yet deeply imbued with many of the Renaissance characteristics, was the whimsical and eccentric Sandro Botticelli (1444–1510). Relatively neglected by art critics until the last

eighty years, this Florentine goldsmith-painter, student of Fra Filippo Lippi, and devotee of the fanatic monk Savonarola was one of the most prolific and eclectic of artists, drawing equally from religious, classical, and philosophical sources for the subject matter of his paintings. Unlike most of his contemporaries, Botticelli was not particularly concerned with scientific naturalism and realism. He was much more interested in revealing subjective charm and delicate grace, and in communicating feeling, than he was in making accurate reproductions of nature. Above all, it is the rhythmic beauty and flow of his lines that make Botticelli one of the great Renaissance painters. His range was vast, extending from classical mythology and history to the great biblical compositions that adorn the walls of the Sistine Chapel along with those of Ghirlandaio and Perugino. His numerous *Adorations* are among the finest produced during the Renaissance.

Botticelli's best-known paintings are the *Primavera*, an allegory on the reign of Lorenzo the Magnificent, depicted as the "return of spring," and the wistful *Birth of Venus*, both painted for the Medici villa at Castello. In the latter painting, Venus, with lithe, undulating body and long golden hair, is wafted by Zephyr (the west wind) toward a newfound shore where a Grace welcomes her with a flowing robe. Like the *Primavera*, its allegorical meaning has been variously interpreted by modern art critics, but contemporaries usually thought it represented the birth of *Humanitas,* patroness of the Medicean humanists. Botticelli's style so influenced his younger contemporary and pupil Filippino Lippi (Fra Filippo Lippi's son), that some works have been attributed to both of them.

Outside Florence, painting also flourished during the Renaissance. Padua, and later Mantua under its benevolent ruler Ludovico Gonzaga, produced one of the most gifted painters in Andrea Mantegna (1431–1506), conspicuous for his idealization of Roman antiquity and for his devotion to mathematically precise perspective. Mantegna's skillful craftsmanship is revealed in many works in copper and bronze as well as in oils and frescoes. The poet Ariosto considered him the most illustrious painter of his day, along with Leonardo da Vinci and Giovanni Bellini. Mantegna's brother-in-law Gentile Bellini (1429–1507) introduced many of Mantegna's techniques into Venice, including the extensive use of oil, which was only gradually replacing egg tempera as the principal painting medium. From their father's workshop, Gentile Bellini and his more famous brother Giovanni (1431–1516) produced some of the most colorful yet delicate paintings of the period. Their forte was color and composition, and their popularity derived from deeply touching religious scenes as well as from portraiture and historical scenes glorifying the Venetian state. Giovanni Bellini is perhaps most famous for his brilliant paintings in the Council Hall of the *doges'* palace and his portrait of Doge Leonardo Loredan. The linear quality of his

MANTEGNA'S "THE DEAD CHRIST." *The most dramatic example of Mantegna's interest in and mastery of perspective is this unusual picture, painted sometime in the 1470s. (Alinari/Editorial Photocolor Archives*

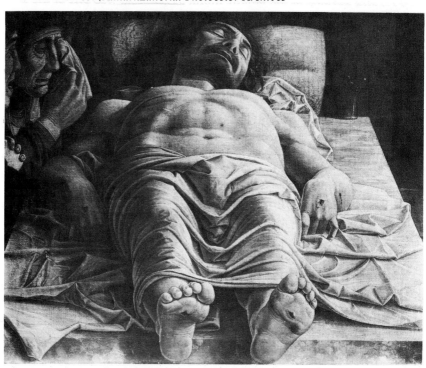

paintings reminds one of Botticelli, but his use of color was more vivid and daring.

The Art of the High Renaissance

The High Renaissance (especially the years between 1500 and 1520) was the culmination and fulfillment of the aspirations and techniques of the earlier Renaissance artists. The problems of perspective, light and shade, foreshortening, space composition, painting in oil, texture, and movement had all been variously solved. Artists could now apply the techniques they had learned to creating masterpieces of harmony and strength to glorify their great age. As the painters' techniques were perfected, they concentrated more on using this medium for powerful portrayals of man's personal accomplishments and also his partnership with God. In architecture, sculpture, painting, and music, as well as in the lofty Latin epics and vernacular histories, this was a period of reconciliation and culmination. Projects of artists and patrons were on a grand and heroic scale—building the richest homes in Rome, the finest palaces in Italy, and the largest churches in the world. The affinity felt with the ancients also made this par excellence, the age of classicism. Now, as masters of their media, Renaissance artists and builders could create the kind of art they deeply felt, the kind of art the ancient Greeks and Romans had conceived. Nature was no longer something merely to be copied—it was to be transcended.

The High Renaissance coincides also with the decline, and in some cases the collapse, of political democracy in Italy and with the growing power and importance of the aristocracy. Art of this period was the art of the great princes, popes, and potentates, reflecting their thoughts and aspirations. In almost any sector one chooses to look—religious, economic, political, intellectual, or artistic, in deeds of virtue, heroism, or villainy—one will find proof that the High Renaissance was an age of giants. Whatever the enterprise, it was neither too vast nor too difficult for a Leonardo da Vinci, Ariosto, Machiavelli, Julius II, Christopher Columbus, Amerigo Vespucci, Cortés, Charles V, Martin Luther, Francis I, Thomas More, Erasmus, Rabelais, Henry VIII, or Michelangelo. Whereas Florence had been the focus of Quattrocento culture, now Rome became the center to which the greatest artists converged and out of which the finest art emerged. But Rome was not the only center of artistic production; Milan too had its moments of glory and disgrace in the High Renaissance, as did Florence and especially Venice. This was also the age when Renaissance art ceased being primarily an Italian phenomenon and spread rapidly to other parts of Europe in the wake of the French invasions.

In the arts we have been describing, three figures tower above all the rest in the High Renaissance: Leonardo, Michelangelo, and Raphael. Each was unique in personality, style, and significance; yet all three shared the spirit of creative genius and left masterpieces conceived in heroic proportions.

LEONARDO DA VINCI'S UN-FINISHED "ADORATION OF THE MAGI (KINGS)." *Few Renaissance artists could match the compositional skill of Leonardo. His use of space and his attention to balance and harmony are remarkable. (Editorial Photocolor Archives)*

Leonardo da Vinci

Of the three artists, Leonardo da Vinci (1452–1519) was born the earliest. Chronologically, he belongs with Botticelli and Ghirlandaio and the artists of the late Quattrocento, and his almost complete rejection of Roman models is unlike the flowering classicism of the early sixteenth century. But his powerful, protean mind and versatile style place him on the frontier of his age. His grandiose projects mark him as a man of the High Renaissance. He was born at Anchiano, near the village of Vinci just west of Florence, of a lawyer father and peasant mother, but was Florentine by training. Leonardo received his early apprenticeship under Verrocchio, who soon recognized his pupil's precosity and provided him with opportunities to work on some of the most important contracts. His *Baptism of Christ* and *Annunciation* are now legendary. In 1481 Leonardo was commissioned to paint an *Adoration of the Kings* for a monastery outside Florence. This unfinished work (and most of Leonardo's works are unfinished) is one of the finest examples of his mastery of composition and movement, and the figures that are completed reveal his unrivaled facility for interpretive facial expression. Two years later, he was in Milan where he painted the controversial *Virgin of the Rocks.* During the last years of the century, Leonardo worked in the monastery of Santa Maria della Grazie, in Milan, on his most famous masterpiece, the *Last Supper.* Here is a supreme example of artistic composition, rhythmically arranging the apostles in groups of three contrasting types, balancing each other as they harmonize the whole in the person of Christ at the moment of emotional drama evoked by the Lord's pronouncement that one of his apostles would betray him.

With the fall of Milan to the French in 1499, Leonardo left the Sforza employ and returned to Florence where he remained for the next six years, creating, in addition to the *Mona Lisa*, a charming *Madonna and Child with Saint Anne*, numerous preliminary studies for great paintings that were never finished, and a mammoth fresco of the *Battle of Anghiari* for a wall of the Great Hall of the Palazzo Vecchio in Florence, which he was employed by the *Signoria* to paint in competition with his archrival Michelangelo. He also served as military engineer to Cesare Borgia during that tyrant's campaign through the Romagna. He then returned to Milan, this time in the employ of Milan's new ruler, the king of France. For four years (1513–17), he resided in Rome under the patronage of Giulio de' Medici before accepting Francis I's offer to come to France, where he joined other Italian artists invited by the king to carry Renaissance ideas and art to that country. He was given a home and shop in Amboise near the court, where he died two years later at the age of sixty-seven.

From whatever position he is viewed, Leonardo was a remarkable and unusual man, gifted beyond most of his contemporaries in the intellectual and technical skills of his profession. But he was not satisfied with being only an artist, although he considered painting the highest of all callings. His restless mind and thirst for knowledge would not allow him repose as he vacillated between painting, engineering, designing, writing, sketching, building, dissecting, and contemplating. During much of his wandering, he kept notebooks in which he jotted down thoughts and impressions on innumerable subjects and sketched hundreds of objects and figures from life. Some of these were used in his paintings, most of them were not, but they reveal the turmoils and trials of his life, as well as the brilliance of his insights and his ability to describe them in pictures.

His philosophy of art is important for understanding his own mind and for appreciating his painting and other art of the Renaissance. Like Alberti, Leonardo believed painting was a science because it is based on mathematical perspective and on the study of nature. No other artist of the Renaissance made such close and detailed observations of nature, including anatomy, as did Leonardo. Surface appearance was not sufficient. He had to know the inner construction and functions of all parts and organs before he felt he could adequately paint the human body in lifelike actions and moods. For this reason, he performed many dissections of animal and human bodies and in so doing added much to his knowledge of human anatomy. But Leonardo believed the artist's role was different from that of other scientists, for in the end it resulted in a creative work of art. Thus the painter is both scientist and creator. In his *Treatise on Painting*, Leonardo argued that painting is superior to science, because it transcends it, being both contemplative and operative. He also maintained that painting is a higher art than sculpture, architecture, and music, and is equal, if not superior, to philosophy and poetry (considered since ancient times the greatest of the liberal arts).

Leonardo's artistic genius is best shown in his complete mastery of the art of composition and in his ability to penetrate beyond the outward appearance of things and reveal their inner reality. His portraits breathe character as well as personality; even his landscapes possess a quality of "lifeness" through the delicate and misty gradations of light, known as *sfumato*, that are the hallmarks of Leonardo's paintings.

Michelangelo

Like the versatile Leonardo, Michelangelo Buonarroti (1475–1564) was also a universal man. He was a painter of unequaled power and feeling, an imaginative architect, an engineer, a poet of depth and sensitivity, a knowledgeable authority on anatomy, and the greatest sculptor of all time. Yet in a sense, he was a simpler person than Leonardo, motivated and unified by a single driving passion to create. Whereas Leonardo found it difficult, usually impossible, to carry a project through to completion, Michelangelo was so compulsively impelled to finish a sculpture once begun that he frequently worked day and night without food or sleep until it was completed. Leonardo was fragmented by his conflicting interests and talents, and by his restless, inquisitive mind, which drank in knowledge as fast as he could find it. Michelangelo was integrated by his powerful urge to produce, to create, in whatever medium available or with whatever technique required. His capacity for work was almost inhuman, yet he drove himself even further because of the unquenchable fire that burned within him. He was full of majestic and noble art that had to be released. The very walls and stones contained magnificent forms and ideas that had to be liberated. It was his life's work to free them.

Michelangelo's ideal of beauty was related to nature; yet true beauty, spiritual beauty in the Platonic sense, transcended nature. It was the divine reflection of God in the material sphere. He disclosed this conception of beauty in his poems as well as in his art:

> He who made the whole made every part;
> Then from the whole chose what was most beautiful,
> To reveal on earth, as He has done here and now
> His own sublime perfections.*

The spark of this Divine beauty is revealed to people both physically, as we see, hear, and absorb the visible and audible world about us, and spiritually as we receive an inner image of ideal beauty from the interaction of mind and soul. In other words, true beauty is communicated from God to people, and from one person to another, not just by the senses or even by a rational faculty of "beauty-truth," as Alberti

---

*Translated by K. T. Butler, in Anthony Blunt, *Artistic Theory in Italy, 1450–1600* (Oxford: Clarendon Press, 1940), p. 62. Reprinted by permission of Oxford University Press.

maintained, but by a combination of sensory, rational, and spiritual manifestations:

> The beauty you behold indeed emanates from her [the
>   visual image]
> But it grows greater as it flows
> Through mortal eyes to its nobler abode—the soul.
> Here it becomes divine, pure, perfect
> To match the soul's immortality.
> It is this beauty, not the other,
> Which ever outruns your vision.*

Born in Florence, Michelangelo was the son of a petty shopkeeper and merchant (a descendant of a minor noble family) who would have liked nothing better than to have his son carry on the Buonarroti family business and eventually acquire land and nobility. It was with deep disappointment, therefore, that he finally consented to apprentice young Michelangelo, who was interested in nothing but art, to the painter Ghirlandaio. The arrangement was only a compromise, however, for the boy's real passion was sculpture. As an infant, he had been sent to a stonecutter's wife to nurse. Vasari proudly quotes Michelangelo as saying to him, "Giorgio, if I am good for anything, it is because I was born in the good mountain air of your Arezzo and suckled among the chisels and hammers of the stonecutters." Michelangelo was a bright student and learned much about the tech-

*Ibid., p. 63.

MICHELANGELO'S "PIETÀ". In this monumental work, done when he was twenty-five years old, Michelangelo depicts both tenderness and agony, and reveals a complete mastery of design and form. One almost forgets that his medium was Carrara marble and not flesh and bones. (Alinari/Editorial Photocolor Archives)

nique of fresco painting in the Ghirlandaio workshop. Soon, however, he was taken into Lorenzo de' Medici's circle of artist friends and trainees, where he became acquainted with many important people, with the intellectual impact of Plato, and with the prominent sculptors of Florence.

With the fall of the Medici in 1494, Michelangelo went to Bologna and from there to Rome in 1496. Here he began the most productive period in his long career. His first significant sculpture was the famous and long-loved *Pietà*, remarkable for its combination of naturalistic beauty and deep religious feeling. It stands in the Capella della Pietà in Saint Peter's Basilica. Michelangelo's fame was well established when he returned to Florence at the age of twenty-six to begin work on several commissions from the Florentine *Signoria*. One of these was the giant white marble statue of *David*, poised in classical masculine beauty and power anticipating the encounter with Goliath. This masterpiece of grandeur and dignity, which stands proudly under the cupola of the Academia in Florence, has probably been copied and reproduced more than any other statue. It has become a symbol of Michelangelo and of Renaissance art. While in Florence, he also completed other sculptures, including the life-size Bruges *Madonna and Child* and a tempera painting of the Holy Family, and competed with Leonardo da Vinci's battle scene on the wall of the council chamber with a cartoon for his own *Battle of Cascina*.

Michelangelo was recalled to Rome in 1505 by the 62-year-old Pope Julius II who, like the artist himself, was a restless and impatient doer. Julius not only set himself the task of expelling the French from Italy and establishing a politically powerful Papal State but also began the creation of a new and more beautiful Rome, complete with grandiose plans for statues and paintings equal to the heroic history of the city, and a mammoth new cathedral that would be the wonder of Christendom. He did not live to see his vast ambitions fulfilled, but he did bring the greatest artists and builders to Rome and inaugurated a brief age of Roman splendor. Michelangelo's first commission from Julius was for a huge tomb requiring no fewer than forty greater-than-life-size statues and innumerable smaller figures and designs. As it turned out, this work became the continuing burden of Michelangelo's life. No sooner had he begun work on the immense project than Julius's money ran out, and Michelangelo was forced to divert his energies to other work, including a bronze statue of Julius in Bologna and the fresco painting of the Sistine Chapel ceiling. After Julius's death, the contract was renegotiated with his heirs for a new tomb, this one considerably smaller and less expensive. But the fortunes of Italian politics were such that few long-range projects could be carried to conclusion. Eventually, five separate contracts were signed, each contradicting the former and causing endless litigation and recriminations over a period of forty years, before the remnant of Julius's original idea was completed. In its greatly diminished form, the tomb now stands in the small church of

San Pietro in Vincoli (Saint Peter in Chains), crowned with the majestic marble statue of *Moses*.

The Sistine ceiling is a saga of its own, an unbelievable undertaking of fortitude, inspiration, and grandeur. The ceiling, covering some 6,300 square feet and containing, when finished, over 300 figures and all that goes with them, was completed by Michelangelo in the amazingly short time of four years. He was offered assistants but refused them (except for two men who mixed pigments and helped transfer Michelangelo's cartoons to the wet plaster), insisting on designing and executing the entire work himself, most of it while straining on his back or crouching over scaffolding in a feverish act of creation. Despite discomfort, fatigue, pain, and sickness (and violent disagreements with Pope Julius), Michelangelo not only completed the massive work but produced a masterpiece of such power and impact as to constitute the supreme Renaissance harmonization of the mortal and divine. In eight huge center panels, the completed vault depicts the story of Genesis from the Creation to Noah, surrounded on the sides of the vaulting by other scenes from the Bible, colossal figures of prophets and sibyls, and in the remaining arches and lunettes, the ancestors of the Virgin, suggesting the expectation and preparation for Christ's coming. Not only is the total rendition monumental, but each individual figure is a masterpiece of composition, movement, and deep meaning surpassing anything that had been painted before. Raphael, who was at the same time painting the Stanza della Segnatura only a few corridors away, pronounced them divine.

The Sistine ceiling notwithstanding, Michelangelo considered himself a sculptor, not a painter, and with hammer and chisel in hand he returned to the pope's tomb. During the next four years, he completed the *Moses* and two *Captives* for the tomb, and a life-size *Christ Risen* for another Roman patron. In the meantime, Julius II was succeeded by Leo X, Lorenzo de' Medici's second son. Leo ordered the abandonment of Julius's tomb and sent Michelangelo to Florence to design and build a new façade for the church of San Lorenzo, the Medici family church. After two years of designing, quarrying, and cutting Carrara marble, and fighting with his patrons, the project was abandoned because of excessive expenditures on Saint Peter's and other lavish papal projects. In 1520 Michelangelo was put to work on a tomb for the Medici family, to be located in the New Sacristy of San Lorenzo, which, after many interruptions (once to rebuild the fortification of Florence against the assault of an imperial army), he completed in 1534, under the aegis of another Medici pope, Clement VII.

The last thirty years of Michelangelo's life were spent in Rome in the successive employ of four more popes, while shunning the invitations of such princes as Charles V, Suleiman the Magnificent, Francis I, and the *doge* of Venice. At the age of sixty, Michelangelo began work on his *Last Judgment*, a mammoth fresco commissioned by Pope Paul III, covering the entire west wall of the Sistine Chapel. More than any of his other works, the *Last Judgment* shows the effects on Michelangelo of the great religious upheaval that was then tearing Europe apart. Here again he displayed a grandiose conception of his subject, but much of the grace and beauty of his earlier works was missing, not because his hand was failing but because he was no longer so interested in physical beauty for its own sake. Now, more than ever before, he employed art for conveying an idea, or more precisely, for revealing a spiritual condition. Deep religious feeling pervades most of Michelangelo's later works and reveals the impact of the Reformation and Counter-Reformation on Renaissance art, transforming it into what art critics now call manneristic—tense, disturbed, exaggerated, distorted, and above all, symbolic and allegorical. Michelangelo's long, productive life (he died in his ninetieth year, still working on the cupola of Saint Peter's Basilica) extended far into the period of Mannerism, and provided a sturdy bridge from the High Renaissance.

Raphael

The youngest of the artistic trio to make the High Renaissance a period of fulfillment and synthesis, as well as the culmination of classicism, was Raffaello Sanzio (1483–1520). Son of a court painter and poet in Urbino, Raphael grew up in the same courtly atmosphere that Castiglione found so attractive under Urbino's cultured duke, Guidobaldo da Montefeltro. After the early death of his parents, Raphael learned painting from a minor local artist before moving to Perugia in 1500 to study under the renowned Pietro Perugino. Perugino taught him much about space composition and form, but young Raphael was soon ready to move on to other ideas and styles. At the age of twenty-one, he settled in Florence in order to learn from the celebrated Leonardo da Vinci. With his unique ability to learn and absorb from many sources and styles and to synthesize and utilize without imitating any of them, Raphael was able to assimilate the best of Umbrian, Perugian, and Florentine art without sacrificing his own originality and style. When he moved to Rome in 1508, he was only twenty-five but already one of the finest painters of Italy.

Julius II invited Raphael to Rome to redecorate some of the rooms in the Vatican Palace at the same time Michelangelo was brought there to paint the Sistine ceiling. Here, in the Stanza della Segnatura, Raphael completed some of his greatest compositions, including the *School of Athens*, which depicts, in almost flawless harmony of composition and arrangement, the Greek philosophers Plato and Aristotle surrounded by numerous other scientists and thinkers of Europe and Asia; the *Dispute of the Sacrament (La Disputà)*, which brings together many heavenly figures, representing saints and prophets surrounding the Savior, the Virgin Mary, and John the Baptist, overlooking an assembly of church dignitaries on earth taking part in the controversy over the Eucharist; and *Parnassus* (sometimes called *Apollo and the Muses*), another group fresco, which glorifies poetical life and cultural refinement. Many other noteworthy frescoes, depicting the cardinal virtues, civil and canon law, poetry, astronomy, justice, theology, and several scenes from the

RAPHAEL'S "THE SCHOOL OF ATHENS." *Raphael links his own times with the classic age by representing the greatest minds of ancient Greece in likenesses of his own contemporaries. Plato (in the center talking with Aristotle) is Leonardo da Vinci; Euclid (at lower right drawing on a board) is Bramante; Heraclitus (sitting in front center) is Michelangelo. (Alinari/Editorial Photocolor Archives)*

RAPHAEL'S "MADONNA IN THE MEADOW." *This beautiful group of the Madonna, Jesus, and the infant John the Baptist, exudes tenderness and compassion, and also shows Raphael's harmonious use of landscape.* (Kunsthistorisches Museum, Vienna)

Bible and from history, adorn the walls and ceilings of the Raphael rooms. All of these Stanze paintings, from the *Jurisprudence* (personifying fortitude, prudence, and temperance), the *Mass of Bolsena*, and *The Expulsion of Heliodorus from the Temple*, to *The Liberation of Saint Peter*, *Fire in the Borgo*, and *The Meeting of Pope Leo I and Attila the Hun*, achieve near perfection in the techniques of figure painting and at the same time unrivaled skill in composition and visual imagery. The grandeur and scope of these Vatican paintings reflect the High-Renaissance style at its best.

Unlike Leonardo, Raphael was a prolific painter. Working quickly and almost effortlessly, he completed literally hundreds of frescoes, portraits, and oils. He was also a versatile artist, adapting his style to the requirements of the subject or patron. Undoubtedly, Raphael is most famous for his portraits and for his soft and modeled Madonnas. While in the employ of Popes Julius II and Leo X, Raphael made several portraits of these pontiffs and of the cardinals. The best known are portraits of Julius II, Leo X with Cardinals Ludovico de' Rossi and Giulio de' Medici, and Baldassare Castiglione. Raphael's most renowned Madonnas are the *Sistine Madonna* (Dresden), *Madonna di Foligno* (Vatican), the *Ansidei Madonna* (London), *Madonna del Gran' Duca* (Florence), and *Madonna in the Meadow* (Vienna). In all of these, and in the 114 other identified Raphael paintings (plus some sixty done by students from his sketches and under his supervision), we see the variety and scope of an artist who assimilated his surroundings assiduously and transformed his experiences into graceful and imaginative compositions that will always delight the lover of beauty. In 1520 Raphael succumbed to pneumonia and died, at the age of thirty-seven.

Other Artists of the High Renaissance

The foregoing trio so dominated the High Renaissance that it is sometimes forgotten that there were also others who, had they not been contemporaries of Leonardo, Michelangelo, and Raphael, would be considered the most eminent artists of the Renaissance. The leading architect of the second half of the fifteenth century and first years of the sixteenth was Donato d'Agnolo Bramante (1444–1514), born in Urbino but trained in Mantua, Milan, and Rome. Specializing in church and palatial architecture, Bramante became the most respected and prolific builder in Rome, being responsible for the Guiraud Palace, the Palazzo della Cancelleria, and several courts of the Vatican. He climaxed his career by designing and supervising the early construction of Saint Peter's Basilica in Rome, the largest church in the world. Bramante planned the church in the form of a huge Greek cross, with a rounded choir and gigantic dome over the center. Upon Bramante's death, his friend Raphael was placed in charge of construction. Disagreements between Raphael and his associates over the relative merits of preserving the Greek shape or altering it to form a Latin cross (favored by Raphael) caused the work to stagnate under him and his successor, Antonio da Sangallo. Recognizing the superiority of Bramante's design, Michelangelo returned to the basic plan when he became the chief builder in 1547.

Venice, Rome's bitterest peninsular rival at the close of the fifteenth century, also enjoyed its artistic heyday in the High Renaissance. From Vittore Carpaccio (1455–1526) to Paolo Veronese (1528–88), Venice was glorified and exalted by her artists in splendid color and magnificent portrayals. For the unifying use of light and color in balanced compositions that seem to sum up the Italian Renaissance, no artist is more important than Giorgione (ca. 1477–1510), even though he died very young. A pupil of Giovanni Bellini, Giorgione reflects in his pastoral scenes and classical themes his master's interest in landscapes and his regard for expressive colors. His paintings are softer and more delicate than many of his contemporaries but still reflect the temper and spirit of the time. He broadened the scope of Venetian painting by paying increased attention to allegory and to the nude figure, and introduced classical mythology into his works.

The greatest painter of the Venetian School was Tiziano Vecellio, better known as Titian (1477–1576). Living to be ninety-nine years old, Titian, like Michelangelo, bridged the transition from the grand style of the High Renaissance through the allegorical religious tensions of Mannerism, to the early Baroque. Also like his Florentine contemporary, he expressed a spontaneous, energetic lust for creation, but unlike

GIORGIONE'S "ADORATION OF THE SHEPHERDS." *Known also as the "Allende Nativity," this pastoral painting reveals Giorgione's skill at integrating all the features of his panel into a unifying focus on the infant Jesus. (Courtesy of the National Gallery of Art, Washington, D.C. Samuel H. Kress Collection)*

Michelangelo he did it mostly in powerful portraits of his contemporaries. It is through Titian's eyes that we see many of the great personalities and events of three-quarters of a century of European history. Two other genres in particular attracted Titian during his long creative career: themes from Greek and Roman mythology, in which he displayed unusual imagination and verve; and religious scenes, such as in the graceful *Noli me Tangere* (Touch Me Not), which he approached with a Giorgionean respect for beauty and human relations, but which he carried beyond his friend's level in feeling and expression. His exuberance for life may be seen in his triumphal *Assumption of the Virgin*, as well as in his *Sacred and Profane Love* or in the *Bacchanale*. Most of Titian's life was spent in the service of great princes of Europe—the Venetian *doge*, the duke of Ferrera, and the emperor Charles V.

Venetian art, as well as power, also penetrated into the surrounding areas in the sixteenth century. Titian's younger contemporary from Parma, Antonio Correggio (1494–1534), was one of the most skillful painters of the High Renaissance, especially in his use of light and shadow and his ability to depict texture. Influenced as much by the Florentine style as the Venetian, and especially by Raphael, Correggio was still related to the Venetian school in his exuberant use of color and in his fascination with ceremonial pomp and grandeur.

The Artist in Renaissance Society

The social position of Renaissance artists has been alluded to but not yet examined or explained. Unlike the fifteenth-century humanists, who were predominantly wealthy and influential, the artists of the Renaissance were in most cases from the lower classes, men of modest means whose social and economic fate depended entirely on their patrons. Quattrocento artists were almost all attached to the workshops of master craftsmen who kept, taught, and worked their apprentices in much the same way as other medieval and Renaissance guildsmen did theirs. Artists who showed unusual promise could look forward to joining the guild some day as journeymen or masters and employing their own workers. Artistic production was done almost entirely by contract with the patron (contractor) specifying not only the general type and purpose of the work but also frequently prescribing its mood, composition, colors, and even technique. It is little wonder that the patrons were considered the real creators of early Renaissance art, not the craftsmen who applied the paint or the stonecutters who pounded the chisel. This is the reason Quattrocento art, although actually executed by men of the middle and lower classes reflected the tastes and interests of the upper bourgeoisie and nobility.

But whatever we say about Renaissance society, we cannot call it static. Any generalization about classes and categories must be modified by the recognition that they changed, that what was true at one time or place was not necessarily true at another. During the course of the fifteenth century, many social changes occurred, among the most significant of which was the gradual transition of the artist from a manual laborer, or at best an artisan, to a semi-independent creator and supplier of valued artistic commodities. This process was slow and uneven, and did not apply to all artists, many of whom remained at the lower levels of society and continued to serve as apprentices and journeymen in painting "factories." But by the early sixteenth century, artists with genuine talent were able not only to acquire wealth but also to occupy a position of respect and admiration in society. No one provides a better example of this triumphal rise than the artists we have just discussed, especially Michelangelo, Raphael, and Titian. Here were men no longer looked upon as laborers or craftsmen; they were at least "gentlemen" and at best—in the case of Michelangelo—"divine." Indeed, it is more than a coincidence that the art of the High Renaissance was stately, majestic, sublime, and pretentious; this is what the artist had become.

Why had this transformation taken place during the late Renaissance? Certainly the conscious efforts of the artists themselves to enhance their social position without abandoning their trade had its effect. Many, such as Alberti, Leonardo, and Michelangelo, not only spoke as men of means and authority, they also wrote treatises and poems justifying and exalting their profession. Through the writings of the humanists also—those who came to recognize their own cultural kinship to the artists—many of the social barriers were lowered or removed, and the artists were able to assume a higher role in society. As they did, pictorial art came gradually to be accepted alongside poetry as one of the liberal arts. Furthermore, the greater mobility of Italian guilds in the

Quattrocento allowed a geographical and occupational flexibility to some of its members that permitted them to do an increasing amount of work outside of the guild itself.

A final factor was the increasingly favorable position occupied by the artists as the demand for their work increased and they were thus able to free themselves from the control of patrons as well as from the restrictions of the guild. Artists now became independent producers instead of contracted laborers, able to determine their own themes and subjects, and free to set their own prices. This process was well under way by the High Renaissance. Art by contract continued to flourish through the sixteenth century, but alongside it now grew independent art produced for sale on an impersonal market to anyone willing to pay the artist's price. In the century of Italian cultural flowering, the artists themselves were emancipated.

Suggestions for Further Reading

GENERAL

Some of the classic interpretations of Renaissance art include Erwin Panofsky, *Studies in Iconology: Humanistic Themes in the Art of the Renaissance*, 2nd ed. (New York, 1962), and *Renaissance and Renascences in Western Art* (New York, 1969), both thought-provoking studies of the character and uniqueness of Renaissance art; Anthony Blunt, *Artistic Theory in Italy, 1450–1600*, rev. ed. (Oxford, 1968); André Chastel's superb *The Flowering of the Italian Renaissance*, tr. by Jonathan Griffin (New York, 1965); and Wylie Sypher, *Four Stages of Renaissance Style* (Garden City, 1955).

Among the many art-history books covering the Renaissance, the following are outstanding: Frederick Hartt, *History of Italian Renaissance Art* (Englewood Cliffs, 1969), a magnificent volume; Andrew Martindale, *Man and the Renaissance* (New York, 1966), brilliantly illustrated and concisely written; Michael Levy, *Early Renaissance* (Penguin, 1967), who sees the early Renaissance dominated by humanity and human forms; Peter and Linda Murray, *The Art of the Renaissance* (New York, 1963); and my favorite, Alastair Smith, *The Renaissance and Mannerism in Italy* (New York, 1971), in the Harbrace History of Art, which emphasizes the religious inspiration and the tragic tone of many Renaissance masterpieces.

ARCHITECTURE, SCULPTURE, AND PAINTING

Peter Murray, *The Architecture of the Italian Renaissance* (New York, 1963), and Rudolf Wittkower, *Architectural Principles in the Age of Humanism* (New York, 1965) are both vivid descriptions of Renaissance architecture. On Quattrocento sculpture, see especially John Pope-Hennessy, *An Introduction to Italian Sculpture*, 2nd ed. (London and New York, 1971), a comprehensive one-volume work with many illustrations and 144 full-page plates; also his *Essays on Italian Sculpture* (London and New York, 1968). The meaning of Renaissance painting is brilliantly presented by the famous art critic Bernard Berenson in *Italian Painters of the Renaissance* (New York, 1957). Others include *The Portrait in the Renaissance* (London, 1966), by John Pope-Hennessy; and Michael Baxandall,

Painting and Experience in Fifteenth-Century Italy (Oxford, 1972), an interesting and well-illustrated book showing how the style of art was partly determined by social facts. Joan Gadol, *Leon Battista Alberti, Universal Man of the Early Renaissance* (Chicago, 1969) is a stimulating narrative.

THE HIGH RENAISSANCE

Linda Murray's *The High Renaissance* (New York, 1967) is a good introduction to the art of this period, and can be supplemented with Michael Levy, *High Renaissance* (Penguin, 1975), which shows that accomplishment and confidence characterized the High Renaissance. Rome was the focus of the High Renaissance and is featured in Paolo Portoghesi, *Rome of the Renaissance,* tr. by Pearl Sanders (London, 1972), and Bonner Mitchell, *Rome in the High Renaissance: The Age of Leo X* (Norman, 1973), the latter very brief and quite superficial, but suggestive. The most complete study of Rome in the first half of the sixteenth century is Peter Partner, *Renaissance Rome, 1500–1559: A Portrait of a Society* (Berkeley, 1976).

LEONARDO DA VINCI

The basic life of Leonardo is Sir Kenneth Clark's *Leonardo da Vinci: An Account of His Development as an Artist,* rev. ed. (Baltimore, 1963). Morris H. Philipson, (ed.), *Leonardo da Vinci: Aspects of the Renaissance Genius* (New York, 1966), and Robert Wallace, *The World of Leonardo, 1452–1519* (New York, 1966) are also fascinating and insightful. Although it is old, Antonina Vallentin, *Leonardo da Vinci: The Tragic Pursuit of Perfection* (New York, 1938) is still a very provocative thesis and well worth reading. Maurice Rowden's *Leonardo da Vinci* (London, 1975), in the Great Lives series, is a brief but fully illustrated text.

MICHELANGELO

The most complete single-volume summary available is by the leading Michelangelo authority, Charles de Tolnay. The book is *Michelangelo: Sculptor, Painter, Architect,* tr. by Gaynor Woodhouse (Princeton, 1975). Tolnay is also the author of *The Art and Thought of Michelangelo* (New York, 1964), and the definitive five-volume *Life of Michelangelo*. Other very readable and reliable accounts are Charles H. Morgan, *The Life of Michelangelo* (New York, 1960), and Howard Hibbard, *Michelangelo* (New York, 1974). Robert J. Clements, *Michelangelo's Theory of Art* (New York, 1962) is both informative and pleasant reading. Robert Coughlan, *The World of Michelangelo* (New York, 1966) is a broad view of Michelangelo and his time.

RAPHAEL AND OTHER ARTISTS

Oskar Fischel, *Raphael* (London, 1964), tr. by Bernard Rackham, painstakingly analyzes Raphael's work in relation to his historical background, but is heavier reading than John Pope-Hennessy's more recent and better written *Raphael* (New York, 1970). The best discussion of the artists' social role is by Arnold Hauser, in *The Social History of Art: Vol. 2, Renaissance, Mannerism, Baroque* (New York, 1960). Also see De Lamar Jensen, "The Artist in Renaissance Society," *The Western Humanities Review,* 16 (1962), 321–37. The entire age is vividly revealed in *The World of Titian* (New York, 1968) by Jay Williams. Giorgio Vasari's contemporary classic, *The Lives of the Artists,* may be read in a convenient and lucid translation by George Bull (Penguin, 1965).

CHAPTER SIX

Science and Technology

HEN JACOB BURCKHARDT wrote his *Civilization of the Renaissance in Italy* (1860), there was little interest in the contributions of the Renaissance to science. From the generally favorable impression of that civilization left by Burckhardt's work, most writers in succeeding years assumed that it must have been a time of great creativity and progress in science as well as thought, literature, and art. But during the past forty years, many scholars have challenged this point of view, maintaining that the Renaissance contributed little, if anything, to the understanding or development of modern science. Some have gone so far as to accuse the humanists of retarding the progress that had been made in the Middle Ages. Such charges, however, have added little to any real understanding of scientific development, either in the Renaissance or in the Middle Ages, and have created much confusion and ambiguity.

Humanism and Scientific Thought

The Italian humanists have frequently come under attack by positivist historians who tend to judge an age solely by its contribution to scientific knowledge. The danger of this is obvious. Why should Ficino be condemned for making no significant contribution to science any more than a scientist for not composing music? The humanists were primarily literary people, interested in the improvement of Latin oral and literary communication and in the promotion of moral thought based on the ideals of classical writers. Therefore, they should be judged by artistic and literary criteria, not by the norms of science.

Nevertheless, the humanists did contribute to scientific success in several ways. For example, in their eager pursuit of classical writings, the humanists discovered, transcribed, restored, and made available many scientific treatises of Greek and Roman writers. Obviously, the ancients were not always correct, but their knowledge and observations of nature provided an essential point of departure for future achievements, especially in mathematics. The Renaissance humanists made available almost all of Greek science, notably that of the productive Hellenistic period (ca. 300–150 B.C.), which was little known in the Middle Ages. The treatises of Archimedes, Apollonius, and Celsus were collected and translated, and Strabo's *Geography* was made available. Furthermore, preeminently concerned with the exact words of an original, the humanists' texts of previously known works were usually more reliable than the available Arab translations.

Humanist veneration of Plato also had important consequences for the future development of scientific thought, because it caused an enthusiasm for numbers and mathematics that eventually affected all phases of science. Not only did this revived interest in Plato stimulate the study of mathematics per se, it also suggested the underlying permanence of "form," which is a fundamental assumption of all scientific "laws."

One of the best examples of the application of Platonic mathematics to cosmological thought can be seen in the writings of Nicholas of Cusa (1401–64), the reform-minded and highly controversial cardinal who had some important things to say about science as well as philosophy, theology, and church organization. Although born in the Rhineland, Nicholas of Cusa studied mathematics, astronomy, Greek, Hebrew, and civil law at the University of Padua, and later returned to Italy to spend his last years in study and writing. His best-known work, and the most significant, as far as science is concerned, *De docta ignorantia* (On Learned Ignorance), was written in 1440 during a lull between ecclesiastical controversies. Here, while negating the ability of the mind to conceive infinity or the absolute, he advocated an almost infinite universe comprehensible only in mathematical concepts beyond rational understanding. Unlike the finite and geocentric universe pictured by the Middle Ages (and by Aristotle), Cusa's universe was limitless, without circumference and without center. The earth, therefore, could not be at the center, since the center was everywhere—an infinite location occupied only by God. The earth moved, Cusa explained, as the entire system moved, relative to the positions and motion of every other object. For him it was easier to conceive of the earth revolving about its north-south axis every twenty-four hours than of all the fixed stars rotating around the earth in the same period of time. Although there is much mysticism in Cusa's thought, it did suggest alternatives to the generally accepted Aristotelian cosmology and opened up new possibilities for the application of mathematics to explaining the universe.

Finally, the respectful attitude engendered by the Italian humanists toward nature and our physical surroundings further added to the eventual desire to understand and even manipulate them. Again the effects were not always immediate, but they soon became noticeable. Uninterested in theological subtleties, the Italian humanists turned more intently to the physical world for aesthetic pleasure and for answers to the problems and mysteries of life. Of course the nature worship of the humanists was a far cry from the later systematic examination of all physical phenomena, but at least it was a turn toward things and reason, both of which are fundamental to any scientific investigation.

Aristotle and the Scientific Method

Traditionally, Aristotle has been linked with the "false" concepts of science and geography, those finally "overthrown" by the heroic deeds of Galileo and Francis Bacon. It is true that in most areas of science little change had been made in Aristotle's descriptions and explanations of the world in over 1500 years. His thought and writings had encompassed such a vast amount of information and had provided plausible and even demonstrable proof of so many physical phenomena that few saw any merit in disputing Aristotle. The longevity of the Aristotelian system is due more to its many strengths and consistencies than to any institutional opposition from the church. To a greater degree than is usually realized, Aristotle's science was founded on common sense and observation, and its prolongation and renewal throughout the Middle Ages was accompanied by experimentation. The Aristotelians themselves provided the earliest and most persistent criticisms and adjustments in the Aristotelian system, and anticipated the methodological tools for its eventual supplantation.

We have already noted the steps taken by the fourteenth-century Franciscans of Oxford, and later by others in Paris, to provide an experimental base for science. In so doing, they rejected many of the accepted notions of Aristotle on the dynamics of matter. The successor to Oxford and Paris in the development of experimental science during the Renaissance was the University of Padua, since 1404 a dependency of the Venetian Republic. The Averroist tradition at Padua, especially among the natural philosophers, promoted a critical attitude toward the church and toward the use of Aristotle as a prop for the priestcraft that all too frequently prevailed in medieval theology. Moreover, the Aristotle of Padua, where attention was given to his writings on physics, natural philosophy, and scientific methodology, was not the same Aristotle that was studied at the Sorbonne and other centers of scholasticism. Emphasis on these scientific aspects of Aristotelian thought led to the examination of contending explanations of physical phenomena and to a more critical attitude toward classical authority itself. This in turn resulted in the gradual development of methods of discovering truth that were based on a more systematic analysis of specific facts of nature.

It is worth noting, however, that the Paduan professors gave much more attention to the theory of the scientific method than they did to its application in solving particular problems of medicine or physics. Nevertheless, their arguments did not go unnoticed, and Padua became the molder of some of the greatest minds of the fifteenth and sixteenth centuries, including Nicholas of Cusa, Paolo da Venezia, Jacopo da Forlì, Agostino Nifo, Regiomontanus, Zabarella, Copernicus, and Galileo.

Just as it can no longer be maintained that Aristotelianism thwarted the development of empiricism and experimentation, so the accusations of its modern advocates that Renaissance humanism and Platonism caused a setback in the otherwise continuous development of science from the Middle Ages to the seventeenth century must also be viewed with caution. Aristotelianism remained, as it had always been, basically qualitative in its approach to nature, categorizing and evaluating rather than weighing and measuring. The quantitative emphasis, which was to become characteristic of seventeenth-century science, was more a result of the mathematical traditions of Plato and Pythagoras than of Aristotle. But the most important fact to remember is that no single tradition or single individual gave birth to modern scientific methods; they are the result of countless contributors and centuries of development.

Art and Science

One usually does not think of art and science in the same terms, but in the Renaissance they were very closely related. Implicit in Renaissance art theory and in the artists' methods of achieving artistic reality were mathematical and physical principles that led to greater knowledge of both nature and people. One such concept was mathematical, or linear, perspective—systematically applying mathematical principles to the problem of depicting visual reality.

One of the greatest innovators in this field was Filippo Brunelleschi, who was as much an engineer as an artist. As a builder with a keen mind and a clear conception of what he wanted to create, he applied imagination and insight to solving the problems he encountered. He also experimented, observed, and tested until he fully understood the nature of his problems, and then reduced these to geometric principles that he could reapply to succeeding problems. In constructing the vast dome of Santa Maria del Fiore, Brunelleschi visualized and utilized mathematical relationships that had an immediate effect on Renaissance architecture and an eventual impact on the study of mathematics itself. He also devised several optical instruments that he used during

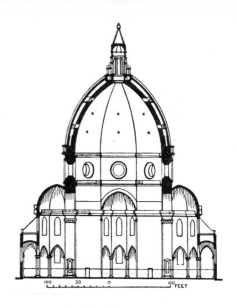

DIAGRAM SHOWING THE CON-
STRUCTION OF THE CATHEDRAL
DOME IN FLORENCE. *Brunelleschi
was a master engineer and builder,
solving the problem of spanning a
huge 140-foot enclosure with a
graceful and harmonious cupola 130
feet above its base.*

the construction of the dome and that may have led to later speculations in optics. With Paolo Toscanelli, the Florentine astronomer and geographer who influenced Columbus's geographical views, he built into the dome a giant astronomical instrument with which Toscanelli made frequent observations.

Associated with the theory of linear perspective in the minds of Renaissance artists and craftsmen were the related problems of visual space. Interest in these problems caused them to contemplate and examine the qualities of air, light, mass, and weight, and to transmit this knowledge pictorially, and sometimes verbally, to later generations. They also paid attention to the chemistry of pigments and studied the effects of light on color and form. Some of them were not content merely to observe and study the outward reality of nature. Many artists sought to see and understand the inner construction and operation of living organisms, including the human body. In this way they became as earnest students of anatomy as the physicians of the time. Sometimes the results of their study were made available in sketches, drawings, and sculptures; but even when such was not the case, the artists contributed to the breakdown of stigmas against human dissection and added to the likelihood of arousing wider curiosity about physiology and about the nature of "things" in general.

Leonardo da Vinci, Scientist and Engineer

For remarkable universality of mind and perceptive insights into the structure and operation of nature, no other Renaissance figure surpassed the searching genius of Leonardo da Vinci. From earliest youth, Leonardo possessed an insatiable appetite for knowledge. In his lifelong quest for learning, he considered the great teacher to be nature itself, not books, traditions, or authorities. He was not only an acute observer of nature, perhaps the greatest of his age, he was also a discoverer of its characteristics and properties.

Recorded in cryptic notes and thousands of sketches, his observations were apparently not meant for publication or demonstration outside his own circle of friends and followers. This peculiarity has led some historians to discredit Leonardo as a scientist. The most John Herman Randall could bring himself to say of Leonardo, after declaring that he was not a scientist, is that he was at least "the anatomist of nature. He could see, and with his draughtsmanship depict clearly, the bony skeleton of the world." It can be granted that many of the scientific principles deduced from Leonardo's observations were known before his time, particularly by scholars in Padua, Bologna, and Paris. But there is little evidence that Leonardo learned these things from other scholars rather than independently from his own observations and thought. Knowing hardly a word of Latin and being a notoriously reluctant and poor reader, he is not likely to have known of most of the available scientific literature, let alone to have read it.

Paramount in understanding Leonardo as a scientist is to remember that he was more interested in the nature of things—the operation of forces; the problems of weight, movement, and pressure; the theories of mechanics and dynamics—than he was in the successful operation of any particular machine. In the words of one modern writer, he was "a scientific explorer rather than a colonizer," a visionary more than a practitioner. Leonardo considered mathematics the basis of all science, and he was aware of mathematical proportions in nature, believing mathematical principles could be used to explain and measure all physical phenomena. "The economy of nature," he wrote, "is quantitative, or one may say, mathematical."

The range of Leonardo's interests is impressive. In his notebooks he recorded, sketched, and diagrammed his observations and experiments on hundreds of scientific topics. He contemplated the heavens and concluded that the universe was a celestial machine, governed by laws of mathematical precision. He declared also that the earth was similar to the sun in giving off rays of heat and light that could be observed if one were far enough away from the surface. From his observations of water, he drew many conclusions about the pressure of fluids and their movement through channels and orifices. Water power fascinated him and he devised numerous ways of harnessing it for useful mechanical purposes. He even suggested a wave theory of light based on its similarity to the movement of waves on water. Leonardo was also enchanted by air and by the challenge to conquer it. He recorded almost endless observations of birds in flight and of the functions of their various parts as they climbed, soared, and alighted. These analyses of the processes of flight in birds led him inevitably to suggestions for flying machines of various types, and the recommendation for a parachute made like a "tent roof of which the pores have all been filled." But Leonardo's enthusiasm for flight did not preclude his practicality, as the following note, accompanying one of his designs, reveals: "This machine should be tried over a lake, and you should carry a long wine skin as a girdle so that in case you fall you will not be drowned."

Exploring the high Alps in search of fossils and other geological artifacts, Leonardo concluded that the earth was much older than anyone had previously suspected, and that the presence of salt-water fossils suggested great physical upheavals and changes in the earth's surface since the first appearance of plant and animal life. While investigating the physical properties of matter and the nature of various forces, he gave meaningful thought to such factors as the tensile strength of different materials and to the effects of friction. Perhaps his most impressive experiments and observations, based on his personal dissection of some thirty cadavers during his lifetime, were in the fields of anatomy and physiology. He described the results in hundreds of unique drawings and sketches.

As a civil and military engineer, Leonardo da Vinci was more ambitious than his patrons could afford or his resources would allow. His prospectus to Ludovico Sforza, master of Milan, offered some thirty-six reasons why the duke should employ him. Most of the justifications were for his skills as a military engineer, including his ability to build "light and strong bridges effective in any military campaign"; his knowledge of trench drainage and of how to build easily portable trench mortars; the skill to undermine fortified places, even if they were

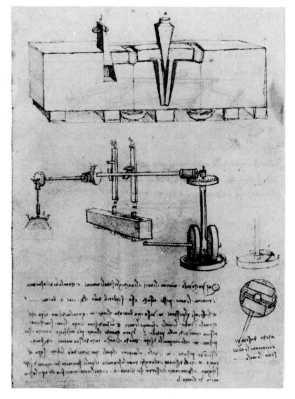

PAGE FROM THE NOTEBOOKS OF LEONARDO DA VINCI. *This machine for making olive oil, Leonardo explains in his cryptic, reverse handwriting, "grinds the nuts [olives] and rakes them under the rollers, extracts the oil with the press, mixes them thoroughly on the fire, and produces six barrels of oil a day." (Facsimile edition of* Codex Madrid I *(New York: McGraw Hill, 1974), fol. 46v. Courtesy of Brigham Young University Special Collections Library).*

surrounded by trenches or rivers; proposals for building armored vehicles "which, entering among the enemy with their artillery, there is no body of men so great but they would break them"; the invention of catapults, flamethrowers, and other types of missile weapons for siege or bombardment; and, almost as an afterthought, "I can carry out sculpture in marble, bronze, or clay, and also I can do in painting whatever may be done, as well as any other, be he who he may." In his years of military service to Ludovico Sforza and later to the *Signoria* of Florence, Leonardo was able to fulfill some of his engineering promises. However, most of his plans went no further than sketches in his notebooks. Nevertheless, Leonardo loved machines and designed many ingenious instruments for accomplishing countless mechanical chores, including an engine for digging canals, portable cantilever bridges, breech-loading and multifiring guns, and prefabricated cartridges.

Leonardo was also fully subject to human error and prejudice. From his dissections and observations of the human body, he might have discovered the circulation of the blood. Some of his cryptic notes almost suggest that he did. Instead, he relied on the authority of Galen that the blood ebbed and flowed in the veins, and that it passed from the right to left ventricles of the heart through invisible holes in the wall of the septum. In his drawings, Leonardo made them visible. But before we cast our stones at either the Hellenistic physician or the Florentine painter, we should reflect on the number of invisible things that *do* exist even though we cannot see them ourselves.

Renaissance Achievements in Mathematics and Science

Activities and accomplishments in the various fields of science during the Renaissance were diverse and uneven, in some fields showing vitality and progress, in others relative stagnation. Although the specific achievements of this period are not as impressive as those of the seventeenth century, some notable attainments were made, especially in the fields of anatomy and astronomy. Thanks largely to the invention and development of printing that used removable and reusable type, and the accompanying increase in literacy, the scientific knowledge that had formerly been the ken of a few was now becoming the heritage of thousands.

Mathematics

The growth of interest and competence in mathematics is a good example of this expansion of knowledge. The new translations and multiple publications of Euclid and Plato only partly explain the growing attention given to mathematics in the universities and the general interest awarded it by the public. The value of theoretical mathematics in the training and discipline of philosophy had long been recognized, but

now its more practical functions were also emphasized. Applied mathematics was invaluable to merchants in keeping their accounts; to civil and military engineers as they designed bridges, buildings, and improved ballistics; to ocean navigators calculating positions and courses. So much in demand were the skills of this "new math" that a whole class of practical mathematician-teachers arose who began giving instruction to both laymen and professionals in applied geometry and trigonometry.

In the realm of mathematical ideas, progress was slower but nonetheless substantial. The methods and functions of trigonometry were revived from Greek, Arabic, and Hindu mathematicians by the German humanist and astronomer Johann Müller, better known as Regiomontanus (1436–76), and his teacher, Georg Peurbach (1423–69). Regiomontanus's first mathematical work was a detailed analysis of Ptolemy's *Almagest* (The Greatest), an encyclopedic work on the motions of the sun, moon, and planets. In 1464 he completed his most important study, *De triangulis omninodis* (On Triangles of All Kinds), the earliest systematic exposition of plane and spherical trigonometry, although it was not published until 1533. After Regiomontanus, all of the important mathematicians for more than a century were Italians. Notable among them were Luca Pacioli (ca. 1445–ca. 1509) of Florence, a Franciscan friar who lectured on mathematics at Pisa, Venice, Milan, and Rome; and Niccolò Tartaglia (1500–57), the greatest mathematician of the early sixteenth century. Tartaglia's most important books were the *Nova Scienza* (A New Science), a study of falling bodies and projectiles, and *Questi et inventioni diverse* (Diverse Questions and Inventions), in which he demonstrated the solution of cubic equations. This was a significant accomplishment because it demonstrated that Europeans had now so thoroughly mastered the Hindu-Arabic numerical techniques that they could advance into new mathematical territory. Closely linked with Tartaglia was his rival, Girolamo Cardano (1501–76), who was a capable enough mathematician but who plagiarized a major part of his principal work, *Artis magnae* (Great Arts), from Tartaglia.

Physics and Chemistry

Advancement in physics did not keep pace with mathematics during the Renaissance. The great breakthrough in mechanics, which was almost achieved by Buridan and Oresme in the early fourteenth century, failed to supply a satisfactory corrective to Aristotle's explanation of motion. Their theory of impetus had many interesting possibilities but was relatively unknown outside the University of Paris. During the next century and a half, it made little impact on the development of scientific thought. The eventual seventeenth-century emergence of Galilean mechanics and the concept of inertia was perhaps as much a reaction against impetus physics as it was against Aristotle.

As in the preceding millennium, fifteenth- and sixteenth-century chemistry consisted mainly of alchemy. It was based on some plausible theoretical foundations (the mutability of many substances) and developed many sound methods (distillation, amalgamation, and precipitation, for example). But it was so obsessed with the transmutation of base metals into gold that much of the energy and thought expended were lost effort. Here, as in other aspects of Renaissance science, can be seen the close relationship between science and magic. But what we call magic may simply be theory no longer accepted. Transmuting mercury into gold is "magic" *unless* it is done with a cyclotron; then it is "science." The mystical and secretive nature of alchemy also limited its success, although many practical applications of the discovery of different chemical properties might be attributed to the alchemists.

Medicine

No one had greater difficulty distinguishing between magic and science than the bombastic Swiss-German physician, teacher, and controversial alchemist, Paracelsus (1493–1541). Paracelsus typifies the amalgam of scientific genius and quackery. Experts still disagree over the proportions of each he possessed, but, whatever the ratio, he was some of both. A pioneer in the rejection of authority in the fields of chemistry and medicine, he put Galen and other Greek philosophers aside and boldly proclaimed the experimental method in the discovery and treatment of disease. Yet inextricably entangled with his scientific method was a dogmatic belief in spiritualism as a determining factor in human physical life. Believing that herbs and chemicals possessed "virtues," or spirits, that could be extracted and used in the cure of disease, he thus pioneered in the application of chemistry to medicine (iatrochemistry). Paracelsus also contributed to many other fields such as pharmacy, homeopathy, and hydrotherapeutics.

Not all Renaissance contributions to medicine were as esoteric as those of Paracelsus, but few were entirely noncontroversial. The fifteenth and sixteenth centuries are not usually thought of as a progressive period in medical science, yet some very important advances were made, particularly in anatomy. Unfortunately, the application and utilization of medical knowledge lagged far behind its theorization. The role of the University of Padua in the advancement of theoretical medicine has already been mentioned. The neighboring Venetians also gained a reputation for medical knowledge and experimentation. The Spanish doctor and theological renegade Michael Servetus roughly described the pulmonary circulation of the blood as early as 1553. In 1546 Girolamo Fracastoro of Verona proclaimed his belief in the germ theory of disease, although without the microscope he was unable to prove his case. He also wrote a notable Latin poem praising the therapeutic qualities of the West Indian herb known as *guaican* in the treatment of syphilis.

The study of anatomy made the greatest strides during the Renaissance. In the fourteenth and fifteenth centuries, autopsies were practiced in Padua, Bologna, and other Italian cities. The use of cadavers in medical schools was equally common. But in the rest of Europe, the practice of dissecting the human body was looked upon with disapproval. It is not surprising, therefore, that until the second quarter of the sixteenth century, all of the important discoveries in anatomy were made by Italian physicians and artists. The greatest anatomist of them all, the Flemish-born Andreas Vesalius (1514–64), received much of his medical training in Padua, and became professor of medicine there at the age of twenty-three. Unlike his predecessors, who traditionally sat far removed from the cadaver, reading Galen's descriptions of the body organs to their students while a barber-surgeon located each one as it was described, Vesalius applied the knife himself and at the same time pointed out where Galen and others since him had erred. From his numerous lectures and dissections of human and animal bodies, Vesalius wrote anatomical tables for use in other universities. In 1543 he published his great *De humani corporia fabrica* (On the Structure of the Human Body), which carefully and minutely described in words and pictures, the parts, organs, and functions of the human body. Here, in one book, was the highest and most useful achievement of Renaissance anatomy. The importance of the *Fabrica* does not lie in its break with the ancient traditions but, as with Copernicus's *De revolutionibus orbium coelestium* (On the Revolutions of the Heavenly Spheres), published the same year, in its advancement and culmination of those traditions.

Suddenly in 1544 Vesalius left the university to spend the last twenty years of his life as court physician to Emperor Charles V and his son Philip II of Spain. During this period of his life, Vesalius made significant, if less renowned, contributions to medical practice and particularly to the art of surgery. In the field of surgery, Vesalius was surpassed only by Ambroise Paré, whose long (1510–90) and active life was spent mostly in the service of the French monarchy, both at court and on the battlefield. Many of Paré's surgical methods (such as his rejection of cauterizing wounds by pouring boiling oil into them) were in advance of his times, and he wrote some treatises on surgery.

We are reminded of just how unique Vesalius and Paré were, however, when we read a typical mid-sixteenth-century medical prescription for the treatment of open wounds: "In one pound of olive oil cook ten green lizards and filter through linen; add one measure of marjoram and wormwood; cook slowly and set by for use." Or, if one prefers: "Take earthworms washed in wine and place them in a closed jar; cook in a double vessel for one day; when they are liquified add either properly prepared balsam, or resin of the fir or larch tree. This quickly heals any new wound and especially wounds of the head."

Natural Science

Closely related to the study of medicine was the work of the natural scientists, particularly in botany. Botanical gardens were maintained and used by the medical schools of Padua, Bologna, Pisa, and elsewhere, and herbs were assiduously cultivated both for experimental and therapeutic use. Beautifully and accurately illustrated herbals were published in the early sixteenth century, giving greater popularity not only to the work of Pliny and the ancient naturalists but also renewing interest in observing and collecting plants, particularly those with medicinal value. At the same time, bestiaries were enlarged and improved until a zenith was reached in the magnificent zoological encyclopedia published in the 1550s by Conrad Gesner. The greatest stimulation to these Renaissance naturalists came with the discovery of the New World, with its endless varieties of previously unknown flora and fauna. Yet as much as these naturalists contributed, they did little to advance the knowledge of how these organisms themselves functioned. Even when they were right about the medicinal value of some herb, it was usually for the wrong reason. Serious plant and animal morphology had scarcely begun by the end of the sixteenth century, and the investigation of the processes of life was still further in the future.

Copernicus and Astronomy

However people choose to picture or interpret the Renaissance contributions to mathematics, physics, chemistry, medicine, or natural history, they usually think of it as a period of revolution in astronomy, a time when the old errors were put aside and the "modern" universe revealed. Some important new thinking was directed toward the problems of astronomy and cosmology—both inseparable from theology—but the framework and content of this thinking were as much a part of the past as were those of the other scientists and humanists. Yet it did herald a new age by serving as the catalyst for the discussions and experiments of the following centuries.

The fifteenth-century universe was still the universe of Aristotle: closed, finite, unified, and intelligible, even though it was enigmatic and vast. Furthermore, it was essentially a commonsense universe based primarily on the apparent realities of visual observation. The earth was believed to be at rest while the sun, moon, plants, and starry heaven rotated around it, not because this was a more respected conditions theologically (since it was not), but because there was no observable evidence to the contrary. Oresme had suggested the possibility of a rotating earth, but rejected it for lack of evidence, as so were Nicholas of Cusa's propositions weak and without proof.

The most persistent and important contributions to astronomy in the fifteenth century were made by the mathematicians Peurbach and Regiomontanus. Much of Ptolemy's (second century A.D.) refinement and adjustment of Aristotle's cosmological system was unknown in the West during the Middle Ages, although Ptolemy was intensely studied and commented on by Arab astronomers. By translating Ptolemy's *Almagest* and by making new observations of the principal stars, it was Peurbach's intention to make Ptolemy's description of the universe available and comprehensible in the West. Regiomontanus and his patron-pupil Bernard Walther continued Peurbach's observations and calculations until shortly before Copernicus began his work in 1507. Their restoration of Ptolemy in the fifteenth century provided the framework for Copernicus's attempt to further refine and perfect this classical universe.

Nicolaus Copernicus (1473–1543) was born in the busy commercial city of Toruń on the Vistula River in Poland. He was educated at the University of Cracow in theology and law, and became interested in the study of astronomy. Passionately devoted to science and mathematics, Copernicus soon left for Italy where he could best satisfy his intellectual thirst. For ten years he remained there, studying Greek, mathematics, law, and astronomy at Bologna, canon law at Ferrara (receiving the doctorate in 1503), and medicine at Padua. In 1512 he returned to Poland as canon of Frauenburg Cathedral and physician to his uncle, the bishop of Ermeland. During the last thirty years of his life, he made such stellar observations as his poor eyesight would permit. He computed, contemplated, and wrote down his conclusions in his great work, *De revolutionibus orbium coelestium* which was finished in 1530, although it was not published until the very month of his death in 1543.

In his magnum opus, Copernicus put forth the view, which he had found in Aristarchus of Samos, the Hellenistic mathematician and astronomer, that the sun was motionless at the center of the universe, that the earth (while rotating on its own axis every twenty-four hours) revolved in a circle, as did the planets, about the sun, and that the stars were motionless at the circumference of the universe. His new system was a monumental exercise of the mind to maintain the closed and finite spherical universe of Aristotle while simplifying and reducing the number of planetary motions added by Ptolemy to explain the observable phenomena of the skies. There was much of a revolutionary nature in Copernicus's suggestions: first, the idea that the earth was in constant motion and the apparent movement of the sun and stars was relative motion caused by the rotation of the earth; second, the implication that the "qualities" imparted to the bodies in the universe by the Creator, such as heaviness and sphericity, caused their continued motion; and third, the suggestion that the circumference of the universe is much greater than had previously been imagined. The theological impact of Copernicus was potentially revolutionary as well, because he broke down the Christian-Aristotelian distinction between heavenly and earthly by giving the earth both motion and a place in the heavens.

Yet despite his innovations, Copernicus was essentially conservative, intending to rectify and reform the Ptolemaic system rather than replace it with a radical new concept. All elements and conditions remained the same: the circular and uniform motion of the planets in

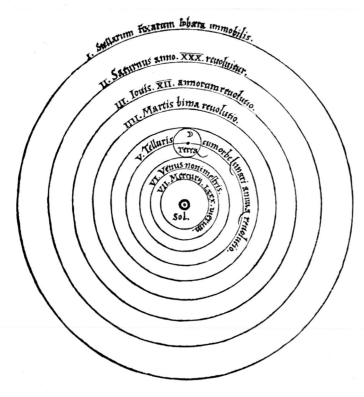

THE ROTATION OF THE PLANETS ACCORDING TO COPERNICUS. *This drawing from De Revolutionibus (Nuremberg, 1543) shows the sun at the center of the system, around which rotate Mercury, Venus, Earth with its moon satellite, Mars, Jupiter, and Saturn. The fixed stars occupy the outer ring. (Courtesy of Brigham Young University Special Collections Library)*

crystalline spheres was retained, the teleological assumptions of the system remained, and the nature of the rotational force was the same. The only real difference between Copernicus's universe and Ptolemy's was the interchange of the sun and earth. He viewed his own role as that of a restorer of Aristotle rather than a destroyer. The Ptolemaic system, with its eighty-some orbits, eccentrics, and epicycles, had violated Aristotle's basic simplicity and uniformity, which Copernicus now sought to recover. By his mathematical adjustments, he could reduce the movements to thirty-four, thus satisfying his Platonic urge for simplicity and harmony while at the same time retaining the manifest nobility (and ease of mathematical calculation) of sphericity and circular motion. Furthermore, the sun, that most exalted of all spheres, should occupy the noblest position (which, according to Copernicus, was the center of the circle) and remain at rest, the noblest state. What he wanted, and got, was a more economical and simpler mathematical explanation of the old universe.

There were many disadvantages to the Copernican system, however. The problem of motion was still unsolved. Why does the earth revolve and rotate? Copernicus could only answer that it was the nature of spherical bodies to turn. The only satisfactory explanation of motion was the Aristotelian, and that would explain the rotation of the older crystalline spheres better than it would the revolutions of the heavy earth. In fact, without an entirely new framework of physics to account for the many phenomena adequately explained in the older system by Aristotelian mechanics, Copernicus's system created more unanswerable problems than it solved.

As far as consequences are concerned, there were no immediate results from Copernicus's work. He had not been interested in publishing it himself; when it was issued just before he died, it was received with very little excitement, partly because of Andreas Osiander's spurious preface, which insisted, contrary to the body of the text, that this was just another set of mathematical devices to facilitate celestial calculations, rather than a statement of physical facts. However, whether or not they believed its assumptions, astronomers did begin to use the book because it was the best available. What theological objections there were came mostly from the Protestants. Unaided observation vindicated Ptolemy as much as Copernicus, and most people let it go at that.

Nevertheless, the role of Copernicus, like that of Tartaglia, Paracelsus, Vesalius, and the other Renaissance scientists was important, though for different reasons than are usually given. In each case, these men brought the scientific work of the Greeks to its logical culmination. In so doing, they also raised issues and problems that helped stimulate renewed activity during the following century. This in turn led to the eventual overthrow of Aristotelian science and the creation not only of a new cosmology but also a new understanding of the dynamics by which it operates.

Renaissance Technology

Technological development in the Renaissance was not so concerned with classical antiquity as were science and the arts. In the application of machine power and tools to supplement and increase human strength, there was no break between the Middle Ages and the Renaissance. Old techniques were improved and new ones invented, but the inspiration and motivation for both came from the contemporary problems and challenges that faced Renaissance technicians, not from the examples or methods of classical writers.

Agriculture

In agricultural technology, little change in either methods or tools took place during the fifteenth and sixteenth centuries. Fields were still tilled by ox- or horse-drawn wooden plows, leveled by wooden harrows, and sown by hand. Reaping and harvesting, also, were accomplished by the same methods as they had been for centuries, with only slight modification or improvement in machinery. Great expansion did take place, however, in reclaiming and using farm lands and in applying wind and water power to milling, fulling, and pumping. Here the Dutch took the lead. For centuries they had fought a defensive war against the sea. By the early 1400s, they had been victorious enough that they could devote more of their time and skill to the offensive, to draining the numerous inland lakes and seas and making their soil productive. The construction and maintenance of dikes and polders was a cooperative enterprise in the Netherlands and brought many spectacular results. By applying the windmill to an Archimedean screw or a series of buckets, they could not only keep the seawater outside the dikes but even pump out the inland lakes and greatly multiply the amount of useful land. By 1500 over 285,000 acres of land had been reclaimed or safeguarded from the sea, and by the middle of the sixteenth century this area was more than doubled. Stimulated by the Dutch, a veritable revolution took place in the technology of swamp and marsh drainage and irrigation. By tunneling through the mountains enclosing Lake Trasimeno in central Italy, for example, many of the surrounding valleys were enriched with life-giving water. But in the sixteenth century, people had not yet succeeded in conquering such vast swamps as the Pontine Marshes in Italy or the English Fens, although they did make ambitious attempts.

Mining and Metallurgy

Mining and metallurgy had declined sharply in the second half of the fourteenth century, following the Black Death and the decades of depression. But they revived again in the middle of the fifteenth century in a great mining boom that lasted until the beginning of the influx of New World metals in the 1530s. Increasing population; expanding needs for silver, copper, and other metals in coinage; and the massive employment of bronze, brass, and iron in the manufacture of cannons all contributed to this metallurgical renaissance. New seams of ore were found in central Europe and many abandoned mines were reopened. After centuries of neglect, brass was again produced on a large scale in the early sixteenth century, following the discovery of rich calamine deposits in the Tyrol. This in turn increased the demand for copper, which was alloyed with calamine to make brass. Another fifteenth-century invention that added greatly to the demand for copper was the development of a process for separating silver from argentiferous copper ore by the use of lead. In the sixteenth century came the discovery of the amalgamation process of extracting silver with mercury. Even more momentous, because of the extent of its application, was the invention of the blast furnace, and with it, the manufacture of cast iron. Bronze, which melts at a lower temperature than iron, had been cast since the Middle Ages. Now with the use of water-driven bellows, furnaces were constructed that could produce sufficient heat to liquify iron, which could then be cast in the same manner as bronze.

The two greatest challenges to Renaissance mining engineers were the problems of water drainage and providing adequate ventilation for the miners. The best authority on sixteenth-century mining was Georg Agricola (1495–1555), a practicing physician who was interested in all aspects of mining and metallurgy. He traveled extensively in Saxony and Bohemia observing the practices and equipment of mining, which he then recorded and published. In this book, *De re metallica* (On the Principles of Mining, 1556), a masterpiece of detail and thoroughness, he described some of the mammoth drainage operations of that day, such as the one at Schemnitz in the Carpathian Mountains, where water was raised from 660 feet underground through a series of pumps turned by ninety-six horses. Water power was also widely used in these pumping and ventilating systems.

Manufacturing

In the various manufacturing industries, many improvements in tools and machines helped increase both productivity and efficiency. The spinningwheel, for example, was widely used in the Middle Ages; but the flyer, which made possible simultaneous spinning and winding, was apparently not added until the fifteenth century. More advanced flyer mechanisms are shown in Leonardo da Vinci's *Notebooks*. The Florentines and Luccans guarded the secrets of their silk mills very carefully, so its is impossible to tell exactly when and how they developed their efficient reeling and throwing machinery. It was another two centuries before these were significantly improved. Special looms were also developed in the fifteenth century for weaving the fancy fabrics that by then had become an Italian stock-in-trade. The use of the crank and connecting rod for converting continuous rotary motion to reciprocating motion, and vice versa, greatly interested Leonardo. His sketches show many uses and modifications of this system. Some precision tools and instruments underwent improvement during this period, such as the spring-driven clock permitting the construction of more compact time mechanisms, the improvement of various kinds of observatory instruments, and the improvement of eyeglasses. But on the whole, the revolution in precision instruments did not come until later.

Transportation and Communication

The methods of land transportation and communication did not change much during the Renaissance—as they had not for twenty centuries or more and would not for another three—but the amount and facility of travel increased severalfold. Roads, which scarcely existed outside Italy in the Middle Ages, were multiplied and improved, particularly in France, and the all-important inland water transportation was stimulated by digging canals, dredging rivers, and improving locks and bridges. The development of mitred lock gates permitted building larger and more dependable lock systems and consequently contributed to the expansion in canal building. The most extensive projects were carried out in northern Italy during the mid-fifteenth century where Bertola da Novate, chief engineer for the duke of Milan, began the construction of an entire network of valuable canals, including the Bereguardo and Martesana canals still used today. The former, completed in 1458, linking Abbiate and the Grand Canal from Milan to Bereguardo on the Ticino River, has a fall of 80 feet made possible by 18 locks. The Martesana Canal connects Milan to the Adda River. Leonardo da Vinci's mitre gates for the San Marco Lock were installed there in 1497 while he was engineer to Ludovico Sforza.

Naval Technology

The fifteenth century was the great age of naval technology, resulting in the designing and building of ships that for the first time were capable of practical and extended navigation across the oceans. For more than a thousand years, the standard vessels of the Mediterranean had been the cumbersome single-masted, square-rigged sailing ships (cogs), and the faster, more maneuverable, oared galleys. For the relatively sheltered waters of the Mediterranean, both of these were adequate; but on the open sea, with mountainous waves and changeable winds, neither was satisfactory. Major changes in the hull construction of sailing ships were made in the late Middle Ages by altering the length/beam ratio, making them longer and narrower, and especially in the invention of the sternpost rudder, which made it possible to steer a ship of any size with relative ease by lengthening the tiller arm or by using other means of increasing the mechanical advantage.

PORTUGUESE AND SPANISH CARAVELS, *according to a water color in the Museo Naval, Madrid. These four-masted* caravelas redondas *show alternative rig variations combining both lateen and square sails. (Museo Naval de Madrid)*

The greatest changes in Renaissance ship design, however, came in rigging. The first notable alteration was the adoption of the Arab lateen sail, used on the Indian Ocean for many centuries. The long, triangular lateen rig provided efficient all-weather service with relatively little bulk. But it had shortcomings for ocean travel, where extreme wind changes required frequent resetting of the sail. The lateen rig also restricted the size of a ship. Therefore, European seamen and shipbuilders took the ingenious step of adding one or two additional masts in order to increase the total sail area, and rigged ocean-going vessels with both multiple-square and lateen sails to utilize the positive characteristics of each. The result was the development of the famous Portuguese three-masted caravel, a sleek 25- to 100-ton craft, usually carrying three lateen sails, or two lateens and one square rig. The most effective of the ships used in the Portuguese and Spanish expansion was the *caravela redonda* (round caravel), with a larger hull design and four masts, two lateen-rigged and two square, although other combinations were sometimes used.

In the course of the sixteenth century, sailing ships took over much of the cargo work of the galleys and eventually even their military role. The Spanish *nao* (ship), larger than the caravel and usually sporting a high stern superstructure to provide more adequate accommodations for the captain and officers and to give them a height advantage when engaging an enemy, was another type of ship used extensively in the late fifteenth and early sixteenth centuries. The technological revolution in ship design finally produced the finest of all sailing ships, the galleon. Longer and narrower than its nearest relative, the huge cargo carrack, the galleon was built primarily for war. Ranging from about 200 tons to over 1,000 by the end of the century, these powerful warships were the ultimate in sixteenth-century technological development and design.

The need for navigational aids in this era of oceanic expansion brought some modest technological progress here also. The simple compass needle, floating on a block of wood in a container of water, had been known and used in the West since the Middle Ages. During the fifteenth century, the compass was improved by providing a pivoting needle and a compass card marked off in degrees. By the end of the century, gimbal rings had been added to allow the compass to remain relatively level while the ship rocked and pitched, thus making this instrument, for the first time, a practical, all-weather navigational aid.

Instruments for celestial navigation also underwent practical improvements in this period. The astrolabe, adapted from the Arabs in the Middle Ages, was the principal fifteenth-century device for calculating latitude by measuring the angle of the north star or other known points in the sky. Another instrument for making sightings was the quadrant, which many seamen preferred to the astrolabe because of its simplicity. During the sixteenth century, solar sighting was usually accomplished with the cross-staff and later the back-staff. Accurate tables of solar and stellar declination—necessary if such a measure was to have any meaning—were provided by Regiomontanus and the Spanish geographer Abraham Zacuto.

Instruments for measuring speed and distance remained very rudimentary. A knotted line, or log line, was usually employed for calculating speed by measuring the time required for a given number of knots to pass a marker as the line was allowed to run out. The lack of a precision timepiece, however, kept this from being more than a fair approximation of speed; it also prevented the accurate measurement of longitude, one of the continuing handicaps to early modern navigation.

Naval armament also underwent change during the fifteenth and sixteenth centuries. Whereas the common warship of medieval Mediterranean Europe was the galley, Renaissance naval experts soon saw military advantages in the sailing ship. Larger and without oarsmen, sailing ships could carry more fighting men and equipment. Furthermore, their design lent itself to the construction of high "castle" decks fore and aft to give gunners, archers, and boarders the advantage of height over their adversaries. The greatest technical innovation, however, was the gradually developing idea of using the ship not primarily as transportation for men-at-arms, but as a gun platform to concentrate heavy firepower against enemy vessels or ports. As this concept slowly emerged, warships were equipped with increasing numbers of heavy cannons mounted on the deck and below deck, which could fire broadside from open ports in the hull. As ship design and construction made boarding difficult and technology provided more firepower, naval gunnery became increasingly important.

Renaissance Navigational Instruments

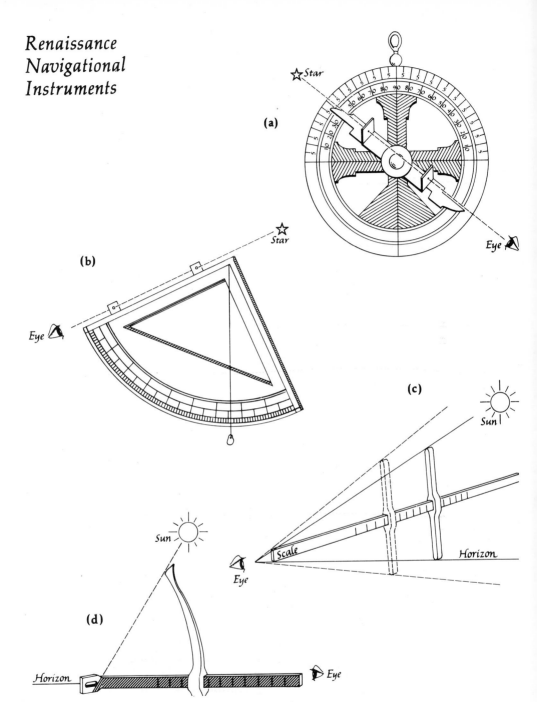

(a)

(b)

(c)

(d)

RENAISSANCE NAVIGATIONAL INSTRUMENTS *included, in addition to the magnetic compass, several devices for measuring the elevation of the sun or a known star, from which latitude could then be computed. Shown here are (a) an astrolabe; (b) quadrant; (c) cross-staff, functional only when the horizon was visible; and (d) back-staff, a later sixteenth-century invention, which had the advantage of allowing the viewer to have his back to the sun.*

Land-based Military Technology

During the fifteenth and early sixteenth centuries, land-based military technology went through a stage, similar to what we have seen in other fields, of elaboration and adaptation of medieval precedents. By the end of the fourteenth century, gunpowder and siege cannons had practically replaced the catapult as a siege weapon; this development also brought about the beginning of a radical change in the design and building of fortifications. Nevertheless, fourteenth-century artillery was still very primitive and, except for siege use where the target was large and stationary, cumbersome to use. Cannons were not made with sufficient precision to have uniform bores, and even if they were, the missiles being fired—sometimes rocks or other easily expendable material—were far from standard in size. Nor did the powder always ignite when it was supposed to. Occasionally, it exploded with more force than the piece could contain, killing the gunners and others nearby. It was not until the early sixteenth century, during the struggle for the domination of Italy, that artillery became accurate or plentiful enough to play a decisive role in a pitched battle between two armies. By this time, many technical innovations (including the casting of iron cannons) had been made, giving artillery an essential role in any successful army, despite Machiavelli's belief that it was only a passing fancy. However, harnessing gunpowder on such a massive scale turned out to be enormously expensive and was therefore restricted, like atomic energy today, to the already strong and wealthy states.

Small-arms weapons (pistols, arquebuses, matchlocks, or muskets) did not replace the sword, spear, halberd, and pike in battle. Even the crossbow had its greatest day during the first two centuries *after* the invention of gunpowder, as did the picturesque full-plate armor, which was supposed to have become obsolete. The size, weight, inaccuracy, and reloading time of hand firearms seriously limited their practicality after the first volley was fired. Nevertheless, this was one of the fields of great experimentation and improvement. It was also an era of elaborate artistic expression. In the sixteenth century, the beautiful casting, engraving, embossing, and inlaying of arms and armor reached its all-time height.

Printing

None of the technological innovations we have mentioned has had a greater effect over a longer period of time and upon more people than the invention of printing in the mid-fifteenth century. Some scholars have pronounced it the single most important development of the Renaissance and perhaps of the entire modern world. Certainly no one can deny that its initial impact on Europe significantly shaped much of European life and thought, and that its continued importance is incalculable.

The Invention of Movable Type

To better understand the nature and significance of this revolution in writing, we need to be as precise as we can in describing its nature and origins. In the first place, it was not printing that was invented in fifteenth-century Mainz, it was *typography*—that is, multiple printing with removable, reusable type. Printing from hand-carved wooden blocks had been practiced since the twelfth century and in China long before that. The impracticality of this process for large pages of tiny print, however, is obvious. Each letter had to be carved anew on the block whenever it appears, and a new block prepared for each page to be printed—and, of course, they all had to be cut in reverse. That is why wood-cut printing in the West had generally been used only for religious pictures and playing cards. The essential steps in typographical printing are simple and effective: First, a single model (known as the punch) of each letter or character is cut in a hard metal. With this punch, a matrix, or mold, is struck, with which an unlimited number of types may be cast in molten lead. These lead types can then be set side by side in a case, or plate, in the proper sequence for a page of print. The plate is then inked with a large porous bag filled with printer's ink, attached to the pressure frame, and pressed against the paper to make a printed page.

The second point of clarification is that the development of printing was a long, evolutionary process, with many contributors. It was not "invented" full-bloom either by Johann Gutenberg of Mainz, Germany, or by Laurens Janszoon Coster of Haarlem, Holland (who runs a not-too-close second as the alleged inventor). Many previous developments in printing and in the materials of printing aided in the eventual discovery of the typographical process: the development of relief printing on fabrics and parchment; the invention of printer's ink (a lampblack or powdered charcoal pigment ground in linseed oil); the construction of the press for transferring ink to the paper; and the improvement in the quantity and quality of paper, without which the whole process would have been impossible. In the latter development, the papermakers of Fabriano, Italy, were great contributors.

Details of the exact origin or first use of movable type are unknown, but they are relatively unimportant compared with the results that followed. Indirect evidence points strongly to Gutenberg, but we cannot say for sure just when he began or how much knowledge and skill were provided by his partners, Johann Fust, a fellow goldsmith, and Fust's son-in-law, Peter Schöffer, who soon formed a printing establishment of their own. Furthermore, since Gutenberg's imprint is not on any surviving book, it is difficult to identify positively which of the early books were actually printed by him. With what has been learned in recent years about early printing, it can safely be said that sometime between 1445 and 1450 the final steps were taken in perfecting the process and that Gutenberg had a leading role in it.

The earliest printed fragments (a poem on the Last Judgment and an astronomical calendar) have been dated between 1445 and 1448. Although the printer of the fragments is not known, it was probably Gutenberg and Fust. The earliest example to bear a printed date is a thirty-one-line indulgence of 1454, issued by Pope Nicolas V to anyone who would give money for the campaign against the Turks, who had just conquered Constantinople the previous year. This indulgence has been identified, through type headings, as Gutenberg's work. From the same year and the same press came a twelve-page leaflet entitled "A Warning to Christendom against the Turks." The first substantial book to be printed from movable type—and one of the finest—is the so-called Gutenberg forty-two-line (per page) Bible (1455 or 1456), although it was evidently, at least, completed by Fust and Schöffer. Many other Bibles appeared in the next few years, none of them as fine as this one. The earliest book giving the date and printer's name is the beautiful 1457 *Psalter*, bearing the imprint of Fust and Schöffer. Since Fust did not part company with Gutenberg until November, 1455, this Psalter was probably begun when the two were working together and, like perhaps all of the books up until this time, should be attributed to both of them. A rare thirty-six-line Bible, identified by its typefaces as Gutenberg's, appeared in 1460 or perhaps a little earlier. Another remarkable book from this early period is the Mainz *Catholicon* (1460), an ambitious encyclopedic dictionary by Johannes Balbus containing the title-page notation, "Printed without help of reed, stylus, or pen but by the marvelous concord, proportion and harmony of punches and types," and further on, "by the aid of the All-Highest, who often reveals to the humble what he hides from the wise."

The sack of Mainz in 1462 during the Bishops' War (a violent and bloody altercation between rival claimants to the bishopric of Mainz) temporarily upset the infant printing industry there. Three years later, however, Fust and Schöffer were publishing again, including some editions of the Latin classics. After Fust's death in 1466, Schöffer continued the business alone. In 1469 he issued the first list of books and pamphlets printed in Mainz and available for purchase from him. It lists twenty items, with brief descriptions of each.

The Spread and Impact of Printing

The rapid and widespread expansion of printing throughout Europe during the last half of the fifteenth century suggests not only that people were ready for this development, but also that many technicians were prepared to produce what the people wanted. Within a few years after the forty-two-line Bible, presses were working at full capacity throughout Europe, producing almost every kind of book, pamphlet, article, and tract. As early as 1458, there was a press in Strasbourg, where Johann Mentelin printed a number of large but little-used tomes. In Bamberg, Albrecht Pfister was turning out many books addressed to a

(a)

(b)

(c)

(d)

SCENES OF THE PRINTING PROCESS.
From Jost Amman's Ständebuch
(1508) come these woodcuts of various steps in making of a book: (a) a wood block cutter at work; (b) paper making; (c) casting type; (d) printing; and (e) bookbinding. (Reproduced by Courtesy of the Trustees of the British Museum)

(e)

more popular audience after 1461. By 1470 there were several presses in Nuremberg and others followed soon after. Basel, Switzerland (then part of the Holy Roman Empire), was another early center of printing. It is impossible to determine accurately who the first printers there were, but after 1491 and during the first quarter of the next century, Johann Froben became the best-known publisher in Basel. Froben, in collaboration with the great humanist scholar-writer-editor Erasmus, produced a galaxy of significant titles, mostly religious.

The first press established outside the empire was in Italy at the Benedictine Abbey of Subiaco, near Rome, in 1464. It was founded by Conrad Sweynheym and Arnold Pannartz, who had left Mainz after the Bishops' War. Within a decade, there were more than a dozen printers in Rome, and in the 1470s, printing firms were established in all of the city-states. The first book printed in Venice, the city that was soon to become almost synonymous with printing, was Cicero's *Letters* (1469), by Johannes de Spira, a goldsmith from Mainz. In 1470 Nicolas Jenson, a Frenchman who is reputed to have learned printing at Mainz by order of the French king, established himself in Venice. His handsome Roman type, one of the first to depart from the close imitation of the handwritten Gothic manuscripts, has been much admired and imitated right up to the present day. In a 1482 advertising blurb, Jenson's partners affirmed that "His books do not hinder one's eyes, but rather help them and do them good. Moreover, the characters are so intelligently and carefully elaborated that the letters are neither smaller, larger, nor thicker than reason or pleasure demand." By 1500 Venice had nearly one hundred printers, more than in all of the other Italian cities combined, and had produced about two million volumes since 1480.

Undoubtedly, the greatest name associated with the early history of printing is Aldus Manutius (1450–1515), a humanist scholar in his own right, who led a crusade to create the best books and make them available to the largest possible audience. In 1490 Aldus established his first printing office in Venice, and for the next fifty years the Aldine Press set the standard for accurate and beautiful publications. Particularly interested in printing the Greek classics, he assembled a group of competent humanists and a body of technicians and began his self-imposed task of printing all of the unpublished classics. Aldus was interested not only in reviving and publishing the ancient classics but also making them available in a small, convenient size and at a price low enough that they could be owned and carried by all interested scholars. The typical Aldine book is in octavo size, or smaller, clearly printed in a small and legible Roman typeface, or else in the famous *italic* (modeled from the chancery script), first used by Aldus. So popular was the Aldine type that it was quickly pirated by less scrupulous printers. Likewise, Aldus's motto, "Make haste slowly," depicted by a dolphin entwined around an anchor, symbolizing the combination of speed and stability, was soon copied by others.

Printing was begun in France in 1470 by two Sorbonne professors, Jean Heynlyn and Guillaume Fichet. They were soon joined by Antoine Vérard and other printers, who combined to make Paris the publishing center of France. The most notable achievements in Parisian printing were made by the Estienne family of scholar-printers. Henri Estienne began publishing Greek and Latin classics in 1502, producing more than one hundred editions during his first eight years. His son, Robert Estienne, took over the firm in 1524 and achieved considerable fame compiling and publishing Latin, Greek, and Hebrew dictionaries, as well as many other beautiful and scholarly works. Second only to Paris was Lyon, where Guillaume Le Roy introduced printing in 1473. By the beginning of the sixteenth century, Lyon had become the center of the French book trade, with an emphasis on popular rather than scholarly books. Chivalric romances, fables, histories, and other forms of popular literature flourished there, along with the lawbooks used by the law school of Lyon.

Printing flourished in the Low Countries from 1473 on; in fact, some contend that printing originated in Haarlem in the 1440s. Many signed and dated books were published at Utrecht, Delft, Gouda, Deventer, Zwolle, and Leiden in the 1470s. Antwerp, Louvain, and Bruges in the southern provinces of Flanders and Brabant (in modern Belgium) were the locations of active printing houses. Printing in Spain, introduced there from Flanders and Germany, began as early as 1474. Presses operated in Tortosa, Valencia, Zaragosa, Barcelona, and Seville before the end of the decade, and in 1481 Salamanca (which was later to become an important book center) began printing.

The first book printed in the English language was William Caxton's translation of Raoul le Fevre's *Collection of the Histories of Troy*, printed at Bruges in 1473. This is a medieval chivalric romance retelling the story of the Trojan War. After producing six different books from his press in Bruges, Caxton moved to London in 1476, and there, during his last fifteen years became the most active English printer of the period. Caxton's press was inherited by his foreman Wynkyn de Worde, who continued the tradition and even the types of his master. Most of the English printing was done in London, but presses were also established at Oxford, Saint Albans, York, and Cambridge.

Printing also spread into eastern Europe during the decades following Gutenberg. The first printing at Pilsen, in Bohemia, was by the "printer of Guido della Colonna" in 1468; in Budapest by Andreas Hess in 1473; in Cracow, Poland, in 1475; in Vienna in 1482; and in 1482 and 1483, Johann Snell, of Lübeck, produced books from his branch printing offices in Odense, Denmark, and Stockholm, Sweden.

By the close of the fifteenth century, only fifty years after the first books were printed, some forty thousand titles (between 8 and 10 million separate books) had been published by over one thousand printers. Not all of these were new or original books; in fact, most of them were reprints of previous works. But the effect of the sudden availability of texts and commentaries hitherto unobtainable or unknown was tremendous. Over half of the books printed in this period were religious—Bibles, commentaries, liturgical works, devotional books, and sermons. Next in frequency were ancient classics, medieval grammars, legal handbooks, philosophical works, encyclopedias and almanacs, and chivalric romances. Soon printing became one of the largest industries in Europe, requiring great advances of capital, numerous technicians, and writers. The impact of printing upon the labor and money markets was immense.

Beyond the immediate social and economic sphere, the effects of printing are harder to determine but perhaps even more profound. Multiple-copy printing opened up new horizons in education by drastically altering the role of the teacher and making it possible for students to read texts and commentaries themselves instead of having them dictated by the professors. Furthermore, the reciprocal effects of printing and literacy were soon felt even in the remotest parts of Europe, for just as increasing literacy during the Renaissance helps account for the immediate and widespread acceptance of printing, so did the latter stimulate an ever-larger reading public. Printing also influenced the development and standardization of languages in each country and had a profound effect on literature. The introduction of mass reading in the fifteenth and sixteenth centuries had an effect (though perhaps in the opposite direction) comparable to the impact of television in the twentieth. Finally, in the field of scholarship, as well as in that of mass propaganda, the effect was immediate and long lasting. The wide distribution and availability of identical texts (inaccurate as well as accurate ones) was not only a boon to scholarly research but also made it possible for scholars to compare texts and exchange their own opinions and discoveries with others, as well as to make their results known to a wider public. Denounced by many as a disrespectful vulgarization of learning, printing nonetheless opened a new era in humanity's long struggle to attain knowledge.

Suggestions for Further Reading

GENERAL

The most satisfactory summary of Renaissance science is Marie Boas, *The Scientific Revolution, 1450–1630* (New York, 1962), although several older books are still useful. See, for example, A. C. Crombie, *Medieval and Early Modern Science*, vol. 2 (Garden City, 1959); Alexandre Koyré, *From the Closed World to the Infinite Universe* (New York, 1957), emphasizing the spiritual revolution underlying Renaissance science; and Herbert Butterfield's lively, *The Origins of Modern Science, 1300–1800* (London, 1949, 1962). George Dubus, *Man and Nature in the Renaissance* (Cambridge, 1978) is short and stimulating. Alan G. R. Smith, *Science and Society in the Sixteenth and Seventeenth Centuries* (New York, 1972) is a brilliantly written and profusely illustrated volume in the History of European Civilization Library.

ART AND SCIENCE: LEONARDO

George Sarton's dated *Six Wings: Men of Science in the Renaissance* (London, 1957) shows a deep appreciation of Leonardo's role. More recently, Boris Kouznetsov, "The Rationalism of Leonardo da Vinci and the Dawn of Classical Science," *Diogenes*, 69 (1970), 1–11, has briefly discussed the nature and meaning of Leonardo's relationship to the development of science. Ivor B. Hart, *The World of Leonardo da Vinci, Man of Science, Engineer and Dreamer of Flight* (New York, 1962) is well worth reading. Also his *The Mechanical Investigations of Leonardo da Vinci*, 2nd ed. (Berkeley, 1963), and *Leonardo da Vinci, Supreme Artist and Scientist* (London, 1964). Richard B. McLanathan, *Images of the Universe: Leonardo da Vinci, the Artist as Scientist* (Garden City, 1966) is evocative. The most recent contribution is by Charles H. Gibbs-Smith, *The Inventions of Leonardo da Vinci* (Oxford, 1978).

MATHEMATICS AND MEDICINE

To George Sarton's distinguished lectures on mathematics, medicine, and astronomy, published as *The Appreciation of Ancient and Medieval Science during the Renaissance, 1450–1600* (Philadelphia, 1955), one should add Paul L. Rose, *The Italian Renaissance of Mathematics: Studies on Humanists and Mathematics from Petrarch to Galileo* (Genoa, 1975); John H. Randall, *The School of Padua and the Emergence of Modern Science* (New York, 1961); Eugenio Garin, *Science and Civic Life in the Italian Renaissance*, tr. by Peter Munz (Garden City, 1969); and Hugh Kearny, *Science and Change, 1500–1700* (New York, 1971), which affirms that new approaches to mathematics and experimental techniques overthrew the traditional assumptions about nature. On medicine, see Charles D. O'Malley, *Andreas Vesalius of Brussels, 1514–1564* (Berkeley, 1964), and Carlo M. Cipolla, *Public Health and the Medical Profession in the Renaissance* (New York, 1976).

COPERNICUS

Maria Bogucka, *Nicholas Copernicus, the Country and Times* (Warsaw, 1972) is an admirable general life of Copernicus. See also Robert S. Westman, ed., *The Copernican Achievement* (Berkeley, 1975), papers from the UCLA Center for Medieval and Renaissance Studies symposium on the 500th anniversary of Copernicus's birth. Other worthwhile studies are Edward Grant, "Late Medieval Thought: Copernicus and the Scientific Revolution," *Journal of the History of Ideas*, 23 (1962), 197–220, and Edward Rosen, "Copernicus and Renaissance Astronomy," in Robert Schwoebel, *Renaissance Men and Ideas* (New York, 1971), 95–106.

TECHNOLOGY

Charles J. Singer, ed., *A History of Technology: From the Renaissance to the Industrial Revolution*, vol. 3 (Oxford, 1957) is the most detailed general survey. For decades, Lynn White, Jr., has been the most active promoter of the study of medieval and Renaissance technology. In addition to the works cited in Chapter One, see his *The Expansion of Technology* (London, 1969), and *On Pre-Modern Technology and Science: A Volume of Studies in Honor of Lynn White, Jr.*, edited by D. C. West and B. S. Hall (Malibu, 1976). More specific and detailed studies include William B. Parsons' distinguished but very technical *Engineers and*

Engineering in the Renaissance (Cambridge, Mass., 1939 and 1976), and B. Gille, *Engineers of the Renaissance* (Cambridge, Mass., 1966), which is not so favorable to Leonardo.

PRINTING

S. H. Steinberg, *Five Hundred Years of Printing*, 3d ed. (Harmondsworth, 1974) is old but continues to be a serviceable introduction. See also R. Hirsch, *Printing, Selling and Reading, 1450–1550* (Wiesbaden, 1967), and especially L. Febvre and H. J. Martin, *The Coming of the Book: The Impact of Printing, 1450–1800* (London, 1976). Elizabeth L. Eisenstein's "Some Conjectures About the Impact of Printing on Western Society and Thought," *Journal of Modern History*, 40 (1968), 1–56, and "The Advent of Printing and the Problem of the Renaissance," *Past and Present*, 45 (1969), 19–89, offer some notions that are challenged by Theodore K. Rabb in "The Advent of Printing and the Problem of the Renaissance: A Comment," *Past and Present*, 52 (1971), 135–44. Ms. Eisenstein's latest contribution is a monumental two-volume work entitled *The Printing Press as an Agent of Change: Communications and Cultural Transformations in Early Modern Europe* (New York, 1978). It is the most up-to-date and challenging discussion of the impact of printing. A very enlightening recent book on one phase of the development of printing is Martin Lowry, *The World of Aldus Manutius: Business and Scholarship in Renaissance Venice* (Oxford, 1979).

CHAPTER SEVEN

Religion and the Renaissance Church

HE POWER AND PRESTIGE of the medieval papacy was greatly reduced during the fourteenth and fifteenth centuries, and the entire church went through a period of serious trial. The problems were widespread, involving both jurisdictional conflicts and moral decline. Political rivalries among the European states also involved the church, and when these led to clashes between civil and religious authority, the problems increased. As the papacy declined in real power vis-à-vis the territorial monarchies, its pretensions grew bolder and more reckless.

The Avignon Papacy and the Great Schism

Unable to see that the medieval papal claim to the right of intercession in the affairs of secular rulers was unrealistic in an age of rapidly growing national powers and unwilling to admit that papal strength depended greatly on the support of at least some of those rulers, Pope Boniface VIII (1294–1303) made the grave mistake of challenging the authority of the king of France without protecting himself with the support of some other princes. Indeed, by his bold promulgation of the bull *Unam sanctum*, which reiterated the papal claim to unchallenged universal supremacy, even in secular affairs if an issue of moral law was involved, Boniface not only infuriated Philip IV, but effectively alienated all other rulers, including those who might otherwise have been unwilling to sit back and watch the French king preempt the papacy. Boniface's bluster cost him his papal throne and his life, and brought to a close, for three-quarters of a century at least, the Roman see.

Since Petrarch's time, the period from 1305 to 1378 has been known as the Babylonian Captivity, suggesting in the subservience of the popes to France during their residence in Avignon a parallel to the Israelite bondage in Babylon. The phrase is picturesque, though not very accurate. After the death of Boniface VIII, the papal see was transferred to Avignon, and for the next seventy-three years the French influence was strong. The seven succeeding popes were all from France or from territories owing allegiance to France; most of the curial officials were recruited from Provence, Languedoc, Limousin, and Dauphiné; and most of the cardinals were French. However, of all the popes, only Clement V (1305–14) kowtowed to the French king. Most of the popes were able and energetic men who directed papal affairs more systematically and effectively than they had been handled for years. Furthermore, Avignon did not belong to France. When the papal curia settled there, it was a fief of the king of Naples and was subsequently purchased by the papacy. It was surrounded by French dependencies and fiefs, but it was still several hundred miles away from the French king.

At Avignon, administrative centralization was carried out with great vigor by several of the popes, especially by John XXII (1315–34). Tighter jurisdiction over the provinces of the church was achieved through exercise of the papal right of reservation; that is, the power claimed by the papacy to the direct appointment of vacant benefices, overruling the normal rights of secular patrons and other clerical bodies. The administrative structure of the curia was also centralized with the final development of the *camera apostolica*, the body responsible for papal revenues. But tightening the central controls of the church was also fraught with serious dangers. As the bureaucracy grew in size, it also multiplied in immobility and corruption. Some parts of it, especially the College of Cardinals, became menacingly obstreperous during the Avignon period. Furthermore, as church administration became more centralized, secular rulers became increasingly suspicious and aggressive. They intervened by imposing new restrictions and limitations upon papal jurisdiction. The English king, for example, induced Parliament to enact the Statute of Provisors in 1351, which forbade the popes to bestow English benefices on non-English subjects, and the Statute of Praemunire, two years later, which outlawed appeals to the papal court unless authorized by the crown. Similar steps were taken against the papacy in France, Spain, and the Holy Roman Empire.

As the rivalry and recrimination mounted and the corruption and worldliness of the curia intensified and spread, the church entered another crisis that left it weakened and discredited. During the 1360s

THE PAPAL PALACE AT AVIGNON. *The curia at Avignon became one of the most sumptuous courts of Europe, and this massive palace the center of a government whose branches reached into every corner of the continent, and beyond. (French Government Tourist Office)*

and 1370s, there was increasing pressure on the papacy to return to Rome. Urban V did reside in Rome for almost three years after 1367, but was forced back to Avignon by the turbulence of Italian politics and wars. In 1378 Pope Gregory XI died in Rome, to which he had retreated the previous year. Increasing pressure to elect an Italian pope resulted in the selection of the neurotic and tempestuous archbishop of Bari as Pope Urban VI (1378–89). Quickly repenting their actions, thirteen of the cardinals, resentful of Urban's immediate attack on the opulence of the cardinals and fearful for the loss of their power, met at Fondi to proclaim the election of Urban VI invalid and to elect Robert, Cardinal of Geneva, the new pope, as Clement VI (1378–94). Instead of meekly resigning, however, Urban promptly excommunicated the rebel cardinals along with their pope and appointed an entirely new college of cardinals consisting mostly of Italians. Clement VI returned to Avignon with the majority of the old cardinalate and the Great Schism began.

For the next forty years, papal policy consisted of mutual excommunications and denunciations by the rival popes, while each attempted to win as large a segment of Christendom to their respective allegiance as possible. In the meantime, while English and French armies battled each other in the Hundred Years' War, the prestige and power of the papacy withered. Europe became hopelessly divided into two contending camps. Allegiance to Rome was professed by part of the German Empire, northern and central Italy, Flanders, England, and

Ireland; the rest of the Empire, France, Savoy, Naples and Sicily, Castile, Aragon, Navarre, Portugal, and Scotland paid homage to Avignon. Corruption and confusion now ran rampant in the church while plague, depression, and war desolated much of Europe.

Clerical Abuses and Popular Devotion

Clerical Abuses

The period of the Great Schism (1378–1415) corresponded with the worst moral degeneration of the church for centuries. While the two papacies vied with each other for ostentation and pretense, the clergy seemed to compete for the depths in debauchery, slothfulness, and graft. Wherever one turns in the literature of fourteenth-century Europe, the same picture of avarice and debasement is drawn. We see it, for example, in the abuses of the secular clergy, in which absenteeism and neglect pervaded every level of the clerical hierarchy. Archbishops and bishops were frequently guilty not only of worldliness and all that goes with it, but at times even of criminal actions. In their competition with each other and with the princes for power, prestige, and pleasure, some of these men seemed to forget entirely their spiritual responsibilities. Absenteeism, ignorance, venality, concubinage, and slothfulness were common among priests as well as bishops.

In the religious orders, the abuses were also flagrant. Splintering and fragmentation of the orders in the fourteenth century contributed greatly to their decline in effectiveness, as rivalries developed and material competition replaced piety and devotion. Violations of the rules of poverty, obedience, and chastity were far from uncommon in the monasteries, while many monks and friars appeared to take pride in their ribaldry. Such abuses did not go unnoticed. Literate members of the church became increasingly outspoken in their criticism and protests.

Indulgences

Also during the Renaissance, the institution of indulgences, in connection with the sacrament of penance, came into wide use and abuse. Penance involved four important steps: *contrition*, or sorrow for sins committed; *confession* to a priest, who then granted *absolution*, which freed the penitent from the guilt of sin and from eternal punishment; *satisfaction*, or the outward manifestation of sorrow through performing prescribed works of penance, thus satisfying the divine demand for the temporal punishment of sin. If for any reason insufficent penance was imposed, or if the sinner died before performing all that was required, the temporal punishment would continue in purgatory. Originally, penance was a public ceremony involving confession before the congregation, which then required satisfaction from the penitent. An indulgence, then, was the permission, also granted by the congregation, to relax or remit all or part of the *temporal punishment*—usually because a person was physically unable to perform it.

With the conversion of penance into a sacrament and its change from a public to a private rite, many abuses developed in the granting of indulgences. The authority to issue them was taken over by the priests, then the bishops, and finally the popes. During the Crusades the church began granting plenary (full) indulgences to those who would participate in a crusade. Partial indulgences were also given for pilgrimages and other forms of religious devotion. Eventually they were granted for cash donations. In the thirteenth century, papal theologians formulated the theory of a "treasury of merit" (the storehouse of surplus good works accumulated by Christ and the saints) that could be drawn upon and distributed by the pope through papal indulgences. In the fifteenth century, the remission of temporal punishment by purchased indulgences was extended to include souls already in purgatory.

Theologians made careful distinctions between *contrition* (sorrow prompted by love) and *attrition* (sorrow prompted by fear of retribution), between *temporal* punishment (required of all absolved confessants) and *eternal* punishment (decreed for all *un*confessed, and therefore unabsolved, sinners), and between the *guilt* of sin (which could be forgiven by a priest) and the *penalties* of sin (which had to be paid either in this life or in purgatory, unless remitted by indulgences). Yet despite these distinctions, many ordinary people, confused by such subtleties, simply thought they were buying salvation when they purchased indulgences, whether they were contrite, confessed, and absolved, or not. The curia's active promotion of indulgences for raising revenue further perverted their original intent. The increased venality of the papacy may be seen in the second half of the fifteenth century, when printing indulgences became one of the important activities of the newly established printing houses, and circulating and selling indulgences involved not only the curia and the indulgence sellers but also bankers, lawyers, and secular rulers.

Popular Devotion

Despite corruption and vice, the teachings of the church were generally accepted by the common people without unusual clamor. The majority of Christians in the fourteenth century were neither antagonists nor fanatics but simple believers who accepted the dogmas of the church and conformed to its discipline and sacraments without complaint. For most, the church was an integral part of their lives and promised the only recognized path to salvation. Relatively few understood or worried about the subtleties of doctrine or the arguments of theologians. What affected people personally and collectively were the ritualistic devotions

provided for them in the Catholic liturgy: the Mass and other sacraments, prayers and pilgrimages, rosaries and relics.

These rites of popular devotion took on new importance and meaning to the masses of Europe as the ecclesiastical hierarchy became further separated from them. Mariology, the cult of the Virgin, grew from the early medieval respect and compassion for a sorrowing mother to the doctrine of Intercession and finally Immaculate Conception, still hotly debated by theologians in the fourteenth and fifteenth centuries. In spite of continuing perils to travel, pilgrimages became increasingly popular as a form of religious expression and devotion. For those unable to win merit as pilgrims, there were other forms of sacrifice and physical chastisement, such as rosaries, fasting, and self-inflicted bodily punishment. The contemplation of Christ in agony was believed to aid the penitent sinner, and for this purpose the realistic paintings and sculptures were aids. It is paradoxical, yet typical of the Renaissance, that this awareness and preoccupation with death should coincide with the renewed concern and exuberance for life. The cult of the saints in the fourteenth and fifteenth centuries also led to a veritable boom in the buying and selling of relics, which, properly preserved and adored, were counted as righteousness to the owner. Another form of devotion was the rise of the flagellants in the fourteenth century, especially in the first decades following the Black Death. These were bands of penitents in hooded robes with large red crosses on their backs who wandered about Europe publicly chanting, praying, and inflicting bodily punishments on themselves, while calling on others to do likewise as a sacrifice to placate the god of woes.

Reform, Mysticism, and Heresy

Reform

The flagrance of religious abuse stimulated many scattered attempts to reform the clergy and ameliorate the problems. Frequently, pious and well-meaning prelates made gestures and sometimes took meaningful measures toward reforming the abuses within their jurisdictions. But the problems were usually too broad or too interrelated with others to be successfully attacked on a piecemeal basis. Churchwide action by the papacy itself was needed, but it was not forthcoming.

What came nearer to succeeding in many specific instances were the reforms and interventions of secular rulers, and the legal and moral emphasis applied by the humanists and other writers of the time. During the fourteenth century, the English kings in particular locked horns with the papacy on many occasions and enacted legislation, as in the statutes of Provisors and of Praemunire, limiting or curtailing papal jurisdiction in England. In France, too, royal as well as Gallican (referring to the independent attitude of the French clergy toward the papacy) opposition made papal policy in France a tentative arrangement at best. A culmination of the long series of struggles came in 1438, with the promulgation of the Pragmatic Sanction of Bourges, giving the French church a favored position vis-à-vis the papacy. Similar, though by that time not so inclusive, concessions were achieved in Aragon, Castile, and Scotland.

Even earlier, during the fourteenth-century struggle between the conflicting interests of church and state, many political and religious writers took an active part in the theoretical delineation of papal authority. None of these was more important than Marsiglio of Padua, a long-time student of Roman law and, after 1313, rector of the University of Paris. In his famous treatise, *Defensor pacis* (Defender of Peace, 1324), Marsiglio not only denounced papal pretensions to temporal authority along with clerical claims to coercive and disciplinary action but also defended the independent territorial state as the legitimate tenant of sovereignty and the custodian of religious and civil law. He summarily refuted the claims of the clergy to autonomy within and above the state and denounced the papal assertion of special prerogatives. These usurpations of power, he maintained, bolstered and protected behind the curtain of canon law, should be exposed and subordinated to the legitimate authority of the state (not the "universal" state of the German emperor and of Dante's *De monarchia*, but the rising monarchical states of the various European powers), from which all jurisdiction, both temporal and ecclesiastical, derives. Marsiglio's theories were to have an increasing impact during the next two centuries.

Mysticism and "Modern Devotion"

Another kind of reaction to ecclesiastical abuse is revealed in the lives and writings of the mystics. By the beginning of the fourteenth century, mysticism (the belief and practice of direct and ecstatic contact with God through living a detached and Christlike life and communing with the Divine through devotional prayers and exercises) was becoming more and more detached from clerical or even monastic life. Although many of the mystics were friars themselves, their influence and following was strongest among the laity. Several congregations of mystics, obedient to church authority but more concerned with the necessity of spiritual experience, came into existence in the fourteenth century. One of these groups, known as the Friends of God, was active in the Rhineland area. Their desire for union with God through the cultivation of love and the renunciation of the material world was typically mystical and was considered suspect by the outward church of that day.

Another movement, which was to have great influence during the early years of the sixteenth century, was the Brethren of the Common Life, developing out of the teachings and examples of the Augustinian Jan van Ruysbroeck and his influential disciple Gerhard Groote (1340–84). Groote's emphasis on living an ascetic and meditative life modulated by an active, evangelical devotion to personal reform, was incorporated into the *devotio moderna* (modern devotion) of the Brethren. Akin to the mystics in their fasting, self-denial, and systematic meditations, they also stressed Bible study and the use of Scripture as the surest guide to a good life. Like the monks, they lived communally (although without taking the monastic vows) and devoted much time to copying medieval manuscripts. Their activism is best revealed in their establishing and operating numerous schools, in which humanist methods of classical education were introduced. The Brethren of the Common Life had their nucleus in The Netherlands, at Deventer (headed by Alexander Hegius, Erasmus's most influential teacher), Delft, and Zwolle, and soon spread into Flanders and many cities and towns of northern and western Germany. From one of these communities of Brethren came the most important devotional book of the Renaissance, the *Imitation of Christ*, written by Thomas à Kempis (1380–1471).

Heresy: Wyclif and Hus

The line between sainthood and heresy was never thinner nor more poorly defined than in the fourteenth and fifteenth centuries. At some time or another, nearly all of the saints were charged with heresy by someone, while the various congregations of mystics were always under a partial condemnation by the papacy or were the targets of suspicion and distrust. However, from its medieval experiences with the Albigensians and Waldensians in southeastern France, the Beguins and Beghards of the Rhineland, and the Fraticelli in Italy, the church had developed some guideline definitions of heresy. The problem with diagnosing heresy lay in the fact that few cases were clear-cut enough to put into one category or the other. In the latter part of the fourteenth century, however, two groups came clearly under the stigma of heresy: the Lollards in England and the Hussites in Bohemia.

John Wyclif (ca. 1320–84), an Oxford don who had many independent ideas about church government and doctrine, was the founder of English Lollardy. Wyclif's notoriety began with his frequent condemnations of clerical abuse and corruption and his support of Edward III's criticism of papal exploitation and wealth. But his attacks did not end there, nor did his influence. Like Marsiglio of Padua, he denied clerical ownership of land and property, and with it, papal and clerical jurisdiction in temporal affairs. Wyclif's doctrine of dominion, as set forth in his early works *On Divine Dominion* (1375) and *On Civil Dominion* (1376), declared that all people are the tenants of God who "makes, sustains and governs all that He possesses." Only the righteous, as God's stewards, have political authority in the full sense—that is, the moral right to dominion and to the holding of possessions. The wicked, on the other hand, whether they be nobles, kings, or popes, have no such rights, although even they may exercise temporary "legal" power or have the "use" of property when God so wills it. Wyclif believed that churchmen living in mortal sin—including the pope, whom Wyclif eventually declared was the antichrist—relinquished their rights as God's stewards and should be deprived of their property and authority.

As direct tenants of God, with no intermediaries between them, Christians are responsible to know and keep God's law, and this is possible, he affirmed only through the Bible. For Wyclif, the Bible was not only the standard of faith, it was also the source of authority. That is why he advocated that the Bible be made available in the vernacular tongues, and he pointed the way by starting an English translation himself. Wyclif's Bible was completed by colleagues after his death.

Rejecting all ceremony and organization that were not mentioned in the Bible, Wyclif renounced transubstantiation, disdained the sacramental power of the Roman priesthood, and denied the efficacy of the Mass. He also objected to the whole network of rituals, rites, and ceremonies that pervaded the church, on the grounds that they were unnecessary and actually detracted from the true worship of Christ. Taking an Augustinian view of the church as the predestined body of true believers, he maintained that salvation comes not through the sacraments of the church nor through people's worthless efforts to save themselves, but through divine grace alone.

Wyclif's attacks on ecclesiastical property brought him many followers, and his English Bible later became very popular, but the Peasants' Revolt of 1381 discredited the socioeconomic aspects of his movement. He was placed under house arrest in 1382 and died there two years later. Persecution by King Henry IV forced the Lollards to go underground after 1401.

A more serious threat to the church appeared in Bohemia with the teachings and following of the Czech theologian-priest John Hus (ca. 1370–1415). For many years, Prague had been a center for evangelical-minded reformers like John Milvič and Matthew of Janov, who were continually at odds with the clergy. The writings of Wyclif were also widely known in Prague and formed the basis for many heated theological exchanges at the University of Prague, where Hus became a leading spokesman for church reform. It was in this environment of devotional piety and reformism that John Hus became preacher of the Bethlehem Chapel in Prague in 1402 and rector of the University of Prague a short time later. Although as a theologian he took a more moderate stand than Wyclif on many issues—such as transubstantiation—the peculiar social and political strains in Bohemia caused by German-Czech tensions in the Holy Roman Empire soon brought Hus into conflict with the church.

As a parish priest, Hus was under some pressure to denounce the Lollard heresy, but as rector of the university he led the fight against clerical abuses and German domination. In 1409 the Germans were expelled from the university and Prague became a seedbed of reformism in the heart of the Empire. The schismatic Pope John XXIII ordered Hus to appear at Rome for trial, and when Hus flatly refused, he and his followers were peremptorily excommunicated. Riots followed in Prague, and Hus appealed to the patriotism of the people against the popes (there were three by this time) and against the German clergy that dominated the church in Bohemia. This defiance of authority, with all of its social as well as religious connotations, was the opening salvo of the Hussite wars that continued to plague the church and Empire for the next half-century. Hus was persuaded by King Wenceslas to leave Prague, but he continued to write theological tracts and produced an important book entitled *On the Church*.

The Dilemma of the Jews

The mobilization of church discipline against the Hussites also proved a dangerous threat to the Jewish community in Prague as well as to Judaism throughout Europe. Inevitably, the fate of the Jews was bound up with the history of both church and state. Jewish life in early medieval Europe had been relatively calm compared with what they had suffered earlier and would be forced to endure again. The peak of Jewish cultural flowering was reached in Spain during the twelfth and thirteenth centuries, especially in the reign of Alfonso X the Wise (1252–84), and in southern Italy (notably Naples, Salerno, and Palermo) where Emperor Frederick II's patronage provided a haven for Jewish intellectuals and enterprising merchants.

Beginning with their expulsion from England in 1290, however, European Jews went through a century of terror and oppression that left them weakened and deluded. In France the repressive Lateran Council decrees of 1215 were vigorously enforced by Saint Louis and his successors, and in 1306 Philip IV ordered all Jews expelled from France. This proved to be bad business from an economic point of view, so they were allowed to return for short periods, only to be alternately protected and exploited until they were permanently expelled in 1394. Oppression did not come from the rulers only. Christians in general feared and hated the Jews with almost pathological intensity. In 1320, for example, an abortive shepherds' crusade, known as the *pastoureaux*, unleashed its frustrations on the Jews of southern France, massacring thousands of them. A year later, Jews were ruthlessly attacked again when a rumor spread that Jews and lepers were planning to poison the drinking water of all Christians in France.

In Germany some Jewish financiers and "court Jews" found favor with several of the rulers, and played a key role in the commercial life of the Empire. But mostly they lived in almost perpetual terror as bands of *Judenschläger* (Jew slayers) systematically sought to exterminate them. The worst years were 1298, 1336, 1337, 1338, and 1348. Towns as well as princes extorted money from them by borrowing from them and then expelling them to avoid repayment. Even in the best of times, they were heavily taxed and shamelessly exploited. In most of the German towns they were required to live in designated areas, wear identifying in-

PERSECUTION OF THE JEWS. *A vivid woodcut from the* Liber Chronicarum mundi *(Nuremberg, 1493) represents the burning of Jews in fourteenth-century Cologne. (Courtesy of Brigham Young University Special Collections Library)*

201

signias, and were sharply restricted in the occupations they could follow. Throughout Europe, they were blamed for the Black Death and were hunted down and slaughtered by frightened mobs.

In the course of that terrible century, violence against the Jews boiled over into Spain, where anti-Semitic outrages scarred the land that had once been their safest home. The violence reached a climax in the bloody massacre of 1391 in Seville and spread from there into the rest of Castile and Aragon. Following this carnage, tens of thousands of Spanish Jews abandoned their ancient religion and accepted baptism. These "new Christians," or *Marranos*, as they were called, played an increasingly active role in Spanish life during the fifteenth century. They were prominent in the universities, in civil service and the legal profession, and in finance. They also intermarried with Christians now, especially those of wealthy noble families, and rose to positions of power and wealth. Yet all did not go well with the *Marranos*. Their former Jewish brothers considered them traitors and cowards; their new Christian colleagues suspected them of deceit, using their nominal Christianity for personal safety and as a cover to undermine the Catholic church. Many of these crypto-Jews did take their Christian vows very lightly and continued to believe and practice the Jewish rites in secret.

By the last quarter of the fifteenth century, the "*Marrano* problem" had become a major issue in Spanish life. Unlike the continuing Jewish persecutions, which were primarily religious, the *Marrano* issue involved an increasing concern over *limpieza de sangre* (purity of blood) and over suspected *Marrano* subterfuge. This growing fear led to the establishment of the Spanish Inquisition in 1478 as an instrument "to counteract *Marrano* cunning." These "new Christians" were subject to its jurisdiction, of course, whereas the unconverted Jews were not. After a slow beginning and much opposition, the Inquisition soon became an awesome weapon of religious bigotry and social persecution. In 1483 Friar Tomás de Torquemada was appointed the first inquisitor-general of Castile. Later in the same year, the Inquisition's jurisdiction was extended to Aragon, and Torquemada became head of it there, also.

The problem of the unconverted Jews in Spain was "solved" in 1492 by a royal decree ordering their expulsion within four months. Even the pleas of the venerable and trusted Isaac Abrabanel, who had been close to the crown for many years, could not change Ferdinand and Isabel's resolve to "purify" the blood of Spain. A few accepted baptism and thereby joined the *Marrano* ranks, but the majority of the estimated 150,000 Spanish Jews opted for exile. Most of them went to Portugal, where a few years later they were subjected to forced conversion by King Manoel. Others stopped temporarily in Naples or moved to other parts of Italy, while many settled in Moslem lands of the southern Mediterranean and the Ottoman Empire. Some found their way into eastern Europe, especially Poland.

In western Europe, only in Italy was life relatively tolerable for the Jews. For many centuries, Jewish communities had existed there, especially in Rome and in the south, where a long tradition of Jewish activity prevailed. Then, from the late thirteenth century on, the Jewish population began moving northward, due partly to persecutions in the south and partly to the invitation from some of the city-states to Jews to establish loan banks (pawnshops) in the north to help the needy—a usurious activity forbidden to Christians. These Jewish moneylenders opened the way to the eventual relaxation of restrictions in other occupations. In the next two centuries Jewish immigration from northern Europe, especially Germany and later Spain, increased the cosmopolitan flavor of Italian Jewry, and by introducing new traditions and values, tended to make it more compatible with the cultural Renaissance. Indeed, in the fifteenth and early sixteenth centuries, many Jews in Italy achieved a unique and remarkably successful synthesis of Hebraic and Christian-Renaissance cultures.

Under the more-or-less benevolent patronage of the Italian despots, many Jews not only found intermittent safety but a degree of identification and fulfillment unheard of north of the Alps, as they participated in the economic and cultural life of the time—although always under a shadow of suspicion and prejudice. Rome was an important center of Italian Jewry where, under the patronage of the Renaissance popes, Jewish scholars and financiers found a compatible environment. Further north in the cultured court of Urbino, they were protected and patronized by the Montefeltro dukes, as they were by the Bentivoglio in Bologna.

In the Florence of Lorenzo de' Medici several distinguished rabbis examined Latin texts while studying the Talmud and expounding the mysteries of the Cabala. One of these was Elijah del Medigo (1460–97), a distinguished physician as well as philosopher and teacher, who introduced Pico della Mirandola to the intricacies of Cabalism. In Ferrara under the d'Este family (where the exiled Abrabanel family settled for a time) and especially in Mantua under the Gonzagas, not only were Jewish moneylenders active, but others established themselves as traders, goldsmiths, and craftsmen, while some participated in court life as well as in scholarship, music, and the other arts. Padua had many Jewish students and some Jewish teachers, including Rabbi Judah Minz and the renowned Hebrew grammarian and Bible scholar, Elias Levita (1469–1549)—known also by the epithet "Bahur," meaning Young Man—who was later offered a professorship by Francis I.

Venice began supporting an important Jewish colony in the early sixteenth century, made up both of refugees of the Italian wars and of German immigrants, reinforced by some Spanish and Portuguese exiles. One of the conditions of settlement in Venice was that all of the Jews must live together in a designated area of the city. In 1516 they were established in the New Foundry (*Getto nuovo*) near Santa Geremia—hence the term *ghetto* to designate the Jewish quarter. This action is noteworthy not only because it established a precedent (although Jews had earlier been restricted to certain quarters of some towns in Germany and elsewhere) but also because it forced Sephardic Jews (those from Spain), with their distinct liturgy, customs, and language, to live with Ashkenazi ("German rite") Jews, who had a very different history and tradition. Venetian rule was relatively light in spite of the ghetto, and Jews in Venice continued to intermingle quite freely with Christians until after mid-century.

Nevertheless, even this degree of harmony was not destined to last, and the brief Renaissance reconciliation came to an end. Growing jealousy of Jewish financial successes throughout Italy, suspicion that they had conspiratorial intentions, and fear of their threat to the Christian religion, combined to cause continued prejudice and sporadic persecutions. The increasing vigor of religious polemics in the sixteenth century gradually drowned out the voices of tolerance and moderation. Zealous monks like Bernardino da Feltre and eager saints like John Capestrano were among the most persistent persecutors of the Jews, whose dilemma was not only how to adapt themselves to Latin-Christian culture without losing their own identity and faith but also how to survive.

Conciliarism and the Council of Constance

During the years of the Great Schism, as the papacy continued to lose face, the cry was heard with increasing frequency to convene a general council of the church to end the schism. Among those calling for a council were some of the leading lawyers, theologians, and scholars of that time: Jean de Gerson, chancellor of the University of Paris; Pierre d'Ailly, cardinal and professor of theology at Paris; Henry Langenstein of Hesse, a German doctor at Paris; Dietrich von Nieheim, bishop of Verden; Cardinal Francisco Zabarella; and a few years later the renowned cardinal, scientist, and philosopher, Nicholas of Cusa. At first the conciliar appeal was based on necessity—to end the schism. But gradually the assertion was made that ultimate authority in all ecclesiastical matters rested with the church itself, not with the pope. In other words, the supreme governing body of the church was a general council that could be spontaneously convened without papal convocation. Pierre d'Ailly declared in writing that the unity of the church consisted in its unity with Christ, not with the papacy. From Christ, therefore, comes the authority to summon a council to restore the unity destroyed by the popes. This opinion was further strengthened by the brilliant lawyer and theologian Jean de Gerson who declared that in cases such as this where neither municipal nor canon law applied, recourse must be made to natural and divine law, both of which clearly authorized the convocation of a council, and which demanded that a thorough reformation of the church, in head and members, be carried out.

Pressured further by popular feeling, a contingent of cardinals from Rome and Avignon decided to settle the schism in a general council which they called to meet in Pisa beginning in March 1409. The Council of Pisa was not well attended. After rehearsing the crimes and outrages of the two popes (Gregory XII in Rome and Benedict XIII in Avignon) and declaring them both deposed, the twenty-four cardinals went into conclave and elected as pope the cardinal archbishop of Milan who took the name Alexander V. It was one thing to depose two popes and elect a third but quite another to make it hold. Neither Gregory nor Benedict recognized the validity of the council's actions, and the new pope commanded so little popular support he was unable to force their submission. Christendom was now "blessed" with three popes: one a simple but senile puppet in the hands of his cardinals, nephews, and the king of Naples, one an obstinate Aragonese noble, and the third a naïve and incompetent Cretan. A year later Alexander died and was succeeded by the hardened and ruthless *condottiere*, Baldassare Cossa, as Pope John XXIII.

Now the pressure was on the newly elected Holy Roman Emperor Sigismund, king of Hungary, to apply his office toward settlement of the schism, not only to end the woes of the church but also in the hope of averting a political crisis in Bohemia, where Sigismund's brother, Wenceslas, was king. Supported and urged by the University of Paris and by influential voices in all the countries of Europe, Sigismund summoned a council to convene at Constance, an imperial retreat on the Bodensee, in the autumn of 1414. The Council of Constance was undoubtedly the most significant assembly of the century. Present in the

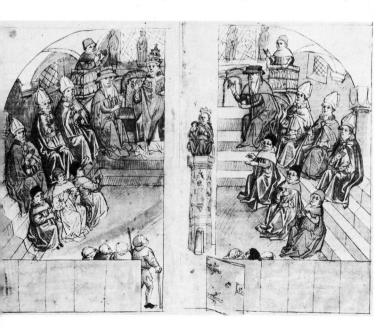

THE COUNCIL OF CONSTANCE. *Sessions of the council as depicted in Ulrich Richental's remarkable* Chronicle, *the best of the first-hand accounts of the activities at Constance.* (Rosgartenmuseum Konstanz)

tiny city of normally 6000 inhabitants, according to Ulrich Richental's detailed record, were several thousand ecclesiastics including two popes, five patriarchs, twenty-nine cardinals, thirty-three archbishops, many abbots, bishops, doctors of theology from all the major universities of Europe, and innumerable laymen, from tradesmen and lawyers to princes, kings, and the emperor. To give full play to the interests of the princes, the delegates were divided into five nations, each voting separately on all matters of procedure, reform, and reorganization. The agenda of the council called for action in three well-defined areas to end the schism, deal with existing heresies (meaning the Hussites and Lollards), and reform the church "in head and members." The success of the agenda also diminished in that order.

In the spring of 1415, Pope John's case was tried. Charged with fornication, adultery, incest, sodomy, and poisoning his predecessor, he was convicted and summarily deposed. One month later, Gregory resigned, leaving only the stubborn Avignon pope, Benedict XIII, to deal with. Believing he could withstand the council and with the continued loyalty of southern France, Aragon, Castile, Navarre, and Scotland, he prolonged his claim of preeminence until he was finally deposed by the council in 1417. In fact, even then he retired with four faithful cardinals to his ancestral stronghold in Aragon and continued to demand recognition as pope until his death in 1423 at the age of ninety-four. In the meantime, the council proceeded to elect the Roman cardinal Oddone Colonna as Pope Martin V. The disastrous schism of thirty-nine years was ended—almost.* In the meantime, the doctors in Constance took time to declare, in the most solemn decree, *Sacrosancta*, that "this holy Council of Constance . . . has its authority immediately from Christ; and all men, of every rank and condition, including the pope himself, are bound to obey it in matters concerning the Faith, the abolition of the schism, and the reformation of the Church of God in head and members." No pronouncement could more clearly affirm the ascendancy of conciliarism. By the decree *Frequens* in October 1417 the council further announced the policy of frequent and regular councils to carry out their duties as head of Christendom.

The problem of heresy was not so successfully liquidated, although at the time it seemed to the divines at Constance that their solution was final. Summoned in 1414 to answer charges of heresy, John Hus willingly proceeded under a safe conduct from Emperor Sigismund, hoping that once heard, his views would be accepted and his name cleared. He was first interrogated on his doctrinal unorthodoxy, and particularly on his attitude toward Wyclif's writings, which had been previously condemned by the council, and then thrown into prison to await a later hearing by the whole council. Seven months later, he was brought out of his dungeon and subjected to even greater abuse before

---

*Today the Roman Catholic Church does not recognize any of the schismatic Avignon and Pisan popes: Clement VII, Benedict XIII, Alexander V, and John XXIII.

the prelates. Still refusing to denounce, *en bloc,* all of Wyclif's teachings, although he did not agree with many of them, and resisting the council's pressure to force him to submit unconditionally to the authority and judgment of the church, Hus was condemned as a heretic and handed over to the secular authority for punishment. Sigismund immediately ordered him burned at the stake. As a final gesture, his friend and associate, Jerome of Prague, was likewise condemned and burned. Hus was disposed of, but the Hussites were not. Both the church and the Empire were soon to learn that he was more disturbing in death than he had been in life.

In their third avowed objective, reformation, the Council of Constance had its least success. Early in 1415 a reform commission, consisting of eight members appointed from each of the five "nations" plus three cardinals, was selected and instructed to make recommendations to the council. In October 1416 the commission submitted its report, outlining in vague terms the more flagrant abuses—simony, papal dispensations and exemptions, concubinage, and absenteeism—but offering no formulas by which they should be ended. The council then appointed a second commission, this one composed of twenty-five members, five from each nation, to revise the work of its predecessor. In the end, a very mild document containing only seven reform decrees was published in 1418. This called for some stabilization of the college of cardinals, some changes in the allocation and collection of revenue, and some limitations prescribed on papal reservations and procurations. Most of the other problems needing attention, such as episcopal exemptions, reform of the law courts, dispensations and indulgences, were left to the new pope to solve. On 22 April 1418 the Council of Constance adjourned.

The Council of Basel and the Hussite Revolt

The era of conciliarism was not yet over, however. Five years later, the next council met in Pavia and then transferred to Siena. Poorly attended, the council did little more than select Basel as the site for the next council seven years later. The Council of Basel was a different matter. Suspected by the pope from the beginning, the council soon found itself on a collision course with the pontiff on almost every issue. The first act of the new pope, Eugenius IV, was to issue a bull immediately dissolving the council, which the council in turn answered by boldly reaffirming conciliar supremacy over the pope. The emperor upheld the council's position and it proceeded to the work at hand, including the Hussite problem; formulating an effective denunciation of the Jews; the question of reuniting the Latin and Greek churches, which was anxiously solicited by the Byzantine emperor; and still "the reformation of the church in head and members."

The Hussite issue was thorny and seemed to get worse each year. After the execution of Hus, Bohemia became a hotbed of discontent and hatred against Germans, emperors, nobles, clerics, papists, conciliarists, and anyone else who might have been in any way responsible for Hus's betrayal and murder. Four separate crusades were launched against the Hussites, all of them ending in disaster for the imperial forces. The wars that racked the Empire for the next thirty years were social and national as well as religious, but the Hussites did have strong religious views and were determined to stand by their beliefs against all odds. These beliefs were succinctly set forth in the Four Articles of Prague in October 1419. This document demanded (1) the sacrament in both kinds, that is, the cup as well as the bread, to be given to the laity, not just the bread as was the custom; (2) freedom of preaching in Bohemia; (3) that the clergy be removed from temporal activity; and (4) that the clergy be subject to civil law the same as the laity. Under their brilliant leader Jan Žižka, whose military genius is only beginning to be recognized by Western historians, the Czech artisan and peasant army crushed every German-papal invasion sent against it. After Žižka's death in 1424, his lieutenant, Prokop the Great, continued to lead them to victory.

But Prokop was not as successful as Žižka had been in holding the Hussites together as a single movement. From the beginning, different factions developed and soon they were fighting each other. The more conservative Utraquists (from *sub utraque specie*, meaning "both the cup and the bread") refused to go beyond Hus's moderate proposals of religious liberty and anticlericalism. The demand for the sacrament in both kinds was their trademark. The more radical Taborites, however, particularly strong among the lower classes, rejected everything in the church, both liturgy and doctrine, that could not be specifically located in the Bible. They denounced transubstantiation on the same grounds and denied the efficacy of all but two of the sacraments (baptism and the Lord's Supper). They vigorously objected to the use of Latin in the Mass, rejected the cult of the saints and with it purgatory, indulgences, and prayers for the dead. Finally, they demanded the right to choose their own priests. In economic matters, they were equally as emphatic, calling for the ending of luxurious living and the abolition of all economic activity except agriculture. It was from these Taborites that Žižka and Prokop drew their most willing and able fighters.

At the end of 1431, three months after the Czechs had destroyed an imperial army sent against them, the council invited them to Basel to discuss peace and a religious settlement. Negotiations dragged on for months without success. The Utraquists were willing to make compromises in order to reach an agreement, but the Taborites would have none of it. In Bohemia, the Hussite split soon culminated in a massive armed conflict between Utraquist and Taborite armies, numbering together over 40,000 combatants. In May 1434 the outnumbered Taborites were defeated in a bloody battle, and the way for a compromise with the council was opened. Finally, in 1436, a compact was signed, recognizing the Hussites as members of the Catholic church by conceding them the cup. The Taborites recognized no part of the compact and continued to annoy the papacy and harass the Empire for another fifteen years. Even with the Utraquists, the agreement turned out to be only a truce, but at least for the time being, attention could be turned to other vital questions.

The thorniest of these problems was the continuing division between the pope and the council, threatening a second great schism. Any actions by the council were certain to be countermanded by Eugenius IV and vice versa. From July 1433 to June 1435 the Council of Basel issued a flurry of reforming decrees, all of which in some way or another curtailed or reduced the authority and resources of the pope. Annates and chancery fees, which made up a large share of papal income, were suppressed by the council, and papal reservations were abolished. In August 1435 the council declared that all revenues to the *Camera apostolica* should be sent to the council instead of to the pope. Eugenius countered by again dissolving the council and ordering its resumption in Ferrara where he could keep it in tow. This time a majority of the delegates yielded. The translocation of the council from Basel to Ferrara in 1437 was a turning point in the history of conciliarism, for not only was it a victory for the pope over the council, it also marked the transfer of allegiance of the greatest of the conciliarists, Nicholas of Cusa, from the council to the pope. For many years, the cardinal of Cusa had been the leading spokesman of conciliarism. Now, with the reunification issue looming in importance, Cusa shifted his allegiance to Eugenius in order to promote the projected union of the eastern and western churches.

Reunion of the Latin and Greek churches had mildly interested the papacy for a century or more; now it was brought to a head by the serious Turkish threat to conquer Constantinople and overrun the rest of the Eastern empire. The problem was further compounded by the existence of the Council of Basel, which insisted on negotiating with the Greeks independently from the pope. But Eugenius was not to be bypassed. The council proposed meeting the Greek representatives in Avignon, but the pope persuaded them that Ferrara or Florence was safer. Thus, while the rump council in Basel deposed Eugenius and elected a new pope, Felix V, and Eugenius in turn excommunicated Felix and everyone left in Basel, the entourage from Constantinople, headed by the Byzantine emperor himself, John VIII Palaeologus, began arriving in Ferrara to negotiate reuniting the eastern and western churches. In this sense, the Council of Ferrara-Florence was more an ecumenical council than any had been since the formal East-West split in 1054. The necessary compromises were not easy to make, but from both sides there seemed to be more desire for agreement than ever before: from the East because of the imminent Turkish threat and the hope of securing aid in the defense of Constantinople; from the West because of the feud between papacy and council. The issues were systematically considered: the dogma of purgatory, the procession of the Holy Ghost, the use of leavened or unleavened bread in the Eucharist, and the thorny question of the primacy of the pope (the latter helped by the opportune death of the patriarch of Constantinople in June, 1439). In February 1439 the council was transferred to Florence where it continued until its triumphant conclusion in July. The decrees of union, in Latin and Greek, signed by the representatives of both sides, were publicly read in the Cathedral of Florence beneath Brunelleschi's recently completed dome.

Largely through his own diplomatic skill, Pope Eugenius had seemingly brought about a favorable settlement of the five-centuries-old dispute. It was a short-lived achievement, however, since the union was immediately repudiated by the people of the eastern church, and was rendered ineffective by western failure to comply with the military terms of the treaty. Yet the papacy profited from the negotiations, and Eugenius (with the help of conciliar bungling) discredited the theorists of conciliarism and began rehabilitating the papacy as the real head of western Christianity.

The Renaissance Papacy

Three features especially characterized the Renaissance papacy from Martin V (1417–31) to Leo X (1513–21): (1) the endeavor to win back papal ecclesiastical supremacy over the church after the era of schism and conciliarism; (2) the drastic secularization of the church as Renaissance popes competed with princes and *condottieri* in the politics of Italy; and (3) papal patronage of arts and letters during the heyday of the cultural Renaissance. The popes did not contribute or participate equally in all of these areas, but taken as a whole, the popes of the fifteenth and early sixteenth centuries did pay more attention to these three activities than any of their predecessors—or successors. Furthermore, they devoted much more energy to these activities than they did to spiritual matters.

The first few popes after the restoration of the papacy in 1417 were those hardest pressed by conciliarism yet the ones to make the most headway against it. Owing his papal tiara almost entirely to the Council of Constance, Martin V had to exercise particular caution in reclaiming the ancient role or he might have found himself in the same condition as the deposed Benedict XIII. He was additionally handicapped by the threat of the Hussite wars and the immediate stigma of the schism. Nevertheless, he did manage to survive one council without mishap and live to summon another. His successor, the young and autocratic Venetian monk Eugenius IV, achieved eminent success in his contest with the councils. The capstone was put on the new papal edifice by Pope Pius II when, in 1460, he issued the bull *Execrabilis*, anathemizing any future appeal to a council. The irony of this pronouncement was that it was made by a man who, before his elevation to the papacy, had been one of the more outspoken critics of the popes and an advocate of conciliarism.

The Papacy and Italian Politics

The preoccupation of the papacy with Italian politics was not a new thing in the fifteenth century—after all, the pope was a temporal lord as well as a religious leader—but it was unusual for the pontiff to largely abandon his other roles to play that of an ambitious Italian prince. Nevertheless, the times demanded tough-minded popes as well as princes, and Renaissance popes were a hardy lot who could deliver blows as well as take them. Martin V was confronted with the political and military problems of the Papal States as soon as he assumed office, and it was not until 1420 that through diplomacy, division, and deception, he was able to enter Rome and begin the consolidation of papal territory. Fourteen years later, Eugenius IV was expelled from the city and did not return until 1443, and then only because of a useful alliance he had made with the king of Naples.

The era of continuous and unequivocal involvement in Italian politics began with the reign of Sixtus IV (1471–84), the ambitious and unscrupulous Francesco della Rovere, who launched a period of nepotism that has never been equaled. Nepotism was a valuable tool for ambitious pontiffs who could not, as could hereditary monarchs, build a dynasty over a period of several generations. Papal dynasticism depended on having enough right people in the right places at the right times. At this strategy, Sixtus IV was a master. In quick succession, he raised five of his nefarious nephews to the cardinalate and established them in key positions of power. To twenty-eight-year-old Giuliano della Rovere (the future Pope Julius II), he gave a cardinal's hat and the jurisdiction of Bologna, Lausanne, and Constance; to Piero Riario, who rivaled the Borgias in debaucheries, he assigned the direction of papal politics until his premature death in 1474; Girolamo Riario, lord of Imola and son-in-law of the duke of Milan, he made a cardinal in 1477; Giovanni della Rovere was established as prefect of Rome; and Leonardo della Rovere, who was married to the daughter of the king of Naples, was made duke of Sora. Sixtus's foreign policy was usually directed against the Medici of Florence, but he did not neglect other vital areas, both in Italy and across the Alps.

Sixtus's Genoese successor, Innocent VIII (1482–92), also practiced nepotism and in so doing reversed most of Sixtus's policies and connections. Marrying his son to the daughter of Lorenzo de' Medici was only the first step in cementing papal relations with Florence. In 1489 Innocent promoted his fourteen-year-old nephew, Lorenzo's son, Giovanni de' Medici (the future Pope Leo X) to the cardinalate.

The most notorious result of nepotism is seen in the pontificate of the Aragonese, Rodrigo Borgia, Pope Alexander VI (1492–1503), who had

POPE SIXTUS IV APPOINTING PLATINA VATICAN LIBRARIAN. *Melozzo da Forlì shows Bartolomeo Platina kneeling before the pope, surrounded by four of the pope's nephews: Giovanni della Rovere, Girolamo Riario, Giuliano della Rovere (the future Pope Julius II), and Rafaelle Riario. (Alinari/Editorial Photocolor Archives)*

been elevated as a child-cardinal by his uncle, Calixtus III (1455–58), and who now scandalized the papacy not only by his own carnal life, but by placing his detestable son, Cesare Borgia, in a favored position in papal affairs and using him to conquer the northeastern half of the Papal States. The debauchery of the Borgia years has overshadowed the fact that Alexander VI was at the same time an effective administrator and an able diplomat.

Borgia influence ended in 1503 when the Borgias' bitterest enemy, Giuliano della Rovere, became Pope Julius II (1503–13). Of all the Renaissance pontiffs, none was so completely taken up with politics and war as was Julius II. This fiery warrior-pope led his papal armies against all foes, whether French, Spanish, Venetian, or Florentine. Yet even he found time and inclination to direct Raphael to remake the Borgia apartments and to cajole Michelangelo into painting the Sistine ceiling.

Papal Patronage

Whatever their shortcomings as men, ministers, or monarchs, the Renaissance popes helped to promote and perpetuate a remarkable cultural flowering. Starting with Martin V, they proved their patronage of Renaissance culture by sponsoring, supporting, and sometimes stimulating some of the greatest writers and artists of the age. Bracciolini, Bessarion, Alberti, Botticelli, Perugino, Valla, Ghirlandaio, Raphael, Bramante, and Michelangelo are only a few of those patronized by the papacy.

Nicholas V (1447–55) was the first real papal devotee of the "new learning" and arts, and the first to carry out an ambitious and systematic program of refinement and beautification of Rome. The Rome he found when he became pope was still a dark and dingy medieval town of dilapidated buildings and mountains of debris; "a mere cowpasture," commented one chronicle, with wolves stalking the streets. When he left it only eight years later, it had begun to take on the appearance of a thriving Renaissance city. The massive clean-up project begun by Martin V, but curtailed for fifteen years, was resumed by Nicholas. He constructed a new Vatican palace, rebuilt the Trevi fountain and other monuments, and with the advice and supervision of Leon Battista Alberti, began rebuilding Saint Peter's Cathedral. But Nicholas's most important edifice was intellectual. With his avid collecting of Greek and Latin manuscripts, documents of medieval and classical times, poetry, literature, and translations, Nicholas V began the Vatican library, his greatest heritage to the modern world. To assist him in his passion for books and learning, he employed some of the greatest minds of his day to collect, translate, and write.

Before he became Pope Pius II (1458–64), Aeneas Sylvius Piccolomini was one of the well-known humanist writers and collectors of Italy. He had studied in Florence under Francesco Filelfo and entered church

service at an early age as a secretary and humanist writer. Intelligent and witty, Aeneas Sylvius possessed his share of virtuosity as well as subtlety. As a young man, he wrote a felicitous novel called *Lucretia and Euryalus*, which in its licentiousness was typically Italian and Renaissance. Under Pope Nicholas V, he served as papal legate in Germany, where he learned much about affairs in the east and saw the first impact of the fall of Constantinople to the Turks in 1453. Historians are particularly indebted to Pius II for his delightful and informative autobiography, called the *Commentaries*. By the time he became pope, he had turned away from the looseness of his early life and devoted himself to piety and service to the church. As pope he continued to patronize artists and writers, and to augment the Vatican collections.

Sixtus IV, Alexander VI, and Julius II also contributed greatly to the advancement of Renaissance culture in Rome, although their patronage is sometimes overlooked and overshadowed by their more sensational political activities. Sixtus was a willing patron and builder whose greatest monument is the Sistine Chapel, although recent scholarship shows that he was not as munificent as he is credited with being. As pontiffs during the first two decades of the High Renaissance, Alexander and Julius were partly responsible for the shift from Florence to Rome as the center of artistic activity.

The last great papal patron of the Renaissance was Giovanni de' Medici, Pope Leo X (1513–21). Politically ambitious like his predecessor, Leo was nevertheless more content to "enjoy the papacy, since God has given it to us," (according to the Venetian ambassador) than to lead armies in combat. This was the High Renaissance, and love of life, music, literature, and art pervaded the Vatican during his tenure. But a grave lack of understanding of the religious and social problems of the time also permeated the papacy as Leo's encounter with the Augustinian monk, Martin Luther, soon disclosed.

The Church on the Eve of the Reformation

Looking back from 1517, the year Luther challenged the theologians with his *Ninety-Five Theses*, it is easy to see that the papacy had come a long way in the 100 years since the dark days of 1417 when no one knew for sure where the Holy See was located, or who, or how many, or if any popes governed the church. Since that time, the curia had been permanently returned to Rome—a larger, more cultivated and cosmopolitan Rome—and the popes had resumed their role as vicars of Christ, custodians of the words of God, and fountainheads of the priesthood. In addition, they were also the recognized rulers of an Italian principate three times as large as it had ever been before, second only to the kingdom of Naples in size and to the duchy of Milan in population.

But to an experienced eye in 1517, there was cause for concern. The victories of the papacy had not been won without cost; their gains were not without comparable losses. As popes paid greater attention to political, military, and artistic matters, they allowed abuses to go unnoticed and uncured. By Leo's time, the curia itself was as corrupt as it had been in the days of Wyclif and Hus. With corruption of the head also went decomposition of the body. Even more than in the previous century, the vices of the clergy were jubilantly revealed by reformers, satirists, lawyers, libelists, laymen, and clerics alike. Little was hidden from the public eye. These disclosures sometimes made entertaining reading, but they also signaled trouble that the papacy was unwilling or unable to face.

The Renaissance papacy had serious financial problems as well. The regular revenues consisted of *tithes*, an irregular tax on ecclesiastical incomes; *annates*, the first year's income from a newly appointed benefice; *servitia*, or services collected from the various candidates for office; *procurations*, charges made for the visitations of bishops and archdeacons; *sealing* and *registry* for the bestowal of benefices (the *pallium*, for example, paid by archbishops for their symbol of authority); *medii fructus*, or the income from vacant benefices; and the sale of offices and other "free will" offerings. Of growing importance in the fifteenth century were certain irregular sources of income, such as dispensations, issued on payment of fees for all manner of breaches of canon and moral law, and indulgences. Added to these was the "temporal" income from the overlordship of Rome and the Papal States, including profits from the Tolfa alum mines. But still the papacy suffered from a chronic financial crisis that grew worse each year. Financing a huge institution, paying salaries, building churches and monasteries would not have been easy in any time. But the Renaissance popes encumbered the church with such massive new expenditures—increased luxury and pomp, patronage of art, and above all the enormous cost of war—that they were hard-pressed to find resources to meet their needs.

Many new problems had also arisen over which the papacy had relatively little control. The growing power and influence of national monarchies, for example, placed additional pressures on the papacy and added to its dangers. Relations between the Holy See and the king of France were strained most of the time, and during the pontificates of Pius II and Sixtus IV, their quarrels reached the point of open hostility. Louis XI restored the Pragmatic Sanction in 1463, making himself the virtual master of the church in France. In the war following the Pazzi conspiracy, the French king sided with Lorenzo de' Medici against the pope and even cut off the flow of money to Rome for ecclesiastical benefices. After the French invasion of Italy in 1494, the papacy was at war with France most of the time. Except during the pontificate of Alexander VI (1492–1503), relations with Castile and Aragon were also frequently abrasive, even when they were partners in the campaign against the Moors of Granada. At best, relations between the Renaissance papacy and the national states were secular and diplomatic, with arrangements regarding pensions, appointments, and privileges being worked out between them on an *ad hoc* basis. The effect of this was to put national ecclesiastical patronage predominantly in the hands of the princes, while the papacy retained the right of confirmation and the collection of annates and other fees.

Regionalism within the church was another cause of difficulty. Gallicanism, as expressed in French clerical independence, was repeated in the attitude of princes and prelates in other countries. By the sixteenth century, the Spanish church had succeeded in winning a large degree of autonomy from Rome, including the independent Spanish Inquisition and the *Patronato Real* (Royal Patronage) which gave the ruler of Castile final ecclesiastical authority in the New World. In Germany, distrust and hatred of the papacy was especially strong, partly because of a long tradition of rivalry between popes and emperors, more immediately because of the lack of national controls or limitations on papal intervention in the Empire. In place of imperial regulation, however, the church in Germany was largely dominated by the princes and magnates who played the key role in imperial politics. Uppermost among these were several powerful German bishops and archbishops whose policies were seldom any more helpful to the church than they were to the Empire. In this touchy situation, it boded no good to have the papacy increase its interference with elections to bishoprics and other offices in the German states, and to continue to misuse papal courts in Germany.

Fundamental changes in the relationship between faith and creed were also taking place in the late fifteenth century, as were the devotional needs of the people. More and more, faith was being directed toward belief in the imminent coming of Christ. This conviction gave rise to a devotional urgency that had not been seen in the church for over 200 years. Aware of the uncertainty of life and the nearness of death, the people increased their ardor for meaningful religious expression. But the church as an institution seemed unable to satisfy the spiritual or social needs of all its people. Conditions were ripening for a major religious upheaval.

Suggestions for Further Reading

AVIGNON AND THE GREAT SCHISM

The standard work on the Avignon papacy is Guillaume Mollat, *The Popes of Avignon, 1305–1368*, tr. by Janet Love (New York, 1963). Yves Renouard, *The Avignon Papacy, 1305–1403*, tr. by Denis Bethell (Hamden, 1970) is another broad survey. J. B. Morrall, *Gerson and the Great Schism* (Cambridge, Mass., 1960) is an important work on the schism. The most recent, and in some ways most penetrating, inquiry is R. N. Swanson, *Universities, Academics and the Great Schism* (New York, 1979). Peter Partner reveals his usual perceptivity and insight in *The Lands of St. Peter: The Papal State in the Middle Ages and the Early Renaissance* (Berkeley, 1972).

ABUSES, REFORM, AND HERESY

Gordon Leff, *Heresy in the Later Middle Ages, c. 1250–c. 1450*, 2 vols. (New York, 1967) is a valuable study of hetrodoxy and heresy. Also John Stephens, "Heresy in Medieval and Renaissance Florence," *Past & Present*, 54 (1972), 25–60, and Richard Kieckhefer, "Radical Tendencies in the Flagellant Movement of the Mid-Fourteenth Century," *Journal of Medieval and Renaissance Studies*, 4 (1974), 157–76. On Wyclif and Hus, see William Cook, "John Wyclif and Hussite Theology," *Church History*, 42 (1973), 335–49, and Matthew Spinka, *John Hus, A Biography* (Princeton, 1968). Spinka's translation of Peter of Mladoňovice's account of the trial and condemnation of Hus, in *John Hus at the Council of Constance* (New York, 1965), is revealing. Heiko Oberman, *The Harvest of Medieval Theology* (Cambridge, Mass., 1963), an analysis of Gabriel Biel and the Nominalists, and *Forerunners of the Reformation* (New York, 1966), are both very useful. R. R. Post, *The Modern Devotion: Confrontation with Reformation and Humanism* (Leiden, 1968) is a somewhat revisionist view of the Brethren of the Common Life. Charles Trinkhaus (ed.), *The Pursuit of Holiness in Late Medieval and Renaissance Religion* (Leiden, 1974), is the result of a conference held at the University of Michigan.

THE JEWS IN RENAISSANCE EUROPE

Cecil Roth, *The Jews in the Renaissance* (Philadelphia, 1964) is the standard account. His *A History of the Marranos*, 3rd ed. (New York, 1966) and *History of* the *Jews in Venice* (New York, 1975) are also first-rate studies. There is much of value in S. Dubnow, *History of the Jews: From the Later Middle Ages to the Renaissance,* vol. 5, rev. ed. (New York, 1969), and especially Moses A. Shulvass's superb *The Jews in the World of the Renaissance* (Leiden, 1973). Jacob Katz, *Tradition and Crisis: Jewish Society at the End of the Middle Ages* (New York, 1971) is a detailed internal examination of Jewish life. On the *Marranos,* in addition to Roth, see Benzion Netanyahu, *The Marranos of Spain from the Late XIV to the Early XVI Century, According to Contemporary Hebrew Sources* (Millwood, 1966, 1972).

CONCILIARISM AND THE COUNCIL OF CONSTANCE

According to Brian Tierney, *Foundation of the Conciliar Theory* (Cambridge, 1955), the origin of conciliarism was the late-medieval canonists. The phenomenon can be further studied in E. F. Jacob, *Essays in the Conciliar Epoch,* rev. ed. (South Bend, 1963); A. J. Black, *Monarchy and Community: Political Ideas in the Later Conciliar Controversy, 1430–1450* (Cambridge, 1970); and James E. Biechler, "Nicholas of Cusa and the End of the Conciliar Movement," *Church History,* 44 (1975), 5–21. L. Loomis, *The Council of Constance,* edited by J. H. Mundy and D. M. Woody (New York, 1961) is a valuable source on the council.

THE HUSSITE REVOLT

Frederick G. Heymann, *John Žižka and the Hussite Revolution* (Princeton, 1955) is slightly dated but still indispensable. It should be supplemented by his *George of Bohemia, King of Heretics* (Princeton, 1965); Josef Macek, *The Hussite Movement in Bohemia* (London, 1965); Howard Kaminsky, *A History of the Hussite Revolution* (Berkeley, 1967); and, most recently, John M. Klassen, *The Nobility and the Making of the Hussite Revolution* (New York, 1978). Otakar Odložilik, *The Hussite King: Bohemia in European Affairs, 1440–1471* (New Brunswick, 1965), studies the reign of George of Poděbrady, king of Bohemia.

THE RENAISSANCE PAPACY

Peter Partner, *The Papal State under Martin V* (London, 1958) is the only study of the pontificate of Martin V. On Eugenius IV, see Joseph Gill, *Eugenius IV: Pope of Christian Union* (Westminster, 1961). The best on Pius II are Robert Schwoebel, "Pius II and the Renaissance Papacy," in *Renaissance Men and Ideas* (New York, 1971), 67–80, and R. J. Mitchell, *The Laurels and the Tiara: Pope Pius II, 1458–1464* (New York, 1963). Pius II's own *Memoirs of a Renaissance Pope* (New York, 1962), an abridged version of *The Commentaries of Pius II,* tr. by F. A. Gragg and ed. by L. C. Gabel, gives a delightful inside view of the Renaissance papacy. Nothing comparable to the above exists for Nicholas V, Calixtus III, Innocent VIII, or Julius II. Egmont Lee's recent *Sixtus IV and Men of Letters* (Rome, 1978) calls Sixtus "a parvenu in cultural matters" rather than a real patron. On the Borgia dynasty, see Michael Mallet, *The Borgias* (Toronto and New York, 1969), a sound and unbiased account. Thomas N. Tentler, *Sin and Confession on the Eve of the Reformation* (Princeton, 1977) discusses some of the problems in the Renaissance church.

CHAPTER EIGHT

The States of Europe: Government and Society

T HE EUROPEAN WORLD at the end of the fifteenth
century was complex and varied. Its topography
and soil ranged from the arid deserts of La Mancha
in Spain and the dry mountains of Greece to the
rain-drenched lowlands of Holland and the ver-
dant, snow-covered Alpine slopes cutting across
Europe from east to west. The Alps had always
held a key place in the history of Europe and were
never more important than during the Renaissance, when they signified to Italians the boundary between civilization and barbarity, and to
northern Europeans the division between virtue
and all manner of vice. Before the end of the fifteenth century, there had been considerable intercourse between Italy and the rest of Europe—
economic, political, intellectual, and religious—
but there was still very little understanding. By the
end of the fifteenth century, these barriers were
rapidly crumbling as European armies turned the
peninsula into a half-century battleground and as
Italian artists, poets, and scholars helped shape
new cultures beyond the Alps.

Europe Beyond the Alps

What, then, was this Europe of the late fifteenth
and early sixteenth centuries like? Who were its
people, and how were they governed? First of all,
it was a relatively populated area. At the beginning of the sixteenth century, Europe between the

Atlantic and the Carpathian-Dniester-Vistula line was composed of some 75 million people living in an area of slightly over 1 million square miles. Since the devastations of the Black Death in the mid-fourteenth century, the population had recovered considerably but probably did not yet equal that of the early 1300s. Yet, despite its small area, Europe in the sixteenth century was very large in terms of human geography. Transportation was slow and hazardous, communications sporadic and uncertain. In terms of the time required to cross it, the Europe of the early 1500s was considerably larger than the entire world today. Had it not been for the numerous inland water routes, it would have been larger still.

The urban life that we saw in Renaissance Italy did not exist in any other part of Europe, although town and city growth was one of the distinguishing characteristics of the time. By far the largest percentage of people still lived outside the cities, in thousands of small villages and hamlets. But this condition was slowly changing by the end of the fifteenth century. City growth was noticeably rapid along the water trade routes in the Netherlands, on the Baltic coast, and along the Rhine and Danube rivers. Southern Germany was an area of many rich and ancient cities whose importance increased with the growth of trade between northern Europe and Italy, as did those of Flanders and Brabant, where the northern cloth trade had its center. Danzig on the Baltic and Ragusa on the Adriatic were also flourishing commercial ports.

Spain, too, was a country of numerous cities, many of which still religiously guarded their medieval charters, or *fueros*, of privileges and freedoms. But urban life did not expand noticeably in Castile and Aragon during the fifteenth century, and there was some decline in the eastern regions of Catalonia and Valencia. In England, London experienced its first prolonged period of population growth in the fifteenth century, although many famous medieval cities showed no sign of expansion for another 200 years. Paris did not yet dominate the cultural, economic, and political life of France as it has since the seventeenth century; however, with its convenient location along the Seine, Marne, and Oise waterways, it was destined to play an important role, along with Lyon, Marseille, Bordeaux, and La Rochelle, as Europe's commercial center gradually shifted from the Mediterranean to the Atlantic seaboard.

Within the radius of the Christian commonwealth, many types and philosophies of government prevailed. We have already examined in some detail the city-states of central and northern Italy. But in the broader picture, that development was unique. The southern German cities were independent of princely control and exercised almost unlimited authority over their respective populations; but their jurisdiction, with few exceptions, extended only to the city walls and did not serve as a force for continuous political rivalry and territorial expansion. A characteristic of German towns was to band together in confederations or leagues, such as the Hansa, the Swabian League, and the

Rhenish League, for the protection of their political and economic independence. But this did not lead to the consolidation of territorial power in the Italian manner. Politically, Europe was a patchwork of overlapping personal and institutional jurisdictions ranging in size from a castle courtyard overlooking the Rhine to the vast domain of the king of Poland. East of the Rhine, feudalism still dominated the social and political pattern; but by the end of the fifteenth century, several European monarchs had successfully expanded the area and range of their dominion and consolidated their power within that domain. This was the most fertile period in the emergence of the national, territorial state.

The Revival of France

For most of the time between 1350 and 1450, large areas of France were under English occupation. The French monarchy was weak and ineffective (except during the reign of Charles "the Wise," 1364–80), and the institutions of government were in chaos. The situation was made even worse by the disruptive rivalries of the powerful noble families of Anjou, Berry, Orléans, and Burgundy, who undermined the royal government. When the English were finally expelled from France and the Hundred Years' War ended, a new era began in the evolution of the French nation. But the war had left France prostrate. The population had declined during those years—especially between 1360 and 1430—and much of the formerly fertile countryside was left desolate. Furthermore, the independent power and privileges of the French nobility made royal domination uneven at best and impossible at worst. The dukes of Brittany and Burgundy, for example, were completely independent of royal jurisdiction as late as 1477, and all of the nobility possessed varying degrees of judicial and administrative autonomy. They were not only able to command the loyalty and services of numerous knights and retainers, they were also exempt from direct taxation by the government.

Nevertheless, in two important ways, Louis XI (1461–83) and his successors held a unique advantage in their struggle with the nobility and against other rival princes. During the last phase of the Hundred Years' War, the Estates General had granted the king the right to collect, by his own authority and without summoning a meeting of the estates, an annual direct tax known as the *taille*. This was retained after the war, and under Louis XI it became a permanent tax imposed by royal authority. The importance of this independent source of revenue, over and above the normal feudal levies authorized to the king, can hardly be overemphasized. With it, the king of France was able to meet the rising costs of administration and war without selling his soul either to the nobles or to the estates, and he could also acquire the skeleton of a standing army. Louis XI was the first Renaissance king able to afford the large-scale employment of cast-bronze cannons in a field army.

Under the "Spider King," Louis XI, France began to take on the shape of a Renaissance monarchy. Louis was an unattractive personality, unscrupulous and suspicious, but he was at the same time a clever, calculating, and effective ruler. Unpretentious in dress and demeanor—occasionally mistaken for a servant or gardener—Louis was a diligent and practical man who laid the foundation on which subsequent French kings could build. The greatest obstacles to his statebuilding were the great nobles, such as "Good King René" of Anjou, who controlled Maine and Anjou as well as Bar and Provence in the south, a vassal of the king but also his uncle; Duke Francis II of Brittany; Philip "the Good," duke of Burgundy, and his son, Charles "the Bold"; the duke of Bourbon; and Louis d'Orléans, whose grandmother Valentina Visconti gave him a claim to the duchy of Milan. Louis XI gradually wrested some of the political and economic control from the nobles and let it fall into the eager hands of the bourgeoisie. But he made the mistake of trying to reduce the nobles all at once. They responded with insurrection (known as the War of the Common Weal); but through skillful management and manipulation, Louis succeeded in putting down the revolt and emerged from the ordeal stronger than before—except that he was forced to grant the nobles perpetual exemption from the *taille*.

Even then, Louis XI's financial position by the middle of his reign was enviable. The ordinary revenues of the crown consisted primarily of income from crown lands, the *demesne*, tenants' dues of various kinds, and judicial income from court fines, confiscated estates, letters of pardon, ennoblement, legitimation, and so forth. In addition to this personal income of the king were the extraordinary revenues developed over the years. Among these were indirect taxes such as *aides*, or excises on the sale of goods; duties and tolls levied on the transit of goods from province to province; and the *gabelle*, the hated but lucrative salt tax, assessed as a crown monopoly on the sale of salt. In the fourteenth century, the French kings also acquired from the papacy the *régale*, or income from vacant ecclesiastical benefices. Finally, the *taille*, a variable direct tax, usually on land or property, occasionally a head tax, sometimes amounted to as much as all the other levies combined. Laboring as they did under all these taxes, the financial burden on the French peasants was extremely heavy. These revenues gave the French king a much greater income than his neighbors had, and thereby, an important margin of advantage over them. By 1475 he had secured his position sufficiently to give primary attention to his most dangerous vassal and rival, Charles the Bold, duke of Burgundy.

The Burgundian Challenge

The case of Burgundy in the middle of the fifteenth century is interesting and instructive. Charles the Bold, duke of Burgundy, was the most colorful ruler of the century, but when pitted against the institutionalized and systematic intrigues of the French monarch, his

COURT OF THE DUKE OF BURGUNDY. *Seated on his throne at left is Duke Charles the Bold receiving a copy of Commines'* Memoires. *This miniature is taken from an early edition of Commines. (Bibliothèque Nationale, Paris)*

medieval knight-errantry seemed anachronistic. By various separate titles, some inherited from his illustrious father, Philip the Good, others acquired by himself, Charles the Bold possessed some of the richest territories in Europe, including the duchy of Burgundy in France, the free county of Burgundy (Franche-Comté) lying within the Holy Roman Empire, Luxembourg, upper Alsace, and most of the Netherlands. During the half century following the Hundred Years' War, the dukes of Burgundy were perhaps the strongest rulers in Europe. But their domains were not united or their power complete. Charles would not be contented until he could humble his arch-rival, the king of France, and carve out of central Europe a Burgundian kingdom that would be respected and honored by all the world. Already his court at Bruges, in Flanders, was the richest and most garish in Europe, boasting the most famous nonroyal order of knighthood on the continent—the Order of the Golden Fleece. If he could enclose the territories lying between Burgundy and Luxembourg, fill out the Netherlands, and perhaps acquire additional holdings in the Rhineland, Charles would indeed be a monarch, ruling a wealthy and populous kingdom.

But not all Renaissance monarchies materialized. Alarmed by the pretensions of the chivalrous duke and incited by the stealthy diplomacy of Louis XI, the duke of Lorraine, along with many of the Rhineland towns, formed an alliance with the wary Swiss against Burgundian encroachment. During the autumn of 1476, in a series of encounters with the ferocious Swiss pikemen at Grandson and Murten (Murat), the Burgundian knights were defeated, and in January, 1477, Charles him-

France and Burgundy

French Crown Lands in 1461

Seized by Louis XI in 1477

Added to French Crown, 1477-83

Added by Charles VIII and Louis XII, 1483-1515

Added by Francis I, 1515-47

Burgundy in 1477

Added by Charles V

Lost to France in 1477

Held briefly, then lost to other nobles

Under Burgundian influence

—— Boundary of the Holy Roman Empire

Bishoprics of:
1 Metz
2 Toul
3 Verdun

✗ Sites of battles

HOLLAND
UTRECHT GUELDERLAND
ZEELAND
BRABANT
Calais
Bruges
FLANDERS
ARTOIS
LIÈGE
Limburg
HAINAUT
NAMUR
PICARDY
Amiens
LUXEMBOURG
Rouen
VALOIS
NORMANDY
Reims
Paris
CHAMPAGNE
3
1
BAR
2
1
Strasbourg
Nancy
MAINE
NEMOURS
LORRAINE
ORLEANS
BRITTANY
ANJOU
BLOIS
Nantes
TOURAINE
Dijon
FRANCHE-COMTÉ
BERRY
NEVERS
BURGUNDY
✗ Murten
Poitiers
Grandson
POITOU
BOURBON
LA MARCHE
ANGOULÊME
Lyon
LIMOGES
AVERGNE
Grenoble
Bordeaux
GUYENNE
DAUPHINÉ
ALBRET
RODEZ
AVIGNON
ARMAGNAC
TOULOUSE
Toulouse
LANGUEDOC
PROVENCE
BÉARN
Marseille
FOIX
Narbonne
Montpellier
ROUSSILLON

Rhine R.

self was killed in battle at Nancy. Since he had no male heir, Charles's French territories (primarily the duchy of Burgundy) reverted to the French crown. But the marriage of his daughter, Mary, to Maximilian of Austria, son of the Holy Roman Emperor Frederick III, prevented Franche-Comté and Flanders from also falling into French hands.

The Consolidation of France

Before Louis himself died in 1483, he had recovered the counties of Picardy and Artois and received by *escheat* (the reversion of a fief to the crown if its holder died without a legitimate heir) the provinces of Anjou, Maine, Bar, and Provence. Of the major nobles who owed some degree of fealty to the French crown, only the duke of Brittany still stood completely outside the royal jurisdiction, although there remained some smaller enclaves of non-French territory within the exterior boundaries of France, and some provinces in which the king's authority was severely limited. The problem of Brittany was temporarily solved by Louis's son Charles VIII (1438–98) who married Anne of Brittany, heiress to the duchy. When Charles died eight years later, his Orléanist cousin and successor, Louis XII (1498–1515), quickly repudiated his own wife and married Anne himself, thus continuing the containment of Brittany for another generation.

Next to the king, the most important organ of French government was the Royal Council, composed of the princes of the blood, the peers of the realm, and additional members as the king saw fit to appoint. The body was obviously too large, numbering some sixty or more during the reign of Louis XI, but was reduced to manageable size by Charles VIII and Louis XII. Some of the more contentious litigation was handled by a subcommittee of the council. The three estates of France (the clergy, the nobility, and the rest of the population) were represented in the Estates General, which was summoned, as was the Parliament of England, at the wishes of the king. In both cases the organ was still in its developmental stage, and it was too soon to say whether it would become a more powerful or a less significant part of the government. Monarchs in the past had summoned the Estates General to grant taxes, ratify treaties, and advise the king on whatever matters he put to them. But with the evolution of the *taille* the necessity for frequent convocation was reduced. Charles VIII's Estates General of 1484, which chose to criticize and oppose the king rather than support him, was the last to meet for seventy-five years. In the meantime, provincial estates continued to function throughout the sixteenth century.

The chancellor of France was the highest judicial officer of the crown. His appointment was for life, and during the Renaissance he became an important and influential man. The *parlements* were the principal judicial and administrative organs in the provinces. During the second half of the fifteenth century, these bodies had been established in Languedoc, Dauphiné, Guyenne, and Burgundy. Louis XII instituted them in Provence and Normandy. The Parlement de Paris occupied a special position in that it constituted the highest judicial tribunal in the kingdom, and it legalized royal edicts and decrees by registering them in its records. Its full potential as a restraint on the power of the king was not realized until later. Other offices of administration, many of them created or regularized by the organizational ordinances of 1498–99, such as secretaries of state, masters of request, and the superintendent of finance, rounded out the important governing machinery of Renaissance France.

This imposing structure, however, should not lead us to assume that by 1500 the French crown had achieved the "absolute" monarchy that has so often been attributed to it. Despite its undeniable achievements and advantages, the French monarchy of the Renaissance was still limited in several important ways. The French nation was made up of numerous corporations and institutionalized bodies, from sovereign courts and *seigneurial* (semi-independent) towns to the provincial nobility and the Gallican church. Every estate and order religiously guarded its privileges and exemptions against encroachments from any direction, especially from the king. The legal actions of the monarch were circumscribed within well-defined limits and conditions. In addition, no Renaissance king was able to exercise the full powers he legally possessed. The delays of travel and inadequacy of communications saw to that. Furthermore, the bureaucratic machinery and administrative organization of the time was entirely inadequate for making any king absolute. Nevertheless, when the dashing young Count d'Angoulême became King Francis I in 1515, he ruled the largest single kingdom in Europe—numbering between twelve and fifteen million subjects—whose geographical location and natural resources promised to make Francis not only the wealthiest but the most powerful monarch in Christendom.

Francis I: The Chivalrous King

Francis I (1515–47) was a flamboyant and colorful monarch, exemplifying the "Renaissance prince." He was an exuberant, well-proportioned, and chivalrous king who loved the rigors and excitement of the hunt and the spectacle and grandeur of the tournament. But his physical prowess was not just for sport or for show. He was also a skillful and eager warrior. Loving combat, he was seldom more in his element than when leading a cavalry charge against a real enemy. His reign began in the glory and excitement of military victory at Marignano in northern Italy.

Yet *le roi chevalier* was also the most generous and sympathetic patron of art, literature, and building in Renaissance France, and the personification of its spirit. Under Francis I, the French royal court surpassed the Burgundian in brilliance, gaiety, and display. The most beautiful and original of the Renaissance chateaux were built for Francis I. He invited some of the greatest Italian humanists, artists, and thinkers to France to stimulate and inspire the arts in his country. He also patronized promising French artists and men of letters, and made the humanist Guillaume Budé master of the royal library. Francis's thirst for books was insatiable, although he read very little himself. He bought them whenever he could, and even commissioned his ambassadors at foreign courts to keep their eyes open for new books and manuscripts that he might acquire. Perhaps recognizing his own intellectual inferiority, the king became the leading benefactor of culture outside of Italy.

But Francis was not all congeniality and benevolence. He was also a hardened and wary strategist by the time he was twenty, fully able to compete in the jungle of sixteenth-century international affairs. Opportunist enough to make the most of his resources, he was likewise cynical enough to be wary of the craftiness of others. Although unhampered by overly cumbersome principles, Francis was not without objectives and goals in his foreign policy, though at times the goals may have had a very limited and personal range. With the potential power at his command, he hoped to regain all rights, incomes, or possessions to which he had some legal claim. Beyond that, he saw in the encircling and strangling arms of the Habsburg-Burgundian-Spanish empire an immediate and deadly threat to France, which he felt compelled to break at any cost.

Francis was brought up by a devoted mother, Louise of Savoy, and a loyal older sister, Marguerite d'Angoulême, the cultured queen of

FRANCIS I ABOUT 1525. *This famous Louvre portrait of the French king, by Jean Clouet, shows him at the height of his power (probably prior to the battle of Pavia) dressed in the royal silks and satins. (Photographie Giraudon)*

Navarre, who gave him both affection and a feeling for refinement. He was not without male companions as he grew up, but in their role as competing sons of rival nobles, they never became more than playmates or adversaries to the young Count d'Angoulême. As a boy, Francis had never learned to trust men, and he could not bring himself to change as a king. He had counselors, secretaries, and favorites enough, but he never listened to them for very long. He was much more amenable to the counsels of his mother, sister, wives (Claude, heiress of Brittany, and after her death, Eleanor of Austria), or mistresses, Françoise de Chateaubriand and the duchess d'Estampes.

By nature and tradition, Francis I was the typical autocrat, and continued to build the strong state bequeathed him by his predecessors. Few structural changes were made during his reign, but he did revive the office of constable—the supreme military officer of the realm—and began the development of the secretaries of state, who were destined to play a leading role in French affairs later in the century. Francis reduced the independent authority of the Gallican church early in his reign (along with that of the *parlements*), taking over many of its functions himself. Nevertheless, although he was tolerant of reformers and sympathetic to the humanists, he remained a staunch Catholic and strengthened royal ties with the papacy. His subsequent negotiations and alliances with the German Lutherans and the Ottoman Turks were for political and commercial reasons. In terms of religion, as well as politics and culture, Francis I was the French king *par excellence*.

England and Scotland

By the end of the fifteenth century, although still a small country of no more than three million people, England was on its way to becoming a stable and relatively integrated national monarchy. This trend was of recent origin, however, since most of the century had been spent in chaotic domestic disturbances and endemic war with France. The final failure of the English kings to make good their claims to the throne of France in the latter phases of the Hundred Years' War led to disillusionment and upheaval at home. Unable to content themselves with peaceful pursuits, the restless nobility were soon at one another's throats, while the excitable masses rose in Cade's Rebellion (1450) against corruption and the chaotic conditions of government. Many of the great nobles returned from the French wars with numerous private armed retainers owing them fealty and homage, which they continued to hold and use against their rivals and enemies at home. The result was a degeneration and disorder such as had not been seen in England since the dark days of Henry III's reign.

The civil turmoil, known as the Wars of the Roses, not only pitted the houses of Lancaster and York against each other but also sucked in most of the aristocratic families of England. When Henry Tudor, duke of Richmond, defeated the last Yorkish king, Richard III, at Bosworth Field in 1485, no one knew that the convulsive Wars of the Roses had come to an end and that a new era was dawning in England. It was in fact several years before Henry felt secure on the throne (although he was of Lancastrian descent, had married the Yorkist heiress Elizabeth of York, daughter of Edward IV, and had had Parliament declare him king), and many more years before the final plot against his reign was squelched. Although there were still many overlapping jurisdictions and corporate limitations on his authority by the end of Henry VII's reign, the first Tudor king nevertheless succeeded in reducing the internal disorders and threats to the crown and establishing a respected and strong monarchical government.

England under Henry VII

Early in his reign, Henry VII launched a frontal attack on the feudal privileges of the English nobility, now obviously weakened by the civil wars. He established the Court of Star Chamber, a government-controlled court pronouncing jurisdiction over the hitherto unrestrained nobles, and used it to suppress much of their irresponsible activity. The court was actually an older institution, but Henry revived it after he came to the throne, giving it statutory authority and the full support of the crown to enforce the law. Its judges were members of the Privy Council, hand-picked for their ability and integrity. Punishment meted out to the barons by Star Chamber usually consisted of heavy fines rather than the death penalty. To consolidate and strengthen the monarchy, Henry needed money and loyalty more than blood. Through the judicious use of Star Chamber, he also confiscated the lands and wealth of many recalcitrant peers and, by abolishing "livery and maintenance" (the practice by wealthy nobles of maintaining private armies of followers who committed themselves to their lord's service), deprived them of their medieval privilege and ability to wage private war. When an army was needed in an emergency to put down conspiracies or disorders, Henry issued Commissions of Array to trusted nobles. These commissions authorized raising a specified number of men for use in a given campaign. When their purpose was fulfilled, the troops were disbanded.

The king recognized that the perennial weakness of the feudal monarchy was its complete dependence on the nobility for military support. But he also knew that money could buy strength and that with sufficient regular income the crown could largely emancipate itself. Henry VII's success in acquiring such funds, without at the same time overburdening and alienating the gentry and middle class from which he drew much of his support, was one of his foremost accomplishments. Henry made very few innovations in the financial structure of the crown. He did, however, make it function more efficiently, and he drastically reduced unnecessary expenditures. By enlarging crown holdings, expanding the income from punitive justice, and increasing the revenues from the customs duties on expanded foreign commerce, he was able to meet his growing expenses without frequently summoning Parliament to grant him funds.

English commercial activities—especially the vital wool trade with Flanders—involved Henry in an entangling and sometimes precarious foreign policy. But, unlike some of his contemporaries, he was able to wade through relatively unscathed and at times even make some profits from his continental rivals and allies. In 1489 Henry concluded the Treaty of Medina del Campo with Ferdinand of Aragon, committing the English king to join in war against France, but also bringing Henry a financial subsidy and a handsome dowry for the marriage of his eldest son, Arthur, to Ferdinand's daughter, Catherine. The favorable conclusion of valuable commercial treaties with the Burgundian Netherlands, the successful marriage alliances with Scotland, and the growing prestige of England in European affairs, all attest to Henry's diplomatic ability. When the fifty-two-year-old king died in 1509, he left to his son, Henry VIII, a stable and prosperous government with a degree of unity and strength unrealized by any of his predecessors.

Scotland

Since 1314 Scotland had been an independent country. Independent, that is, from the previous domination of English lords and kings, but not freed from the ravages of Scottish nobles, nor from financial and military dependence on other rulers. For half a century, the crown was thrown about among rival clans until the Stuart line was established by the accession of Robert II in 1371. Fearing the encroachment of England, the Scottish rulers turned to France for support and began the two-century commitment of Scottish affairs to the foreign policy of France. Based primarily on aristocratic acceptance of the rule of the king, governmental institutions were less sophisticated in Scotland than in England. A rudimentary parliament developed in the fourteenth and fifteenth centuries along the lines of its English counterpart, but it was less an instrument of royal control. The lesser knights as well as the great nobles preferred to maintain their individual independence from the crown as much as possible. In 1499 Henry VII attempted to wean the Scots away from their French allegiance by proposing the marriage of his daughter, Margaret, to the Scottish king, James IV (1473–1513). It was the beginning of the last and most tumultuous stage of Anglo-Scottish relations.

Henry VIII: The Impetuous Monarch

Upon his accession in 1509, Henry VIII (1509–47) showed promise of becoming England's greatest king. Unlike his shrewd and calculating father, Henry was carefree, outgoing, glamorous, and affable. At just under eighteen years of age, he was also handsome, robust, and ath-

HENRY VIII. *This portrait by the Antwerp painter Joos van Cleve shows the English king in the vigor of his reign, probably before his break with Rome. (By permission of Her Majesty, Queen Elizabeth II)*

letic. In addition, he was a competent musician, a fair writer, intelligent and well-read both in theology and in the "new learning," and a devoted patron of the arts. The transition to the new reign was without the usual bloodshed of English successions (except for the trumped-up execution of Henry VII's fiscal judges, Epson and Dudley, but they were unpopular anyway and their murder only increased Henry's popularity). The coronation was accompanied by the greatest rejoicing and merriment. Henry reaffirmed his father's alliance with Spain by immediately marrying Catherine of Aragon, who was crowned Queen of England. The people rejoiced. Prospects for the future had seldom looked better.

But Henry VIII possessed other traits too, and these were soon to dominate his reign. Overbearing and dogmatic, the king's obsessive willpower and compulsive vanity prevented him from seeing many of the real needs of the country, and drove him to launch other enterprises that were intended only to enhance his image and glory. Along with a lifelong jealousy of Francis I, these traits also caused him to become implicated in the disastrous European wars and to exhaust the treasury left to him before he had been on the throne two years. He could also be petty and cruel, as his later domestic affairs would show, and at all times he was unscrupulously ambitious. He could brook no competition and no opposition. Enthralled with the privileges and prerogatives of kingship, Henry was nevertheless unwilling to devote the time, energy, or thought to fulfilling its responsibilities. Administration bored him, so he turned much of it over to his remarkably competent ministers.

Few monarchs, however, have been more successful in symbolizing the office and power of kingship through its embodiment in a single person. Henry had no peer in projecting his personal image as monarch and tying them together in the minds of his subjects. He was a great showman as well as opportunist and successfully combined his personal ambition and exalted view of kingship into a symbol of power and authority that made an indelible impression on his country and on the entire age.

The concept of monarchy by Divine right certainly was not alien to Henry VIII's mind and temperament. Nevertheless, he was not completely master of his own destiny. No one can deny that he held the right of final decision in all matters whether domestic or foreign, but it is also evident that sometimes the ideas or initiative for many of those decisions came from the ministers and not from the king. This may account for much of the drastic fluctuation in foreign policy during his reign or even his kaleidoscopic family affairs. It is certainly strongly intimated in the frequent upheavals of his administrative and advisory councils. The contrasting minds and philosophies of his great ministers, Cardinal Wolsey, Sir Thomas More, and Thomas Cromwell, are discernible in the policies of their respective administrations. But their sudden and calamitous fall also suggests that Henry listened to other, less competent, voices as well. Yet through it all remains the profound imprint of Henry VIII's impetuous personality and will.

Spain under Ferdinand and Isabel

The process of unification in Spain proceeded along very different lines than it did in either England or France. Modern Spain emerged from a conjunction of various peninsular powers, each of which possessed its own institutions, laws, and monarchs, whereas France and England were created from the expansion and strengthening of their respective political centers.

During the course of the Middle Ages, the kingdoms of Galicia, Asturias, León, and Castile had at different times merged to form the large kingdom of Castile, covering the whole central plateau and all of north-central and northwestern Spain. To the east, the kingdom of Aragon was composed of the institutionally separate realms of Aragon, Catalonia, and Valencia. Northward lay the saddleback kingdom of Navarre and in the far south the Moslem kingdom of Granada. In the west was the rival monarchy of Portugal, which was rapidly consolidating its own autonomy under the Avis dynasty (1385–1580) and becoming a power to be reckoned with, especially after the wealth of the East Indies began flowing into Lisbon. Under João II (1481–95) and

Spain During the Reconquest

The Christian reconquest:

• • • • • by 1037

+ + + by 1100

•+•+• by 1200

———— by 1264

Kingdoms in 1500:

Portugal

Castile

Navarre

Aragon

FRANCE

La Coruña
Santiago de Compostela
GALICIA
Oviedo
Santander
ASTURIAS
ALAVA
Pamplona
NAVARRE
León
Burgós
Ebro R.
LEÓN
OLD CASTILE
Zaragoza
CATALONIA
Barcelona
ARAGON
Tarragona
Oporto
Duero R.
Tordesillas
Valladolid
Medina del Campo
Salamanca
Segovia
Ávila
Alcalá
Madrid
Teruel
Coimbra
Toledo
VALENCIA
PORTUGAL
Tagus (Tajo) R.
NEW CASTILE
Valencia
LA MANCHA
Gandia
Lisbon
ESTREMADURA
Guadiana R.
MURCIA
Murcia
Córdoba
Guadalquivir R.
ALGARVE
ANDALUSIA
Seville
Granada
MOSLEM
K. OF
GRANADA
(until 1492)
Palos
Cape
St. Vincent
Málaga
Cádiz
Algeciras

AFRICA

his brother, Manoel I (1495–1521), royal power was firmly established and Portugal took its place among the successful monarchies of the Renaissance.

The separatism and jealous individualism resulting from these political divisions, and from the topographical separations of the peninsula, were pronounced from earliest times. Not only were regions, kingdoms, and provinces split, but within each of these, many of the cities and domains of the smaller nobles jealously guarded their distinctive rights and *fueros* against all attempts to integrate them into larger units. During the long centuries of the *reconquista*, many of these characteristics and divisions became hardened into a complete way of life, institutionalizing and maintaining political differences.

In 1479 the kingdom of Castile and Aragon unexpectedly became allies as a result of the marriage of their respective sovereigns, and the slow evolution of territorial consolidation began. Castile, much the larger of the two realms (with an estimated population of between six and seven million, while that of the combined Aragonese territories was less than one million) was an agricultural and grazing land, dominated by powerful noble families preoccupied with the expulsion of Moors, Arabs, and Berbers from the peninsula, and with maintaining their racial and religious integrity. Aragon, on the other hand, was an aggregate of three geographic regions with little in common except that the reconquest had ended there several centuries earlier than it had in Castile and their concern was more Mediterranean and European than it was internal and African. In other words, the two kingdoms stood back to back, Castile facing southward, and later, westward; Aragon looking eastward and northward.

The institutions of the two kingdoms were likewise distinct, though they also had much in common. The crown in Castile was weak, not only in comparison with those of other countries, such as England and France, but in relation to the Castilian nobles. The *Cortes* (the Spanish representative assembly) had also declined in strength in the fifteenth century but still had impressive theoretical powers. In Aragon, too, the depressions and dislocations of the late fourteenth and early fifteenth centuries had created a difficult situation for the crown. But here even its theoretical position vis-à-vis the nobles and burghers was more limited. The Aragonese *Cortes* was a more powerful and impressive institution, which saw to it that kings did not step out of line. The king of Aragon could not legislate without the *Cortes*, and his conduct was closely watched by the *Justiciar*, an appointed guardian of constitutional liberties.

Immediately upon the accession of Ferdinand and Isabel, steps were begun by the two rulers to control the great magnates more effectively and strengthen the limited royal control of the instruments of government. Many administrative offices, which usually went automatically to the nobles, were assigned to able members of the middle class, especially to the lawyers and the clergy. Isabel also arranged to have Ferdinand appointed grand master of the three great Castilian military orders—Santiago, Calatrava, and Alcántara—increasing the crown's prestige and power, and providing an important additional source of revenue. This was important to Ferdinand and Isabel because the lack of money plagued them constantly. By the end of the Middle Ages, the strength of the Castilian nobility was based on their wealth. So deeply set were their economic foundations that it would have been folly for the new monarchs to attack them there, so they directed their assault against the political privileges of the aristocracy rather than against their land or their immunity from taxation. In Aragon the Catholic Kings were unable to make much headway even against the independent political authority of the magnates, so they generally left them alone.

Ferdinand and Isabel also made use of the towns to implement their policy of state building. For example, they revived and reorganized the medieval *hermandades* (brotherhoods), which had been protective leagues of the municipalities for the purpose of maintaining law and order, and converted them into a governmental institution resembling a national militia. Since the "public peace" was usually disturbed more often by the grandees than by anyone else and since the *hermandad* was paid for by the municipalities, it became a weapon wielded jointly by crown and town against the landed nobles. At the same time, central power began to extend into the cities, too, as corrupt and ineffective municipal counselors and officials were gradually replaced by able crown-appointed *corregidores*, who influenced municipal decisions and kept tabs on the financial potential of the cities.

COAT OF ARMS OF FERDINAND AND ISABEL. *Beneath the quartered emblems of León, Castile, Aragon, Catalonia, and Valencia is the pomegranate of Granada. The words refer to the phrase "Tanto monta, monta tanto Isabel como Fernando," symbolizing the joint and equal jurisdiction of the two "Catholic Kings." (Foto Archivo Espasa-Calpe)*

Ferdinand, the wary, suspicious, calculating, and skillful organizer of the Spanish union, demonstrated his administrative ability by making some significant readjustments in the use of government institutions. When the *Cortes* of Castile was summoned—usually to obtain additional revenue—the nobles were frequently not invited to attend, and the body became increasingly amenable to the king's wishes. The *Cortes* of Aragon (where the nobles attended by legal right rather than by invitation, as in Castile), which was less pliable, was simply ignored as much as possible. In place of the *Cortes*, the king accelerated the development of government by crown-appointed councils that could handle the functional details of administration and also serve as royal advisors. The principal organ of this conciliar system was the Royal Council (known as the Council of Castile after 1494 when a separate Council of Aragon was created). This council was composed of eight or nine lawyers, two or three knights, and one clergyman. The grandees (upper nobles) were not included, and when on occasion some of them did attend, they were not allowed to vote. The Council of Aragon was similarly structured around the jurists, who could be relied upon to give the king trustworthy and competent advice.

At the time of the marriage of Ferdinand and Isabel, Spain was divided by more than political, economic, and social differences. There were also three large religious groups—Christians, Moslems, and Jews—coexisting in a tolerable but precarious balance. During most of the Middle Ages and even when campaigns were being waged in the *reconquista*, the three got along surprisingly well. But now, due to the feared and actual difficulties of maintaining political order with such a division and owing to Isabel's pious zeal and deep concern for religious orthodoxy, the queen began actions that were intended to preserve the religious predominance of Spanish Christianity and protect its doctrinal purity. Several extreme steps were taken, including the establishment of the Inquisition, the conquest of Moorish Granada, and the expulsion of the Jews. These actions won for Ferdinand and Isabel the formal title of "Catholic Kings" (granted by Pope Alexander VI in 1494).

Because of Ferdinand's stealthy involvement in almost every international negotiation and conflict from 1479 until 1516, Aragon—and now Castile as well—became committed to a leading role in European affairs, a commitment that outlived the Catholic King by more than a century and that, despite continuing economic backwardness, brought Spain prestige and power unequaled by states with twice its population and many times its natural resources. During the reign of Ferdinand and Isabel, Navarre, as well as Granada, was incorporated into their realms. Spanish influence was also extended from Sicily and Naples northward into the rest of Italy, and the conquest of the New World was begun. Nevertheless, by the time of Isabel's death in 1504, the two kingdoms were still no more unified socially, or even politically, than they had been half a century before. Each retained its own political organs, laws, economic institutions, coinage, speech, customs, and courts. Royal power had been greatly enhanced by the joining of the two realms and by the complementary personalities of the two monarchs, but separatism and resistance to centralization were as strong as they ever were.

Nevertheless, a dynasty was born, and in that age of dynastic nationalism this could be more important than centralized institutions and unified laws. In many respects, the Catholic Kings' greatest success, like that of the Habsburgs, was in the field of dynastic marriage diplomacy. Isabel, their oldest daughter, was married to Alfonso of Portugal. Juan and his younger sister Juana were joined to the house of Habsburg-Burgundy by their double marriages to the daughter and son of Maximilian and Mary. María provided a continuing tie to Portugal by marrying Manoel, the heir to the Avis dynasty. Catherine was given to the prince of Wales, and later to Henry VIII. After the untimely deaths of both Isabel and Juan, the dynastic destiny of Aragon and Castile rested with Juana and her husband, Philip the Handsome, Habsburg duke of Burgundy. Had it not been for the machinations of Ferdinand, these two might have taken the Castilian throne in 1504. But when Philip suddenly died in 1506 and Juana suffered a mental breakdown, Ferdinand became regent of Castile until Juana's and Philip's son, Charles, came of age to assume the throne. How unpredictable were the dynastic politics of the Renaissance!

Austria and the Holy Roman Empire

The Holy Roman Empire

It is difficult to conceive of a greater discrepancy between theory and fact than that existing in the Holy Roman Empire of the late fifteenth century. Theoretically, the emperor was the temporal ruler of all Christendom and, jointly with the pope, responsible only to God for his actions. In reality he was hardly more than one of innumerable princes who vied with one another for status and influence in the chaotic labyrinth of imperial politics. It is true that in prestige and honor the emperor stood above them all, but the German and Bohemian princes never allowed him to forget that he owed his position to the seven electors who chose him. Nor did they fail to remind him that his only power, outside that of his own hereditary domains, depended on the willingness of the princes to support him. There was no imperial army, no sources of imperial revenue, and no active imperial institutions, other than the emperor himself.

By the end of the fifteenth century, the Empire was a vast area encompassing all of the German-speaking states of central Europe plus most of the Netherlands, all of Lorraine, Franche-Comté, Savoy and northwestern Italy as far south as the Papal States, the kingdom of Bohemia, Moravia, and some of Polish-speaking Silesia. The total population of the Empire is estimated at between 15 and 20 million and

Central and Eastern Europe in the Fifteenth Century

Bergen •
NORWAY
Oslo •
SWEDEN
• Stockholm

R U S S I A

• Novgorod

Moscow •

Kalmar •
DENMARK
• Copenhagen

TEUTONIC
KNIGHTS

• Smolensk

Danzig •
TEUTONIC
KNIGHTS

• Vilna

LITHUANIA
(to Poland, 1386)

Lübeck
Hamburg •
• Bremen
Stettin •
BRANDENBURG
• Berlin

Warsaw •

Kiev •

NETHERLANDS

HESSE
Cologne •
SAXONY

S I L E S I A

POLAND

• Cracow

PODOLIA

PALATINATE
WÜRTTEMBURG

BOHEMIA
• Prague
MORAVIA

GALICIA

JEDISTAN

BAVARIA
Munich •
Innsbruck •
SWISS
CANTONS
TYROL
Vienna •
AUSTRIA
STYRIA
CARINTHIA
Buda •
Pest
HUNGARY

MOLDAVIA

CARNIOLA
Venice •

WALLACHIA

CROATIA
BOSNIA

SERBIA

BULGARIA

O T T O M A N

Constantinople •

E M P I R E

Shaded areas show
the seven Imperial Electors

1 Archbishopric of Mainz
2 Archbishopric of Trier
3 Archbishopric of Cologne

——— Boundary of the Holy Roman Empire

— — Boundary of the Ottoman Empire in 1500

was made up of some 300 separate, sovereign, and semisovereign states, not counting the petty territories of the imperial knights. The Golden Bull of 1356 created a loose imperial diet, or *Reichstag*, composed of the leading princes in one house and the seven electors in the other, but the princes chose to play independent roles within the Empire rather than work together as a parliament in the broader interests of the Empire itself. Later, representatives of the free imperial cities were also allowed to attend meetings, but they still had relatively little influence.

The role of the seven electors was special and they made the most of it. Leading the group in rank and size of territory was the king of Bohemia. The position of Bohemia in the Empire was unique, enjoying more autonomy and fewer feudal duties to the emperor than any of the other imperial states. The elected king of Bohemia was always a voice to be reckoned with in the diet, not only because he religiously guarded Bohemian interests in the Empire, but because he was also a spokesman for the Jagiellonian dynasty that ruled Poland and Hungary as well as Bohemia during much of the fifteenth and early sixteenth centuries. Furthermore, the Bohemian kings *were* the Holy Roman emperors from 1347 until 1437.

Northwest of Bohemia lay the margravate of Brandenburg, a flat and heavily forested region ruled by the Junker landowners and by the house of Hohenzollern, whose ancestral seat was the Burg Hohenzollern in Southern Swabia, just north of Switzerland. Still relatively unauspicious in the fifteenth century, Brandenburg, governed from its capital at Berlin, was destined to occupy the central role in the creation of the modern German state. Under several of the late-fifteenth-century electors, adjacent territories were added to their dominion and much internal consolidation accomplished. The Hohenzollerns' control over revenues, army, and courts was already the envy of many neighboring princes.

Immediately to the south of Brandenburg was the duchy of Saxony, wealthiest of the electorates, governed since the early fifteenth century by the Wettin dynasty. The dukes of Saxony reaped the benefit of the richest copper, iron ore, coal, and salt-mining region of the Empire. In 1485 Saxony was divided between the two brothers Ernest and Albert, with the electoral title and privilege going to the former and the ducal title to the latter. Ernest's son, Elector Frederick "the Wise," was Martin Luther's first patron and protector, while his cousin, Duke George, remained the reformer's bitterest enemy.

The last of the secular electors was the Count Palatine of the Rhine, who governed his busy upper-Rhineland possession from his capital at Heidelberg. The other three electors were also Rhinelanders, but they were ecclesiastical princes: the archbishops of Mainz, Trier, and Cologne. Although their territories were smaller, these three electors commanded unusual prestige and influence at imperial diets, especially the archbishop of Mainz, who acted as chairman. Other German princes who exercised considerable independent power in German affairs were the Wittelsbach dukes of Bavaria, the dukes of Württemberg, and the landgraves of Hesse.

The Habsburgs

Of greatest importance, as far as sixteenth-century Europe is concerned, was the flamboyant role played by the Habsburgs of Austria. The house of Habsburg was founded in the Middle Ages by one of the petty landowner-counts of eastern Switzerland (immortalized as the oppressors of William Tell). From there the family nucleus moved eastward, gradually acquiring the mountainous regions of Tyrol, Carinthia, Carniola, and Styria, and finally the duchies of Upper and Lower Austria along the Danube plain, and becoming one of the largest landholders in the Empire. The Habsburg capital at Vienna was both wealthy and cultured. Under Count Rudolf of Habsburg, elected Holy Roman Emperor in 1273, the family began playing a leading role in German politics. But it was not until near the middle of the fifteenth century that they began exerting a continuous influence on European affairs. In 1438 Albert II of Habsburg Austria succeeded Sigismund of Hungary and Bohemia as Holy Roman Emperor, initiating an almost dynastic succession of the house of Habsburg for the next 400 years.

Politically secure in Austria (except for the Turkish threat after 1453), the Habsburgs began playing serious European politics. The success of their policy, however, was due much less to military and economic strength than to the gradual and favorable resolution of a carefully executed policy of dynastic marriages. An early Habsburg motto ran: "Leave the waging of wars to others! But thou, happy Austria, marry; for the realms which Mars awards to others, Venus transfers to thee." Through such marriages, the Habsburgs had succeeded by 1519 in forming a dynastic ring around France, intended to neutralize the growing wealth and military strength of the Valois monarchy. In 1476 negotiations were concluded between the emperor and the duke of Burgundy for the marriage of Maximilian, heir to the Habsburg possessions, to Mary, daughter and heiress of Charles the Bold of Burgundy. Although Maximilian and Mary were not able to prevent the French king from seizing the duchy of Burgundy after Charles's death, they did retain Franche-Comté, Luxembourg, and the valuable Netherlands. The Netherlands was not kept without some struggle, however, for the independent-minded Netherlanders demanded a written guarantee of their privileges and freedoms (a set of articles known as the Grand Privilège) before they would recognize Mary's sovereignty. Upon her death in 1482, their son Philip the Handsome became ruler and, after lengthy negotiations, Maximilian was recognized as regent during Philip's minority. In the northern provinces (the modern Netherlands), Habsburg rule lasted for 100 years, and in the south (Belgium) it continued until 1790.

The Reign of Maximilian

In 1493 Maximilian became Holy Roman Emperor and was immediately drawn into the treacherous European diplomatic whirlpool created by the French invasion of Italy in 1494. Like his father-in-law, Charles the Bold, Maximilian was an adventurous, quixotic knight, a holdover from the days of chivalry. There was also an idealistic nobility and a congeniality about Maximilian that made him loved, though not always respected, by his subjects. He was unusually sensitive to the artistic and intellectual influences of the time, and was a very cultivated man in his own right. But he was a strangely visionary figure, out of touch with the realities of sixteenth-century power. His policies were vacillating and capricious with little apparent rationale or direction.

In the midst of his involvement in the Italian imbroglio and his preparations for a crusade against the Turks, Maximilian summoned the imperial diet, hoping to reorganize and centralize the administration of the Empire. Three new institutions were proposed: a moratorium on private wars within the Empire; an imperial law court (*Reichskammergericht*) to administer the Roman law throughout Germany; and the Common Penny (*Gemeine Pfenning*), a graduated property-income-poll tax to be assessed in all of the states for the purpose of paying the expenses of government and the raising of an imperial army. A reform party of the Reichstag, headed by the elector archbishop of Mainz, favored these reforms but insisted that they be controlled by the electors and great princes, not by the emperor. Five years later, in 1500, an imperial council (*Reichsregiment*) of twenty-one nobles chosen by the electors and other princes was created to represent the emperor in his absence and carry on the continuous executive functions of government. But without the support of the emperor, it failed to work, just as the other reforms had failed without the cooperation of the princes.

For the rest of his reign, Maximilian was continually plagued by the controversial issues of organizational reform, which caused friction and disorder and seriously hampered his sporadic Italian campaigns. Eventually all of the new organs failed, and Germany resumed its proud anarchy. In the meantime, the reform proposals not only raised protests from the haughty Swiss, who passionately disliked the Habsburgs, but led to a disastrous war. Objecting to the tightening of imperial government—which meant reducing the independent position that the Swiss occupied within the Empire—and resenting their total exclusion from the imperial councils and courts while being included in the tax, the Swiss struck in force against Maximilian's Swabian League allies in 1498. Maximilian personally entered the fray the following year only to have the bulk of his army of 30,000 annihilated by the Swiss pikemen.

In the end, Maximilian's hopes for dynastic aggrandizement had to come from his marriage diplomacy rather than from arms. In 1491 he began negotiating a double marriage treaty with Ferdinand and Isabel of Spain. In fulfillment of this agreement, Maximilian's daughter, Margaret, was married to the Spanish heir, Juan; and the emperor's son, Philip, was married to the Catholic Kings' daughter, Juana. As events unfolded, Juan died shortly thereafter and the inheritance of all four lines—Habsburg, Burgundian, Castilian, and Aragonese—converged through Philip and Juana on their son Charles, born at Ghent in the Netherlands in 1500.

Charles V: Step-Father of Europe

From the moment of his birth, Charles of Ghent was destined to become the pivot around which European politics, diplomacy, and religious controversy rotated for almost half a century. In 1506, at the age of six, Charles inherited all of his father's Burgundian territories, including by that time Franche-Comté, Luxembourg, and the Netherlands from Artois northward to Friesland (governed during his minority, and frequently thereafter, by his remarkable aunt, Margaret of Austria). In 1516, upon the death of his maternal grandfather, Ferdinand of Aragon, he became King Charles I of Aragon, Catalonia, Valencia (also possessing the Mediterranean territories of Majorca, Minorca, Sardinia, Sicily, Naples, and a claim to the duchy of Milan), and Castile. In addition he became ruler of all the Castilian territories overseas: the Canary Islands, the West Indies, and in a few years the New World empires of Mexico and Peru. Charles was still only nineteen when his other grandfather, Maximilian, died, leaving him the Austrian inheritance and opening the way for his subsequent election to the Holy Roman Empire as Charles V.

The contrast in appearance, personality, and character of Charles V with his life-long rival, Francis I, and with his other contemporary antagonist-ally, Henry VIII, is both striking and significant. Physically he was quite unlike them both. With his protruding lower jaw, bulging eyes, and sallow skin, Charles was not likely to inherit the epithet of his father, Philip "the Handsome." He was slow and stammering in speech but possessed considerable linguistic ability. His native language was Flemish, but he was also fluent in French and eventually mastered Castilian. He read Latin and conversed haltingly in German and Italian. According to a Spanish anecdote, he "spoke Italian with the ambassadors, French with the ladies, German to the soldiers, English to his horse, and Spanish with God." Charles showed an active interest in humanism and history and was well read in the classics. He was a knowledgeable patron of painting and music, and revealed more than a passing fascination with science.

In spite of his titles and dominions, Charles V was pious and reserved, and he took his responsibilities with the utmost seriousness. Abandoning his earlier amorous pursuits for political and military success, he became an astute and respected leader. His strong regard for justice sometimes shaded into vindictiveness, and his sense of responsi-

EMPEROR CHARLES V. *A portrait, painted by Bernard van Orley, of the youthful emperor just prior to the Diet of Worms (1519 or 1520). Around his neck hangs the collar of the Golden Fleece. (Institut Royal du Patrimoine Artistique, Copyright A.C.L.-Brussels)*

bility added to the seriousness of his demeanor, but there was much of the chivalric knight, with a commitment to high ideals and noble deeds, in the emperor. Perhaps a trace of humor in his personality might have lightened his burdens, but there was none. His sense of duty kept him from retreating from any of his onerous tasks, but assured him of ultimate disappointment and defeat.

His policy in all of his realms, reflecting both his temperament and situation, was to conserve the territories he had already inherited and to acquire others he believed were legally his. He hoped moderation, balance, and constancy would preserve his legacy and the unity of Christendom. But his task was overpowering, even for a great ruler, and Charles was only too aware of his own limitations. Internal problems alone, in an empire so diverse and widespread and in an age without adequate communications or administrative bureaucracies, would have taxed the ablest sovereign. But Charles also had the Ottoman Turks to contain, Protestantism to vanquish, the pope to contend with, colonies to preserve, and always the French to fight. It is small wonder that Charles's youthful imperial ideal of ruling the world, of being in fact the temporal head of all Christendom, slowly died after the death of his brilliant and enthusiastic grand chancellor, Gattinara, who had inspired and animated the young emperor through his first decade of rule.

On the Frontiers of the Empire

Scandinavia

The age of Viking expansion and conquest had ended by the eleventh century, and a new era of internal consolidation and conflict began in Scandinavia. A new landholding aristocracy arose that dominated the political and social life in the north for the next three centuries while the hard-working peasants were reduced to semiservile status.

The election of Waldemar IV (1340–75) to the throne of Denmark began a resurgence of the monarchy and a revival of Danish influence in the Baltic. It also led to a series of disastrous confrontations with the Hanseatic League. The sting of defeat in these encounters was partially removed when Waldemar's enterprising daughter, Margaret (wife of King Haakon of Norway), succeeded in uniting the crowns of Denmark, Norway, and Sweden under her own control after the death of her husband. The Union of Kalmar (1397) institutionalized the arrangement, leaving each kingdom autonomous but establishing a personal union of all three under a single monarch. Margaret ("the lady king," as she was styled) managed the union until her death in 1412, skillfully maintaining order while repressing the powerful nobles and reestablishing Danish ascendancy, The union never functioned as successfully after her death. Bitter rivalries among the noble houses, the economic dominance of the Hansa, unrest among the Swedish peasantry, and the active interference of the clergy in political affairs eventually led to revolution and separation.

Poland

The struggle between crown and aristocracy to control the lives of the one million people living on the vast plains east of the Oder was equally bitter and prolonged. The Polish nobles were particularly jealous of their privileges and opposed every effort of the monarchs to dominate or control them. The native Piast dynasty had some success, however, especially when they mobilized the nobility in territorial expansion and created a viable monarchy with an administrative bureaucracy, a law code (the "Statutes of Casimir the Great"), and a royal chancery. They also made Cracow the cultural center of Poland. But Casimir III's (1333–70) attempts to expand northward to the Baltic met with failure at the hands of the Teutonic Knights, who held tenaciously to the coastal area east of Pomerania.

The death of Casimir ended the Piast dynasty and inaugurated an era of foreign domination and aristocratic resurgence. In 1374 the Polish magnates obtained the first of many "capitulations" from the crown granting them broad tax exemptions and privileges. Twelve years later, Jagiello, the Grand Prince of Lithuania, married the cultured and capable Polish queen, Jadwiga, and was duly accepted as king of Poland (as

Wladislaw II, 1386–1434). Thus a new dynastic union was made with the huge territory of Lithuania, which lay between Poland and Muscovite Russia to the east. In 1410 a Polish-Lithuanian army (supported by Bohemian mercenaries under Jan Žižka) crushed the knights of the Teutonic Order at Tannenberg and relieved the pressure on the Polish northern frontier, for a time at least. Internal deterioration resumed during the reign of Jagiello's minor son, Wladislaw III (1434–44), who was simultaneously king of Hungary. Wladislaw's brother, Casimir IV (1447–92), was able to curtail some of the power of the magnates and finally secured an outlet to the Baltic Sea. But by the end of the century, Jagiellonian preoccupation with affairs in Bohemia and Hungary, plus wars with both the Russians and the Turks, led to the breakdown of royal authority within Poland and the further growth of aristocratic power. The national diet (Sejm), composed mostly of magnates, lesser nobility, and prelates of the church, became the supreme legislative organ of government. The principal loser in this process was not the crown but the peasants, who were completely reduced to serfdom by act of the Sejm in 1511.

Bohemia, Hungary, and Russia

Neighboring Bohemia was part of the Holy Roman Empire, but Czech ties with other Slavic peoples, especially Poles and Slovaks, and their distrust of the Germans gave them a basis for cultural and political association with their northeastern neighbors. The Hussite wars further alienated Czech allegiance to the Empire, and in 1458 George Poděbrady, an Utraquist nobleman and leader of the Hussites, was elected king of Bohemia. His condemnation as a relapsed heretic was ignored by everyone but the Hungarian king, who eagerly sought to defend the faith by opposing him. After George Poděbrady's death in 1470, the Bohemian diet elected Casimir IV's son to the throne as Vladislav II (1471–1516). Seven years later, he was also chosen king of Hungary. The Jagiellonian dynasty came to an end in Bohemia and Hungary in 1526 but continued in Poland until 1572.

The kingdom of Hungary had prospered in the fourteenth century under the Angevin rulers Charles I (1308–42) and Louis the Great (1342–82), even though the magnates continued to rule at times like "little kings" as they had in the previous centuries, and the lesser nobles controlled much of the administration through their provincial governments (Comitats). But a marked decline set in with the selection of Sigismund of Luxembourg as king in 1387 (he became Holy Roman Emperor in 1410 and king of Bohemia in 1436). Royal authority decayed under the absentee reign of Sigismund and did not revive until the election of Matthias Corvinus as king (1458–90).

In the meantime, Hungary and the Serbian states to the south stood directly in the path of Ottoman expansion into the Balkans. Sigismund himself led a Christian crusade against the Turks in 1396 that was utterly destroyed at Nicopolis. A result of that crusade was Sigismund's loss of the upper Dalmatian coast to Venice. In the year of Sigismund's death (1437), John Hunyadi, a Transylvanian border lord, won the first of several victories against the Turks. Encouraged by these successes, the new Hungarian king, Ladislas I (Wladislaw III of Poland) led another ill-fated crusade that ended in disaster at Varna in 1444.

John Hunyadi's son, Matthias I Corvinus, was elected king of Hungary in 1458, and for thirty-two years ruled with an intelligent combination of firmness and finesse that brought Hungary to the peak of its Renaissance glory and made it the dominant power in Eastern Europe. He succeeded in breaking the stranglehold of the magnates and created the rudiments of a central administration. Like his western counterparts, Louis XI, Henry VII, and Ferdinand of Aragon, Matthias Corvinus increased crown revenues and created the nucleus of a standing army. He was also a true "Renaissance prince," the greatest benefactor of humanism, literature, and art in the East. He brought several Italian scholars and artists to his capital at Buda and made it the most brilliant court outside of Italy. His own court poet, Janus Pannonius, was lauded throughout the West for the grace of his written works. After Matthias's death in 1490, Hungary returned to a weak, absentee king (Vladislav II of Bohemia) and the work of Matthias Corvinus was gradually undone.

In the meantime, Muscovite Russia, expanding westward under the rule of Ivan the Great (1462–1505) after throwing off the Tartar yoke, annexed Novgorod in the north and then invaded Lithuania, attaching much of the Polish-Lithuanian territory to Russia. As more land was acquired, the free-lance warriors known as *boyars* gradually became landholding nobles. With their strong voice in the regional assemblies of nobles (*dumas*), these landlords were able to tie their peasants to the land, just as the Polish nobles were doing, and create a rigid form of serfdom.

The Ottoman Empire

The major threat to the entire Balkan area came from the steadily advancing Ottoman Turks. In previous centuries, the predominant influence in southeastern Europe had been the Byzantine Empire, the center of Greek Orthodox Christianity and a barricade between the Moslem Middle East and the Latin West. From Justinian's magnificent metropolis of Constantinople, the Roman law had gone forth to the rest of Europe, and from that center, Byzantine art and ideas had influenced much of the West, especially commercial centers like Ragusa and Venice. In subsequent centuries, Constantinople had fallen on hard times, but nothing was more devastating than the diverted Fourth Crusade (1204) which subjected this "Second Rome" to the horrors of conquest and pillage from which it never fully recovered. The

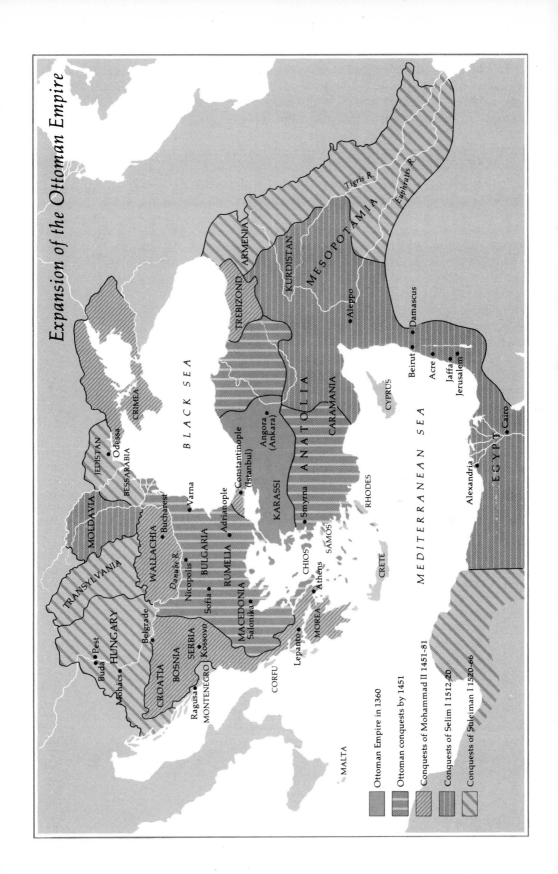

Expansion of the Ottoman Empire

BLACK SEA

MEDITERRANEAN SEA

Tigris R.

Euphrates R.

Danube R.

ARMENIA

TREBIZOND

KURDISTAN

MESOPOTAMIA

Aleppo

Damascus

Beirut

Acre

Jaffa

Jerusalem

Cairo

Alexandria

EGYPT

CYPRUS

ANATOLIA

CARAMANIA

KARASSI

Angora (Ankara)

Smyrna

RHODES

Constantinople (Istanbul)

Varna

Adrianople

BULGARIA

RUMELIA

Nicopolis

Sofia

MACEDONIA

Salonika

Athens

MOREA

Lepanto

CHIOS

SAMOS

CRETE

CORFU

MALTA

Odessa

JEDISTAN

BESSARABIA

CRIMEA

MOLDAVIA

WALLACHIA

Bucharest

TRANSYLVANIA

HUNGARY

Pest

Buda

Belgrade

Mohacs

CROATIA

BOSNIA

SERBIA

Kossovo

MONTENEGRO

Ragusa

Ottoman Empire in 1360

Ottoman conquests by 1451

Conquests of Mohammad II 1451–81

Conquests of Selim I 1512–20

Conquests of Suleiman I 1520–66

Palaeologus dynasty (1260–1453) tried hard to restore Byzantine authority in the Balkans, but attacks, by Serbia on one side, under its ambitious king, Stephen Dushan, and by the Turks on the other, spelled its doom.

Ottoman expansion westward was almost continuous after they first crossed into Europe in 1345. Under Sultan Murad I (1359–89), they conquered Adrianople, eastern Bulgaria, Macedonia, and defeated a large Balkan army at the Battle of Kossovo in 1389. Constantinople itself was saved only by the Tartar Tamerlane's appearance in the Anatolian Peninsula and his victory over the sultan at Ankara (1402). But the Ottoman pressure on the Byzantine Empire resumed. Emperor John VIII Palaeologus sought help in the West, even supporting the unification of the Greek and Latin churches (at the Council of Ferrara-Florence) in order to win Western support. But it was all in vain. When Mohammed the Conqueror (1451–81) laid siege to Constantinople in 1453, only a handful of Westerners came to its defense.

The fall of Constantinople opened the Balkans to increased Ottoman penetration. Three years later Athens fell, and soon after that all of the Morea, thus ending Christian rule in Greece, followed by the conquest of Trebizond, the last of the Greek states. The Turkish advance continued with the subjugation of Serbia, Bosnia, Herzegovina, and Albania, leading inevitably to a prolonged and bitter confrontation with Venice for control of the Adriatic. Under Selim I (1512–20), the Turks consolidated their eastern flank by conquering eastern Anatolia and Kurdistan, and pushing the Persians beyond the Euphrates. Selim then turned south, overran Damascus, took possession of Palestine, and defeated the Mameluk rulers of Egypt. With some justification, the sultan declared himself protector of the entire Islamic world. Now controlling the eastern centers of the Levant trade and possessing a formidable galley fleet, the Turks were prepared to exert renewed pressure on the West, both in the Mediterranean and up the Danube Valley toward Vienna. Papal appeals for a crusade against the Turks fell on deaf ears, and the burden of resisting their advance fell mainly to the Holy Roman Emperor Charles V.

Suggestions for Further Reading

GENERAL

Joseph R. Strayer, *On the Medieval Origins of the Modern State* (Princeton, 1970) covers a broad spectrum, as does A. Marongiu, *Medieval Parliaments: A Comparative Study* (London, 1968), which includes the entire early modern period. The selections in A. J. Slavin (ed.), *The New Monarchies and Representative Assemblies* (Boston, 1964) point up the complexities in the development of the Renaissance monarchies. J. H. Shennan, *The Origins of the Modern European State, 1450–1725* (London, 1974) is broad and informative.

FRANCE AND BURGUNDY

J. Russell Major, *Representative Institutions in Renaissance France, 1421–1559* (Madison, 1960) interprets the Renaissance crown as a limited monarchy, whereas R. J. Knecht sees it as absolute. Compare his short *Francis I and Absolute Monarchy* (London, 1969), and "The Court of Francis I," *European Studies Review*, 8 (1978), 1–22. P. S. Lewis (ed.), *The Recovery of France in the Fifteenth Century* (New York, 1971) presents a collection of important essays on fifteenth-century France, to which should be added C. T. Allmand, "The Aftermath of War in Fifteenth-Century France," *History*, 61 (1976), 344–57. Paul Murray Kendall, *Louis XI: The Universal Spider* (New York, 1971) is a brilliant recreation of the life and reign of Louis. The following two reigns are briefly assessed in R. Doucet, "France under Charles VIII and Louis XII," *The New Cambridge Modern History* (New York, 1957), I, 292–315. No adequate biography of Francis I has appeared yet, but Desmond Seward, *Prince of the Renaissance: The Golden Life of François I* (New York, 1973) is a good popular account that is both suggestive and well illustrated.

Joseph Calmette, *The Golden Age of Burgundy*, tr. by D. Weightman (New York, 1963) has now been superseded by Richard Vaughan's *Philip the Good: The Apogee of Burgundy* (London, 1970); *Charles the Bold: The Last Valois Duke of Burgundy* (London, 1973); and his single-volume overview, *Valois Burgundy* (Hamden, 1975). C. A. J. Armstrong's *New Cambridge Modern History* chapter on "The Burgundian Netherlands, 1477–1521," I, 224–58, also contains much useful information.

ENGLAND AND SCOTLAND

The best study of early-Renaissance England is J. R. Lander, *Crown and Nobility, 1450–1509* (London, 1976), to which can be added Charles D. Ross, *The Wars of the Roses: A Concise History* (London, 1976), and A. L. Rowse, *Bosworth Field: From Medieval to Tudor England* (Garden City, 1966). Paul M. Kendall's *The Yorkist Age* (London and New York, 1962) is social history at its best, and his *Richard the Third* (London and New York, 1955, 1965) is still the definitive biography of that strange, enigmatic monarch.

For the first Tudor king, S. B. Chrimes, *Henry VII* (Berkeley, 1972), is highly recommended. It is a solid study showing the impact Henry had on the government of England. R. L. Storey's *The Reign of Henry VII* (New York, 1968) is also informative. Neville Williams, *The Life and Times of Henry VII* (London, 1973) is richly illustrated, as is the same author's *Henry VIII and His Court* (New York, 1971). The principal biographies of Henry VIII are A. F. Pollard's very dated *Henry VIII* (New York, 1902, 1966); Lacey Baldwin Smith's probing *Henry VIII, The Mask of Royalty* (Boston, 1971); and especially J. J. Scarisbrick, *Henry VIII* (Berkeley, 1968).

On the Scottish rulers, see Robert L. Mackie, *King James IV of Scotland* (Edinburgh, 1958 and Westport, 1976), and Caroline Bingham, *James V: King of Scots, 1512–1542* (London, 1971). Jennifer M. Brown (ed.), *Scottish Society in the Fifteenth Century* (London, 1977) is wide-ranging. Anglo-Scottish diplomacy is skillfully treated in Richard G. Eaves, *Henry VIII's Scottish Diplomacy, 1513–1524: England's Relations with the Regency Government of James V* (New York: 1971).

SPAIN AND PORTUGAL

The literature on early Renaissance Spain continues to grow. A good starting point might be Derek W. Lomax's compact *The Reconquest of Spain* (London and New York, 1978). The essays in Roger Highfield (ed.), *Spain in the Fifteenth Century, 1369–1516* (New York, 1972) cover many aspects of Spanish growth. J. M. Batista i Roca, "The Hispanic Kingdoms and the Catholic Kings," in *The New Cambridge Modern History*, I, 316–42, is succinct and systematic. The most recent and detailed analysis is J. N. Hillgarth's authoritative *The Spanish Kingdoms, 1250–1516: Vol. II, Castilian Hegemony 1410–1516* (New York, 1978). Ralph A. Giesey, *If Not, Not: The Oath of the Aragonese and the Legendary Laws of Sobarbe* (Princeton, 1968) debunks the myth of the famous Aragonese oath, but shows them to have been very freedom loving, anyway. On the reign of the Catholic Kings, see J. H. Mariéjol, *The Spain of Ferdinand and Isabella*, tr. by Benjamin Keen (New Brunswick, 1961); Townsend Miller, *The Castles and the Crown: Spain, 1451–1555* (New York, 1963), a well-written family portrait of Ferdinand, Isabel, Philip, and Juana; and Marvin Lunenfeld, *The Council of the Santa Hermandad: A Study of the Pacification Forces of Ferdinand and Isabella* (Coral Gables, 1970).

AUSTRIA AND THE HOLY ROMAN EMPIRE

Geoffrey Barraclough, *The Origins of Modern Germany* (New York, 1963) is both readable and reliable. Another fundamental work is Francis L. Carsten, *Princes and Parliaments in Germany* (Oxford, 1959), and the R. G. D. Laffan chapter, "The Empire under Maximilian," in *The New Cambridge Modern History*, I, 194–223, is informative, though uninspired, writing. For a fascinating new look at the chivalric emperor, see Louise Cayler, *The Emperor Maximilian I and Music* (New York, 1973). Gerald Strauss has edited a useful collection of ten essays in the Stratus series, *Pre-Reformation Germany* (New York, 1972). Karl Brandi's long-standard biography of *The Emperor Charles V*, tr. by C. V. Wedgwood (London, 1939) has been greatly updated but not replaced by Manuel Fernández Alvarez, *Charles V: Elected Emperor and Hereditary Ruler* (London, 1975).

ON THE FRONTIERS OF THE EMPIRE

The chapter on "Eastern Europe," by C. A. Macartney, in *The New Cambridge Modern History*, I, 368–94, is a good, short synthesis. Paul W. Knoll, *The Rise of the Polish Monarchy: Piast Poland in East Central Europe* (Chicago, 1972) is a recent analysis by a leading authority on medieval and Renaissance Poland. Also consult the appropriate chapters in A. Gieysztor, et al., *History of Poland* (Warsaw, 1968); S. Harrison Thomson, *Czechoslovakia in European History* (Princeton, 1953); C. A. Macartney, *Hungary: A Short History* (Edinburgh, 1962); and S. Guldescu, *History of Medieval Croatia* (The Hague, 1964).

On the Ottoman expansion, see especially Franz Babinger's definitive *Mehmed the Conqueror and His Time*, tr. by Ralph Manheim (Princeton, 1978); Ducas, *Decline and Fall of Byzantium to the Ottoman Turks* (Detroit, 1975); and Steven Runciman's classic, *The Fall of Constantinople, 1453* (Cambridge, 1965). For the continuing "Turkish menace," see V. J. Parry, "The Ottoman Empire, 1481–1520," *New Cambridge Modern History*, I, 395–419.

CHAPTER NINE

Europe and the Italian Wars

A S THE OTTOMAN SPECTER hung over Europe, Italy again became the focus of activity when a huge French army crossed the Alps and marched southward toward Naples, ostensibly to attack the Turks. No one knew what a profound effect the invasions and subsequent wars of Italy would have on the life of Europe. The peninsular upheaval burst upon Italy at the very height of the flowering Renaissance, in some cases bringing immediate repercussions and in every case leaving lasting scars. The cultural leadership of Florence declined rapidly. Although many important Florentines still contributed to literature, art, and building, most of it was done outside of Florence. The pinnacle of the High Renaissance was reached in Rome and Venice, the two states least damaged by the wars. The political and economic impact on Italy was no less intense. Just as Italians had much to teach the invaders about culture, diplomacy, and style, they learned many lessons from these "barbarians" about warfare and government. After 1494, Italy became the cockpit of Europe, the focal point of international diplomacy and war, and the catalyst for the evolution of a European system of national states.

The French Invasion of 1494

The political situation in Italy invited interference from outside. The once-powerful duchy of Milan, guardian of the passes over the Alps across which northern invaders might descend onto the Lombard plain, was in a period of frustration and disorder. Economically, the duchy was in good condition, but there was growing unrest among the opponents of the Sforzas at home and abroad. Tension increased after 1476 with the accession of the infant Gian Galeazzo Sforza as duke and the assumption of actual power by his ambitious but incompetent uncle, Ludovico Sforza, known to his contemporaries as *Il Moro* (The Moor) because of his swarthy complexion. Neighboring Venice was riding the crest of a period of prosperity and expansion at the expense of Milan on the west and the Papal States to the south. The Venetian government was strong, its hold on its mainland satellites secure, and its wealth unequaled. But as a consequence, the jealousy and hatred of the surrounding states was keen. The papacy was particularly piqued by Venetian intrusions into the Romagna and constant pressures on the buffer duchy of Ferrara, a papal fief ruled by the popular house of d'Este. Naples was still dominated by restless nobles who canceled out one another's power by their continuous rivalry and disorder. The house of Aragon had ruled Sicily since the thirteenth century and had conquered mainland Naples in 1435, but there was always a threat from the supporters of the French Anjou dynasty that had previously ruled there. When Alfonso V, "The Magnanimous," of Aragon died in 1458, his kingdoms were divided between his brother, Juan II, who became king of Aragon and Sicily, and his illegitimate son, Ferrante, who assumed the throne of Naples. In 1494, King Ferrante died, and the Italian political bubble burst.

From early in his reign, there were many pressures exerted on young Charles VIII (1483–98) of France to lead an army across the Alps into Italy. Charles's distant claim to the throne of Naples through his great-grandfather, Louis II of Anjou, was at best ephemeral, but it made a useful pretext—along with an avowed crusade against the Turks. Charles was persistently urged by Ludovico Sforza to intervene in Italy on behalf of *Il Moro*'s niece, Isabella, wife of the legitimate Milanese duke, Gian Galeazzo Sforza, to prevent an anticipated attack on Milan by the violent young Alfonso of Calabria, Ferrante's son (who now assumed the Neapolitan throne as Alfonso II). Whether the French king responded or not, the threat of intervention could be a valuable shield to Ludovico against his foes. After Ferrante's death, the doors also opened for *Il Moro*'s claim to at least a share in the Neapolitan spoils through his sister, Ippolita, who, as the wife of Alfonso II, now became queen of Naples.

Other influential individuals at the French court who also appealed to Charles for intervention in Italy included the disgruntled Neapolitan nobles; the disaffected Giuliano della Rovere (the future Pope Julius II), arch-enemy of the present Borgia pope, Alexander VI; and the king's hot-blooded counselors. But Charles VIII really needed no coaxing. What could provide a more glorious or profitable means of occupying the restless French nobles and divert them from nefarious activities against the crown than an exhilarating march through Italy? Resistance should not be strong, if reports of Italian disunity and rivalry were correct, and the opportunities for booty and ransom were great. Besides, Charles had more of the medieval knight-errantry in him than his father had, and he easily fancied himself in the role of a benevolent conqueror. Misshapen in body and weak in intellect, the almost illiterate king was brought up on the tales of chivalry and conquest that he now intended to emulate.

In September, 1494, Charles led an army of some 30,000 heavy cavalry, Swiss pikemen, Scottish archers, and a huge train of artillery across the Alps and onto the Lombard plain, supported by a sizable fleet providing flank cover and supplies. No one in Italy had ever seen such an array of military strength. Ludovico Sforza probably began repenting his rash invitation before the last column of French troops had passed through Milan. The new king of Naples, Alfonso II, prepared a land and sea defense that collapsed faster than it was built. Alfonso's Florentine ally Piero de' Medici was supposed to delay the French advance through Tuscany, but the people of Florence would have none of it. Its economy crippled by a French embargo on Florentine cloth and its outlying defense ring corrupted and weak, the once-proud city surrendered passively to the French king, submitting almost unconditionally to French protection, and agreed to help finance the invasion of Naples. Similarly, Charles VIII passed through Rome after receiving papal permission to traverse the Papal States. Five months after he had crossed the Alps, Charles VIII arrived triumphantly in Naples, frightened Alfonso and his young son, Ferrantino, across the straits of Messina into Sicily, and had himself crowned king of Naples. A kingdom had been won without fighting a battle.

But the fortunes of war changed quickly in Renaissance Italy. Neapolitans soon learned that French rule was as corrupt and oppressive as the Aragonese had been, and that offices as well as landed estates were quickly distributed to the invaders. Soon riots and insurrections against the French regime were mounting. Charles elected to withdraw northward before his retreat route was cut off. Bolstered by assurances and reinforcements from Ferdinand of Aragon, Alfonso returned to the mainland and raised the standard of revolt against the French. At the head of an Aragonese and Castilian army transported across from Sicily came the "Great Captain," Gonzalo de Córdoba, soon to become the most successful military organizer and tactician of the age.

Meanwhile, in the north, Pope Alexander VI was negotiating a "Holy League" (sometimes called the League of Venice) between the papacy, Venice, Milan, Emperor Maximilian, and the king of Aragon, ostensibly for the purpose of a crusade against the Turks, but in fact, as Charles correctly suspected, intended to drive him from Italy. The French army made a hurried withdrawal and was able to retreat successfully across the Alps with only one major encounter, the battle of Fornovo (claimed as a victory by both sides), before the full force of the League could be mobilized.

Three years later, Charles VIII was dead, but the French fascination with Italy was not. For more than half a century, Italy was the battleground of recurring French invasions, Spanish counterinvasions, imperial incursions, and frequent internal feuds. It was also the scene of cultural disruption and international turmoil, as the European giants jostled for position and advantage in a new world of national and dynastic rivalries.

Savonarola and the Florentine Republic

In Florence the effects of the French invasion were immediate and decisive. For several years, the indomitable Dominican friar Girolamo Savonarola had been stirring the people of Florence into a frenzied revivalism against immorality, frivolity, and corruption. Speaking as the mouthpiece of God, Savonarola called upon the sinners to repent, and pronounced the condemnation of hell on those who refused to listen. His prophetic warnings of the imminent punishment and cleansing of Florence at the hands of a heaven-sent avenger seemed to be fulfilled when Charles VIII's conquering army marched into Tuscany. Savonarola and his followers hailed the French king as their deliverer and savior. Piero de' Medici was banished from Florence for life, and a modified republican government emerged. Some of the Medici institutions were abolished and others were transformed into less autocratic organs. The nucleus of the new republic was the Great Council, in which a large share of the citizens participated. Political activity and interest increased as partisans of differing philosophies of government debated their relative merits in private and public disputes.

Yet due to its apocalyptic foundation and the continuing agitation of the Dominican friar, the new government was something less than a democracy, even by Florentine standards. The Medici were gone, but so was the classical balance and moderation of the Renaissance city. In its place was Savonarola. During the ensuing four years, the austere friar became the virtual dictator of Florence. With vitriolic words and actions, he tried to cleanse the city of all vices and sins, and establish a republic of obedience and virtue. The Renaissance in all of its forms and expressions, from secular art to frivolous and bawdy drama, was repudiated. Savonarola showed the way in his dramatic Burning of the Vanities—in which instruments of sin, from cosmetics and jewelry to light-minded literature, were put to the torch. His political program, like his religious revivalism, was preached in the name of God. Anyone dissenting from it disobeyed God's will, not just the friar's.

For a time, Savonarola's position was unchallenged. But his relentless sermons soon began to wear thin and started winning him more enemies than converts. His uncompromising attempts to reform the church and the morals of the papacy brought him into a clash with Pope

Alexander VI. No group or practice in Florence or Rome was exempt from Savonarola's probing sermons. Early in 1497, he began attacking the papacy openly, not only for its low morals but for its political policies. Unresponsive to papal warnings, Savonarola was excommunicated. Now his enemies counterattacked viciously. Early in 1498 he was baited by the rival Franciscans of Florence into an abortive show of miraculous powers—a medieval spectacle that cost him much of his popularity with the people, and with it his power. A severe economic crisis in the winter of 1497–98 did nothing to help his cause, and the expulsion of the French and the death of his protector in 1498 spelled the end of his regime. Charged by the Florentine *Signoria* with plotting to overthrow the constitution, the erstwhile prophet was tried, convicted, and on May 23, hanged amid a jeering crowd in the Florentine piazza. His body was subsequently burned and the ashes thrown in the River Arno.

The Struggle for Italy

In 1499, Charles VIII's Orléanist cousin and successor to the French throne, Louis XII (1498–1515), led a second massive invasion of Italy. Louis's actions are more difficult to explain than were those of his predecessor. Humane, tolerant, and unusually generous by nature, Louis XII was a good judge of people and an able administrator of the laws of France. For his wise domestic rule (due in large part to his principal advisor, Georges d'Amboise, archbishop of Rouen), he was accorded the title of "Father of his People." He also gained popularity by his relaxation of the tax burdens and his general leniency in most areas of royal administration. But Louis XII had no military ability and very little sagacity in the jungle of international politics. He was hardly a match in the European arena for the wily Ferdinand of Aragon or Henry VII. By all measures, he should have remained in France and reaped the rewards of a sound and just administration.

But Louis d'Orléans was a prince, born to rule and to fight. Whether he had ability in the profession or not, his lot, like that of all French nobles, was to wage war. By ignoring the Sforzas, Louis's claim to the duchy of Milan—through his grandmother Valentina Visconti, daughter of the last Visconti duke, Gian Galeazzo—was irrefutable. But why should the Sforzas be disregarded? Mainly because the legitimate duke had died in 1494 and the regent-usurper, Ludovico *Il Moro*, was more interested in tournaments and banquets than he was in resisting a French attack. Secure behind the assurances and recognition of Emperor Maximilian (who had formally invested him with the duchy in 1495) and confident in the ability of his 10,000 Swiss mercenaries and the skill of his newly employed military engineer, Leonardo da Vinci, Ludovico approached the impending invasion with confidence and ease. How little he had learned about either politics or war!

Other Italian potentates were making more careful preparations to guarantee their own security in the ensuing campaign, and if possible, to make a meaningful advancement of their own interests. The Florence government made sure the French king remembered their alliance, reminding him of their close relations since Cosimo's day when the Medici were given the right to add the *fleur de lis* to the Medici coat of arms, and assuring him that they supported his claim to Milan. Alexander VI saw the possibilities of using French arms to extend papal control into the Romagna; so he sent his illegitimate son, Cesare Borgia, to the French court with the papal dispensation the king had requested for the repudiation of his wife, freeing him to marry his predecessor's widow, the valuable Anne of Brittany. Borgia also took a cardinal's hat for Louis's trusted counselor Amboise. After long and bitter negotiations, even Venice made an alliance with the French king, guaranteeing to lend aid to the invasion.

The campaign for Milan was short and decisive. After two of his ablest commanders deserted to the French and the Milanese defenses collapsed under artillery bombardment, Ludovico fled to Austria under protection of the emperor. Six months later, his attempt to retake the duchy with the support of a contingent of German *landsknechts* and a large number of Swiss pikes was a great fiasco. Ludovico's Swiss, refusing to fight against their countrymen in Louis XII's army, laid down their arms, and Sforza was forced to flee again. Captured and sent to France, he died there in 1508.

Having thus secured Milan, Louis XII turned covetous eyes on far-off Naples, as the Cardinal d'Amboise deftly pursued the scent of the papal tiara. In November, 1500, a strange agreement known as the Treaty of Granada was concluded between the French king and Ferdinand of Aragon, by which they agreed to conquer and partition Naples between them, Louis to rule the northern half and Ferdinand the southern. Seven months later, the pope sanctioned the predatory pact in return for the two monarchs' recognition of His Holiness's right to the dominion of central Italy, including Emilia and the Romagna.

Yet it became increasingly apparent to Alexander VI that it would require more than the formal recognition for his claim by two foreign rulers to achieve control of the midlands. The task of gaining and consolidating papal rule there was given to the pope's nefarious son, Cesare Borgia, once cardinal of Valencia, now duke of Valentinois. Borgia was a cold and malevolent creature whose reputation for violence and ruthlessness was already well established. He stopped at nothing to achieve his ambitions, including the murder of his elder brother, the duke of Gandia. In January 1500 Cesare Borgia began his three-year despoilment of the Romagna. With French forces under his command, and through perfidy and murder, he destroyed the independent power of the petty Romagna princes and began to carve out a large principality of his own under the suzerainty of his father, the pope. Successful in his first campaign, he next began exerting pressure on neighboring Florence and intimidating the Florentine government. But

CESARE BORGIA. *The nefarious son of Pope Alexander VI ruthlessly conquered the petty rulers of Emilia and the Romagna but failed to establish a permanent or stable regime there. (Alinari/Editorial Photocolor Archives)*

at the height of his power, Cesare Borgia's fortune suddenly changed with the death of his father in August 1503. His empire quickly collapsed around him and the former scourge of the Romagna withdrew ignominiously to Naples where he was imprisoned and soon died. The new pope was none other than the Giuliano della Rovere, Pope Julius II, the Borgias' bitterest enemy.

The Treaty of Granada was scarcely two years old before it was scrapped by both Ferdinand and Louis as a result of continuing rivalry over the division of their Neapolitan spoils. Aragonese control of the seas around Naples and the organizational and leadership abilities of the great Spanish captain Gonzalo de Córdoba proved decisive in the expulsion of the French from southern Italy by the beginning of 1504. In 1505, Louis renounced all further claims to Naples and a year later acquiesced to the marriage of his niece, Germaine de Foix, to Ferdinand of Aragon. Isabel had died in 1504 and Ferdinand hoped to prevent both Castile and Aragon from falling into the hands of his son-in-law, Philip the Handsome, duke of Burgundy and son of the Emperor Maximilian. Yet the strangest episodes of the Italian wars were still ahead.

Julius II and the Holy League

Pope Julius II was unquestionably the dominant political personality of the opening decade of the sixteenth century. Sixty years of age when he assumed the papal throne, he was nevertheless almost superhuman in energy and vigor. Ambitious and uncompromising, he neither shrank from any enterprise, however formidable, that might lead to his objectives, nor faltered at any sacrifice its attainment might entail. But Julius was not only a planner of grandiose enterprises, he was also the active agent and executor of his own ambitious ventures. He was a worldly and militant man who, as contemporaries remarked, "loved the smell of smoke and the blood of battle." Only in Michelangelo did he meet a personality as immovable and indomitable as his own, and even then he tried to be the performer as well as the planner. Julius's immediate ambitions when he ascended to the papacy were to complete the consolidation of the Papal States, then lead the expulsion of the foreigners from Italy.

Julius devoted the first two years of his pontificate to preparations for his enterprises. He tried to regularize and increase papal revenues while cutting down on unnecessary expenditures. With financial firmness came a tightening of administrative policy and the purging of Borgia elements from the curia. For support and safety in his foreign policy, he expanded his diplomatic network and negotiated treaties with the Swiss for infantry units to supplement the regular papal levies. In 1505, Julius began his first military campaign, a march northward through Romagna and Emilia to reaffirm the loyalty of the lords of those areas—many of whom had repudiated their allegiance to Roman government as soon as Cesare Borgia was gone—and to complete the conquest of papal territories not reached by the duke. The climax of Julius's campaign was the surrender of Bologna, which finally opened its gates to his triumphal entry in November, 1506. Here he held court, then returned to Rome in triumph.

In the meantime, shifts in the relations among the great powers were indicating to the pope the direction of his next move—the reduction of Venetian power. Louis XII's sudden descent on Genoa to suppress a revolt there against French occupation forces caused fear in imperial circles that the French king might use control of northern Italy as a lever to promote his own candidacy for the emperorship. A meeting between Louis of France and Ferdinand of Aragon at Savona in June 1507 did nothing to calm either Maximilian's fears or the pope's apprehensions. In February 1508 Maximilian crossed the Alps with a modest force of German knights and mercenaries, only to be intercepted and defeated by an aroused Venice objecting to the passage of troops across Venetian territory. In the ensuing truce, Maximilian was forced to concede Fiume and Trieste to the Venetians. Consequently irritated and resentful, Maximilian joined with Louis XII in the League of Cambrai (December 1508) for the purpose of crushing Venice and dividing her mainland territories between them. Other powers quickly joined the pact in order to exact their pound of flesh from the high-riding republic. Mantua and Ferrara were first into the bargain, but not far behind were Ferdinand of Aragon and Pope Julius II.

In May 1509 the French king crossed the River Adda and defeated the outnumbered Venetians at Agnadello. Imperial and papal-Spanish troops struck from the north and south, and the proud republic was forced to surrender most of its territory. But at the height of his success,

Julius suddenly recognized the advantage offered to France as a result of the Venetian campaign. He also saw his own opportunity for a crucial blow against the extended French lines. Therefore, the pope quickly reversed his field—after having regained all his Romagna towns—and formed another Holy League (1510) with Ferdinand of Aragon against France. The timing was perfect. Disillusioned and provoked by the ruthlessness of French occupation, many of the cities joined Venetian moves to expel the French. The French king was caught unaware by the pope's maneuver, as Maximilian, the Swiss, and Henry VIII (who had just succeeded to the English throne) joined the coalition.

At Ravenna in April 1512, a decisive battle was fought between the bulk of the French army, commanded brilliantly by Gaston de Foix, the king's illustrious nephew, and the Spanish-papal regulars under Raymundo de Cardona, viceroy of Naples. The battle was hard-fought and bloody, ending finally in a French victory, due mostly to the firepower and deployment of French artillery. But in the melee, Gaston de Foix was killed, and with him died the French hopes for mastery of northern Italy. Their withdrawal was orderly, but continuous. Entering Italy through the Saint Gottard pass, the Swiss drove the French out of Milan and restored Massimiliano Sforza, Ludovico's son, to the ducal throne. A year later, the French attempted to return to Milan but were defeated by the Swiss at Novara.

In the meantime, Henry VIII, anxious to win glory and acclaim and goaded on by his father-in-law, Ferdinand of Aragon, entered the arena. The action at Ravenna was over by the time his army of 10,000 reached its landing near Bayonne, but from Ferdinand's point of view,

POPE JULIUS II. *This striking portrait of the crusty "Warrior Pope" is a detail from Raphael's "The Mass of Bolsena," located in the Stanza d' Eliodoro in the Vatican. It clearly reveals Julius's forceful character. (Editorial Photocolor Archives)*

the English force could serve him as well then as before. Used to divert a French force away from Navarre, Henry's army did nothing but mold and die of dysentery as Ferdinand overran the saddleback kingdom of Navarre and attached it to the crown of Aragon. Ferdinand's conquest was complete. But the costly English venture ended in humiliation and mutiny by October 1512. Ready now to withdraw from the coalition and lick his wounds, Henry was persuaded by Pope Julius to renew the attack. Therefore, in the spring, as the French returned to Milan, Henry personally led a new invasion of France from the north. Landing at Calais (the sole English trophy of the Hundred Years' War), the English, with their German allies sent by Maximilian, defeated the French knights in the colorful Battle of the Spurs, and captured the great French captain Bayard, who was, according to legend, *sans peur et sans reproche* (without fear or reproach). Having thus won his own spurs, Henry returned to England childishly jubilant after having gained nothing substantial except a stimulation to his ego and a debt that more than exhausted the treasury his father had left.

The French rout seemed to be complete, and its consequences for Italy were considerable. The council of the church, which had been convened under French auspices at Pisa for the purpose of deposing Pope Julius, retreated with the French armies to Milan, and there disbanded when the French power collapsed. In Florence, the Medici were returned to power and the republican government was overthrown by Spanish arms. The defending Florentine militia, recruited by Machiavelli, fled in disorder when faced by the disciplined Spanish infantry. Lorenzo the Magnificent's two remaining sons, Cardinal Giovanni and his younger brother Giuliano, assumed control of the city (Piero had died in 1503). Upon Giuliano's death in 1516, Piero's weak and ineffectual son Lorenzo governed Florence as a satellite of Medicean Rome. Meanwhile, in February 1513, Julius II died and the papal scepter fell to Giovanni de' Medici as Pope Leo X. The Italian carousel had come a full turn since 1492.

The Invasion by Francis I

Two years later, the political winds shifted again. Leo X had none of the crusading vigor nor the military ambitions of his predecessor, and he lacked the political acumen of his illustrious father. His avowed intention was to enjoy the papacy and its cultural fruits now that God had given it to him. But unhappily, it was not his lot either to relax and enjoy the fruits of his predecessor's sweat or to bask in the glories of the Roman Renaissance. His was to be, even more than Julius II's, a pontificate of upheaval and disorder. Leo would have preferred being only the last of the Renaissance popes. But Martin Luther and Ulrich Zwingli made him also the first pope of the Reformation.

On January 1, 1515, the decrepit old king, Louis XII, died. The crown of France passed to his young and robust cousin, François d'An-

FRANCIS I AT THE BATTLE OF MARIGNANO. *The French invasion and victory in September 1515 opened a new phase of the Italian Wars and marked the debut of the young king in international politics. (Bibliothèque Nationale, Paris)*

goulême, son of the count of Angoulême and Louise of Savoy. Observers at the time believed it would only be a matter of time before Francis I would reopen the Italian wars, even though his legal claims to Milan were slimmer than those of Charles VIII and Louis XII. Such a venture stood an excellent chance of bringing wealth, power, and glory to both France and its illustrious king. What further justification was needed? In August 1515, Francis crossed the Alps with the cream of the French cavaliers, a large array of Gascon infantry and an even larger host of German mercenaries, all supported with the greatest variety and weight of artillery yet seen in Italy. On September 14–15, the French army met and defeated a powerful and hitherto invincible force of Swiss infantry defending the duchy of Milan at Marignano. The battle was a turning point in European political and religious affairs, and was a landmark in military history. It marked the close of a half-century of military domination by the Swiss pikemen, and ended the shorter period of independent Swiss participation in Italian affairs. Machiavelli's fears of two years earlier—that the Swiss would overrun Italy and dominate it by force—turned out to be groundless. By the Treaty of Fribourg, the Swiss were forbidden to fight against French arms and were bound by a system of pensions to the service of France. They also surrendered control of the Simplon Pass, which meant that Francis I not only became duke of Milan but that he would be able to defend it with ease against all intruders.

Pope Leo X quickly made peace with the French king at Bologna, where in December 1515 they concluded the famous concordat that shaped Franco-papal relations for the next century and a half. By the Concordat of Bologna, the papacy conceded to the French king all the privileges and powers enjoyed since the Pragmatic Sanction of Bourges (1438) by the French clergy. Thus, to the crown went the right to make all nominations to vacant bishoprics and abbacies in France, and the political jurisdiction of the French clergy. The pope retained the power of confirmation, of course, and also the annates from newly appointed benefices. Territorially, Leo gave up Parma and Piacenza in exchange for the French guarantee that the Medici rule in Florence would not be disturbed. Since Maximilian was also allied with the papacy in futile resistance to the French invasion, he was forced to relinquish Verona and other Venetian cities he had held since the expulsion of the French two years earlier.

By 1516 all of northern Italy lay under the direct or satellite control of France. Only Spanish Naples stood untouched by the French victory. But in that same year, sixteen-year-old Charles of Ghent became king of Aragon and Castile and a new era of the Italian wars began. With Charles's elevation to the archduchy of Austria three years later (he was already ruler of the Burgundian Netherlands) and his election as Holy Roman Emperor following Maximilian's death, the struggle for Italy became a Europe-wide Habsburg-Valois duel.

The Renaissance Art of War

Like the literature, art, and science of the Renaissance, warfare was also transitional. The successful armies of the time incorporated mercenary, feudal, and national (or royal) elements in various combinations and uses. They also employed artillery, not only for siege purposes, but also for field action against stationary and moving targets. Hand firearms, from pistols to heavy arquebuses, were employed in increasing numbers and effectiveness, although the lance and sword were still considered the soldier's mainstay and the crossbow his deadliest missile weapon.

Raising an Army

Feudal levies still provided the bulk of early sixteenth-century cavalry, especially in the French armies. This was and continued to be the aristocratic arm of all military organizations. In France the *ban* and *arrière-ban* were the feudal levies required of tenants owing military service for their fiefs. In the Middle Ages the *ban* had applied to the king's immediate vassals, or tenants-in-chief, and the *arrière-ban* to those of lower rank. By the sixteenth century, the terms together referred to all who owed military service to the king. Use of the *ban et arrière-ban* was limited to specific needs and for designated periods of time, and consisted primarily of heavy cavalry—mounted nobles with all of their retainers—but some peasant militia likewise owed service. Feudal levies were also retained in the Spanish armies of the Renaissance, but they made up a smaller percentage than in the French, and they consisted more often of light cavalry armed with spears and mounted on fast, lightly armored horses. Light cavalry was effectively used by the Spanish in Italy, and it was decisive in the conquest of Mexico and Peru. As the Inca Garcilaso de la Vega observed, "Spain won a new world *á la jineta*" (on horseback, riding with very short stirrups and spear in the manner of the Moors).

By the outbreak of the Italian wars, the major European monarchs—those who could afford it—also had the nucleus of a professional standing army. In France this consisted of the king's household guard plus the *gendarmerie,* or as they were designated at the time, the *compagnies d'ordonnance.* These companies, paid for on a continuous basis by the king, were composed of one hundred "lances" and their commanders. A lance consisted of a mounted knight (*gendarme*) and his retinue—usually a squire, valet, page, and one or two archers. In the time of the Italian wars, they were the best heavy cavalry in Europe. The Spanish armies also had a standing nucleus of a royal guard, the *guardas viejas,* of heavy cavalry, but this was supplemented in Castilian armies with semipermanent levies from the towns and with reserve volunteers, both of which were infantry. This Castilian standing (reserve) infantry was unique in its time.

Since it was too risky to allow common people to bear arms and it was beneath the dignity of the nobility to fight on foot, most armies hired their infantry on a job basis, just as modern movie producers hire extras for shooting mob scenes. These mercenaries might be local or they might be brought from other countries. By the middle of the fifteenth century, every government recognized the tactical and individual superiority of the Swiss pikemen.

Tactics and Arms

The vaunted Swiss square was the most effective infantry tactic of the Renaissance, not only against mounted cavalry but against other infantry as well. It consisted of a compact formation of some 6,000 men, shoulder to shoulder, eighty-five men across and seventy deep, armed with eighteen- to twenty-foot-long pikes on the front ranks, halberds on the flanks, and swords in the center of the square. This formation was virtually impenetrable by a cavalry charge and could quickly change to the offensive against an army infantry line. Several squares deployed in echelon could be invincible in open terrain. The Swiss success, of course, depended not only on their formation and equipment, but on the discipline and valor of the pikemen themselves. Other nations eventually adopted the Swiss tactics—most notably the German mercenary *landsknechtes*—but with the growing efficiency of field artillery and small arms, their potency declined. They were also ineffective in rough terrain. Other infantry tactics and formations were developed as the square and phalanx declined, but mercenary infantry did not decline. During the whole of the sixteenth century and into the seventeenth, the bulk of the foot soldiers in all armies were hired mercenaries from Switzerland, Germany, Bohemia, Italy, the Netherlands, Wales, Ireland, Scotland, Scandinavia, and eastern Europe.

In the course of the Italian wars, the Spanish army developed into a superior fighting force unequaled for nearly 100 years. Its success was based on the courage and ability of its Castilian infantry and light cavalry, its envied discipline, the variety and flexibility of its tactics, and the competence of its commanders, who were of the caliber of Gonzalo de Córdoba. Great mobility and speed were provided by the light horse, and firepower was increased by the early adoption of hand firearms. Units were divided into companies (*capitanías*) of 500 men and regiments (*coronelías*) of twelve companies each, commanded by a colonel. Even greater mobility and versatility were achieved by the military reforms of 1534, when the famous Spanish *tercio* was first introduced. A *tercio* (third) was composed of an integrated 3,000-man striking force made up of three parts—pikemen, swordsmen, and arquebusiers. To each *tercio* was attached a cavalry unit of 500 to 600 light and heavy horse, and a battery of artillery.

Field artillery was the forte of the French armies in Italy. Largely abandoning the cumbersome and virtually immobile bronze giants of

the preceding decades, the French developed smaller, more portable guns carried into battle on trunnions. They were usually longer barreled than their predecessors but with a smaller bore and greater emphasis on accuracy and faster firing. Yet in spite of improvements, artillery in the early sixteenth century was still extremely inaccurate and unwieldy, when not outright dangerous to the users. The most dramatic change caused by the use of the cannon was in defensive fortifications. Gunpowder had made the tall, thin walls of the medieval castles obsolete and, as a result, both building styles and military tactics changed drastically. The low, thick walls with protruding bastions did not spring up overnight, but the period of the Italian wars marked the beginning of a steady revolution in fortification building and siege tactics.

Naval Warfare

Naval armaments and warfare also grew as a result of the wars in Italy. Supplies and equipment for the land armies battling up and down the peninsula were largely replenished by ships. Ports sometimes had to be attacked and interference by enemy vessels resisted. French and Spanish strength in this field lagged noticeably behind. But Ferdinand could frequently adapt a larger merchant fleet to wartime uses, and this, with the strategic employment of his island possessions near Italy, gave him a considerable advantage over his Gallic foe.

For numbers, size, and strength, however, the fleets of France and Spain combined could hardly compare with the permanent war galleys of Venice which, by the turn of the century, numbered over 100. Of the large national powers, only England maintained a sizable war fleet of sailing ships, though even these had to double as merchantmen. The strength of English seapower was built by Henry VIII around the nucleus of fourteen warships left by his father and the addition of forty-eight more fighting ships ranging in size from 40-ton pinnaces to the 1,000-ton *Henry Grace à Dieu*. By the end of his reign, Henry VIII had an impressive royal navy of sixty or more fighting ships and many additional heavy merchantmen.

The Development of European Diplomacy

The sudden impact of the Italian wars had a profound effect on both Italian and European diplomacy. As the Italian states system was destroyed, a new and broader European states system came into being. No more stable in its origins than the Italian had been, it adopted, modified, used, and developed the techniques and procedures of Italian diplomacy and applied them to the ever-widening scope of European and world relations. As the competition for alliances among the great powers grew more intense, the need for permanent or continuous diplomatic relations was felt.

The leader in this development was the wily Ferdinand of Aragon, notorious for both his hard-nosed realism and his cunning. The latter is exemplified in the story of his interview with the French ambassador, who accused him of twice deceiving his master, the French king. Ferdinand angrily retorted, "You lie! I've deceived him six times."

Ferdinand of Aragon was the first of the Renaissance princes outside Italy to develop a systematic and more or less continuous network of diplomacy. His older contemporary and rival, Louis XI, had intricate diplomatic involvements with some of the northern Italian states and with neighboring rulers in Switzerland, Lorraine, and the Rhineland. But Louis's negotiations were always *ad hoc* and constantly shifting as he conducted his diplomacy through temporary legates or casual visitors. Ferdinand, on the other hand, built up a pattern of relations with other powers, directed and adjusted through the systematic use of permanent embassies. By the beginning of the sixteenth century, Ferdinand had resident ambassadors (mostly Castilians) not only in Rome and Venice, but also in England, the Netherlands, and Austria. These were also the pivots of his dynastic alliances. His intention was obviously the isolation of France. Ferdinand's diplomatic network served him well. It also provided the core of a trained body of diplomatic functionaries, from ambassadors and consuls to clerks and couriers, who helped make the Spanish diplomatic service the strongest in Europe.

During the early years of the Italian wars, each of the major Italian states, already in continuous contact with each other, established resident embassies at the courts of France, Austria, and Spain. Even the papacy sent nuncios to foreign courts. Although they lagged behind Ferdinand, the other monarchs also soon adopted permanent diplomatic relations, first with Rome, then with the other Italian states, and finally with the larger European powers. Under Henry VIII, English residents were established, or reestablished, in Spain, the Netherlands, and Austria, and after Wolsey took over the management of policy, in France. Maximilian and Louis XII were slower in extending legations, other than to Rome, but after Charles V took over the imperial office (and the Spanish diplomatic network of his grandfather) and Francis I began to feel the Habsburg cordon tightening around him, both imperial and French diplomacy were broadened. In fact, Francis I extended the useful instrument beyond Christian Europe and established an embassy at the Sublime Port (Istanbul) to help promote and maintain cooperative ties with the Ottoman Turks. By 1535 the establishment of modern diplomatic relations was well underway throughout Europe.

The primary functions of these diplomatic representatives were to secure and maintain alliances and friendship with other powers and to acquire information that might be useful in formulating policy. The methods of fulfilling these duties varied with personality, occasion, and need. Ambassadors were expected to declare and uphold the rights of their governments while in residence and represent that government at all ceremonial and state functions. More important, they were to establish and operate an effective system of intelligence in order to obtain reliable information. Friendship should thus be cultivated not only among the important personalities at court but also with other ambassadors, servants, merchants, or clerics. To help lubricate the lips of

DIPLOMATIC CEREMONIAL. *A foreign ambassador taking leave from court. A detail from a series of paintings by Vittore Carpaccio illustrating the Legend of St. Ursula. (Alinari/ Editorial Photocolor Archives)*

informants, the more effective envoys discreetly distributed money to knowledgeable courtiers and potential mediaries. The astute ambassadors were able to discern from this potpourri of information and gossip which of it was reliable and useable and which was to be disregarded—or passed on to confuse a rival agent. Residents were also expected to obtain frequent audiences with the rulers to whom they were accredited and learn of their intentions, while reaffirming the policies of their own masters. Sometimes this resulted in verbal duels of mutual deception. In these audiences, formal negotiations occasionally took place, but usually such bargaining and all treaty making was carried on by an ambassador extraordinary or a special agent sent with specific instructions for that purpose.

As the range of European diplomacy widened, the problems of communication multiplied accordingly. The language barrier may not have been as complex as it is today, but there were few facilities for overcoming it. In formal, ceremonial address, and in written treaties and proclamations, Latin was the universal language of diplomacy. Yet relatively little verbal communication was carried on in it, and its written use declined fast after mid-century. Some of the resident ambassadors of the early sixteenth century were unlearned in Latin, and even the majority who were educated had to converse and negotiate with many who were not. To be entirely effective, an envoy should speak the tongue of the country of his residence plus as many of the other languages likely to be encountered as possible. But linguistic ability along with the other traits necessary in a good ambassador were not always easy to find. Rulers, therefore, and ambassadors, too, usually did the best they could with what they had. In Italy, varying dialects of Italian—especially the language of Rome—prevailed, and a surprising number of European diplomats were conversant in Italian. The rapid growth and prestige of vernacular French made it another language frequently used in diplomatic circles, even outside France and the French-speaking Lowlands. English and German were seldom used by other than their own natives. The ambassadors' dispatches and letters from their governments were always in the vernacular. Even the correspondence of the popes with their nuncios was written in Italian, rather than Latin, after the first decade of the sixteenth century.

The other problem of communication was the difficulty in transmitting dispatches over great distances with sufficient safety and speed. In France, Spain, and England, official government posts were established. But these posts were annoyingly slow and dangerously unreliable. When diplomatic pouches of rival, or even friendly, foreign states were carried in the mails, the temptation to peruse the contents or delay the pouch was too much for most officials to resist. Occasionally, reliable travelers were also entrusted with letters when the situation and the need seemed to warrant it. Diplomatic correspondence was sometimes sent by merchant post. Here the service was inexpensive and considerably safer than foreign government post, but it was very slow.

MAXIMILIAN I SENDING A DIPLOMATIC DISPATCH. *By the beginning of the sixteenth century, royal couriers were becoming an important part of the growing diplomatic network in Europe. (Bild-Archiv der Österreichischen Nationalbibliothek, Vienna)*

Consequently, all of the European states employed, in varying numbers, diplomatic couriers to carry and deliver dispatches of an urgent or confidential nature. These couriers were well-paid (though the occupational hazards were great), and most governments of the Renaissance lacked the funds to hire as many as were needed. To improve the factors of safety and rapid delivery, multiple dispatches were sent by various routes and confidential messages were put into diplomatic cipher. The system was far from perfect, but it served a useful and important function during the formative age of modern diplomacy.

Diplomatic Theory and International Law

The evolution of a European system of national states, accelerated by the rivalry over Italy and the development of diplomatic machinery on a Europe-wide scale, brought to the front a number of intellectual problems that now required fresh thought and new interpretations in light of the changing attitudes toward international relations and law. The medieval conception of the Christian commonwealth as a single family of nations adopting a universal view of law and recognizing the universality of the church was rapidly declining in the early sixteenth century. Europe was not a single society. It was a jungle of rival, contending monarchies and states, vying with one another for power and prestige, and with each of the various royal families promoting its own dynastic ambitions. From our vantage point, this all seems obvious. To the people of the time, it was not so clear. How different was the rivalry among the nations from the previous century's equally competitive struggles among the city-states of Italy? Did competition necessarily contradict unity? If the *Respublica Christiana* did not exist, what did? The theorists still talked about the unity of Christendom, but the actions of aspiring monarchs disproved it.

The intellectual dilemmas of early "international" relations were not easy to resolve. From outward appearances, it looks as though the monarchs and diplomats of the early sixteenth century recognized their role as the precursors of modern nation-states. Perhaps some of them did, but by and large they would not have known the meaning of the term. They had personal, dynastic, and sometimes even national interests at heart; but it all operated within a framework of law more familiar to the medieval mind than to our own. With few exceptions, the writers and theorists still conceived of European society as undivided, and more often interpreted the ambassadors' duty as the "preservation of peace and the common welfare" than, as Ermolao Barbaro saw it, "to do, say, advise, and think whatever may best serve the preservation and aggrandizement of his own state." Diplomats themselves were more apt to view the new diplomacy in this way than were the humanists or the canon and civil lawyers. Barbaro was a practicing ambassador as well as a theorist. The Italian wars catalyzed this transition from the medieval concept of the law of nations (which viewed nations as members of a single commonwealth) to the modern view of international law between separate and sovereign states. For the rest of the century, lawyers, theologians, and political theorists generally continued to write as though no change had taken place, whereas those practitioners of diplomacy who were involved in the day-to-day power struggle were keenly aware that it had.

Among the many vexing and sometimes insoluble problems encountered in the spread of continuous diplomacy was that of diplomatic immunity and extraterritoriality. If an ambassador represents a sovereign, independent power at a foreign court that is also sovereign and autonomous, what legal rights and obligations does he possess? Does he carry his own national laws with him or is he subject to those of his host? What about the religious activities of a Catholic ambassador at a Protestant court? How different would his legal status be if the ambassador represented not a sovereign state but a sister power within a family of nations? There were no simple answers to these questions. They were solved in various ways by different governments, and the solutions changed markedly between the beginning of the century and its end. In general, the trend was away from the medieval concept of community and toward the notion of extraterritoriality, which implied the autonomy of national laws and recognized the right of an ambassador to carry the law of his own nation with him. Except when violating a higher law still accepted as universal or when endangering the safety and sovereignty of his host nation, the ambassador of the sixteenth century was granted rather full immunity from the civil laws of the host state. Such immunity, however reluctantly granted or frequently violated, was necessary for a prince to concede in order to receive the same recognition for his own ambassadors abroad.

Roman Law in the Renaissance

The gradual emergence of a conception of international law during the Renaissance accompanied a similar change in attitudes toward civil law and jurisprudence. In the late Middle Ages, particularly the twelfth and thirteenth centuries, there was a great revival of interest in Roman law. This regeneration was most active in Italy and Germany, and was reflected in the numerous commentaries and "glosses" (marginal notes) written on the Justinian Code (the great sixth-century codification of Roman law). The so-called glossators of this period were the lawyers and legal commentators who thus expounded the meaning of the various Justinian texts.

The Bartolists and their Opponents

The next step in the rehabilitation of Roman law came with Bartolus of Sassoferrato (1314–57) and his followers, who attempted through reason and dialectic to apply ancient law to contemporary situations without much regard to their original meaning and without taking into consideration the vast changes in conditions wrought by the passage of seven centuries. Both the glossators and the post-glossators (Bartolists) gave cogency to the concept of *Respublica Christiana* by applying to it the terminology and ideas of the ancient Roman Empire. They also made the study of law extremely popular in fourteenth- and fifteenth-century Italy. The leading law faculties were at Bologna, Pavia, and Pisa, but most Italian universities offered law as one of their major strengths.

The legal profession, especially the methodological approach of the jurist, was severely criticized by the Italian humanists of the Renaissance. Their opposition was based partly on the close relationship between civil and canon law (as a result of which, they saw the lawyers as a class of civil scholastics), partly on the static conception of law engendered by the Bartolists, and partly on their atrocious Latin and their disregard for literary eloquence and beauty. The humanists, who viewed institutions and conditions as developmental, evolutionary processes, reacted against the unhistorical approach of the civil and canon lawyers. In this vein, Petrarch blamed the lawyers because "They do not reflect that a knowledge of the origins of their art and of the great writers brings intellectual pleasure and may serve in the practice of their trade. Their equipment is more appropriate for the practice of the mechanic arts, whereas the purpose of legal studies should be more liberal and honorable."

Undaunted by humanist criticism, however, the Bartolists continued to dominate the teaching and practice of law in Italy. In the meantime, a new generation of legal interpreters replaced the negativism of the humanist critics with a new approach to law, but one that was still based directly on the humanists' historical outlook. This school, known as the *mos gallicus* ("after the manner of the French") because of its wide adoption in France, emphasized the understanding of Roman law in its historical context rather than attempting to apply (or misapply) it to existing conditions. In following this path, the greatest of the early sixteenth-century jurists, Andrea Alciati (1492–1550) and Jacques Cujas (1500–90), established a historical school of jurisprudence but without the humanists' confidence in the applicability of historical lessons. Alciati, an Italian jurist who found a more compatible environment in France, made the University of Bourges the center of this French historical-legalistic tradition, as he returned to the sources to separate the "pure" Roman law from the mountains of comments and annotations of the glossators. Cujas went even further than Alciati in applying a critical and analytical approach to the study and interpretation of law. Both the *mos italicus* and the *mos gallicus* helped stimulate the rapid spread of Roman law in the sixteenth century.

English Common Law

In England the vicissitudes of the law followed a somewhat different course because of the overriding importance of the common law, which grew out of the case decisions of English judges, as recorded in the yearbooks. This does not mean that English lawyers did not borrow from Roman law, but rather that they adopted useful features of it rather than accepting the system. English law, which had developed out of earlier Germanic and feudal customs, as well as continental precedents and canon law, entered a vital period of adaptation and institutionalization during the late fifteenth and early sixteenth centuries. Under Henry VII and Henry VIII, this meant the application of a variety of medieval legal traditions to the creation of an absolute state while at the same time preserving the flexibility and popularity of the traditions themselves. In the theoretical field, such a synthesis had already been advocated by Sir John Fortescue (ca. 1394–1476) in his *De laudibus legum Angliae* (In Praise of the Laws of England). Together, the monarchs and the parliamentary lawyers now made it a practical reality. This reconciliation of medieval law with the modern state, which preserved some of the unique characteristics of each, was one of the great achievements of the Tudor monarchy.

Renaissance Political Thought

The changing conceptions and role of law in the Renaissance are strongly reflected in the related discussions and speculations on politics and the nature of political jurisdictions. Such thinking was taking place on many levels and with varying degrees of cogency in the universities, in the chanceries, and among the ecclesiastical bodies of Europe. The most important concept to emerge from these considerations, and the most original feature of Renaissance political thought, was the concept of the state. Seldom discussed in the way we would today, the idea was elusive and deceptive, even in the fifteenth century. The word *state*, in all of its forms and in every language, from *stadt, stato, estado,* and *état* to *estate, status,* and *station,* was widely employed in medieval litera- ture. But the idea implied by its use never seems to have corresponded exactly with the notion of the state as a political unit of government. "Christendom, the union of the various flocks under one shepherd with divine claims, divine origin, and divine sovereignty," comments J. N. Figgis, "had to be transformed into Europe, the habitat of competing sects and compact nations, before the conditions of modern politics arose."

Of course the absence of a theory of the state in the Middle Ages does not signify the absence of political thought. On the contrary, there were many theories of politics in medieval Europe, all based in one way or another on the principle of contract. Contract theory meant mutual rights, but it also meant the fusion of both public and private rights, and of secular and religious jurisdiction. Furthermore, the emergence of the concept of the state in the Renaissance gave rise to varying interpreta- tions of the role of the state, not only in relation to its subjects but also vis-à-vis the church and the empire (in the few cases in which the imperial idea was still recognized as having "universal" authority).

We have already seen some anticipation of this new theory of state in the sermons and writings of Marsiglio of Padua and Nicholas of Cusa, but not until the chain reaction set off by the French invasions of Italy did the concept begin to emerge in its fullness, and then with great speed, especially in Italy. Immediately after the Florentine revolution of 1494 and the establishment of the republic, there was great speculation in Florence on politics and political theory. The Florentines were not alone in sensing that a new era had begun, not only in the immediate political life of Italy but in the history of Europe. Few people could see exactly what was happening or what its implications were, but they did think more seriously and speculatively about political and historical ideas.

More and Seyssel

In the second decade of the sixteenth century, no less than half a dozen important books were written on the nature and functions of the state, all by men who were active participants in, not just observers of, the revolutionary events of the day. For example, Sir Thomas More's *Utopia*—which scholars still have difficulty deciding whether to call a harbinger of the future or a postscript to the past—delightfully but de- spairingly recounted the evils brought on by "modern" society, and satirically corrected them in his island of Utopia (Nowhere). With remarkable perspicacity, More dissected the Renaissance state and unveiled its cupidity, ruthlessness, and ambition; he described it as one that rejected the sanctions of religion and sought only its own aggrandizement and wealth. He wished it were not so, but it was, and the only remedy seemed to be in flight to fantasy. Yet in the back of his mind, More felt that the seemingly absolute ruler must in the end recognize the sovereign authority of the church and yield to the dictates of natural law. He would one day discover his mistake—but then it was too late.

Two years after the publication of *Utopia*, the French ex-minister and chancellor, scholar, humanist, and bishop, Claude de Seyssel, published his *Le grande monarchie de France* (The Great French Monarchy). Like More, Seyssel saw the realities of the growing power of monarchy, but was more inclined to see its benefits than its dangers. Relatively unconcerned about the form of government, Seyssel emphasized its functions, concluding that the best government is that which governs best, and that appeared at the time to be the monarchy of France—not because it was absolute, but because it was not. Instead, it possessed the ideal balance of power among king, nobles, church, orders, cities, courts, and people. Powerful and wealthy enough to enforce the common law and defend the realm against outside enemies, the monarch was restrained from abusing his authority or usurping more by the limitations and sanctions of religion, law, and custom. But Seyssel was observing through rose-colored glasses. His prosaic state was as idealistic as More's imaginative Utopia.

Machiavelli

The early sixteenth century had its most acute observer and terse commentator on the politics of the state in the Florentine functionary and man of letters, Niccolò Machiavelli. During the first years of the Italian wars, when Florence was dominated by the charismatic personality of Savonarola, Machiavelli was studying the business of government through quiet observation of the newly established republic. In 1498, Machiavelli was appointed chancellor of the Second Chancery, charged with foreign affairs, and secretary to the Council of Ten, the department of war. For the next fourteen years, he served the republic with enthusiasm and efficiency. His duties were not only administrative and secretarial, he was also frequently sent on diplomatic missions to foreign courts. It was as a representative to Cesare Borgia, while this perverse prince was campaigning in the Romagna, that Machiavelli saw first-hand the workings of intrigue and deceit that marked Italian politics and diplomacy. But suddenly, with the retreat of French troops from Florence and the restoration of the Medici in 1512, Machiavelli was removed from office and, after an agonizing interlude of torture, was sent into "retirement" at his ancestral home outside of Florence.

For the next fifteen years, Machiavelli was a moderately prominent man of letters, gaining most of his modest recognition as a satirist. His reputation as the cynical preceptor of tyranny and despotism, however,

NICCOLO MACHIAVELLI.
This well-known portrait by Santi di Tito, in the Palazzo Vecchio, symbolizes the continuing enigma of the Florentine secretary, diplomat, historian, dramatist, poet, and political philosopher. (Alinari/Editorial Photocolor Archives)

resulted from the posthumous publication of a little book called *The Prince*, which he wrote during the latter months of 1513 to instruct Giuliano de' Medici on the methods to use in governing the Romagna. The infamy of Machiavelli's *The Prince* derived from the various reactions to its baldly irreligious and immoral advocacy of deceit, calumny, and even murder as legitimate methods for the use of a prince in securing and maintaining political power. The tendency to interpret it as a book of general political principles, rather than as a treatise written to a particular person for a specific purpose, has added to its disrepute. Over the years, *The Prince* has become the most controversial and elusive piece of political literature to come out of the Renaissance.

Although this is his most famous work, *The Prince* is not Machiavelli's most important political writing. His view of the state, as revealed in *The Discourses on Titus Livy, Florentine History*, and *The Art of War*, as well as in *The Prince*, depicts a new and virile interpretation of the state as an autonomous power, subject to its own rules of behavior and justification, and dedicated to creating a stable, efficient, prosperous regime. He believed in a strong and effective government, whatever its form—though for Florence he much preferred a republic to a monarchy—that could maintain public order and defend itself against all enemies, internal as well as external. To do this, he believed the state had to be entirely secular, with no compulsion or interference from the church, and had to function under the sanction of law. He advocated organized religion, but rather as the necessary mystique that binds people together under common loyalties and aspirations than as an institution that interferes with the functioning of government. His chief criticism of Christianity was based on the belief that in too many cases it divided the people rather than united them. As a further necessity to the stability and order of the country, Machiavelli believed in the creation and maintenance of a citizen militia to replace the hired mercenaries. Finally, the state played an important but intangible role in shaping and maintaining the unique character traits and spirit of its citizenry.

Most of these conceptions represent a sharp break with previous interpretations, although it should be noted how close Marsiglio of Padua came to the same views in his *Defensor Pacis* (1324). Yet Machiavelli's conception of the state was not modern when considered in the framework of the developments of national monarchy. His prince was always a Renaissance Italian prince, and his state the city-state of fifteenth- and sixteenth-century Italy. He conceptually separated and liberated the secular state from the church but failed to understand the real nature of national monarchy as it was then emerging in England, France, and eventually Spain. Machiavelli naïvely insisted that Switzerland was a more powerful and dangerous threat to Italy than was France.

Machiavelli's outlook on the people and society of his day seems to have been pessimistic, or as some writers have insisted, realistic. But did Machiavelli really believe people were all naturally and irredeemably evil, or were they just instinctively egocentric? He does say they are self-centered, ambitious, and usually foolish, but does this mean hopelessly depraved? Elsewhere he affirmed that the people are more to be trusted than princes, and he had confidence enough in the citizens to trust them with arms and the defense of the state. What appears to be pessimism in Machiavelli is more likely a veiled hope—hope in the regenerating power of *virtù* (vitality, valor, and decisiveness), and trust in the recurring cycles of history. In the golden age of ancient republican Rome, people were virtuous, brave, and wise; and according to Machiavelli's own acknowledgement, not only do "Natives of the same country preserve for all time the same characteristics," but "All cities and all people are and ever have been animated by the same desires and the same passions; so that it is easy by diligent study of the past, to foresee what is likely to happen in the future in any republic." But *virtù* involves more than vigor and resolution. People are also victims of *fortuna,* and what serves one person well fortune causes to be the downfall of another. Therefore, the virtuous and fortunate prince is one who can adapt himself to the needs of the time and steer his own ship of state rather than have it buffeted and capsized by the forces he should harness and use.

This was Machiavelli's dream, that Florence's citizens and rulers would rise from their lethargy and become as virtuous as those of old, redeeming their state and all of Italy from the tyranny of foreign powers. But being a dreamer, Machiavelli was out of touch in many important ways with the long-range realities of rule. His was an incisive and clever mind, quick to see the irony and pith of a situation, but sometimes unable to probe deeply into the nature of its causes or the meaning of its effects. He was neither an abstract political theorist nor a completely realistic observer of politics and history. Rather, he was the poet of politics and of human nature, seeing and tersely commenting on the foibles of political life.

Suggestions for Further Reading

THE INVASIONS OF ITALY

Cecilia M. Ady, "The Invasions of Italy," in *The New Cambridge Modern History*, I, 343–67, is a good overview. Another, lighter account, is E. R. Chamberlin, "The French Invasion of Italy, 1494," *History Today*, 22 (1972), 54–61. Clemente Fusero, *The Borgias* (New York, 1972), and Sarah Bradford, *Cesare Borgia, His Life and Times* (New York, 1976), show the role of the Borgias in the Italian wars. The essential Savonarola is Roberto Ridolfi, *The Life of Girolamo Savonarola*, tr. by Cecil Grayson (New York, 1959). Other outstanding accounts are Donald Weinstein, *Savonarola and Florence: Prophecy and Patriotism in the Renaissance* (Princeton, 1970), and Ronald M. Steinberg, *Fra Girolamo Savonarola* (Athens, 1977). Rosemary D. Jones, *Francesco Vettori: Florentine Citizen and Medici Servant* (London, 1972), sheds much light on the period. The climax of Francis I's invasion is analyzed by R. J. Knecht in "The Concordat of 1516," *University of Birmingham Historical Journal* (1963), 16–32.

WAR AND DIPLOMACY

J. R. Hale, *Renaissance Fortification: Art or Engineering?* (New York, 1979) is a fresh examination of an important aspect of Renaissance warfare. It should be read in conjunction with Christopher Duffy's more general, *Siege Warfare: The Fortress in the Early Modern World, 1494–1660* (London, 1979). F. L. Taylor, *The Art of War in Italy* (Cambridge, 1921) is long out of date but contains some useful data on the Italian wars. More current is J. R. Hale, "International Relations in the West: Diplomacy and War," in *The New Cambridge Modern History*, I, 259–91. For diplomacy, see the appropriate chapters in Garrett Mattingly, *Renaissance Diplomacy* (Boston, 1955), and De Lamar Jensen, "Power Politics and Diplomacy, 1500–1650," in Richard DeMolen (ed.), *The Meaning of the Renaissance and Reformation* (Boston, 1975), 327–68.

LEGAL AND POLITICAL THOUGHT

The most helpful general studies of late medieval and Renaissance legal and political thought are Gaines Post, *Studies in Medieval Legal Thought: Public Law and the State* (Princeton, 1964); J. N. Figgis, *Political Thought from Gerson to Grotius, 1414–1625*, with a new introduction by Garrett Mattingly (New York, 1960); Walter Ullmann, *A History of Political Thought: The Middle Ages* (Baltimore, 1965); and M. Wilks, *The Problems of Sovereignty in the Later Middle Ages* (Cambridge, 1963). Although it is very old, C. N. S. Woolf, *Bartolus of Sassoferrato* (Cambridge, 1913) is the only adequate study of the post-glossators and their founder. For later political thinkers, see Francis Oakley, *The Political Thought of Pierre d'Ailly* (New Haven, 1964); Nicolai Rubinstein, "Marsilius of Padua and Italian Political Thought of His Time," in *Europe in the Late Middle Ages*, ed. by J. R. Hale, et al. (Evanston, 1965), 15–43; and M. Watanabe, *The Political Ideas of Nicholas of Cusa* (Geneva, 1963). Myron P. Gilmore, *Humanists and Jurists: Six Studies in the Renaissance* (Cambridge, Mass., 1963) is by one of the leading Renaissance scholars of our time. The most recent and the best discussion of Renaissance political thinking is Quentin Skinner's comprehensive *The Foundations of Modern Political Thought: The Renaissance*, vol. 1 (New York, 1978).

MACHIAVELLI

De Lamar Jensen (ed.), *Machiavelli: Cynic, Patriot or Political Scientist?* (Boston, 1960), presents conflicting opinions on Machiavelli. The best biographies are J. R. Hale, *Machiavelli and Renaissance Italy* (New York, 1960), and Roberto Ridolfi, *The Life of Niccolò Machiavelli*, tr. by Cecil Grayson (Chicago, 1963). The most challenging interpretations are J. H. Whitfield, *Machiavelli* (New York, 1965) and *Discourses on Machiavelli* (Cambridge, 1969), although these are written in a very heavy style; Felix Gilbert, *Machiavelli and Guicciardini: Politics and History in Sixteenth-Century Florence* (Princeton, 1965); Cecil Clough, *Machiavelli Researches* (Naples, 1967); Sidney Anglo, *Machiavelli: A Dissection* (London, 1969); Martin Fleisher (ed.), *Machiavelli and the Nature of Political Thought* (New York, 1972); and J. H. Hexter, *The Vision of Politics on the Eve of the Reformation: More, Machiavelli, Seyssel* (New York, 1973). Alfredo Bonadeo, *Corruption, Conflict, and Power in the Works and Times of Niccolò Machiavelli* (Berkeley, 1973), demonstrates that Machiavelli was extremely worried by factions and that this concern helped shape his political views. J. G. A. Pocock, *The Machiavellian Moment: Florentine Political Thought and the Atlantic Republican Tradition* (Princeton, 1975), analyzes the consequences of the revival of the classical republic in Renaissance Italy.

CHAPTER TEN

The Overseas Expansion of Europe

F ALL THE ACTIVITIES of the period we are calling the Renaissance, none has had a more profound effect on the world during the last 500 years than the global expansion of European ideas, institutions, religions, languages, and customs. This Europeanization, which began in the fifteenth century, reached its climax in the early twentieth. During that period of time, it had such a profound effect as to create, if not a European world, at least a world in which European ideas, institutions, and techniques have come to constitute some of the key features of contemporary civilization.

Even though the cumulative effects of this European expansion increased manyfold in the seventeenth, eighteenth, and nineteenth centuries, the immediate impact of expansion in the early decades of the sixteenth century was still sufficient to make it one of the paramount features of the time. Among other things, the expansion of Europe caused the center of commercial activity to gradually shift from the eastern Mediterranean to the Atlantic seaboard. It promoted first the rapid rise of the hitherto peripheral powers of Portugal and Spain, and later that of the maritime states of England and the Netherlands. It sparked the transition from an almost completely agrarian economy to one of combined commercial and industrial capitalism, and formed the practical basis for the operation of a vigorous mercantilism. It also stimulated further technological and scientific achievements, and in general helped to broaden the intellectual outlook of Europe. At the same time, through the influx of silver from the rich mines of the New World, it contributed to the prolonged sixteenth-century inflation that raised the cost index in some places over 300 percent and had varied repercussions throughout Europe.

The Background and Motives of the Iberian Expansion

What caused Latin Christendom to reverse the trend of a thousand years and launch a vigorous exploration and conquest of much of the world? To help answer this question, it is necessary to understand something about medieval conceptions of the world. Underlying all motivations was an overpowering fascination for the exotic Far East. Asia was a mysterious and therefore alluring place of supposed riches, goods, and magic, where legend and fact were inextricably interwoven. Medieval myths about the land of the Amazons, the Fountain of Youth, and the land of Ophir strongly influenced European notions about Asia. Many of the legends were of classical or Christian origin and tended to become canonized with the passage of time. Asia became identified with Biblical locations and people: the Terrestrial Paradise (Garden of Eden), the home of the Magi, the tomb of Saint Thomas, and the wall of Alexander the Great enclosing the minions of Gog and Magog until the last days. Most persistent was the legend of Prester John, a descendant of the Magi, who was believed to be a fabulously rich and powerful Christian monarch located somewhere in the East.

There had been some trading contacts between Europe and Asia since Roman times, when silk was brought from China by Greek and Syrian merchants over the great "Silk Route." Nobody in the West really knew where it originated. India was a little better known but was still geographically vague and shrouded in magic and mystery. It was the land of many precious stones, aromatic woods, and exotic species—of men with dog's heads (Cynocephali), or with one foot (Monopodes), or with their feet turned backward (Antipodes). Traders recounted stories of Hyperboreans (who lived 1,000 years), Amazons, satyrs, horned pigmies, unicorns, griffins, and gold-digging ants. With the interposition of Moslem power in Central Asia, Europe's isolation from Asia became greater and the myths grew wilder.

In the meantime, one of the many nomadic Mongol tribes of inner Asia succeeded not only in subduing the other tribes of Mongolia but by 1215 had established its rule over most of China as well. Its leader, Genghis Khan ("universal ruler"), aspired to nothing less than dominion over all the world. The zenith of the Mongol Empire was reached under Kublai Khan (1259–94) when it extended from the Black Sea to Korea and from northern Siberia to Afghanistan and southern China. Kublai moved his capital from Karakorum south to Peking where he established a magnificent court, and respectfully entertained visitors from the West.

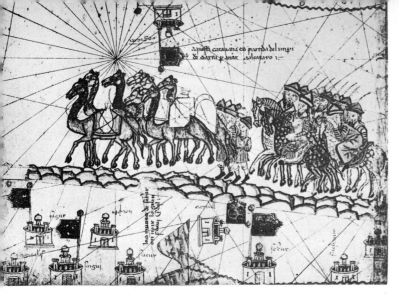

THE POLOS EN ROUTE TO CHINA. *This detail from the 1374 Catalan Atlas of Abraham Cresques shows the Polo expedition crossing central Asia. The cities along their way are indicated beneath. (BBC Hulton Picture Library)*

The Franciscan friar Giovanni de Plano Carpini crossed the interminable Asiatic steppes to China in 1245–47 and was followed soon after by André de Longjumeau and William of Ruysbroeck. In 1256 the brothers Niccolò and Maffeo Polo, merchants of Venice, traveled to China and remained there more than ten years. In 1271 they set out for the East once more, this time taking Niccolò's fifteen-year-old son, Marco, with them. They traveled overland by way of Arabia, Persia, northern India, and Tibet, staying seventeen years this time as guests of Kublai Khan. Marco traveled throughout much of Cathay, as he called it, as the Khan's ambassador and learned about the western island kingdom of Cipango (Japan). The Polos' slow return was via the Malay peninsula, Sumatra, southern India, then overland via the spice route through Tabriz, Trebizond, and Constantinople, finally arriving in Venice in 1295. The experience was intimately reported by Marco Polo in his popular and influential *Travels*.

Other travelers and missionaries followed, including Giovanni de Montecorvino, Odoric of Pordenone, and Giovanni de Marignolli, all official representatives of the pope. They found the Mongols to be very tolerant of diverse religions, and considerable interest in Christianity was expressed by the Khan himself. It was an encouraging field for missionary labors.

But in the middle of the fourteenth century, the overland route to China was severed by the conjunction of the Black Death, the vigorous expansion of the Ottoman Turks, and the overthrow of the Mongol dynasty in China by the first of the Ming emperors, Hung Wu, who established a policy of strict isolation. By the beginning of the fifteenth century, any hope of reviving the overland passage to China was completely obliterated by the conquests of the Tartar hordes under Tamerlane. Some Europeans now began thinking of the possibility of reaching Asia by sea.

The political threat of the militantly expanding Turkish empire was serious, as the hope of a concerted counterattack against Islam grew dimmer each year. The age of European crusades was past, but there was perhaps an alternative course in a flanking movement with the aid of some non-European ally. But where was such an ally? Of the scores of medieval legends concerned with the little-known periphery of Europe, none was more persistently told and believed than the story of Prester John. The tales of Prester John varied with the tellers, but they all agreed that he did exist, that he was a powerful Christian monarch with the command of legions of soldiers, and that he was incredibly rich. If contact could be made with such a prince, the Moslem flank might be turned and Christendom saved. By the early fifteenth century, the legendary land of Prester John was no longer in Asia but somewhere in the center of Africa, at a point where the Nile and "another mighty river flowing westward" had their source. It was partially the thought of reaching this kingdom of Prester John, plus the mounting political rivalries resulting from the rise of the territorial states, that motivated the early Portuguese voyages down the African coast.

The most compelling motive of all, however, was economic. Europe in the last two-thirds of the fourteenth century was economically destitute. The shortage of money in an economy that was coming to depend more and more on a fluid supply of capital was causing an economic depression with widespread and disastrous effects. By the early decades of the fifteenth century, some improvement in the situation resulted from the mining operations in the Austrian Tyrol and in southern Bavaria, but other resources were needed to revive the diminishing gold and silver supplies in Europe and to stimulate the revival of trade.

Among the causes of diminishing capital was the spending of huge sums every year for the purchase of luxury items from the Middle East and spices and medications from India and the islands of southeast Asia. The spice trade, which had grown spectacularly in the late Middle Ages, resulted not only in an unfavorable balance of trade, but also in huge additional costs from the middle-man profits of the Arab traders who carried the precious products from Asia and sold them at exorbitant prices to Venetian merchants in the Levant. Mark-ups of 2,000 percent were not unusual in the transporting of pepper from the Malabar Coast of India to Alexandria; and when the Venetian traders sold their cargoes in Venice to eager northern merchants, they were certain to increase the price sufficiently to make comfortable profits. In light of this situation, it is not difficult to understand the desire of European merchants and statesmen—particularly in Portugal, where shipbuilding and navigation were flourishing activities—to go directly to the source of this prosperous trade and deliver the spices to the northern markets themselves.

But was the level of technology sufficient to permit that kind of navigational feat? Medieval maps, for example, were mostly symbolic representations of the world as interpreted from the Bible rather than

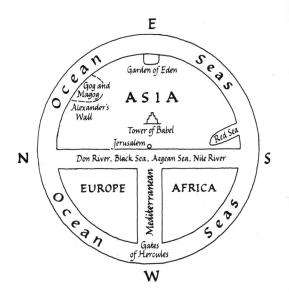

T-O MAP *representing the world as conceived in the Middle Ages, with three continental land masses surrounded by oceans and separated by other waterways. Jerusalem is at the center, with the Garden of Eden at the top (east) and the Red Sea to the south.*

practical charts useful for travel. The stylized Jerusalem maps, or *mappamundi* (world maps), frequently called wheel, or T-O maps by modern scholars, were of little use to the ocean navigator.

The recovery of Ptolemy's *Geography* in 1410 opened a new dimension in cartography. Writing in Alexandria in the second century A.D., Ptolemy described the world in a more realistic manner and projected the spherical earth onto a flat surface by the use of meridians and parallels. Ptolemy's map was a great improvement over the *mappamundi*, but beyond the well-known parts of Europe, it was still very inaccurate and helped perpetuate a number of geographical myths, including a land-locked Indian Ocean.

Of greatest value to the Renaissance seaman were the portolan charts (*portolani*) developed in the thirteenth and fourteenth centuries by Mediterranean navigators and mathematicians. These *portolani* were detailed maps showing very accurate coastal contours, distances between ports, compass readings, and wind lines (loxodromes). The most extensive of these, showing a remarkably accurate Asia, was the *Catalan Atlas* of 1375 made by Abraham Cresques, a Majorcan Jew whose son became the principal cartographer of Prince Henry the Navigator. By Columbus's day, many reasonably accurate maps of the known world were available, and the sudden expansion of geographical knowledge was accompanied by a great flourishing of cartography.

European technological developments, especially in the fields of navigation, cartography, and shipbuilding, made expansion possible and contributed to its continuation and growth in the succeeding centuries. Although many of the technological aids to navigation, such as the compass, astrolabe, and lateen sail, were Eastern inventions introduced into the West in the late Middle Ages, their adaptation and integration into a conscious attempt to cross uncharted oceans and explore new worlds was a European contribution. During the fifteenth century, European shipbuilders, particularly the Portuguese, introduced more innovations and useful changes into the design, building, and rigging of ships than had been made in the previous 1,000 years. The hinged rudder, deep-draught hull, bowsprit, and composite rigging were all developed in a relatively short period. By the time they were needed, Portuguese and Spanish ships were ready to defy the elements and unknown terrors of the open sea.

The men, too, were prepared to match their skill against the fury of nature. European seamen learned fast from the Arabs and from each other. They developed great skill in navigational dead reckoning, estimating speed, calculating leeway and currents, and tacking against the wind. Much of the geographical knowledge accumulated during the early phase of expansion was assimilated by geographers, cartographers, and mathematicians and passed on to future navigators. Fifteenth-century Portuguese seamen made use of Abraham Zacuto's astronomical tables and particularly his *Almanach perpetuum* (Perpetual Almanach). Much nautical knowledge and astronomical understanding were also contained in Sacrobosco's well-known *De sphaera mundi* (On

PTOLEMY'S REPRESENTATION OF THE WORLD, *marked off in grids of latitude and longitude, made a great impact on European geographical thinking in the Renaissance. His conception of Africa and east Asia, however, was very vague and included a landlocked Indian Ocean. (By permission of the Houghton Library, Harvard University)*

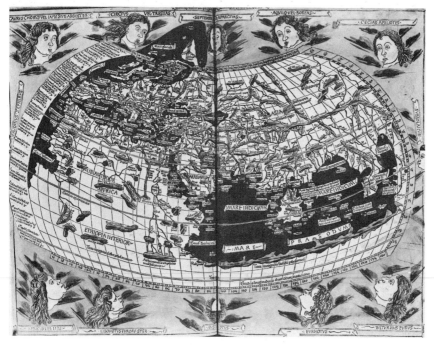

AN EARLY SIXTEENTH-CENTURY COSMOGRAPHER AT WORK. *This engraving by Johannes Stradanus shows numerous nautical instruments of the time: compass, dividers, rule, quadrant, hourglass, globe, armillary sphere, and lodestone. (National Maritime Museum, London)*

the World Sphere, known simply as the *Sphere*). Other navigational manuals followed. The first fully practical manual-almanac was the *Regimento do astrolabio e do quadrante* (Rule of the Astrolabe and the Quadrant), printed in the late 1400s. This was used by da Gama and all subsequent Portuguese navigators.

Finally, it should not be forgotten that plain intellectual curiosity and a spirit of adventure were noticeable characteristics of Renaissance Europe, features that motivated many people during the expansion and ensured its continuation and success.

The Sea Route to India

An almost continuous development of Portuguese expansion can be traced from 1415 to the climactic arrival of Vasco da Gama in India in 1497. The first forty-five years of this period were dominated by the figure and personality of the third son of King João I of Portugal (1385–1433), Prince Henry "The Navigator." According to his earliest chronicler, Gomes Eannes de Azurara (1453), Prince Henry's motives were scientific, economic, military, political, and religious: to explore the coast of Africa beyond Cape Bojador; seek countries with which to trade; see how far the Moorish territory extended; seek a Christian kingdom as an ally; and extend the Christian faith. Following the successful victory over the Moors at Ceuta in North Africa (1415), Prince Henry became the active force in Portuguese maritime activities. At Sagres Castle, not far from Cape Saint Vincent on the southwest promontory of Portugal, Prince Henry attracted the best cosmographers, astronomers, and mathematicians of Europe to establish his school for seamen and navigators. From this point, he supervised annual expeditions southward along the west African coast. As these seamen returned and reported the winds, currents, lands, and astronomical readings

observed on their voyages, this information was studied, evaluated, and made available to the others of Prince Henry's "court." This data soon became part of a growing library of oceanography used in training navigators, cartographers, and ocean pilots.

In 1434, one of Henry's ablest captains, Gil Eannes, rounded Cape Bojador, the first of many imposing obstacles to the circumnavigation of Africa. By 1447 his seamen, led by Antão Gonçalves, Nuño Tristão, Dinis Dias, and Alvaro Fernandes, had reached as far south as present-day Conakry (10° north latitude). During the early years of these expeditions, several groups of islands off the African coast were discovered or rediscovered, settled, and soon developed into important financial enterprises by Prince Henry. The Canary Islands (claimed also by Castile through previous discovery), the Madeiras, the Azores, and eventually the Cape Verde Islands were discovered and claimed by Portugal. In the 1440s, Henry introduced sugar cultivation into the islands, and with it African slaves. In 1455 Madeira produced, in addition to bounteous harvests of Malmsey grapes, almost 200,000 pounds of sugar—double the production of Sicily—and by 1498 this had increased twentyfold.

Although the first profits from Portuguese expansion came from sugar and slaves, a flourishing and profitable trade in African spices, ivory, gold, silver, monkeys, and parakeets also developed. This traffic was made possible in part by the explorations of Alvise da Cadamosto, a Venetian adventurer who had joined the Portuguese enterprise, the first of many Italians to be associated with Iberian expansion. Cadamosto carefully explored the coastal area from Arguim to the Senegal River, and in a second voyage, traveled some sixty miles up the Gambia River. Diogo Gomes penetrated even further into the interior, reaching the city of Kuntaur before sickness forced him to turn back. A subsequent expedition reached Mandinga country and Timbuktu on the upper Niger.

Prince Henry did not live to see the complete fruition of his pioneering efforts. After his death in 1460, there was a decade of inactivity in African exploration before Afonso V (1438–81) and João II (1481–95) took an active interest in it during the 1470s and 1480s. In 1469 a royal agreement was reached with Fernão Gomes, an enterprising Lisbon merchant, to discover 100 leagues of new coast each year. In the next five years, the entire Grain, Ivory, Gold, and Slave coasts were explored and thence south to Cape Saint Catherine beyond the equator. The key fort of Elmina, on the Gold Coast, was built in 1482. By 1484 Diogo Cão had reached the mouth of the Congo River before pressing his caravels on to Cape Saint Mary (13° south) and finally to Cape Cross (22° south).

The climax of the African voyages came with the memorable voyage of Bartholomew Dias, who sailed from Lisbon in August, 1487. Steering straight for the Congo from Cape Palmas, Dias made his way down the coast to Cabo da Volta before he was blown past the final cape in a blinding storm to land at Mossel Bay 200 miles eastward. Threatened with mutiny when he reached the Great Fish River, Dias was forced to turn back, and he returned to Lisbon in December, 1488. Elated by this success in rounding the stormy cape, King João christened it the Cape of Good Hope. Ptolemy had been wrong about the shape of Africa; the all-water route to India was at least possible. The next expedition would make it a reality. Nautical and geographical data acquired by Dias— plus important information about the Middle East obtained by Pedro de Covilhão in an unbelievable overland and sea journey that took him eastward from Barcelona and Rhodes to Egypt, Ethiopia, Arabia, and even to the Malabar Coast of India—was used by the Portuguese government to make the da Gama voyage as successful as possible.

On July 8, 1497, a compact fleet of three fully manned caravels and one large storeship moved gracefully down the Tagus River and out to sea. Nothing had been overlooked in making this the best-equipped and most carefully planned expedition of the century. The latest maps, charts, tables, and instruments were provided by the leading cartographers and mathematicians of the day, and, with the exception of Bartholomew Dias's notable absence, was led and manned by the ablest seamen in Portugal. Vasco da Gama, commander of the expedition, was thirty-seven years of age, almost unknown to the historian prior to that great venture, but apparently with considerable ocean experience and leadership ability—both of which he demonstrated in the next year and a half. From Lisbon, the fleet struck a direct course for the Cape Verde Islands and then stood out to sea in a southwesterly direction before

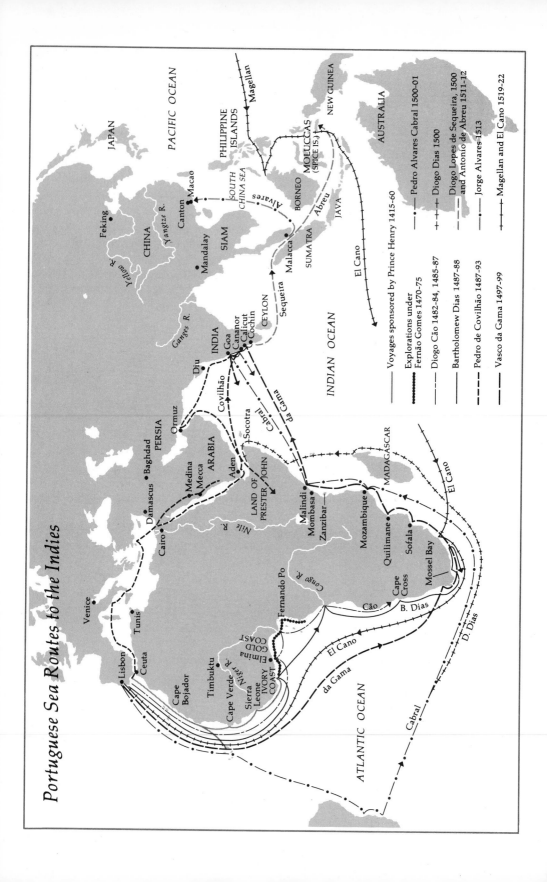

Portuguese Sea Routes to the Indies

making one large tack across the south Atlantic to Saint Helena Bay, just north of the Cape of Good Hope. This navigational marathon from Cape Verde to the tip of Africa, covering some 3800 miles and requiring three months on the open sea, was a remarkable feat of seamanship.

After a week of careening the ships and replenishing the water supplies (and an unfortunate skirmish with the Hottentot natives), the fleet made its way around the cape, and northward along the east African coast. After making stops at Mossel Bay, the mouth of the Zavora River (which they named Rio de Cobre because of the abundance of copper); Quilimane, north of the great Zambezi River; and Mozambique, where they first encountered hostile Moslem settlers; and passing Zanzibar and Mombasa, they arrived at the port of Malindi, about three degrees south of the equator, on Easter day, 1498. After refitting and repairs and engaging an Arab pilot, the fleet rode the monsoons across another 3,000 miles of uncharted sea to the Malabar Coast of India, where it dropped anchor at the teeming port of Calicut on May 20, 1498.

The zamorin of Calicut, a local ruler under the suzerainty of the Hindu empire of Vijayanagar, welcomed da Gama with respect and ceremony. But the amenities soon changed to menacing complaints when the zamorin was informed by Moslem traders that the Portuguese intended to overthrow his rule. The situation was not improved by the array of cheap trinkets brought by da Gama and presented to the zamorin as gifts. It was obvious that the Portuguese were dealing with intelligent and shrewd traders, not, as Columbus had, with gullible savages. Nevertheless, da Gama did avoid a conflict with the Hindus, and in a few weeks had won the confidence of enough native merchants—though not of the zamorin—to engage in selective trading and collect a respectable cargo of pepper and precious stones for the return voyage.

After more unsavory encounters with both Moslems and Hindus, da Gama finally set sail for Portugal late in August, 1498. The return voyage was hard, slow, and costly. Three months were required just to cross the Indian Ocean, and during that time scurvy took a heavy toll of the crews. Two and a half more months passed before the battered fleet rounded the Cape of Good Hope, and almost another four had to be endured before it reached home. Only two ships, carrying a handful of sick and beleaguered seamen, completed the memorable voyage. But the enterprise was financially successful, and the all-water route to India was opened.

The Portuguese Eastern Empire

India had been reached, but the lucrative trade of the East was still entirely in the hands of the Arabs and Turks. It was obvious that any share Portugal was to have in that trade would have to be at Moslem expense. Six months after da Gama arrived at Lisbon, another, larger fleet was assembled to begin the creation of a Portuguese trading empire in India. This time Pedro Alvares Cabral commanded thirteen heavily armed carracks and caravels, and more than 1200 men. In some respects, the voyage was even more remarkable than da Gama's had been, for it laid the basis for Portugal's claim to Brazil. In spite of the long tack across the Atlantic Ocean (which carried them to the northeastern point of Brazil) and an encounter with a hurricane that sent four of the ships to the bottom of the south Atlantic (one of them commanded by the veteran Bartholomew Dias), the fleet made the run to India in the amazingly short time of six months.

Cabral's sojourn in India was short and violent, resulting in the loss of many lives in skirmishes with Arab warships and Indian warriors. But the expedition was still successful, returning to Portugal with valuable cargoes, according to Amerigo Vespucci, of

> Cinnamon, fresh and dried ginger, much pepper, cloves, nutmegs, mace, musk, agallochum, stomax, delicacies, porcelains, cassia, mastic, incense, myrrh, red and white sandalwood, wood aloes, camphor, amber, canes, much lacquer, mummy wax, indigo, and tutty, opium, hepatic aloes, India paper, and a great variety of drugs. . . . Of jewels I do not know the rest, except that I saw many diamonds, rubies, and pearls, among which I saw one ruby in a round piece of most beautiful color, that weighed seven and a half carats.

Before another year had passed, German and other European merchants were arriving in Lisbon to take advantage of the heralded bargains offered by the Portuguese. From 1501 on, annual fleets made the Atlantic circuit to India and were soon cutting deeply into the Mediterranean trade of the Venetians and Turks.

Arab and Turkish traders did not take the Portuguese intrusion lightly. The Indian Ocean was still a Moslem lake and Portuguese ships ventured into its waters at definite peril. In 1505 King Manoel sent Francisco de Almeida east with twenty ships and the title of viceroy of India. As more of the Indian trade was channeled around Africa, permanent bases were established in East Africa at Sofala, Mozambique, Kilwa, and Mombasa. In desperation, a combined Egyptian-Turkish-Arab fleet was mobilized to strike a death blow at the audacious Portuguese encroachment. In February 1509, off the island of Diu, Almeida and his followers met the huge combined Moslem fleet of over 100 sails. Undaunted by the odds, the Portuguese struck into the heart of the enemy armada, and before the day had ended, the Moslem fleet was almost completely destroyed. The Portuguese sea road to India was now secure.

In the same year as the naval battle of Diu, Almeida was replaced as viceroy of India by one of the most illustrious and hardened noblemen of Portugal, Afonso d'Albuquerque. More than any other person, Albuquerque was responsible for converting the tenuous Portuguese foothold into a prosperous and continuing commercial empire. To do this and to enable the Portuguese to maintain a permanent fleet in the

Indian Ocean, Albuquerque set out to secure a ring of commercial-military bases advantageously located for their most expedient use both in trade and naval support.

The first and most important of these bases was Goa, the sheltered island just north off the Malabar Coast of India, which Albuquerque captured from the local zamorins in an audacious sea assault. For the next century and a half, Goa remained the keystone of the Portuguese trading empire, and continued to be a Portuguese colony until it was seized by the government of India in 1961. To Goa were quickly added Socotra, guarding the entrance to the Red Sea; Ormuz, an important and strategically located island at the mouth of the Persian Gulf; and far-off Malacca, commanding the straits through which the spice ships from southeast Asia had to pass. From Malacca, they obtained trading agreements with the ruler of Tennate in the Moluccas and thereby gained an important foothold in the very heart of the Spice Islands. Of the key stations in his master plan, Albuquerque failed to take only Aden, the seaport fortress on the Gulf of Aden just west of Socotra.

As early as 1513, the Portuguese succeeded in opening a trickle of trade with some Chinese merchants, and to help promote this potentially lucrative commerce, they eventually acquired the island of Macao at the mouth of the Canton River. Trade with mainland China was still difficult, since the powerful and self-sufficient Ming emperors of China had for many years discouraged Chinese navigation west of Malacca and had expressly forbidden all commercial and cultural intercourse with foreigners. For the most part, the Portuguese had to be content to trade with the buffer and satellite states with which the Chinese had

PORTUGUESE CARRACKS IN THE EAST. *A detailed oil painting of carracks, naos, and a galley off a rocky coast, attributed to Cornelius Anthoniszoon. (National Maritime Museum, London)*

surrounded themselves—Burma, Siam, Annam, and Ceylon. Except for distance, commerce with Japan was easier. Japanese pirates, active in the China Sea, were also interested in trade, and from the early exchanges with these enterprising seamen developed the most famous annual trading runs of the Portuguese carracks between Japan and Macao.

Less spectacular, but no less successful, were the Portuguese economic relations with the new rulers of India, the Moguls, who moved into the subcontinent from the north soon after the Portuguese had arrived. Under their great monarch and lawgiver, Akbar, the Moguls welcomed commercial intercourse with the Portuguese and made no moves to oppose their system of trading posts around the Indian coast. In fact, for many years the Moguls were even tolerant of the religion and culture of the West.

For the next half-century, all of Portugal was teeming with interest and activity in the Eastern trade. Hundreds of royal vessels were mobilized in the vast network; and hundreds of thousands of people were employed in the shipyards, docks, on the seas, and at the scattered overseas bases from Elmina on the west coast of Africa to Tidore in the Moluccas. Only half of the ships engaged in the India trade ever survived for a second voyage, however, and the combination of disease, shipwreck, and war took a heavy toll of life.

The very vastness and success of this trade contributed to the eventual downfall of the Portuguese empire. As the profits mounted, more of Portugal's European neighbors began interloping and privateering to divert as much of the wealth as possible into their own hands. Underpopulated and hardpressed to keep the flow of commerce going even under favorable conditions, Portugal was unable to cope indefinitely with the additional strains of foreign competition and aggression.

Columbus and the Discovery of the New World

Through most of the fifteenth century, Portugal's immediate neighbors to the east paid little attention to overseas discovery and exploration. Castile was preoccupied with the serious internal problems of *reconquista*, religious orthodoxy, and diplomatic realignment. Aragon was already extensively committed in the western Mediterranean and, under Ferdinand, became intimately involved in the intricacies of European politics and war. Suddenly, in 1492, the year of the Castilian-Aragonese victory over the Moors of Granada, and without a great deal of previous preparation, Castile became a colonizing nation.

Since Christopher Columbus was such a key figure in the opening phase of European expansion, many legends have grown out of the fragmentary evidences of the period, making it difficult to distinguish between the historical and the mythical Columbus. For example, the notion that Columbus was the first person to seriously believe the earth is round is certainly untrue. Geographers, mathematicians, and philos-

CHRISTOPHER COLUMBUS. *This portrait in the Museo Civico Navale di Genova-Pegli, attributed to Ridolfo Ghirlandaio, is considered to be the best likeness of the discoverer. It is a 1525 copy of an earlier lost portrait.* (Alinari/Editorial Photocolor Archives)

ophers for more than fifteen centuries had not only known it, but had calculated its circumference with considerable accuracy. This of course does not deny that many people had strange notions about the earth, including the idea that it was flat, or cubical, or cylindrical; but these fancies made no appreciable impact on the people who were actually involved in geography and navigation. The unique contribution of Columbus was not the concept of a spherical earth, but the tightly argued thesis that it was not as large as people had previously thought it was, and that the navigational problems of sailing around it (as far as Asia at least) were not insurmountable.

A great many factors influenced Columbus in his conclusion that the earth was only a little over 18,000 miles in circumference, when most of his contemporaries believed it was between 25,000 and 26,000 miles. He also assumed that the Asiatic continent was much larger than most people believed and that it extended around the globe to within 2400 miles of the Canary Islands. It is little wonder that Columbus insisted throughout his life that he had reached the outer islands of the East Indies. Among the influences on Columbus were the *Travels of Marco Polo*, which Columbus read avidly; the spurious accounts of the travels of Sir John Mandeville; the book *Imago Mundi* (The World Image, 1410) of Cardinal Pierre d'Ailly, which Columbus owned and annotated profusely; and the cosmographical writings of Pope Pius II, especially his *Historia rerum ubique gestarum* (History of Things that Have Happened Everywhere), also owned and annotated by Columbus. Combined with certain selected passages from the *Geography* of Ptolemy, these sources convinced Columbus of the soundness of his theories. The written approval of his views by the well-known Florentine physician and geographer Paolo Toscanelli and the frequent reports from Portuguese sailors that carved wood objects, trees, and other strange artifacts were frequently washed ashore from the west along the Azores, all strengthened Columbus's convictions and increased his desire to lead an expedition westward to the Indies.

The full motives of the discoverer will probably never be known, but there is evidence that they were not unlike those of Henry the Navigator almost a century earlier—that is, a combination of economic, political, and religious incentives. He hoped to reach an ally beyond the Islamic sphere who perhaps could be induced to lend aid to embattled Christendom, and at the same time provide a fertile soil for the propagation of the Christian religion. In the emperor of China might be found such an ally. At one time, at least, there was every indication that Kublai Khan had been amenable to the introduction of Christianity into his realms. Whatever the full nature of the "Enterprise of the Indies," Columbus had a difficult time selling his ideas to either his countrymen or his neighbors.

Genoese by birth, Columbus spent a good share of his youth on the western Mediterranean and at the bustling Atlantic and west African ports. He knew ships and he loved the sea. For eight years, Columbus tried to sell his "small world" idea and obtain backing to finance a voyage of discovery and exploration. In 1484 he presented his proposal to King João of Portugal, but Columbus's price seems to have been too high. Besides, the return of Batholomew Dias made such a venture unnecessary as far as the Portuguese were concerned. Next he went to Spain to lay his plans and conditions before the Catholic Kings. The proposal was studied carefully by a special commission headed by Hernando de Talavera and the Royal Council. Opinions were divided. If Columbus were correct in his calculations, the project might work; if he were wrong, it would be money down the drain. And neither Ferdinand nor Isabel could afford new enterprises in the midst of their war against the Moors of Granada. Thrice rejected, Columbus turned to the kings of France and England, where his brother Bartholomew went to present his case. A lesser man might have given up in the face of such opposition, but Columbus believed he was divinely inspired to carry out the enterprise. He would not be deterred. His long and frustrating efforts finally bore fruit when Queen Isabel reconsidered—following persuasive appeals by Luis de Santangel, a royal official, and Fray Juan Pérez, head of the monastery of La Rábida, near Palos, where Columbus had left his young son in care of the Franciscan friars.

The tiny expedition of three small ships and ninety men that finally set sail from Palos on 3 August 1492 was a joint enterprise financed partly by Columbus, partly by Queen Isabel, and partly by the town of Palos. The owners of two of the ships, Juan de la Cosa and Juan Niño, sailed with the expedition—the former as master of the *Santa María* and the latter as pilot of the *Niña*. Martín Alonso Pinzón commanded the

Pinta, and his brother, Vicente Yáñez Pinzón, was captain of the *Niña.* Most of the crew were from Palos and adjacent villages, or other towns in Andalusia. Ten came from the northwestern province of Galicia—as did the *Santa María* herself.

At sea, Columbus proved himself to be a capable and meticulous navigator, skillfully skirting the lower edge of the prevailing westerlies to ride the northeast trade winds, just south of the twenty-fifth parallel, all the way to the Bahamas. After exploring some of the coastline of northwestern Cuba and the northern shores of Haiti (Hispaniola), where they obtained small quantities of gold and a number of ornaments from the natives, Columbus established a small settlement with thirty-nine of his crew and began the torturous journey back to Europe in the two remaining caravels (the *Santa María* had wrecked on the Hispaniola shoals on Christmas day, 1492). The reception given the explorer and his news was varied. The Portuguese were skeptical about his fantastic report, but the Spanish monarchs were greatly pleased, if also somewhat incredulous. For a while, Columbus was the man of the hour and duly honored with the titles and privileges previously agreed upon.

But trouble was brewing. King João II of Portugal, believing Columbus's discoveries to have been western islands of the Azores group, immediately claimed them for Portugal; Isabel promptly appealed to the pope, who was the Aragonese Borgia, Alexander VI. In the spring of 1493, the pope issued a number of papal bulls that in substance confirmed that whatever discoveries Columbus had made belonged to the Crown of Castile, and drew an imaginary line of demarcation from the North Pole to the South some 100 leagues west of the Azores, authorizing the Spanish to explore the lands and sea to the west of this line. This demarcation became the basis for subsequent negotiations between the two governments (since Portugal was dissatisfied with the papal pronouncement), and soon led to the conclusion of the Treaty of Tordesillas (1494), which confirmed the Spanish sphere west of a line and the Portuguese to the east, but moved the line 370 leagues west of the Cape Verde Islands. This agreement was later confirmed by the papal bulls of Julius II in 1506 and Leo X in 1514.

The Treaty of Tordesillas was a diplomatic victory for Portugal, since it guaranteed the Portuguese sea route to India and gave them a legal claim (not realized at the time, however, due to the vagueness of the line and the inability to accurately determine longitude) to explore and settle the eastern part of South America, eventually making Brazil Portuguese rather than Spanish. The issue of demarcation was aroused again when Spanish claims resulting from the voyage of Magellan clashed with Portuguese assumptions of influence in Southeast Asia. But at least as far as the New World was concerned, the two spheres were accepted and generally respected by both powers—but by no others.

The impact of Columbus's first voyage was immediate in Spain and

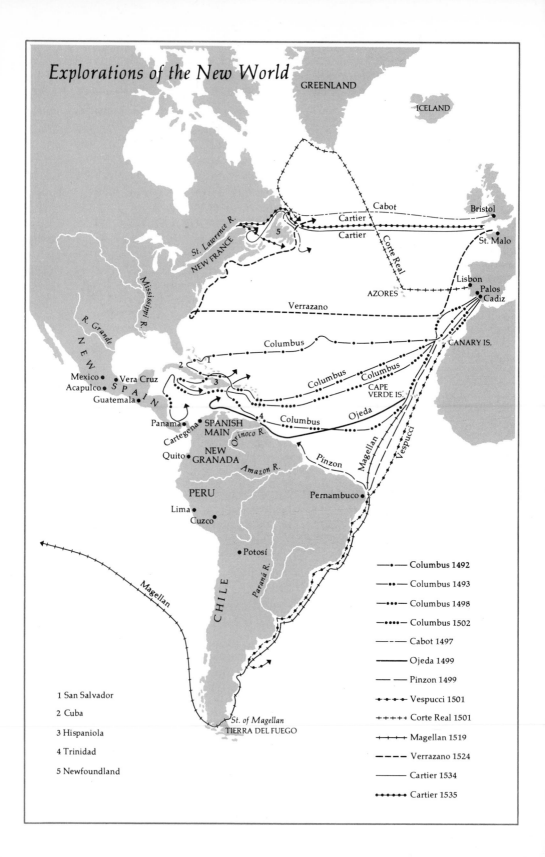

Explorations of the New World

raised considerable curiosity in the rest of Europe. Portugal might have played a greater role in the subsequent discoveries and explorations had she not been so involved in the African route to India and the Spice Islands. As it was, Castile, which had no previous experience in overseas colonization, suddenly became the inheritor and custodian of the New World, a frontier so vast and rich that its full potential could not be realized for centuries. How much this new frontier affected the attitudes and dynamic of the Spanish people is difficult to measure, but certainly it was one of the factors in the vitality and leadership of Spain for the next century and a half.

The Age of Exploration

The Treaty of Tordesillas had not yet been signed when Columbus weighed anchor for his second voyage to the "Indies." Now at the height of his glory, he was given command of a fleet of seventeen ships carrying over 1500 eager sailors, churchmen, officials, settlers, and soldiers of fortune. On 27 November 1493 they reached Hispaniola only to find that the colony left there the year before had been destroyed by hostile Indians. A new settlement was made and Columbus began a five-month cruise of the Caribbean in search of the Chinese mainland. The quest was obviously a failure, but he did discover and explore the coasts of many of the West Indian islands, including Jamaica, the southern shore of Cuba, and the Isle of Pines. Meanwhile, the colony on Hispaniola again almost perished from sickness, disorder, and Indians. Leaving his younger brother, Bartholomew, in charge of a new settlement planted on the southern coast, Columbus returned to Spain in 1496, disappointed but not yet discouraged.

In 1498 he embarked on a third voyage. This time he touched the New World at Trinidad, sailed through the Gulf of Paria between the island and mainland South America, then proceeded northward to Hispaniola. Unable to bring order out of the chaotic colony, Columbus and his two brothers were arrested by the royal commissioner dispatched from Spain and shipped home in humiliation and in chains. Still having the ear and sympathy of Queen Isabel, however, Columbus was eventually freed and given authority to make a fourth voyage, this one to be devoted entirely to exploration. The last Columbian voyage was the most fascinating and adventuresome of all, but it was also the most disappointing. For two years, the admiral groped along the coast of Central America trying desperately to find the route to the Asian mainland, surviving mutiny and costly clashes with hostile natives, and being shipwrecked and marooned, before he finally limped back to Spain where he died at Valladolid a year and a half later.

Columbus's last years were unhappy ones partly because he refused to recognize the nature and meaning of his own accomplishments. He considered his efforts a failure because he had not attained the riches of the East. By the time of his death, many people in Spain and elsewhere had caught the vision and challenge of the new frontier and were energetically rushing to meet it. In 1497, Giovanni Caboto (John Cabot), a Venetian seaman, obtained a license from Henry VII of England to sail into the western sea to discover and explore any islands or mainland he might reach. In his two voyages, Cabot explored the coastline of North America from Labrador as far south as Maryland. Nor was this the first evidence of English activity in the exploring arena. Bristol seamen had been venturing far out into the north Atlantic for many years. Recent discoveries reveal that as early as 1483 some of these explorers may have reached the mainland of America. But these discoveries, just as those of the Scandinavian expeditions four centuries earlier, did not establish a continuing line of communication between the two continents as the voyages of Columbus did.

While John Cabot and his son, Sebastian, explored the New England shore, another Italian, the Florentine shipping contractor, Amerigo Vespucci, accompanied other seamen on voyages along the coast of North and South America and wrote letters to prominent people describing the geography as well as the flora and fauna of the New World. It was due to the early publication of some of these letters by Martin Waldseemüller in his *Cosmographiae Introductio* (Introduction to Cosmography, 1507) that the New World received the name "America." Many have resented the naming of the new continents after Amerigo Vespucci instead of Columbus, but there is little doubt that in the early years of the sixteenth century, it was primarily the voyages of Vespucci and his published (and unpublished) comments about the coastal geography of the New World that first made Europeans aware of the real significance of the discoveries and explorations. Columbus was the discoverer, but Vespucci was the interpreter of the discoveries. From 1505 until his death in 1512, Amerigo Vespucci was pilot major at Seville, where he supervised and licensed all Spanish expeditions to the New World.

During the first two decades of the sixteenth century, many exploring and colonizing ventures were carried out. Alonso de Ojeda and Juan de la Cosa, both veterans of the Columbian voyages, made numerous trips to the New World and explored much of the northern South American coast as did Vincente Yáñez Pinzon and others of Columbus's crewmen. Gaspar and Miguel Corte-Real, French merchant-sailors, explored Newfoundland and entered the Gulf of Saint Lawrence, while Giovanni da Verrazano located the mouth of the Hudson River, sailed into New York harbor, explored Narragansett Bay, and followed the New England coast as far north as Maine. Juan Díaz de Solis and Sebastian de Ocampo confirmed Spanish interest in the Caribbean while others explored the Yucatan Peninsula. In 1513 Vasco Nuñez de Balboa crossed the Isthmus of Panama and discovered the Pacific Ocean. The entire eastern coastline of South America was explored as far south as the Río de la Plata (Argentina), and most of the North American coast as far as 67° north latitude. Augmenting these voyages of discovery and explo-

ration were many colonizing expeditions, which brought thousands of settlers, mostly Castilians, to the New World.

In September 1519 the Portuguese captain Fernão Magalhães (anglicized as Ferdinand Magellan) sailed under a Spanish charter for the New World. His destination is not known for certain, but we do know from the journal of Antonio Pigafetta, who accompanied the expedition, that he planned a long voyage and intended to reach at least the Moluccas. No one knew the distance across the Pacific, so it was not at all certain whether the rich Spice Islands lay on the Spanish or Portuguese side of the Tordesillas demarcation. Apparently the expedition was intended to establish a Spanish foothold in the lucrative spice trade. The voyage appeared to be a defiance of the papal bull of 1514 and was an open threat to the Portuguese. But it was not an age of great respect for international agreements or fear of the pope.

Making careful use of information gathered from Vespucci's 1501 voyage and from survivors of Juan de Solis's Río de la Plata expedition of 1515, Magellan, with a fleet of five overaged caravels, struck boldly south into the Atlantic. More than two months were required for the passage to Brazil and another three to beat along the coast to Saint Julian in Patagonia, near the straits that now bear his name. Here Magellan camped for the winter (from March until the end of August 1520), and here also he weathered a mutiny that deprived him of two of his vessels and almost ended the expedition. After passage of the treacherous straits, the little company of three ships and not more than 150 crewmen began its slow journey across the endless expanse of the Pacific Ocean. In March 1521 they reached the island of Guam, and some weeks later the Philippines. There Magellan met his death, along with several other crewmen and officers, and another of the ships was lost. After trading and exploring among the islands of the archipelago, Borneo, and the Moluccas, the two remaining ships parted company, the *Trinidad* attempting to return across the Pacific, and the tiny 85-ton *Victoria*, commanded by Sebastian del Cano, continuing the voyage across the Indian Ocean, around Africa, and up the Atlantic to Europe. In September 1522 the battered and leaking ship, with its scurvy-ridden remnant of a crew, reached Seville, completing the most harrowing and spectacular ocean voyage of the age of discovery. Of the original 280 crewmen, 18 reached home aboard the *Victoria*. The *Trinidad* was never heard from again.

The Spanish Conquest of America

The creation of a Spanish empire in the New World was not only an unparalleled feat of military conquest but also a landmark in the colonization of foreign lands. It is noteworthy that the *conquistadores* who, through determination, valor, cruelty, and endurance, won an empire for Castile, were predominantly from the same region of the motherland—Estremadura, the hot, hard, and arid southwestern corner of Spain. Many of the later colonizers were also from there and from the colorful region of Andalusia, which adjoins Estremadura on the southeast. These hardy frontiersmen carried with them to the New World their distinctive culture and their particular dialect of the Castilian language. The *conquistadores* were an audacious lot who faced unbelievable hardships with a stoic determination that would never recognize failure or defeat. Their motivations were varied, including, in addition to the recognizable desire for glory and wealth, a religious crusading zeal. The success of their ventures lay mostly with themselves and their greater initiative and enterprise, not just with their superior weapons or materiel. *Conquistadores* from Estremadura, or any part of Castile, had already overcome great hardships just to stay alive. They were not likely to flinch in face of the obstacles offered by the New World.

Another feature worth noting in the conquest of America was the predominantly middle- and lower-class composition of the exploring, conquering, and colonizing expeditions. The New World was not won by official actions of the state or by the higher nobility of Spain, but by the enterprising individuals and groups belonging to the lower levels of society. The financing, organizing, equipping, and directing of these expeditions were done privately rather than by the government as was the case in the Portuguese expansion. The Castilian crown granted a concession, or *capitulatión*, for these ventures, supervised legal matters in relations among settlers and with the Indians, and required a tax on all economic success. But it was not until a later date, after the conquest was virtually completed, that the crown began to play an intimate role in the colonial administration.

Mexico and Cortés

The first major invasion of the American mainland was the Cortés expedition, which left Cuba in February 1519 with sixty-six men, variously armed, and sixteen horses. The epic story of the conquest of Mexico remains one of the great sagas of the age of expansion. From beginning to end, the margin of victory was very slim, but the final result was decisive. Dramatically severing his legal ties with the governor of Cuba, Cortés led his doughty army from the steaming jungles of Vera Cruz into the rugged highlands of the central Mexican plateau, fighting through Indian attacks and ambushes until he reached the majestic island city of Tenochtitlán, capital of the Aztecs. After entering the city and taking the Aztec chieftain, Montezuma, into "protective custody," Cortés was forced to divide his strength to meet the threat of a second invasion from Cuba, this one sent by the irate governor to arrest Cortés. Persuading its leader to join him in the campaign against the Aztec capital, Cortés returned to Tenochtitlán only to find that one of his captains had imprudently desecrated the native temples, and the Spaniards now found themselves trapped inside the hostile island city. Their escape across one of the narrow causeways on the night of 30 June 1520 (*la noche triste*—"the sad night") was nearly fatal, but the remnant of Cortés's army limped back to lands of the friendly Tlaxcalan Indians, healed their wounds, and began laying plans for a second assault on the Aztec capital. By the summer of 1521, a crude but effective navy had been built and a seaborne attack was launched, which finally overthrew the mighty Aztec empire.

THE MEETING OF CORTÉS AND MONTEZUMA. *This Indian depiction of the first meeting of the Spanish commander and the Aztec emperor is from the* Lienzo de Tlaxcala, *1555–64. Cortés's Indian interpreter, Malinche, stands behind him. (Courtesy of the American Museum of Natural History)*

Following the conquest of Mexico, Cortés sent out other expeditions to gather information, explore, plant colonies, and subdue other Indian states they might encounter. Thus the territory north beyond the highlands and south through the land of the Mayas almost as far as Panama, came under Spanish control as a result of Cortés's expedition. The transition from Indian to Spanish rule was not as difficult as might be imagined, but the quarrels and rivalry among the Spaniards themselves, and between the colonists and the Spanish government, were intense. The rugged and violent *conquistadores* did not take well to peaceful pursuits. Consolidation and continuous supervision of the newly won territories eventually had to be done by appointed colonial administrators sent out from Spain for the task.

Peru and the Pizarros

The outstanding example of personal rivalry can be seen in the conquest of Peru, where abundant wealth and the civil upheavals already tearing apart the Inca empire attracted the most enterprising and lawless elements of Castilian society. Its comparison with the American West

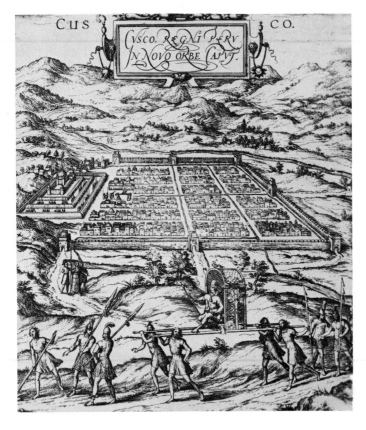

SIXTEENTH-CENTURY CUZCO. *The majestic capital of the Inca Empire stands 12,000 feet high in the Peruvian Andes. Conquered by Pizarro in 1533 and converted into a Spanish city, it still retained much of its Indian population and culture after the conquest.*

during the gold-rush era is not inappropriate. The conquest of Peru was initiated by the strange partnership of an ambitious adventurer, a parish priest, and a hardened soldier. In 1525, the latter, Francisco Pizarro, led a motley expedition down the west coast of South America and to the equatorial tidelands, only to meet with defeat and near annihilation at the hands of the natives. Two years later, enough money and men were raised by his partners, Almagro and Luque, for a second assault on the fabled Inca empire. This, too, turned into failure when the majority of Pizarro's men deserted at the island of Gallo, near the Equator. Now Pizarro was more determined than ever to become the conqueror of the Incas. This time it took a personal appearance before the Emperor Charles V to obtain the needed permission and support for another attempt. While in Spain, Pizarro also secured the active assistance of his brothers, Gonzalo and Hernando, and other relatives who not only helped assure the success of his schemes but also guaranteed that Peru would remain the scene of family feuds and upheavals for years to come.

Late in 1530 the Pizarros began their final assault on the doomed Peruvian civilization with a tiny army of 100 foot soldiers and some 60 cavalry. High in the Andes, Pizarro reached the encampment of the Inca Atahualpa, who was locked in bitter civil conflict with his half-brother, Huascar. Through deceit and treachery, Pizarro seized Atahualpa, used the Inca leader to intimidate, then rout the Indian forces, and finally, when his usefulness had been served, had him murdered. By November 1533 the *conquistadores* were in control of Cuzco, the Inca capital. Compared with the conquest of Mexico, the victory in Peru was easy; but whereas the subsequent goverment and organization under Cortés and his successors was relatively smooth and moderate, the greater bloodshed and turmoil in Peru came after the conquest was over, when the Almagro and Pizzaro factions fell into dispute over the spoils, followed by open civil war after the assassination of both leaders. Rivalries were intense, and they kept Peru in a continuous state of disorder for another two decades.

Two of the richest areas of the New World were in European hands by the mid-1530s, but the conquest was still far from complete. It was several more years before the indefatigable Jiménez de Quesada overcame the hardships and resistance of northwestern South America—New Granada (modern Colombia)—and another ten before the fabulously rich silver mines of the Bolivian highlands were discovered. It was past mid-century before much progress was made along the eastern side of the continent—the valley of the Río de la Plata and the Orinoco basin—and even longer before Pedro de Valdivia's coastal conquests in Chile could be extended against the ferocious Araucanians. Nevertheless, by 1535, organized and extensive governmental agencies had been set up in North and South America in an effort to make the New World a viable extension of the Old.

Relations with the Indians

The consolidation of Spanish power in America was accomplished within the comprehensive and relatively sophisticated legal structure of late-medieval Spain. No European country was more interested in jurisprudence and legal practice than Spain, and this orientation was carried by the *conquistadores* to the New World. Contact with the natives of America caused an immediate problem among the Spanish legal theorists, for until it was decided whether these strange creatures were actually humans or not, it was difficult to fit them into any known legal pattern of the day. For half a century, while the doctors of law debated the issues, the conquest went on and many important decisions regarding relations between the Spanish settlers and the aborigines were made by the settlers themselves.

From the outset, Spanish Indian policy was hopelessly contradictory. Queen Isabel took the first step by forbidding the sale of Indians and declaring them to be direct subjects of the crown of Castile. She further ordered the first colonial governor to protect and Christianize them, and allowed the medieval *encomienda* (an estate or commission granted by the crown) to be instituted in America. This institution gave the Spaniards the right to collect tributes from the natives and use them as laborers. In return, the *encomendero* (holder of an *encomienda*) was required to care for the Indians' spiritual and temporal needs and provide for their protection. Thus the paternalistic policy of the government toward the Indians was left for the settlers to implement. Since the settlers were 3,000 miles from the government, their attitude and treatment of the Indians was more brutal than paternal. The classic attitude of the colonials toward the government in Spain was colorfully expressed early in the conquest: *"Obedezco pero no cumplo"* ("I obey but will not comply"). This constant tension and contradiction of interests between the Spanish crown and the colonists must be recognized if the relations with the Indians are to be understood.

After Isabel's death in 1504, the protective pressure from the crown was relaxed and the Indians were more cruelly exploited by the Spanish settlers. During this period, the Indians gained their most outspoken and tireless champion in the Dominican friar Bartolomé de Las Casas. Las Casas, a former *encomendero* himself, took up the cause of the Indians, and in a series of pamphlets, sermons, and books, called attention to Spanish brutality and put constant pressure on the government of Charles V to intervene in Indian matters. No doubt, much of what Las Casas wrote about the conquest was true, but his accounts—especially the *Brevissima relación de las Indias* (Very Brief Relation of the Indies, 1542)—were frequently exaggerated and misleading, and provided Spain's enemies with ammunition for the "black legend" of Spanish atrocities.

Cruelty was not a Spanish monopoly in the sixteenth century, and its overemphasis distorts the total balance of Spanish influence in the New World. The government did recognize the problem of Indian relations and took increasingly effective steps to alleviate it in the face of bitter opposition from the colonists. The Indian laws that eventually evolved were defective but were surprisingly humane for the time. In the New Laws of 1542, the *encomienda* system was abolished, although the strength of colonial interests was great enough to prevent their complete enforcement. What resulted was an eventual relaxing of tension as the *encomenderos* themselves improved the standard of Indian treatment and as Negro slaves, imported from Africa by English and Portuguese traders, gradually replaced Indian labor on the plantations and in the mines.

Colonial Administration

From 1493 until 1524, the supervision of colonial government was in the hands of a single man, the queen's chaplain and archdeacon of the Seville cathedral, Juan Rodríguez de Fonseca. However, after Cortés's expedition extended the Spanish dominions to the mainland, it became impossible for one person, without modern communications and aids, to coordinate such a vast administration. The Council of the Indies was created to fill this need, and continued to be the principal organ of colonial government for the next three centuries. As an administrative body, the Council of the Indies proposed the names of colonial officials for the king's appointment, supervised their activities in the New World, and oversaw ecclesiastical matters in the colonies. As a judicial body, it acted as a court of last appeals from the colonial courts, and in cases involving the colonies, it had primary jurisdiction. In all of its activities, the council was the right hand of the king in colonial administration.

In the colonies, the organization was more complex. For the first thirty-five years of the century, administration was supervised by colonial governors sent out from Spain. The system worked tolerably well, but with the great expanse of territory after the conquest of Peru, it became necessary to have closer supervision over the various parts and at the same time coordinate the whole into a more consistent and manageable form. The result was the inauguration of the viceroy system, dividing the New World into two viceroyalties—New Spain (Mexico, Central America, and the Caribbean islands), with its viceroy in Mexico City, and Peru (all of western South America), administered from Lima. The viceroy was appointed by the king and represented him directly in the colonies as chief civil and military officer. To assist the viceroy, serve as the supreme judicial body in the colonies, and supervise administration of the laws in the outlying areas, advisory-judicial courts called *audiencias* were created. Local government was made up largely of creole (American-born Spaniards) and mestizo (offspring of Spanish fathers and Indian mothers) elements of the towns. In the sixteenth century, these municipal bodies, called *cabildos*, were locally elected and exercised considerable authority in the jurisdiction and management of municipal affairs, just as their prototypes in medieval Spain had done.

By papal bulls in 1501 and 1508, extensive rights and privileges relating to religious affairs in the newly discovered Americas were granted to the crown of Castile. This *Patronato Real* (Royal Patronage) made the Spanish monarch the secular head of the church in the New World, with authority to nominate all ecclesiastical dignitaries, found and construct churches and monasteries, receive and dispose of all ecclesiastical benefices, collect fees, and approve (or disapprove) papal pronouncements. The various religious orders, as well as the clerical courts, answered directly to the Spanish king rather than to the pope.

From the outset, missionary zeal was rewarding in the New World. To the Indians, it seemed that their own gods had failed them and they turned therefore to the new and more powerful God of the Spaniards. Dominican, Franciscan, and Augustinian friars baptized hundreds of thousands during the first years of the conquest and worked with the *encomenderos* in caring for their religious needs. But the missionary era passed with the coming of the secular clergy and the formal ecclesiastical organization. Parishes and dioceses were established; schools, hospitals, and monasteries were built. The immediate result was bitter rivalry between the seculars and the regulars, and between the European and American clergies. But in the end, there was plenty of room in the New World for both. For three centuries, Franciscan and Jesuit missionaries advanced the frontiers of Christendom beyond the jurisdiction of the organized government and church, establishing a chain of missions as far north as San Francisco and south into Patagonia, while the parish priests, abbots, and bishops worked to organize and consolidate Christianity within the more populated areas.

As early as 1503, the burden of economic matters involving Spain and the New World was so great that these were detached from Bishop Fonseca's responsibility, and a separate board of trade, the *Casa de Contratación*, was created for handling the job. It supervised the outfitting and provisioning of ships bound for the Indies, licensed all persons and cargoes embarking, and registered those who returned. It was also responsible for receiving the royal taxes assessed on the production of wealth from the New World. And to put teeth into its supervisory authority, it was given a judicial arm for trying violations of the commercial code. All trade with the Americas was channeled through Seville, where accurate records could be kept and taxes assessed. Complaints were often voiced, but the Seville monopoly remained for almost two centuries.

Portugal in the New World

Brazil remained the stepchild of the Portuguese empire until late in the sixteenth century. Although not entirely neglected, it received second priority to India and Southeast Asia as far as the Portuguese government was concerned. Its value in the first twenty or thirty years after discovery came mostly from brazilwood, which was shipped from several ports along the northeastern coast. Indians, as well as Negro slaves imported from West Africa, were employed in the forests cutting and preparing the wood and transporting it to the coast for shipment. Although not comparable in value to the spice trade, the brazilwood trade was lucrative enough to attract other Europeans to the Brazilian coast. It was this growing competition and threat from Spanish and especially French traders that moved the Portuguese government to begin the actual colonization of Brazil.

In 1530 Martin Afonso de Souza was sent to drive off the French interlopers and establish a base for subsequent colonization. One fortified settlement was made just south of Pernambuco and another at the site of presentday Rio de Janeiro. As a result of Souza's voyage and subsequent report to Lisbon, King João II initiated the colonization policy and structure thereafter employed in Brazilian settlement. The system, known as *capitaneas* (captaincies), had been used in the colonization of the Madeiras and Azores. It consisted in granting individuals large tracts of land, along with considerable political and economic authority, for the purpose of effective colonization and efficient government. In essence, the system was not unlike that of the later proprietary colonies of Maryland and Pennsylvania. The captaincies were granted by the king in perpetuity and carried with them not only great privilege and honor but also considerable power and opportunity for economic gain. Eventually, a captain general was designated to coordinate and supervise all of the colonies, but the degree of centralization achieved by the Spanish viceroys was never realized by the Portuguese captain generals.

By mid-century, Brazil was producing a variety of agricultural and forest products, including cotton, tobacco, cacao, and wood. But the most important crop was sugar. The Portuguese were not new to sugar production, having cultivated it in the Atlantic islands, but the Brazilian sugar industry was promoted on a much larger scale. Huge plantations of sugar cane, at times covering thousands of acres, were not uncommon by the end of the century, and sugar mills literally dotted coastal Brazil. The soil was ideal and Indian and Negro labor plentiful. It was this sugar economy, like the later cotton economy of the United States South, that largely determined the social development and structure of colonial Brazil. The proprietor was the ruler and judge of his hundreds of "subjects," and from the "Big House" presided over a miniature state. Still the social stratification was not as rigid as might be expected. From early in the colonial period, Indians and blacks played such an intimate role in the economy of the plantation and in daily life at the Big House itself, that personal relationships did not always adhere to the theoretical stratification they were intended to follow.

The Economic Impact of Expansion

It would be difficult to overemphasize the long-range effects of European overseas expansion on the cultural, social, and political development of Europe during the succeeding centuries. In the New World, it was decisive, overthrowing ancient political and social structures while planting European institutions, religion, language, and culture in their place. It is true that in some cases the natives maintained their autonomy and languages, but such examples are rare and even where this happened, aboriginal patterns of life were greatly affected. In Asia, the impact of Europe was much less pronounced and in some areas it was nil. This was due both to the cohesiveness and political strength of the sophisticated civilizations of the East and to the lack of Portuguese attempts to colonize these areas. The "factories" at Goa, Malacca, and Macao had little cultural impact on southeast Asia. Only in the field of religion did the Portuguese have much effect, and even there it was limited.

However elusive the relationship between European expansion and

WORLD MAP OF THE EARLY SIXTEENTH CENTURY. *Drawn by Girolamo Verrazano in 1529, this map shows with remarkable accuracy the coastlines that had been explored and charted by the end of the third decade of the century.* (National Maritime Museum, London)

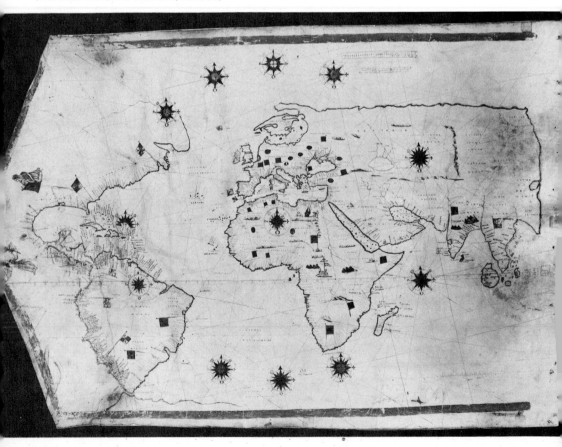

the politico-cultural changes in Europe during the sixteenth and seventeenth centuries may have been, the economic impact was immediate and continuous. Although few Europeans living in the second and third decades of the sixteenth century were conscious of the causes, most of them recognized that great economic changes were taking place. In some quarters, great wealth was amassed while in others the most abject poverty and economic desolation prevailed. Even as acute an observer as Sir Thomas More attributed the economic upheavals of his day only to the cardinal medieval sins of pride and greed. Economic historians now see many causes but generally agree that the increase in volume and area of European trade, and the augmentation of fluid capital due to the expansion, were paramount.

The nucleus of this new commercial capitalism was the Portuguese spice trade, but this was not all of it. The buying and selling of spices stimulated other exchanges until soon all of Europe was drawn into the commercial cyclone that continued to grow. The first effects of expanding trade were felt in the Mediterranean, where the newly emerging states of Portugal and Spain began taking their place alongside the flourishing Italian city-states, eventually replacing them in the volume and value of goods exchanged. Lisbon became the principal entry point of the Eastern trade, not only in spices of every kind but also in sugar, precious stones, dyestuffs, silk, cardamom, camphor, alum, carpets, leather, ivory, porcelain, and perfumes.

Into Seville soon flowed streams of products from the New World: sugar, indigo (blue dye), cochineal (red dye), vanilla, cacao, cotton, and especially silver. New products such as potatoes, corn, coffee, and tobacco were introduced into European society, and older staples were produced in greater abundance. The availability of vast grazing lands and the previous Spanish experience with livestock (particularly sheep and horses) made stock raising one of the chief occupations in the New World. Long before the end of the colonial era, more hides were being produced from the South American *pampas* than from all other parts of Europe combined.

The greatest stimulant to transatlantic trade was the discovery and exploitation of rich silver deposits in the mountainous regions of central Mexico and southern Peru (modern Bolivia). The opening of the famous Potosí mines in 1545 quadrupled in one year the value of previous metal imports into Europe. Employing the latest amalgamation processes, the Spanish were able to increase silver production for the next century and a half. It was this great frontier, with its seemingly endless expanse of land and the limitless production of wealth, that led the American historian Walter Prescot Webb to describe the period from Columbus's voyages to the twentieth century as "the 400-year boom."

But the boom economy of this European frontier did not lend itself to friendship and mutual respect, either among individuals or nations. "Beyond the line" there was no peace. From the return of Prince Henry's first successful African expedition, there was a continual and bitter rivalry among the European powers for a larger share of the valuable cargoes coming from Asia and the New World. Spanish and Portuguese sailors, as well as monarchs, jockeyed for advantageous positions in the race for trade and colonies. Early in the sixteenth century, French seamen began serious efforts to make profitable inroads into the Spanish colonial system, and soon the Dutch were advancing against the Portuguese in Brazil and later in southeast Asia. Free-lance Italian and German merchants, as well as municipal governments and city-states, became wealthy in America or in the American trade. The Welsers and other south German bankers were active in capitalizing on the almost-limitless possibilities for financial gain. In the second half of the century, English privateers were the most serious threat to the Spanish sea-lanes and reaped the greatest economic profits from plunder and piracy. The expansion of Europe was truly an economic catalyst in making the modern world. Trading companies were soon organized, opening vast new areas of commerce that in turn altered the whole configuration of European and world economy. This was not achieved without a high cost, however: inflation, social exploitation and upheaval, and international wars were among the inevitable results.

In the meantime, except for those whose lives were linked with the sea, the immense impact of the expansion was not widely recognized for many generations. Most Europeans still saw both Asia and America more as oddities than as meaningful entities, exotic rather than real. Their interests, worries, and hopes were closer at hand. Their thought and culture were not yet related to the New World, but rather to their own Christian heritage and to the civilizations of classical Greece and Rome as these were being recovered in the Renaissance.

Suggestions for Further Reading

GENERAL

There are many outstanding and fascinating books on the European expansion. The best single-volume general accounts are still Boies Penrose, *Travel and Discovery in the Renaissance, 1420–1620* (New York, 1962), and J. H. Parry, *The Age of Reconnaissance: Discovery, Exploration and Settlement, 1450 to 1650* (New York, 1963). Other important works of J. H. Parry include the much shorter *The Establishment of the European Hegemony, 1415–1715* (New York, 1961), which is the U.S. edition of his earlier *Europe and the Wider World*, and *The Discovery of the Sea* (New York, 1974), which tries to answer the question of why the Europeans, rather than the Arabs or Chinese, made the long oceanic voyages to new worlds. Also very important are Charles Verlinden, *The Beginnings of Modern Colonization*, tr. by Yvonne Freccero (Ithaca, 1970), which shows that Genoese colonization in the eastern Mediterranean provided the model and transition for Iberian expansion; Carlo M. Cipolla, *Guns, Sails, and Empires: Technological Innovation and the Early Phases of European Expansion, 1400–1700* (New York, 1965); and C. R. Boxer, *The Church Militant and Iberian Expansion, 1440–1770* (Baltimore, 1978). Also see the various interpretations in De Lamar

Jensen (ed.), *The Expansion of Europe: Motives, Methods, and Meanings* (Boston, 1967). Leo Bagrow, *History of Cartography*, tr. by D. L. Paisley, rev. and enlarged by R. A. Skelton (Cambridge, Mass., 1964) is the definitive study of maps and map making.

THE PORTUGUESE IN ASIA

Some of the background to the Portuguese expansion may be seen in Henry H. Hart, *Marco Polo: Venetian Adventurer* (Norman, 1967); I. de Rachewiltz, *Papal Envoys to the Great Khans* (Stanford, 1971); and the brief collection of Joseph R. Levenson (ed.). *European Expansion and the Counter-Example of Asia, 1300–1600* (Englewood Cliffs, 1967). The indispensable work is Donald F. Lach's monumental *Asia in the Making of Europe: Vol. I, The Century of Discovery,* in two books, and *Vol. II, A Century of Wonder,* in three books (Chicago, 1965–1977). C. R. Boxer, *The Portuguese Seaborne Empire: 1415–1825* (New York, 1969) is now the standard study of the Portuguese expansion. Excellent shorter accounts are G. R. Crone, *Discovery of the East* (London, 1972), and Christopher Bell, *Portugal and the Quest for the Indies* (London, 1974). W. Bailey Diffie and George D. Winius, *Foundations of the Portuguese Empire, 1415–1580* (Minneapolis, 1979), the first volume in the new Europe and the World in the Age of Expansion series, edited by Boyd C. Shafer, is a useful but uneven book. The figure of Prince Henry the Navigator has stimulated many writings, the most exciting of which is Garrett Mattingly's "Navigator to the Modern Age," *Horizon,* 3 (1960), 73–83. An intriguing thesis, arguing that the Portuguese expansion extended all the way to Australia, is Kenneth G. McIntyre, *The Secret Discovery of Australia: Portuguese Ventures 200 Years Before Captain Cook* (London, 1977).

THE DISCOVERY OF AMERICA

Many outstanding books on the discovery and settlement of America have appeared in recent years. The most engaging of these are two volumes by the renowned historian-seaman, Samuel Eliot Morison, entitled *The European Discovery of America: The Northern Voyages, A.D. 500–1600* (New York, 1971), and *The Southern Voyages, A.D. 1492–1616* (New York, 1974), both up-to-date and refreshingly casual in style. Morison is also the author of the best biography of Columbus, *Admiral of the Ocean Sea: A Life of Christopher Columbus* (Boston, 1942), and a fascinating description of *The Caribbean as Columbus Saw It* (Boston, 1964), with Mauricio Obregón. Many books on Columbus are published every year, most of them nonsense. But some are well worth reading, and even owning. Among these are Björn Landström, *Columbus,* tr. by Michael Phillips and Hugh Stubbs, illustrated by Landström himself (New York, 1967); and Ernle Bradford, *Christopher Columbus* (New York, 1973), important primarily for its many brilliant pictures. John S. Collis's *Christopher Columbus* (London, 1976) is an up-to-date and well-written brief account.

Louise-André Vigneras, *The Discovery of South America and the Andalusian Voyages* (Chicago, 1976) is a brief and challenging account of the early years of exploration. Edmundo O'Gorman's highly controversial *The Invention of America* (Bloomington, 1961) argues that Columbus was not the discoverer of America because the concept of "America" did not exist. It had to be invented, and this was the role of Amerigo Vespucci. Wilcomb E. Washburn answers O'Gorman in "The Meaning of 'Discovery' in the Fifteenth and Sixteenth Centuries," *American Historical Review,* 68 (1962), 1–21. The best discussion of Vespucci and his voyages is Germán Arciniegas, *America and the New World:*

Life and Time of Amerigo Vespucci, tr. by Harriet de Onís (New York, 1955). A very good short summary of the westward expansion is G. R. Crone, *The Discovery of America* (London, 1969).

North American discovery and exploration is thoroughly examined in two new books by David B. Quinn: *North America from Earliest Discovery to Settlements: The Norse Voyages to 1612* (New York, 1977), in the New American Nation series, and *England and the Discovery of America, 1481–1620* (New York, 1974), which argues that England took a significant part in the discovery and exploration of North America. *The Discovery of North America* (New York, 1972) is a detailed and sumptuously illustrated examination by W. P. Cumming, R. A. Skelton, and D. B. Quinn. More general, though superficial, is Louis B. Wright, *Gold, Glory and the Gospel: The Adventurous Lives and Times of the Renaissance Explorers* (New York, 1970).

CONQUEST AND COLONIZATION

Bernal Díaz de Castillo's sparkling eye-witness relating of *The Conquest of New Spain* (Penguin, 1963, and other editions), and William H. Prescott's nineteenth-century classics, *The Conquest of Mexico* and *The Conquest of Peru,* have never been equaled, although there have been many attempts. Hammond Innes, *The Conquistadors* (New York, 1969), is a colorful popularization by a famous novelist. Another is Paul Horgan, *Conquistadors in North American History* (New York, 1963). The standard is Frederick A. Kirkpatrick, *The Spanish Conquistadores,* 2nd ed. (Cleveland, 1968). Few books about the conquest are as delightful to read as R. B. Cunningham Graham, *The Horses of the Conquest* (Norman, 1949). On Cortés, see Salvador de Madariaga, *Hernán Cortés, Conqueror of Mexico* (Garden City, 1969); William W. Johnson, *Cortés* (Boston, 1975); and Jon M. White, *Cortés and the Downfall of the Aztec Empire* (London, 1971). On the Inca demise, see Burr Cartwright Brundage, *Lords of Cuzco* (Norman, 1967).

The role of Las Casas in the conquest and the subsequent relations with the Indians is underlined in Juan Friede and Benjamin Keen (eds.), *Bartolomé de Las Casas in History: Toward an Understanding of the Man and His Work* (Dekalb, 1971), and Lewis Hanke, *All Mankind is One* (Dekalb, 1974), which updates his earlier *The Spanish Struggle for Justice in the Conquest of America.* Carl O. Sauer, *The Early Spanish Main* (Berkeley, 1966) is an excellent book, as is Peggy K. Liss, *Mexico under Spain, 1521–1556* (Chicago, 1975), and James Lockhart, *Spanish Peru, 1532–1560: A Colonial Society* (Madison, 1968). The best overall summation of Spanish colonization is J. H. Parry, *The Spanish Seaborne Empire* (New York, 1966).

THE IMPACT OF EXPANSION

Ruth Pike, *Enterprise and Adventure: The Genoese in Seville and the Opening of the New World* (Ithaca, 1966) is well written and informative; also Kenneth R. Andrews, *The Spanish Caribbean: Trade and Plunder, 1530–1630* (New Haven, 1978). The influence of the expansion on Europe is convincingly explored in G. V. Scammell, "The New Worlds and Europe in the Sixteenth Century," *The Historical Journal,* 12 (1969), 389–412; J. H. Elliott's concise and brilliant *The Old World and the New, 1492–1650* (Cambridge, 1970); and the sumptuous collection of essays on *First Images of America: The Impact of the New World on the Old,* 2 vols. (Berkeley, 1976), edited by Fredi Chiapelli.

CHAPTER ELEVEN

Christian Humanism and Religious Reform

HE RECOVERY OF ANCIENT thought and literature in northern Europe had many characteristics of its fifteenth-century Italian counterpart, but it also contained important differences that justify considering it separately. In the first place, the scholastic pattern of the northern universities represented a closer connection with the medieval church than existed in Italy. In northern Europe (including Spain), there was a deeper religious piety and greater enthusiasm for ecclesiastical studies, although as we have seen, there was also a strong religious flavor to Italian humanism in the last half of the Quattrocento. Furthermore, the northern culture had few roots in the classical past comparable to those of Italy; the northern literary heritage was based primarily on religious writings and medieval books of chivalry and romance. It was not until Italian humanism developed a greater interest in philosophy and theology, near the end of the fifteenth century, that it began to penetrate the intellectual life of northern Europe.

Humanism and Learning in Northern Europe

Just as with Italian humanism, northern humanism emphasized ethics, reason, beauty, classical style, and an attitude of openness toward the world. But instead of expressing these features in the study and imitation of Cicero and Quintilian, they were mobilized in the interest of reforming the church. These so-called Christian humanists believed that the introduction of Greek (and even Hebrew) learning into the schools, the careful examination and correction of Christian sources, and the rational and orderly reformation of the church, using as a guide the Sermon on the Mount, would bring about a renewal of Christian ethics and intellectual balance and correct the sterility of scholastic thought. These humanists did not intend to break away from the church or preach heretical doctrines. They were simply more interested in morals and ethics than in theology or metaphysics.

Placing less weight on metaphysics than did the scholastics, and more stress on reason and logic than the mystics, the Christian humanists accentuated historical study, grammar, "return to the sources," and careful and accurate translation of those sources. Although they did much writing in the European vernaculars, these humanists wrote primarily in Latin, giving their literature a Europewide appeal. But humanism was never a mass movement either by or for the lower classes, and in the non-Italian countries it possessed an even more obvious elitism than it did south of the Alps. It was a philosophy and approach to life and to religion that was both compatible with and restricted to the educated classes.

One of the goals of the Christian humanists was to reconcile the various and seemingly conflicting traditions of pagan and Christian culture. As committed Christians, they looked at the abuses and corruption of the clergy with deep concern. Believing in the basic integrity and goodness of people and in their natural ability to reason and improve, the humanists felt that through education and enlightenment these abuses could be eliminated. In most of their writings, moral values occupied an important place, serving as the common bond among nations, creeds, and people. Thus in all religions and all periods of time, they found the "divine nuggets" of moral truth on the basis of which a thorough reformation of the church could and should be carried out. Whether Christian humanism is easier understood as an intellectual revolution with religious overtones or a religious revival using intellectual methods, it was a conscious attempt by Christian scholars to reconcile reason and faith, and to reeducate people using both Christ and the classics as guides.

Many of the humanists were directly involved in the reform of elementary and grammar school education. They also had something to do with the increase in the number of schools in Europe during the early part of the sixteenth century. As might be expected, one of the major influences was the increasing classical emphasis on school curricula. Cicero's *Letters*, Cato's *Moralia*, and Virgil's *Aeneid* were required reading in many schools by the second decade of the century, and in some, Livy's histories, Cicero's *Rhetoric*, and several Greek authors were, too. In isolated cases, students were even introduced to the study of Hebrew on the grammar-school level. Dictation of texts, memorization, and disputation were the standard methods of teaching, although with the growing impact of printing and the greater availability of printed commentaries, as well as texts, dictation gradually declined.

Of distinct importance in early-sixteenth-century education was the great grammar school of Deventer and other similar schools established by the Brethren of the Common Life in the Netherlands and western Germany. Here young boys were given difficult and challenging study in Latin grammar and the classics, as well as practical Bible training, by some of the best teachers in Europe. Pedagogy was advanced by these teachers and by students trained in their schools. John Colet envisaged the same type of liberal environment in his school in London. The Collège de Guyenne at Bordeaux, where the noted André Gouvéa guided thousands of boys through the stringent curriculum of grammar and classic literature, was another important educational center where humanism set the tone and pattern. Even more renowned was the Strasbourg Gymnasium under Johann Sturm, where Greek was introduced at a very early stage and where the Bible was used as a literary as well as theological text.

In university education, the most remarkable feature was not so much the influence of humanism on the curricula and methods—although it did have some impact here, particularly in the arts faculties—as it was the great proliferation of universities. In France the number doubled during the fifteenth century, and Angoulême, Nîmes and Rheims were added in the early sixteenth. Eleven new universities were founded in Germany in the fifteenth century and half that number in the first half of the sixteenth, Wittenberg soon becoming the most famous. Spanish university expansion was greatest in the early sixteenth century when some sixteen new schools were founded, including the renowned and strongly humanist-oriented University of Alcalá and the University of Granada.

French Humanism and Thought

In many respects, the French Renaissance was most like the Italian. The close linguistic and cultural ties between France and Italy caused a fuller adoption of elements of Italian humanism here than in neighboring countries. There was great interest in Latin literature even in medieval France, and a close bond existed between French and Italian intellectuals. Nevertheless, with the strong conventions of medieval Christianity prevailing in France and the cultural orientation of chivalric feudalism centered there, Renaissance influences were slow to develop. Even after humanism spread to France, it retained many elements of scholasticism that distinguished it rather sharply from Italian humanism. Surrounded by reminders and remnants of ancient Rome on all sides, Italian scholars could hardly avoid becoming classicists. To the French, on the other hand, historical Rome was a foreign and hostile place that inspired more hatred than love. Not surprisingly, therefore, French humanists were very selective in their adoption of classical culture.

Yet, however it resembled or differed from Italian humanism, the French intellectual awakening soon became a vital and active force in Europe, and shortly after the turn of the century, France rivaled Italy as the intellectual center of Europe. Paris and Lyon became centers of printing and the book trade, and French schools rapidly adapted themselves to the New Learning. Teaching was the stock-in-trade of the northern humanists as they expounded scriptures and other Latin texts in a variety of media, from sermons and lectures to pamphlet satires and erudite books. This activity may be partly explained by the eager patronage of Francis I, who subsidized the work of many Italian and French writers. Along with the royal library, he also founded a series of professorships and created a press.

The first of many important humanists to engage in serious classical studies and promote their spread in France was Robert Gaguin (1433–1501), whose admiration for Cicero was scarcely less ardent than that of his Italian colleagues. Gaguin's Latin translations and treatises not only began a trend in France, they also set the tone of that trend in a reconciliation of classical and French, pagan and Christian, which prevailed throughout the French Renaissance. Gaguin may be regarded as the father of French humanism, not only as a writer and scholar but also as a teacher of the New Learning at the University of Paris. The university was not the most compatible place for the incubation of new ideas, but Gaguin was a distinguished professor of law, and in that capacity imbued his enthusiastic students with many of the objectives and methods of humanism.

The foremost classicist scholar of the French Renaissance was Guillaume Budé (1467–1540), who was, like Gaguin, a lawyer, classical stylist, and teacher. But unlike his older countryman, Budé was a wandering scholar, attached to no university or educational institution until he founded his own Collège de France in 1530. Trained in law at Orléans, Budé turned from the legal profession to study and promote the New Learning. He was particularly interested in philology, and published a number of Latin and French translations and an important treatise on Roman antiquities. But his principal love was Greek, to which he applied himself diligently after his first lesson in 1494. At an early age, he made translations from Plutarch and produced some original writings in Greek. His most impressive volume of Greek scholarship was a 1529 Greek lexicon, which confirmed his reputation as a peer of the great Erasmus. In the meantime, Budé was appointed master of the king's library at Fontainebleau and spearheaded the acquisition of Greek manuscripts. He was succeeded in that position by another prominent humanist and wandering scholar, Pierre du Chastel, whose career as a world traveler, teacher of Latin and Greek, soldier of fortune, ambassador, editor, king's reader, archdeacon of Avignon, and bishop of Macon, Tulle, and Orléans, is a saga in itself.

GUILLAUME BUDÉ. *An engraving of the French humanist from André Thevet,* Portraits and Lives of Illustrious Men *(1584). Budé was the most enthusiastic Greek scholar in France.* (Bibliothèque Nationale, Paris)

Many other scholarly luminaries lighted the early sixteenth century in France. Among the more prominent of these was Maturin Cordier, humanist educator at the University of Paris (and one of John Calvin's teachers). But Paris was not the only center of French learning. A crusader against misuse and corruption of classical Latin, Cordier left Paris in 1528 to teach at Nevers for several years, then to the new humanist Collège de Guyenne at Bordeaux, and finally to Calvin's Geneva, where he published his justly famous *Colloquies.* The prominence of Bordeaux in humanistic education has already been mentioned, but similar foci of the New Learning could be found at Nîmes, Bourges (where the great Italian jurist Andrea Alciati taught jurisprudence from 1528 to 1533), and especially Lyon. Largely Italian in culture and orientation, Lyon became a compatible congregating place for Italian humanists and French scholars who preferred the provincial atmosphere, away from the Sorbonne and the French court. From this environment emerged one of the most colorful printers and humanists of the French Renaissance, Étienne Dolet (1509–46), whose pugnacious personality, as much as his enthusiastic and uninhibited pursuit of Protestant ideas, eventually cost him his life at the stake. His *Commentaries on the Latin Tongue* (1536–38) remains one of the lasting monuments of French erudition and style.

The most important of the French scholars was Jacques Lefèvre d'Étaples (1450–1536). Like Pico della Mirandola, who influenced him profoundly during his journey in Italy, Lefèvre was interested in all knowledge, including that of the scholastics and mystics. He had been impressed by the tendency toward mysticism and occultism in Italian Neo-Platonism and by Pico's interest in symbolism and cabalism. He published Ficino's hermetic translations and other works attributed to ancient and medieval mystics. He was also fascinated by the mysticism of Nicholas of Cusa, whose complete works he published in France in 1514. Lefèvre was unusually devoted to Aristotle, but he disagreed with many of the scholastics' interpretations of Aristotle's writings and applied his sharp philological sense to an examination and purification of the Aristotelian texts. Later, at the University of Paris, he delivered lectures on Aristotle that in their literal exposition of the philosopher's writings closely resembled John Colet's approach to the epistles of Saint Paul.

As he grew older, Lefèvre devoted more of his time and thought to the scriptures and devotional literature than he did to the Greek and Roman classics. At one point in his life, he even seriously contemplated renouncing the world and entering a religious order. His serious biblical scholarship began in 1505 with the publication of his translation of the theology of John of Damascus. Between 1505 and 1536, he published many volumes of commentaries, expositions, and textual criticism on biblical and theological subjects, including a translation of the Epistles of Paul, a *Commentary on the Four Gospels* (1522), and a new Latin translation of the New Testament (1523). His study of the Bible and biblical theology, along with his continued mysticism, brought Lefèvre very close to some of the heretical beliefs of the Protestants.

Although he remained staunchly loyal to the Catholic church, Lefèvre's intellectual wanderings and friendship with many Protestants made him a leading influence on the prereformers and early Protestants in France. At Meaux, outside Paris, many of his intellectual and spiritual followers congregated, and, under the pastoral guidance of Bishop Guillaume Briçonnet, formed the nucleus of a growing multitude of Christian humanists who hoped to reconcile Christian dogma with the New Learning and effect a spiritual and moral reformation within the church.

Similarly at Nérac, in the southern duchy of Albret, the refined and learned duchess of Alençon and queen of Navarre, Marguerite d'Angoulême (1492–1549), sister of Francis I, led another group of reform-minded humanists who considered Lefèvre d'Étaples their precursor and friend. Marguerite was undoubtedly the outstanding woman of her time. Brilliant, talented, and charming, she was one of the greatest stimulants to the Renaissance in France and much of the inspiration to her brother, the king, in his devotion to culture. When awarded the duchy of Berry as her *appanage*, she made its university at Bourges one of the leaders of the New Learning. Married in 1527 to Henri d'Albret, king of Navarre, she immediately made her new home the center of humanistic culture for southern France. Having mastered Latin, Italian, and Spanish in her youth, Marguerite applied herself to the command of Greek and Hebrew in order to study the scriptures in their original idioms. She felt a strong kinship with the Florentine Platonists and was influenced also by the writings of Nicholas of Cusa.

Humanism and Religious Thought in Spain

Too often the place of Spain in the flowering of humanism is overlooked. Geographically, Spain is very close to Italy—the Mediterranean being much easier to cross than either the Alps or the Pyrenees—and since Roman days had had close economic and political ties with her. The church provided another link and after 1494, so did war. From the middle of the fifteenth century, very close cultural connections were made between Italy and Spain. Many Italian humanists traveled in Iberia, and some of them taught at Castilian universities during the second half of the Quattrocento. All of the first-ranked Spanish humanists studied at one time or another at universities in Italy.

Foremost of the Spanish scholars of the period was Antonio de Nebrija (1444–1522), a disciple of Lorenzo Valla and a distinguished perpetuator of his philological method in Spain. Thoroughly grounded in the philosophy and methodology of humanism after a ten-year sojourn in Italy, Nebrija launched a continuing crusade against the vulgarities of Latin as it was then used in the church and taught in the universities. He began by publishing a new Latin grammar and followed this with a Latin-Castilian dictionary. Moreover, his productive career was not restricted to lexicography and philology. He wrote a number of books on Spanish geography and antiquities, and a renowned history of Spain, *The Decades*, which brought him the acclaim of Ferdinand and Isabel, and an appointment as royal historian. Above all, he was interested in the Bible and biblical criticism. For many years he taught Latin grammar at the renowned University of Salamanca, but his radical writings on the Holy Scriptures brought his dismissal in 1512. He was immediately given the chair of rhetoric and grammar at the new University of Alcalá.

Nebrija was at the same time a well-known and accomplished Greek scholar. Since the Middle Ages, Spain had been a fruitful soil for the cultivation of Greek and Hellenistic learning. The greatest Arab centers of this study were located in Moslem Spain. At the same time, Jewish theological and cabalistic studies were more extensive in Spain than in any other part of Europe, reaching a climax in the 1480s with the scholarly enterprises of Isaac Abrabanel (1437–1508). The final phases of the *reconquista*, however, and the expulsion of the Jews in 1492 wrought considerable damage to this tradition, although interest in Greek and Hebrew literature never entirely disappeared from some of the Spanish universities. In the fifteenth century, several Greek refugees found compatible homes in the Iberian Peninsula, even at the University of Salamanca. Here the greatest of the Spanish Hellenists, Hernán Nuñez

(1471–1522) was trained and later taught, before moving to the more compatible atmosphere of Alcalá.

The greatest promoter of humanism in Spain was not in a strict sense a humanist himself. This was Francisco Jiménez de Cisneros (1437–1517), confessor to Queen Isabel, archbishop of Toledo and thus primate of Spain, inquisitor general, grand chancellor of Castile, and cardinal regent of Spain. As a conscientious and energetic reformer, Cardinal Cisneros was without peer among his contemporaries. Having no more tolerance for clerical abuses than he did for heresy, he instigated and carried out an ambitious reformation in Spain, beginning with his own Franciscan order. After eliminating the flagrant abuses of the two major orders of friars and extending his reform campaign into the monasteries, he was invited by the queen to plan and effect an overall reform of the secular clergy. So effective was his reforming zeal that by the time of his death, the Spanish church was less in need of overhaul than any in Europe; the Reformation was already completed there.

Cardinal Cisneros was much more than a reformer of ecclesiastical abuses. He was a scholar in his own right and a sympathetic benefactor of humanistic learning in Spain. His philosophy of education was that all study of history, languages (but especially Greek and Hebrew), and texts helped make better Bible scholars and better Christians. In 1509 Cisneros founded the University of Alcalá de Henares near Madrid for the purpose of providing a better and more complete education for the Spanish clergy. Soon Alcalá became the leader in biblical scholarship and in the study of Greek, Hebrew, and even Aramaic.

The most notable scholarly-theological activity to emerge from the first years' operation of the new university was the Complutensian Polyglot Bible, the first significant attempt to produce the complete Bible in original languages. On either side of the official Latin Vulgate were printed the Greek, Hebrew, and Aramaic texts to assist in interpreting the scripture and in clarifying errors. The New Testament was completed in 1514 and the entire Bible of six large tomes, including a Greek-Hebrew-Aramaic lexicon, in 1522; all told, it was a tremendous work of cooperative scholarship and devoted effort. To complete this monumental work, Cisneros attracted scholars from all parts of Spain and beyond, including the Jewish scholars Alfonso de Zamora and Lablo de Coronel.

The greatest of the Spanish humanists, whose Europewide reputation was surpassed only by that of his mentor Erasmus, was Juan Luis Vives (1492–1540), a philosopher, teacher, and man of letters from Valencia. Educated locally until he was seventeen, Vives completed his formal schooling at the University of Paris. His earliest major work, the *Fabula de Homine* (The Fable of Man, 1518), is a penetrating inquiry into human nature, revealing in Vives a mature and probing mind. Although largely Platonic, his view of human nature is even more strongly Christian and humanistic, seeing people as agents of their own free will operating within certain well-defined limits. From Paris, he was attracted to the Low Countries and the University of Louvain, where he became professor of belles lettres. Henry VIII invited him to England, where he became the tutor to Princess Mary and a fellow of Corpus Christi College, Oxford. Opposition to the king's divorce of Catherine of Aragon cost Vives the royal favor, so he was forced to return to the continent where he settled at Bruges in the Netherlands.

Throughout his life, Vives was an advocate of reform—in education, law, historiography, and the church—but in the latter, he was even more careful than most of the humanists to attack only corruption and abuse, not doctrines. In his fifty-two volumes of published works, Vives criticized and corrected current educational practices, called for broad reforms in the teaching and practice of law, and advocated a sounder methodological approach to the writing of history. His educational philosophy was based on the reconciliation of Christianity and humanism, since the primary aim of education, he believed, was morality and goodness, which is realized through the scholarly study of Latin and Greek literature as well as the application of Christian ideals and piety. Yet he also advocated teaching the vernacular, and insisted on sound methodology, that is, beginning with simple facts and concepts and then moving on to more abstract ideas. He believed in secular education, based on Christian principles, of course, but sponsored by municipal governments; and he thought it should be available to more than the sons of the wealthy. In *De subventione pauperum* (On Aid for the Poor) he outlined a program for educating the poor, and in *De institutione feminae Christianae* (On the Education of a Christian Woman) he proposed teaching women as well, albeit in a somewhat different way, because of their different needs. Above all, he recommended observation of nature and performance of experiments as the basis of knowledge instead of undiscerning imitation of ancient, medieval, or even modern authorities. True wisdom, he concluded in his *Introductio ad sapientiam* (Introduction to Wisdom), "consists in judging things correctly, so that we may estimate a thing at its true worth, and not esteem something vile as though it were precious or reject something precious as though it were vile."

In the early decades of the sixteenth century, Spain proved to be a fertile soil for the spread of Christian humanism. Between 1515 and 1530, the popularity of Erasmus in Spain was so great as to almost constitute a cult. And this was not a mere personality worship, for Erasmus never visited Spain; it was an interest and belief in the program and tenets of Christian humanism as expounded by its greatest representatives. A Spanish translation of Erasmus's *Enchiridion militis Christiani* (Manual of a Christian Soldier) in 1526 made this for a time the most popular theological-devotional work in Spain. Offered a position at Alcalá, Erasmus carefully considered the invitation before turning it down, as he resisted every temptation to attach himself to a permanent position. Christian humanism as it radiated from western

Germany and the Low Countries under the influence of Erasmus was naturally attracted to the young Flemish prince who in 1516 became king of Spain, and three years later Holy Roman emperor. But Spain's congenial attitude toward Erasmus cannot be attributed entirely to the influence of Charles V. The previous cleansing of the church by Cardinal Cisneros had a great deal to do with the reception given Christian humanism in Spain.

Less surprising is the eager reception of Erasmian humanism by the more anticlerical elements in Spain and by the many *Marranos* whose ranks had swollen greatly after the Jewish expulsion of 1492. Unfortunately, the receptivity to outside ideas that had characterized Spain in the first third of the century disappeared with the spread of Protestantism. Enthusiasm for reform and learning was replaced by anxiety and fear. Christian humanists who at one time were more highly esteemed in Spain than anywhere else were now suspected of heresy and treason. Both Erasmians and *Alumbrados* (Illuminists or "enlightened" Spanish mystics) were distrusted, then intimidated, and finally persecuted. As the curtain of fear descended, the glow of Christian humanism gave way to the flames of the *auto-de-fé* (literally, "act of faith"—a public ceremony in which the sentences of condemned heretics were pronounced).

The German Humanists

At first glance, it may seem strange that the influence of humanistic thought and literature spread from Italy into Germany as early as it did. However, considering the long-standing political connections between the two countries (a third of Italy was still theoretically within the Holy Roman Empire), the lack of a strong cultural influence from the imperial court, the German tradition of sending their sons south for schooling in the universities of Italy, the desire for cultural expression among the urbanized populations of south Germany, and the receptivity of the many newly founded German universities to the intellectual pressures from Italy, it is not so incredible. Evidence of the close intellectual and literary relations between Germany and Italy may also be seen in the development of printing and its spread.

But even then, the influence of Italian culture on Germany was only scattered and ill-defined by the end of the fifteenth century. Here, just as in the other countries of Europe, Italian humanism had few deep roots until near the end of the fifteenth century, when it adapted itself to the broader philosophical and religious needs of the northern climes. Even then it clashed with the upholders of scholastic traditions, and a sharp cleavage between the new and old schools of thought resulted in the creation of a scattered hybrid humanism, which was neither Italian nor exclusively German. Humanism in Germany differed most from its counterparts in France, Spain, and England in that it exerted a less positive reforming pressure on the church within its territory and a more embittered hostility toward Rome. Thus, humanism was more likely to breed religious discontent and social disorder in Germany than it was elsewhere.

Early relations between Italian and German humanism date from the time of the Council of Constance, which drew many clerics and intellectuals together from both sides of the Alps. The expository writings and teachings of the Italian-trained professor of Latin at the University of Heidelberg, Peter Luder (1414–74), stimulated Italo-German intellectual intercourse, as did the extensive travels and embassies of Pope Pius II in many parts of Germany. More than anyone else, Nicholas of Cusa provided the early link between the thought of the two areas.

A more direct scholarly relationship between Germany and Italy was provided by Rudolf Agricola (1444–85), who is considered the father of German humanism. Born near Groningen in northeastern Netherlands, Agricola was educated by the Brethren of the Common Life in Groningen, studied arts at the University of Erfurt, scholastic philosophy and mathematics at Louvain, and arts and theology at Cologne, before plunging into the cultural stream of Renaissance Italy in 1469. So impressed was he by all he saw and learned there that he remained for the next ten years, reading law at the University of Pavia and immersing himself in the classics at Ferrara. While supporting himself as an organist to Duke Ercole d'Este, he learned Greek, wrote Latin epigrams, and mastered the programmatic literature of the humanists. He was particularly inspired by Petrarch and fancied himself in the role of the Petrarch of northern humanism. Struck by the cultural contrasts with Germany when he returned there in 1479, he devoted the last six years of his life to promoting a cultural and religious renaissance in the north.

Agricola's influence in Germany was strong, and it affected disciples of many differing convictions and temperaments. Conrad Celtis (1459–1508), for example, a student of Agricola's at Heidelberg, became the leading poet of the German Renaissance, as well as an active advocate of religious renewal, and a genial but outspoken champion of classical scholarship while upholding a patriotic attachment to German culture. Celtis was the first humanist to lecture on Tacitus in Germany and published Tacitus's *Germania* as a preliminary to a larger and more comprehensive compilation of German history and geography. He also published a laudatory poem about Germany, ironically, but not surprisingly, written in Latin. Jakob Wimpheling (1450–1528) was another rabid cultural nationalist, who—unlike Celtis, whose attitude toward the church was disdainful when not outright contemptuous—remained a devoted and obedient churchman. Wimpheling's numerous literary barrages against the practices and morals of the clergy (of which he was a member) were all intended to defend, rather than destroy, the structure of medieval Catholicism.

Two other German humanists whose lifespans were almost identical but whose personalities and outlooks were nearly opposite were Willibald Pirkheimer (1470–1528) and Conrad Mutianus Rufus (1471–

WILLIBALD PIRKHEIMER. *A handsome engraving of the notable Nuremberg patrician and humanist, by his close friend Albrecht Dürer. The inscription reads, "A portrait of Willibald Pirkheimer at 53. We live in spirit. All else is mortal. 1524." (Reproduced by Courtesy of the Trustees of the British Museum)*

1526). Pirkheimer was a wealthy, influential, urban aristocrat from the imperial city of Nuremberg. Unlike many of the patrician class, he was a dedicated intellectual who felt a greater urge to gain knowledge than to further wealth. Educated in Italy, as were all of the major German humanists, he was a capable and erudite Latin and Greek scholar, whose loose morals and unrestrained appetites placed him in a rather ambiguous position as a religious reformer. Mutianus Rufus, on the other hand, remained close to the faith of his fathers, advocating a Christian humanism based on the moral teachings of Paul. As leader of the circle of humanists at the University of Erfurt, the stronghold of Occamism in Germany, he attracted many interested students to that city and instilled in them a belief in a more devotional and ethical Christianity, with an emphasis on morals rather than theology.

The most illustrious of all the German humanists was Johann Reuchlin (1455–1522), who enjoyed the respect and admiration of all Europe. Like Pico, whom he acknowledged as his teacher and model, Reuchlin was interested in all phases of human knowledge. During his lifetime, he mastered many areas of knowledge himself. He studied jurisprudence at Orléans, philosophy at Paris, Greek at Basel and Tübingen—where he also taught Greek and served as a civil magistrate—law at Rome, and Plato at Florence. He was an eloquent Latin stylist and one of the most accomplished Greek scholars in Germany. But the real passion of his life was Hebrew, or more precisely, the mystical content of the Jewish Cabala, to which he applied himself after 1493. Like his young mentor Pico, Reuchlin mastered the cabalistic literature and published a study on it before the turn of the century. In

1506 he published a Christian-Hebrew grammar and in 1518 a further treatise on Hebrew studies. His interest and enthusiasm in this direction led to many serious controversies with the orthodox Thomists of Cologne and with others who considered his studies not only radical but heretical. Ironically, his most rabid opponent was a converted Jew named Johannes Pfefferkorn, who had assumed the role of exterminator of Judaism in Germany. Pfefferkorn charged that all Jewish books were wicked and should be destroyed, while Reuchlin defended them as sources of religious and cultural truths. Soon a widening circle of people were involved in the spectacular controversy, with pamphlets, invectives, and condemnations filling the air from Rügen to Rome. In the meantime, a perturbed Augustinian professor-priest named Luther was hurling another kind of challenge at the theologians, soon pushing the Reuchlin-Pfefferkorn controversy into the background. The only abiding result of the affair was the publication of one of the most celebrated satires of the period, *Letters of Obscure Men*, written mostly by two of Reuchlin's humanist defenders, Ulrich von Hutten and Crotus Rubeanus.

Reuchlin's Hebrew scholarship was not an end in itself but a means to the central aim of most of the Christian humanists: to cleanse the church of its follies and redirect its emphasis toward a simpler and more meaningful spiritual experience by restoring it to its pristine form through reliable Christian scholarship. His major philosophical-theological works, *De verbo mirifico* (On the Wonder-Working Word, 1494) and *De arte cabalistica* (On the Cabalistic Art, 1517) both disclose his attempts to weave the divergent threads of ancient and modern philosophy into a convincing and satisfying tapestry of divine truth.

Early Humanism in England

Cultural and intellectual life in England was still predominately medieval by the early sixteenth century. Chivalry was almost as much in vogue as it had been two centuries earlier, and English letters had not changed drastically since Chaucer and Wyclif. Nevertheless, new elements that were gradually being added to the intellectual life were producing a slow but profound change in the pattern of English thought and expression, even though humanism never had as wide a following in England as it did on the continent. In the study of Latin grammar, for example, which was the first field to be revitalized, the humanistic influences from Italy were only beginning to be felt in the last decade of the fifteenth century, as it became more and more common to see Italian scholars in England, at Canterbury, Winchester College, and Oxford.

The strongest impulse toward the New Learning, however, came from a group of English scholars who traveled and studied in Italy, some of them under Ficino and Pico at the Platonic Academy, who then returned to spread their new perspectives in England. One of these early precursors was William Sellyng (d. 1494), prior of Christ Church at

Canterbury, who spent several years in Italy studying Latin, Greek, and philosophy. Among Sellyng's most influential students at Canterbury were Thomas Linacre (1460–1524) and his friend William Grocyn (1446–1519), both Oxonians, who likewise studied in Italy and returned to spread the New Learning in England. Linacre studied medicine, received his degree in 1496 at Padua, and published several scholarly works on the Greek physicians and various translations of Galen. In England, while serving as court physician, he became royal tutor under Henry VII and Henry VIII. Grocyn's inclinations were more literary and philosophical than were Linacre's, and they were particularly important because of his devoted application to the study of theology. Although he did not write as prolifically as many of the humanists, Grocyn was very influential in England. Both Colet and More expressed their indebtedness to him for their interest and respect for classical studies.

Probably the most brilliant and devoted pioneer in applying humanist learning and method to the study and interpretation of theology was the dean of Saint Paul's, John Colet (1466–1519). From his four years in Italy associating with Pico and other luminaries of the Florentine Renaissance, Colet learned to respect and admire the historical and realistically critical method of the humanists, but he also gained a deeper appreciation of Christianity and its divinely established role. Son of a wealthy London burgher, Colet was already well grounded in scholastic philosophy and rhetoric before he went to Italy. His inspiring contact with Plato at the Florentine Academy imbued him not only with a broader outlook on religion in general and the scriptures in particular but also with a sense of dedication to the cause of Christian humanism.

The mission that motivated Colet was the desire to combine scholarship with piety to produce a balanced and harmonious Christian life. He stood for a simple exegesis of scriptures as the inspired but human writings of real flesh-and-blood men to other people, for the purpose of learning humility and devotion. Only through self-denial and almost mystical devotion could people attain the God-given grace that alone produces truth. Colet's criticism of the church, which was always indirect and never polemical, was that it had been obscured and perverted by the narrowly allegorical expositions and definitions of the scholastics. Therefore, in his famous lectures on the Epistles of Saint Paul, Colet sought to understand the meaning of the great missionary's words by interpreting them as the simple, personal, and loving (though sometimes upbraiding) words of a real person with feelings, desires, and biases, who was writing to congregations or individuals with similar human strengths and weaknesses. In thus expounding the scriptures, Colet became a reluctant but persistent critic of ecclesiastical abuses and ignorance.

Although all of the Christian humanists aspired to a reconciliation of faith and scholarship, Christianity and humanism, none was quite as successful in achieving a harmonious balance in both private life and public teaching as John Colet. In order to continue the humanistic exposition of the scriptures and lead the way to a broader and more tolerant Christian scholarship, Colet founded Saint Paul's School in London and set its direction toward sound scholarship and Christian learning. Saint Paul's School reflected its founder's conviction that truth was paramount, that it had to be discovered individually and personally, and that it should be passed on to others.

Sir Thomas More

A more famous humanist of a different type was Sir Thomas More (1478–1535), lifelong friend and admirer of Colet. In contrast to his older associate, More was a layman, a trained lawyer, and an active and wealthy man of affairs who eventually attained the highest political office in the kingdom, next to the king. With an alert mind and a sympathetic heart, he also immersed himself in the New Learning while continuing to deepen his understanding and devotion to the church.

SIR THOMAS MORE. *This well-known portrait was painted by Hans Holbein the Younger in 1527, two years before More became lord chancellor. He proudly wears the collar of a royal secretary. (Copyright The Frick Collection, New York)*

327

Son of a moderately well-to-do London lawyer, Thomas More was given the best educational opportunities available. He was schooled at Saint Anthony's in London where he was first introduced to Latin grammar and acquired a taste for the classics. Then, as the custom among middle-class families was to attach their sons to influential patrons, he was sent to reside as a page in the household of Cardinal Morton, who continued the education of his young client, adding to it a religious facet that it might not otherwise have had. More's liberal arts education was completed at Oxford, where he continued work in the Latin classics and later studied Greek under Linacre and Grocyn. Finally, like his father before him, he studied law at the Inns of Court and began a promising, though reluctant, legal career. His brilliant mind and quick, perceptive personality soon opened many doors of opportunity and challenge to him. In 1504, at the age of twenty-six, he was elected to Parliament, and from that time until his execution thirty-one years later, he was always in the public light. In 1510 More accepted an appointment as undersheriff of the City of London and later became a part of Henry VIII's diplomatic service. In 1515 he was sent on a diplomatic mission to Bruges and Antwerp, where he wrote the second book of his *Utopia*. In 1518 he became a member of the king's council. He was undertreasurer in 1521 and in 1523 was chosen speaker of the House of Commons. For more than four years, he was also chancellor of Lancaster and high steward of both Oxford and Cambridge. In October 1529 he succeeded Thomas Wolsey as lord chancellor of England.

In spite of his active public career, More never lost interest in the intellectual, cultural, or spiritual aspects of life. He was well acquainted and closely associated with John Colet, Cuthbert Tunstall, and other English humanists and from 1500 on was an intimate, cherished friend of Erasmus. He promoted the study of Greek at Oxford and made some contributions of his own to Greek scholarship: a Greek anthology, in collaboration with the Greek scholar William Lily, and some translations from Lucian. He was also an avowed follower of Pico della Mirandola, whose Latin biography he translated into English around 1505, along with a number of Pico's letters. Contemporaries proclaimed More's Latin prose and poetry to be among the best of the time. He was withal a devoutly pious and religious man who spent many hours a week in private and family devotions and prayers, whose dedication to the church was unfeigned, and who practiced charity unstintingly— except to heretics, whom he believed should be killed. His religious dedication, as well as his scholarly distinction and urbane humor, are amply revealed in his great social satire, *Utopia*.

Although still controversial and elusive after more than 450 years, More's *Utopia*, which describes the idealistic life and institutions of the inhabitants of the imaginary island of Utopia, is considered one of the greatest books produced in the sixteenth century. In it the ingredients of a well-read and highly intelligent humanist are combined with the sympathy, brotherhood, and simplicity of the devoted Christian, and with the boldness and clarity of a worldly individual, to produce a provocative and witty treatise that has profoundly affected social and political thought ever since.

More was disturbed by many of the problems and abuses of his day, from the injustices of the laws, to the new monarchies, the economic impositions of the landowners, and the ungodliness of the clergy. He sensed that his society was undergoing a transition and that many of the attributes and assets of the medieval structure were being lost in the changeover to a commercial-capitalist economy, autocratic monarchy, and increasing secularism. But at the same time, he saw the equally abominable vices of the earlier age of serfdom and manorial despotism, and knew that time could not be turned back even if it were desirable. Therefore, he proposed a new social order in which reason, tolerance, and cooperation would replace power, prestige, and wealth as motivating forces. This could result, he maintained, only in a society based on the community of property and goods instead of a crass money economy and private property that are caused by the heinous sin of pride and result in manifestations of greed, vanity, envy, and sloth. Of all God's creations, More lamented, only humans are greedy out of "pride alone, which counts it a glorious thing to pass and excel others in the superfluous and vain ostentation of things."

In Utopia everyone works six hours a day, no matter what their office or calling, and are compensated according to their needs. They are free to use their leisure as they see fit. Without the competitive profit motive and its resulting incentives to greed, dishonesty, corruption, and graft, the Utopians can direct their lives into more fruitful and meritorious channels. As a result, their cultural attainments are prodigious. Sloth at one end and vain ambition at the other are prevented, not by redistribution of the productive instruments as in the later Marxist utopia, but by the regimen of just laws and efficient institutions. More had a deep concern for the common people and gave them the opportunity in Utopia to live lives of dignity and comfort, free from the ruthless exploitation at the hands of the wealthy and powerful. He was harsh on criminals, however. Serious offenders of the law were made slaves, chained, and kept constantly at work. Yet their bondage was still lighter than punishments in other countries, as witnessed by the fact that many of the poor of other nations chose of their own accord to become slaves in Utopia because that was preferable to freedom in their own countries. Their work was lighter than that of other slaves, however, and they were free to return to their homelands if they wished (which they seldom did).

More had no use for the pomp and ostentation of the nobles of his day; in Utopia the governors and lawgivers dressed and looked just like everyone else (except for the priests). The use of jewelry and finery is ridiculed (along with a fitting barb thrown at contemporary diplomatic practices) in the diplomatic entourage of a visiting embassy from the neighboring country of Anemolia. The ambassadors, bedecked in gold

and silver, were scorned by the Utopians, because in Utopia gold was used only for children's toys, prisoners' chains, and chamberpots. "And you might have seen children, who had already thrown away their pearls and gems, nudge their mothers upon seeing the jewels in the ambassadors' caps, and say, 'Look, mother! See that big fool who wears pearls and gems, as if he were a little boy!' Then she would say seriously, 'Hush, my boy. I think he is one of the ambassadors' fools.' " Throughout the *Utopia*, there is an asceticism that reminds us not only of the repugnance More felt toward the social imbalance and injustices of his day but also the deep biblical piety that he longed for himself even while serving in places of importance and grandeur.

In Book One of the *Utopia*, More addressed himself directly to the problem of serving a ruler whose policies and methods he opposed. It was not an easy dilemma for Sir Thomas to resolve. Dedicated as he was to the goals of peace, brotherhood, and righteousness, and after having explicitly declared himself against many of the abuses Henry VIII represented, More could hardly reject everything he had written and stood for when he was asked to join the royal council. But on the other hand, what about his obligation to his king—and to himself? Could he turn his back on the opportunity at least to do what he could to make a situation even minutely better? Here More's ultimate realism stands out above the apparent fanciful idealism of Utopia. He understood human nature and knew that people and practices would not be changed overnight. Yet if no attempt were made to right the wrongs, they could certainly never be changed. His justification for serving the king is an indication of his faith and practicality:

> If evil opinions cannot be quite rooted out, and if you cannot correct habitual attitudes as you wish, you must not therefore abandon the commonwealth. Don't give up the ship in a storm because you cannot control the winds. And do not force unheard-of advice upon people, when you know that their minds are different from yours. You must strive to guide policy indirectly, so that you make the best of things, and what you cannot turn to good, you can at least make less bad. For it is impossible to do all things well unless all men are good, and this I do not expect to see for a long time.

Humanism in the Netherlands

Humanism in the Burgundian Netherlands was affected by a great variety of influences and pressures, which made it perhaps the most cosmopolitan of any. Located at the economic crossroads of Europe, it is not surprising that the Netherlands was touched by every wind of opinion or philosophy that blew across the continent. The chivalric flavor of the Burgundian court at Bruges and Ghent, along with the staid scholasticism of the University of Louvain, set the tone of intellectual stability, but there were few who followed it exclusively. The cultural influences of nearby France were always strong, especially in the southern states of Flanders, Artois, and Hainaut, while the channel separating the Lowlands from England was in many ways narrower than the Rhine. Yet the language of the northern two-thirds of the provinces was Germanic, and the kinship with the neighboring states of Friesland, Münster, Cleves, and Zülich extended into the northern flatlands and up the Rhine Valley. After the marriage of Maximilian of Habsburg and Mary of Burgundy, influence from Austria and the Empire increased, and when this union resulted in the accession of Charles V, king of Spain and Holy Roman emperor, the Netherlands was opened also to Spanish influences.

Still, the most important ingredients making up the cultural sauce of the Netherlands were essentially native. The semimystical groups composing the *devotio moderna* (The Modern Devotion), were centered in the Lowlands and radiated from there eastward and southward. As a persistent effort to strengthen and invigorate Christianity through emphasis on morality, prayer, devotion, and living the Sermon on the Mount, the *devotio moderna* was not unlike many other forms of mysticism that flourished in Europe. But as lived and taught by the Brethren of the Common Life, it was also an educational system bringing its approach and attitude to thousands. The schools of the Brethren of the Common Life brought training first to Deventer, then to scores of other sities in northwestern Europe. Their schools were responsible for training some of the outstanding personalities of the age, and for fusing the methods and motives of humanism with the highest traditions of

Christianity into a meaningful new devotion. The most illustrious of their students was Erasmus of Rotterdam.

Erasmus

As the universally acclaimed "Prince of the Humanists" and a leader among the intellectuals of Europe, Desiderius Erasmus (1466–1536) epitomized and combined the greatness and weakness of sixteenth-century Christian humanism. Educated at Deventer by Alexander Hegius and the Brethren, by early religious and monastic experience, by intensive personal study, and by extensive travel and observation, Erasmus's later life and thought were a synthesis of these varied experiences. Irredeemably impressed by classical literature and good Latin style—and unusually gifted himself with the ability to write lucid and eloquent prose—he abandoned a six-year monastic life after 1492 because of the lack of intellectual challenges there. In 1494 he went to Paris to the Collège de Montaigu, which he later vilified for its "stale eggs and equally stale theology." As yet Erasmus had not been able to reconcile his devotion and obligation to the church with his own secular and scholarly tastes, or even his inner convictions with his outer demeanor. He enjoyed the intellectual companionship of Gaguin and other French humanists, but he could not satisfy his religious longing by either a mundane or a monastic life.

DESIDERIUS ERASMUS. *This portrait by the Antwerp master Quentin Metsys (Massys) was commissioned by Erasmus in 1517 as a gift to Thomas More. The thoughtful eyes and slight smile suggest Erasmus's lucid scholarship and his penetrating wit. (Alinari/ Editorial Photocolor Archives)*

In 1499 Erasmus went to England for the first time, and there experienced a major intellectual reorientation under the influence of Thomas More and John Colet. Seeing Colet's example, Erasmus's eyes were opened more fully to the possibilities and opportunities for employing literary talent, intellectual brilliance, and sparkling wit to the strengthening of Christianity. The English prelate also inspired Erasmus with the value and challenge of scriptures, to which he now increasingly directed his intellectual inquiries. He came to realize that his interest in classical humanism was modified by an equally vital concern for religious truth, not the restricted "inner truth" of Hegius and the Dutch mystics, nor the theological and ecclesiastical truths of the scholastics and clergymen, but the religious truth of right living, honest dealing, and brotherly love and peace.

With this new outlook, Erasmus returned to Paris and Louvain, where he began the most productive period of his creative life. In the next few years, he published the *Adages* (1500), an insightfully annotated collection of classical proverbs; the *Enchiridion* (1503), a penetrating handbook of Christian virtues and practice, summarizing his faith and practical theology; editions of Cicero's and Saint Jerome's Letters; and a critical edition of Valla's *Annotations of the New Testament.* In 1505 Erasmus was back in England where he began work on his own translation of the New Testament. A year later, he made his memorable journey to Italy, where he came into closer contact with the sources and inspiration of Italian humanism. There, at Rome, Bologna, and Venice, he drank deeply from the fountains of classical scholarship. He was particularly impressed by the religious potential in humanistic studies, and reaffirmed his devotion to the work of applying humanistic methods to the recovery and clarification of religious texts in order to promote a revival of true Christianity.

In 1509 Erasmus was on his way to England again, passing the time in transit creating a charming little satire on the mores and foibles of life, which was particularly harsh on monks; it was dedicated to his friend Thomas More and entitled, with a clever play on More's name, *Moriae Encomium* (The Praise of Folly). Although written partly in jest, *The Praise of Folly* had a serious intent and has remained the most read and most enduring of all Erasmus's works. Two years later, he was back in England devoting himself to the New Testament translation and to critical editions of Saint Jerome, Seneca, Plutarch, and Cato. In 1516 Erasmus's New Testament was issued, the first complete Greek New Testament with Latin translation to be published (the Complutensian Polyglot New Testament had been completed two years earlier at Alcalá but was not yet published). At the same time, his *Institutio principis Christiani* (Education of a Christian Prince) was published by Johann Froben at Basel, Switzerland. After that, his wanderings became so frequent and varied, it is meaningless to try to follow him.

Erasmus's writings may be divided into three categories, each of which reveals another facet of his fecund personality. First were his scholarly works, represented by historical writings, lexicons, translations, and scholarly editions of earlier writings. These reveal his great respect for learning and his continual war against ignorance. His view of education was based on the study of the classics and on independent thinking. He believed truth was not only a worthwhile goal, but that it was also recognizable and attainable, for truth is clarity. He was particularly interested in textual criticism and contextual analysis, believing always that the truth was contained in sources. His favorite early writer was Saint Jerome, whose penetrating mind, ready wit, and tolerant imagination were akin to his own. Yet for all of his erudition, Erasmus was aware of the limits of scholarship, and was as ready to criticize scholars and humanists who went overboard as he was clerics and monks. He stood for moderation, abhorring extremism even when exercised in a worthy cause.

His second characteristic, revealed especially in *The Praise of Folly* and the *Colloquies*, was a lively and piercing wit. The *Colloquies*, begun when he was still a student in Paris and published by Froben in 1522, are short, scintillating dialogues and tales drawn from everyday life, employed to ridicule the superstitions and foolishness of people— especially the monks. But all fools are not foolish, he mockingly points out in *The Praise of Folly*, and sometimes folly itself is wisdom. How can that be? Because the only real fool is he who thinks he is not foolish. Reason is sounder than impulse, yet how absurd to believe there is not need for both. The humanists and scholars were not exempt from Erasmus's irony, either, but in the end he reserved his deadliest rapier thrusts for the bigoted clerics, dogmatic divines, supercilious monks, pompous lawyers, and warmongering princes.

Finally, neither Erasmus's erudition nor his humor were ends in themselves but means to a religious goal. He sought a restoration of primitive Christianity. "Plenty of them [Christians] burn little candles to the Virgin, and in the middle of the day, when it does no good," chides Folly, "but how few of them burn with zeal to imitate her in chastity, temperance, and love of heavenly things! That, after all, is the true worship, and it is by far the most pleasing to those above." He viewed his own mission as one of cleansing and purifying the church through the application of humanistic scholarship to the important sources of the Christian tradition. Hence for him, truth and piety were products not of sacraments and rituals but of historical research, though he was quick to admit that relics, observances, and ceremonies helped lead the simple folk to faith and spiritual understanding. The essence of his confessional writings, especially the *Enchiridion*, is the call to discover the biblical Christ and follow the spirit of His message: "Wish for good, pray for good, act for good to all men." Thus did Erasmus hope to reconcile both personal and universal conflicts through moderation and balance.

> He who has said, "Have faith. I have overcome the world," wants you to be confident, but not complacent. If we fight according to His example, we

shall eventually be victorious through Him: therefore, you must steer a middle course between Scylla and Charybdis, shunning both the excessive reliance upon God's favor which would make you slack and careless, and the distrustful anxiety over the hazards of war, which would simultaneously deprive you of your weapons and your stomach for fighting.

Although scarcely read today, another short pamphlet written by Erasmus contains very pertinent thoughts on a subject that is still much with us—war. In his *Querela Pacis* (The Protest of Peace), Erasmus pleads for the consistent and conscientious endeavor on the part of everyone, but especially the princes, to put human relationships on a peaceful basis of mutual respect and Christian forebearance instead of on self-interested rivalries and warfare. Peace ends her impassioned plea with the provocative thought:

> Most of the people detest war and desire peace. A small number, whose accursed happiness always depends upon the misfortune of the common people, want war. Must their inhumanity outweigh the will of so many good people? Look to the past and see that up to now nothing has been definitely established, either by treaties or by family alliances, by force or by vengeance; nothing guarantees against danger so surely as kindness and good will. Wars lead to wars. Vengeance attracts vengeance. Indulgence creates indulgence. Good will invites to good will. Thus those who yield even a small part of their rights will enjoy the greatest consideration.

In Erasmus, the idealism and reforming optimism of the Christian humanists had their most eloquent voice.

Suggestions for Further Reading

GENERAL

The growth of humanism throughout Europe is summarized in Roberto Weiss, *The Spread of Italian Humanism* (London, 1964). Quirinus Breen, *Christianity and Humanism* (Grand Rapids, 1967) points up the relationship between humanism and religion. The most comprehensive and imaginative overview is Robert Mandrou, *From Humanism to Science, 1480–1700*, tr. by Brian Pearce (Harmondsworth, 1978).

HUMANISM IN FRANCE AND SPAIN

Two very valuable collections of articles on French humanism are Werner L. Gundersheimer (ed.), *French Humanism, 1470–1600* (New York, 1969), and A. H. T. Levi (ed.), *Humanism in France at the End of the Middle Ages and in the Early Renaissance* (Manchester, 1970), the latter containing essays in both English and French. Eugene F. Rice, "The Humanist Idea of Christian Antiquity: Lefèvre d'Etaples and His Circle," *Studies in the Renaissance*, 9 (1962), 126–60, provides a brief insight into the thought and influence of one of the leading French humanists. David O. McNeil, *Guillaume Budé and Humanism in the Reign of Francis I* (Geneva, 1975), illustrates the work of another.

Nothing has yet replaced Marcel Bataillon's monumental study of Spanish humanism, *Erasme et l'Espagne*, 2 vols. (Paris, 1937), but we are not without other guides through the labyrinth of Spanish thought. A recent and very thoughtful work is Carlos G. Noreña, *Studies in Spanish Renaissance Thought* (The Hague, 1975), along with his earlier *Juan Luis Vives* (The Hague, 1970). The political aspect of Spanish thought is ably analyzed in J. A. Fernandez-Santamaria, *The State, War and Peace: Spanish Political Thought in the Renaissance, 1516–1559* (London, 1977). Also of interest is Elizabeth Hirsch, *Damiâgo, de Goes: The Life and Thought of a Portuguese Humanist, 1502–1574* (The Hague, 1967).

HUMANISM IN GERMANY AND ENGLAND

Lewis W. Spitz, *The Religious Renaissance of the German Humanists* (Cambridge, Mass., 1963) is an indispensable introduction to German humanism through its leading advocates. Maria Grossman, *Humanism in Wittenberg, 1485–1517* (Nieuwkoop, 1975) is a fresh and pioneering approach. Charles G. Nauert, *Agrippa and the Crisis of Renaissance Thought* (Urbana, 1965) is a scholarly study. A. B. Ferguson, *The Articulate Citizen and the English Renaissance* (Durham, 1965) points to the causes and effects of humanism in England. Dealing more directly with some of the early humanists are Francis Maddison, et al. (eds.), *Essays on the Life and Works of Thomas Linacre, c. 1460–1524* (New York, 1977); Leland Miles, *John Colet and the Platonic Tradition* (La Salle, 1961); and Sears R. Jayne, *John Colet and Marcilio Ficino* (London, 1963), a study of Colet's copy of the Epistolae of Ficino. Stanford E. Lehmberg, *Sir Thomas Elyot, Tudor Humanist* (Austin, 1960) is also enlightening.

SIR THOMAS MORE

On the greatest of the English humanists, see E. E. Reynolds, *The Life and Death of St. Thomas More* (New York, 1978), and E. M. G. Routh, *Sir Thomas More and His Friends, 1477–1535* (New York, 1963). An outstanding new work by one of the leading More scholars is Richard J. Schoeck, *The Achievement of Thomas More: Aspects of His Life and Works* (Victoria, 1976). The once-standard biography of R. W. Chambers, *Thomas More* (London, 1935), is now very dated. J. H. Hexter, *More's Utopia: The Biography of an Idea* (Princeton, 1952) is still one of the most stimulating interpretations. Outstanding essays on More may be found in *Quincentennial Essays on St. Thomas More* (Boone, 1978); *St. Thomas More: Action and Contemplation* (New Haven, 1972), edited by Richard S. Sylvester; and *Essential Articles for the Study of Thomas More* (Hamden, 1977), edited by Richard S. Sylvester and Germain Marc'hadour.

ERASMUS

The literature on Erasmus is extensive. The best general biography is Roland H. Bainton, *Erasmus of Christendom* (New York, 1969). The shorter books by Margaret Mann Phillips, *Erasmus and the Northern Renaissance* (New York, 1965) and J. Kelley Sowards, *Desiderius Erasmus* (Boston, 1975) are also outstanding. On specific aspects of Erasmus's life and thought, see John B. Payne, *Erasmus: His Theology of the Sacraments* (Richmond, 1970); James D. Tracy, *Erasmus: The Growth of a Mind* (Geneva, 1972); Marjorie O'Rourke Boyle, *Erasmus on Language and Method in Theology* (Toronto, 1977); and James D. Tracy, *The Politics of Erasmus: A Pacifist Intellectual and His Political Milieu* (Toronto, 1978). Richard L. DeMolen (ed.), *Erasmus of Rotterdam: A Quincentennial Symposium* (New York, 1971), is an excellent collection of essays, and John C. Olin (ed.), *Christian Humanism and the Reformation: Selected Writings of Erasmus* (New York, 1975) lets Erasmus speak for himself.

CHAPTER TWELVE

The Culture of the Northern Renaissance

ITERARY AND ARTISTIC expression outside of Italy in the early sixteenth century was characterized by a conscious effort to fuse the most desirable features of the Italian Renaissance with the native traditions and styles of northern Europe. With the increasing European awareness of Italian civilization and culture, and the growing worldliness and curiosity of Europeans themselves, there emerged in all of the states an active cultural flowering distinctively non-Italian, yet containing many elements of classical influence derived from Renaissance Italy.

The Twilight of Latin

Beyond humanist circles, the literature of Europe was still predominantly a continuation of the more popular forms of medieval writing. Allegory and epic love poetry based on chivalric tales were widely read, with the standard religious works adding a pious flavor to the fare. But by the beginning of the sixteenth century, medieval institutions and patterns of life were gradually disappearing. The political features of feudalism were retreating before the growing territorial state. With the economic and political realignment of the nobility and the accompanying dissolution of chivalry came also a decreasing interest in the medieval literature of knight-errantry.

The revival of the ancient classics and the large-scale introduction of classical Latin into the poetry and prose of northern Europe had a profound effect on the tone and quality of literary expression, giving it a form and precision it had lacked in the Middle Ages. Thanks to the persistent efforts of the humanists, Latin (not the vulgar Latin of the late Middle Ages but the classical tongue of Horace and Cicero) had become the principal literary medium of the Italian Renaissance. The humanists' obsession with classical purity, however, prevented Latin from becoming a functional language for daily use except for scholars, lawyers, and theologians. Nevertheless, the total impact of Latin on the literature of northern Europe was considerable, and in some cases decisive. In the countries of Roman heritage outside of Italy—principally Spain, Portugal, France, and the southern Netherlands—the Latin roots ran deep, frequently resembling the vernacular dialects very closely. In northern Europe—Germany, the northern Netherlands, England, Scandinavia, Poland, Bohemia, and Hungary—Latin was a foreign import but no less important. In fact, in these countries, where vernacular literatures were more primitive than in Italy, France, or Spain, Latin was a greater literary necessity than in the south. In some cases it was the only literary language.

Latin continued to be cultivated in the sixteenth century not only because of its precision and lucidity as a literary vehicle but also because it was a unifying link among people of differing customs and tongues who still liked to think of themselves as belonging to a single Europe. Scholars of every country wrote in Latin because it emphasized their commitment to scholarship over that to their homelands. Latin was enjoying its last glow of brilliance before the inevitable decline. During this twilight, more Latin works were written than in any previous period of comparable duration; and although overall their quality was not particularly impressive, some very distinguished Latin works flowed from the pens of Erasmus, More, Budé, Vives, and Celtis (not to mention the thousands of theological writings by Melanlanchthon, Luther, Zwingli, Calvin, and other reformers) and later in the century, from those of Manutius, Buchanan, and Montaigne.

Although the greatest bulk of sixteenth-century Latin writing was on theological, scholarly, or otherwise technical subjects, Latinists covered the full gamut of literary genres, from lyric poetry and romances to epics, elegies, and drama. Yet the most impressive contribution of Latin to the sixteenth century is not in the number or variety of its written works but in the salutary influence Latin had on the vernacular literatures of the time. Most sixteenth-century writers were bilingual, and the interaction of such Latin characteristics as precision and order with the emotional expressiveness of the vernacular helped them reach a new level of literary excellence.

Vernacular Literature in France and Flanders

The sixteenth century saw the crystallization of the innumerable languages and dialects of western Europe into national literary forms, just as the fourteenth and fifteenth centuries had seen the Tuscan dialect become the principal literary language of Italy. These vernacular languages had been developing for a long time. French in particular had emerged a century or two before Italian as a popular literary medium. But it was not until the late fifteenth and early sixteenth centuries that it became broad enough in scope to provide a national literature that could rival Latin. Of course most of the dialects continued to be the spoken languages of their particular provinces or areas, as many of them still are today.

In the appreciation and development of secular art and literature, and in its close political and cultural association with Italy, France experienced a cultural revival more like that of Renaissance Italy than did any other country in northern Europe. Italy exerted a significant influence on France, especially after the French invasion of 1494, but there were also many native elements in the French flowering during the age of Francis I. Not the least of these was a literary tradition stemming directly from the "Twelfth-century Renaissance," which had derived largely from the background of the French troubadours and the *chansons de geste.*

Poetry

By the beginning of the sixteenth century, French poetry was developing along two principal lines. One of these was the school of the *Grands Rhétoriqueurs,* the descendants of a long tradition of lyric poets in France and Flanders. Their name is derived from their conviction that verse is the form of rhetoric most congenial to courtly life and that it should be applied with elegance and order. In the late fifteenth century, the *Rhétoriqueurs* were primarily associated with the ostentatious Burgundian court of Charles the Bold and the later regency of Margaret of Austria. The subject matter of their poems was chivalry and courtly love, religion and morals, and occasionally science, art, history, or statecraft. But the conscious and affected elegance of their language, steeped in allegory and filled with stilted Latinisms and artificial idioms, prevented the *Rhétoriqueurs* from achieving the level of excellence many of them were capable of. Among the *Rhétoriqueurs,* Jean Lemaire de Belges, a distinguished Flemish poet, diplomat, and historian, was the most ingenious and the most entertaining. His *Épistres de l'amant vert* (Epistles of the Green Lover, 1511), for example, is the poetic account of the sorrows and eventual death from a broken heart of Margaret of Austria's parrot, and his subsequent sojourn in hell guided by the Roman god Mercury. The parody on Dante's *Divine Comedy* illustrates both the author's familiarity with Italian literature and his typically French disrespect for it.

Another poetic tradition in late-fifteenth-century France stems from François Villon and his followers. Villon was the least likely exponent of Renaissance culture, yet he became the greatest French lyric poet of the fifteenth century and the spokesman of the middle and lower classes.

Raised among the beggars and thieves of Paris, Villon participated fully in the life of the outcast, spending much of his time in vermin-ridden prisons, and being twice sentenced to death by hanging. Yet he discerned much of poetic interest and value in the life he lived; and he revealed his own innermost thoughts, yearnings, pleasures, and fears as no previous poet had done. Few lines have ever been written more poignantly about the meaning of life and death than his *La Ballade des pendus* (Ballad of the Hanged), which he wrote while awaiting what he thought would be his execution. Chivalric romance and courtly love sonnets held no interest for Villon. What did interest him was life in the raw, and with Villon began a poetic counterpoint to the court literature of the *Grands Rhétoriqueurs*.

Under the appreciative patronage of Francis I, French poetry flourished in the early decades of the sixteenth century under the skillful and easy-flowing pen of Clément Marot (1496–1544), although it was not until a generation later, with Ronsard and the poets of the *Pléiade*, that it reached a full flowering. Of Norman ancestry, though born and reared at Cahors in south-central France, Marot developed an independent style that embodied preciseness of language with the ease and natural flow of conversational French. Modulating both the pedantry of the *Rhétoriqueurs* and the jargon of Villon's followers, Marot effected a truly Renaissance reconciliation of three elements: courtly French, the language of the streets, and classical Latin. Although they at times disclose sincere feeling and sentiment, his poems are seldom passionate and never profound. His supreme gift lay in the power to charm and delight with the ease and unaffected freedom of his verse.

More Italianisms (especially the Petrarchan sonnet) and humanistic Latin were introduced into French poetry by Marot's colleagues Mellin de Saint-Gelais and Marguerite d'Angoulême, queen of Navarre and sister of Francis I. Marguerite of Navarre was one of the truly great women of the sixteenth century. Not only was she the protector and regent of the French crown during some of the many absences of her brother, she was a queen in her own right, a respected patron of artists, poets, philosophers, and religious nonconformists, and a devoted Christian humanist. She was also a poet of unusual sensitivity. Although unequal in technical skill to Marot or Saint-Gelais, Marguerite was their superior in emotional power. Her sentiment is particularly expressive in the devotional-mystic poems, *Le Miroir de l'âme pêcheresse* (The Mirror of a Sinful Soul) and *Le Triomphe de l'agneau* (The Triumph of the Lamb). Marguerite's chief literary fame, however, comes from her principal prose work, the *Heptameron*, a collection of seventy assorted stories, told in the manner of Boccaccio's *Decameron*, by ten French lords and ladies who were marooned for seven days in the Pyrenees. Like Boccaccio's tales, these are clever and witty vignettes of Renaissance life, but unlike the former, they are pitched to a higher social level and, in spite of frequent coarseness, reveal the religious and devotional inclinations of their author. Indeed it is this intimate harmonization of the coarse and the fine, the irreverent and the devoted, the profane and the pious, that make the *Heptameron* such a characteristic book of the Renaissance.

The Novel

Marguerite of Navarre's novelettes suggest the popularity in the northern Renaissance, particularly in France and Spain, of the novel—longer, anecdotal, and entertaining narratives interpreting facets of human life. Stemming directly from the medieval *fabliaux*, French novels of the Renaissance were predominantly satirical at a time when satire was becoming overwhelmingly popular throughout Europe. Without doubt, the greatest of the French satirical novelists was François Rabelais (1494–1553). In fact, no literary figure of the time better illustrates the robust enthusiasm, the satirical humor, and the rebellious freedom-loving of the Renaissance than does Rabelais. Born in central France the same year Charles VIII launched his invasion of Italy, Rabelais grew up in the effervescent atmosphere of war, religious controversy, and rapid social change. As a young man, he entered the Franciscan convent of Fontenay-le-Comte, but the monastic life was a prison to this bright and ambitious youth, and he deserted it for the pursuit of letters and scholarship. For a while he was secretary to the powerful Benedictine prior and bishop, Geoffroy d'Estissac, and continued to find timely favor with influential civil and religious figures, including Cardinal Jean du Bellay. With zest and enthusiasm, Rabelais threw himself into his studies, which included not only the *studia humanitatis* but also medicine, science, and mathematics. In 1530 he became a practicing physician. Two years later appeared the first of his literary masterpieces, *Pantagruel*, which tells the lusty story of the giant Pantagruel and his fantastic escapades. In 1534 came the chronicle of *Gargantua*, Pantagruel's illustrious father who was married to the daughter of the king of the Amaurots of More's *Utopia*. Both of these books were peremptorily condemned by the Sorbonne and immediately became "best-sellers," more popular in France than any other vernacular books of the time.

In these and the three additional books treating the heroic deeds and sayings of Pantagruel, Rabelais poured forth his disdain for hypocrisy, bigotry, idolatry, and sham, and boldly, if crudely, declared people's right to freedom and the full enjoyment of life. At times with robust humor, at times with coarse sardonic wit, Rabelais satirized his times; and in so doing he gives us a feeling not only of his own lust for life but also an incisive glimpse into the turbulent society of his day. His outlook on people was optimistic and condescending. He believed that when unencumbered by the tyranny of political and religious institutions or the greed and cruelty of zealots, people are by nature good; life is good, since it all comes from God. The Christian concept of original sin had no place in Rabelais's thought, although he did have religious

FRANÇOIS RABELAIS. *A portrait by an unidentified artist of the French School shows Rabelais wearing his doctor's bonnet and looking at the viewer with a sardonic smile. (Musée Versailles, Cliché des Musées Nationaux)*

convictions. He accepted life and everything as he found it without shifting blame to premortal divine dictate. He took pain and sorrow in the same stride with which he embraced all forms of worldly pleasures and joys. Renounce not the God-given things of this life, Rabelais implored (Bk. II, Chap. 34) in reaction to the monks, only the

> rabble of squint-minded fellows, dissembling and counterfeit saints, demure lookers, hypocrites, pretended zealots, tough friars, buskin monks, and other such sects of men, who disguise themselves like maskers to deceive the world. . . . Flee from these men, abhor and hate them as much as I do, and upon my faith you will find yourselves the better for it. And if you desire to be good Pantagruelists, that is to say, to live in peace, joy, health, making yourselves always merry, never trust those men that always peep out at you through a little hole.

The Beginning of Spanish "Golden Age" Literature

Except for a short time in Valencia and Catalonia, the cultural flowering in Spain came later than in France and had a more religious flavor. Spanish life and thought were deeply influenced by the medieval church, and—although intimate contact between Aragon and southern Italy was continuous from the thirteenth century, and after the 1490s, relations with Flanders and the rest of Italy were just as close—the church continued to give the Spanish Renaissance a distinct flavor throughout the sixteenth and early seventeenth centuries, the *Siglo de Oro* (golden century) of Spanish literature. Nevertheless, the cultural, political, and economic proximity of Italy to Spain could not help influencing Spanish customs and letters, especially after 1494. Many of the literary figures of Spain in the late fifteenth century spent time in

Italy and were motivated by the elegance of Italian culture. As early as the middle of that century, the poet Iñigo López de Mendoza, Marquis of Santillana, had introduced Italian meters into Castilian verse. But it was many years before this had any noticeable effect on Spanish literature as a whole.

Meanwhile, a brief blossoming of Catalan literature was taking place in the northern and eastern parts of Spain. Catalan literary prose had been created in the late Middle Ages by the Mallorcan writer, scholar, missionary, and scientist Raymond Lull. The tradition was continued, although without Lull's independence and versatility, in the works of several fourteenth-century authors. The reform of the royal chancery in the latter part of that century, and the growing impact of Ciceronian Latin on the Catalan vernacular led to what some have called the Catalan Pre-Renaissance, and is reflected in the writings of Bernat Metge and Antoni Canals, among others. Its climax was reached in Valencia with the love poetry and moral poetry of Ausias March (1397–1459), particularly his *Cants de mort* (Songs of Death), and with the elegant prose of Joanot Martorell's (ca. 1410–68) *Tirant lo Blanc* (Tirant the White—a noble knight), a realistic story about love and war in the early fifteenth century. Nevertheless, the Pre-Renaissance failed to ripen into full fruition. After Martorell, there were no major writers in Catalan for 400 years. With the union of Castile and Aragon, Castilian quickly became the literary language of Spain.

The Novel

Spain was imbued, as much as was France, with the medieval romances. It was from these traditions, and from the powerful influence of Spanish realism, that the Renaissance novel reached its fullest expression. The most important romantic novel of the period was *Amadís de Gaula* (Amadis of Gaul), given its final form in 1508 by Garci Rodríguez de Montalvo. Like the Arthurian cycle and other chivalric romances including the medieval ballads so popular in both Spain and England, *Amadís* is a blending of ideal knight-errantry with a medieval chivalric love theme. Yet there was much in the conduct of Amadís that was appealing to the people of the Renaissance. Like Castiglione's courtier, Amadís was loyal to his patron and master; like Machiavelli's prince, shrewd and clever; like More's utopians, confident and unperturbable; like Ariosto's Orlando, brave and devoted; like Rabelais's Pantagruel, devoid of pretense or sham.

An even more important development in the Spanish novel is represented in *La Celestina* (ca. 1493), a masterfully written tragicomedy, realistically depicting human character and passions. *La Celestina* is a simple yet tragic love story of the high-born Calisto and the exquisitely beautiful and charming Melibea, complicated by the machinations of the bawdy enchantress Celestina. Written originally as a sixteen-act play by Fernando de Rojas, *La Celestina* quickly became the most renowned novel in Europe, spreading in translation to all of the major countries and running through more than fifty editions in Spain. It is still considered one of the great pieces of Spanish literature, showing in its mixture of lusty vulgarity and lofty idealism the dichotomy of the Spanish character.

In literary circles, Spain is even more noted for the development of a new type of novel, the so-called picaresque novel, focusing on the life and knavery of society's *pícaros* (rogues and vagabonds). Unlike Amadís and similar noble heroes, the *pícaros* are low-born rascals and social outcasts who subsist by deceit and dishonesty, yet they succeed as well as a knight who obeyed the rules of chivalry. The rogue-hero might be a renegade monk or a vagrant pickpocket, but the character was always depicted with stark realism, as were his surroundings and the other recognizable types drawn to complete the picture. The medium had limitless possibilities for social satire and was widely used for that purpose, though its powers of sheer entertainment were not overlooked. In their characterizations, Machiavelli's Callimaco (in the *Mandragola*), or Celestina (and several of her cohorts) might be considered *pícaro* types, but *La vida de Lazarillo de Tormes* (The Life of Lazarillo of Tormes) is generally considered the first, and in some ways the greatest, of the picaresque novels. Published anonymously in 1554, though written in 1539 or 1540 (the authorship is still a matter of dispute, although most believe it was written by the Castilian nobleman-diplomat-historian, Don Diego Hurtado de Mendoza), *Lazarillo de Tormes* soon became one of the most read and talked-about books of the period. As morally ambiguous as it is artistically complex, *Lazarillo de Tormes* is a devastating satire on many aspects of Spanish life, and a superb characterization of social behavior. This and subsequent picaresques provided notable steps in the evolution of the modern realistic novel.

Finally, sixteenth-century Spain also contributed to the popularity and spread of the pastoral novel, patterned after Sannazaro's *Arcadia*, which depicted the idealized life of the free and noble shepherds. The best of the Spanish pastoral romances is *La Diana*, written by Jorge de Montemayor in 1559. In alternating prose and verse, it tells the touching story of the shepherd Arsenio and his tragic encounters with life and death.

Drama

Closely associated with the development of the novel in Spain was that of drama. Religious drama in the form of mystery plays existed in medieval Spain, as it did in all of Europe, but we know very little of its specific nature prior to the end of the fifteenth century. In the early sixteenth century, the foundations were laid for the great flowering of Spanish drama under Lope de Vega 100 years later. Juan del Encina (ca. 1468–1529) contributed to these foundations by rejuvenating the old religious dramas and infusing a lyrical quality into the secular plays.

Contact with Latin and Italian literature in Rome added greater variety and better structure to his dramatic works and won for him recognition as the father of the Spanish theater. Of equal importance was Gil Vincente (ca. 1465–ca. 1536), a contemporary Portuguese goldsmith who wrote poetry and plays in both Portuguese and Castilian. Vincente's forte was comedy and farce, which gained wide popularity in Spain. The popularization of the Spanish theater during the first half of the sixteenth century was due primarily to the barnstorming of Lope de Rueda (1510–65) who not only composed lively farces himself but traveled about Spain presenting one-night stands at the inns and marketplaces.

Poetry

Poetry did not make the strides in Spain that prose did during the early Renaissance, although the Marquis of Santillana wrote sonnets in the Italian manner by mid-fifteenth century, and the *Cancionero general* (General Songbook, 1511) of Hernando del Castillo did contain a number of pleasingly polished lyric poems. Garcilaso de la Vega (ca. 1501–36) was the best Spanish poet of the time, and it was he who introduced the finest of Italian literary methods into Spanish verse. Garcilaso, as an erudite Latin and Italian scholar, talented musician, eloquent speaker, successful diplomat, and valiant soldier (he gave his life in the service of the emperor), was the ideal Renaissance courtier. Despite his own active life, his poetry was a model of tranquility and mellow yearning for peace. Yet under the surface is also revealed a depth of feeling unusual in poetry of such balance and precision. Some of the pathos can be felt in this lament over the loss of his beloved:

> More hard than marble to my mild complaints,
> And to the lively flame with which I glow,
> Cold, Galatea, cold as winter snow!
> I feel that I must die, my spirit faints,
> And dreads continuing life; for, alienate
> From thee, life sinks into a weary weight,
> To be shook off with pleasure; from all eyes
> I shrink, e'en from myself despised I turn,
> And left by her for whom I yearn,
> My cheek is tinged with crimson; heart of Ice!
> Dost thou the worshipped mistress scorn to be
> Of one whose cherished guest thou ever art;
> Not being able for one hour to free
> Thine image from my heart?
> This dost thou scorn? in gentleness of woe
> Flow forth, my tears, 'tis meet that ye should flow!*

*Source: Jeremiah H. Wiffen, tr., "Egloga Primera," in Eleanor L. Turnbull, ed., *Ten Centuries of Spanish Poetry* (Baltimore: Johns Hopkins Press, 1955), p. 41.

Renaissance Literature in Germany

Germany and England were less influenced by Italian literature than were France, Spain, and the Netherlands. In the case of England, this may be explained in part by the inaccessibility of Italian sources and the obvious cultural lag. But Germany was geographically much closer to Italy than was England and actually participated with her in the revival of learning. Why, then, did German literature lag behind that of the other continental countries? And why were German writers so reluctant to adopt Italian literary forms?

German literature, especially poetry, was slow in maturing largely because the valuable lessons of precision, form, order, and balance, which Italian literature could teach, were still being resisted in Germany. Perhaps the Germans had too much contact with Italy. We find many examples in the early sixteenth century of strong German biases against Italians, and not just over religious issues. South German merchants and bankers were the most aggressive rivals of Italian capitalists. And the competition between Italian and German iron manufacturers was sometimes bitter. Resentments from political causes also went deep. For five centuries, German emperors had tried to make good their claim to Italy as a part of the Holy Roman Empire and impose their rule on the Italian communes. For an even longer period of time, papal jurisdiction in Germany had aggravated nobles, princes, and peasants. The chronic imperial-papal struggle had repercussions lasting much longer than the ensuing Ghibelline-Guelf duels of the fourteenth and fifteenth centuries. Outside the immediate circle of German humanists, there was also a strong resentment against Italian cultural domination. This, along with the great dissimilarity between the Italian and German languages, may partially explain the lack of Italian influence on the German literature of the period.

The literary language of Germany in the fifteenth and early sixteenth centuries was a hybrid vernacular in the process of flux and development from the Middle High German of the medieval *Minnesänger* to the High German of Lessing and Schiller. As a literary language, it had not yet reached the degree of formality that French, Castilian, and especially Italian had, although it was vivid and could adequately express the thoughts and feelings of the people. Not until the second third of the sixteenth century, under the impact of Martin Luther's powerful pen, did Germany have a literary language comparable to those of its neighbors. In the meantime, two figures loom above the rest in their expressive use of the German vernacular to portray life as it was experienced by the people of the time.

Satire

The first of these was Sebastian Brant (1457–1521), a versatile jurist, humanist, poet, artist, and civil magnate from southwestern Germany. Although he wrote many legal works and edited some medieval jest books, Brant's real contribution to the literary history of his times was the composition of his lively satire, *Das Narrenschiff* (The Ship of Fools), first published in 1494. *The Ship of Fools* not only exemplifies the great popularity of social satire in the Renaissance, it was the model for that genre for the next fifty years. Brant's *The Ship of Fools* is a long allegorical poem, bluntly but adeptly poking fun at the vices, stupidity, and general foolishness of mankind. No class or group was immune to Brant's scorn. He denounced with equal gusto the pedantry of scholars, the perversion of the clerics, and the slothfulness of the magistrates. The book is divided into 112 short chapters, each devoted to a particularly type of "fool," from gluttons, idlers, and beggars to gamblers, thieves, and adulterers. In addition to his exhortations against these flagrant offenders, Brant also ridiculed the presumptuousness of pride and boasting, the disgrace of usury, and the annoyance of prattling in church. There is also much broader wisdom in many of his couplets. Take the following for example:

> Who never girds before he'd ride,
> And shows no care in proper tide,
> Is scorned when falling off the side.

or

> By those who build it should be heeded
> What sums of money will be needed,
> Or else the task will not be speeded.*

Like Erasmus and the German humanists, Brant accepted and defended the traditional church, and was even less prone than they to criticize all established institutions. His sarcasm was aimed more at people who perverted those institutions. Yet despite his deep religious convictions and his negative reaction to Luther's early disturbances, Brant was not blind to the abuses in the church. In his chapter, "On Becoming a Priest," he wrote:

> Another type I'd have you mark
> That on the fool's ship should embark
> Has recently been much increased,
> For every peasant wants a priest
> Among his clan, to dodge and shirk
> And play the lord, but never work.**

Poetry and Drama

In lyric poetry, the German counterpart to the French *Rhétoriqueurs* were the *Meistersänger*, composers and singers of light verse in a variety

*Source: Edwin H. Zeydel, tr., *The Ship of Fools* (New York: Columbia University Press, 1944), pp. 86, 94.
**Ibid., p. 242.

of meters and rhymes. Special schools and guilds developed to teach and standardize the composition of poems, and participants went through the same stages of apprentice, journeyman, and master that any other craftsman would. The guild of *Meistersänger* flourished in southern Germany during the early sixteenth century, especially at Nuremberg. It was here that the best of them, the shoemaker and poet Hans Sachs (1494–1576)—immortalized in Richard Wagner's *Die Meistersinger von Nürnberg*—lived, worked, and composed over 4,000 lyric poems and no less than 2,000 other short verses, dialogues, and plays. He drew his themes from the daily activities in and around his cobbler's shop, putting his minutest observations and reflections into fast-moving pieces of delightful verse. In addition, he wrote about religion, saints and sinners, historical and legendary figures, and variations on the great medieval themes. A particularly noteworthy contribution of Hans Sachs was the carnival drama or Shrovetide Play (*Fastnachtspiele*), a series of short farces in verse intended to entertain the people at carnival time. In this genre, he was an innovator and generally proclaimed father of modern folk drama in Germany. Much of Sachs's literary energy in the last half of his life was spent in versified religious polemics. Nuremberg was one of the first of the southern German cities to accept the Reformation, and Sachs threw himself whole heartedly into the mainstream of religious controversy.

HANS SACHS MONUMENT. *This Nuremberg landmark shows the Meistersinger as a jovial but thoughtful entertainer in the very act of poetic creation. (Courtesy of German Information Center)*

The Emergence of Vernacular Literature in England

The development of a literary vernacular in England was slower than in the other major countries of Europe for several reasons. In the first place, it had a later start. The early development of Anglo-Saxon as a literary language was stemmed after the Norman conquest by the vogue of French, which for the next three centuries was the spoken as well as literary vehicle of the ruling class in Britain. The flowering of Old English in the age of Chaucer was only a temporary plateau in the evolution of the English language. In the fifteenth century, it continued to change so rapidly that it was hardly the same language from one generation to the next. At a time when Italian and French had become relatively stable idioms, English was still being formed. Consequently, English literature retained its medieval characteristics long after they had been lost on the continent. A casual comparison of the publication lists of Manutius in Venice and Caxton in London during the first decade of the sixteenth century will reveal the literary gap between Italy and England. English did not become the primary literary language of England until the second half of the sixteenth century. The principal writing was done in Latin, and almost until Thomas Wyatt's time, the second language was French. Sir Thomas More's popular *Utopia* was not printed in English for twenty-five years after it was first published in Latin in 1516.

Poetry

But even in far-off Britannia, the winds of the Italian Renaissance were beginning to be felt by the early sixteenth century. The first true lyric poet of Renaissance England was Sir Thomas Wyatt (1503–42), who should not be confused, as he frequently is, with his more notorious son of the same name who led the unsuccessful rebellion against Queen Mary in 1554. There were earlier versifiers in England, like Alexander Barclay and John Skelton (whose crude but lively poetry had won him considerable acclaim), but the best poems between Chaucer and Wyatt were the popular late-medieval ballads that had been passed down orally over the years until the printing press finally fixed their form in the late fifteenth century. Thomas Wyatt was an active man of affairs as well as a sensitive poet during the middle years of Henrician England. He served Henry VIII in various capacities, including special ambassador to France, Spain, the Empire, and Italy. As a courtier, Wyatt had the misfortune of being attracted by the same dark, alluring eyes that had captivated the king. Whether Wyatt's Petrarchism demanded of him a Laura, in the person of Anne Boleyn, or whether her appeal was a real physical attraction, we can only conjecture; but his name was one of several linked with the queen's alleged adultery, and he soon found himself in the Tower of London. More fortunate than five others who were beheaded along with Anne Boleyn, Wyatt managed to regain the king's favor for another five years before he was imprisoned on a charge of treason. Released again in 1541, he resumed his active role in public affairs until his death a year later at the age of thirty-nine.

In English literature, Wyatt is remembered mostly for his introduction of the Petrarchan sonnet into English, although his lyric poems, written with little foreign influence, better reveal the strength and personality of his verse. Here, for example, in the opening stanza of his "Lute Song" can be seen his command of meter and rhythm:

> My lute, awake! Perform the last
> Labor that thou and I shall waste,
> And end that I have now begun;
> For when this song is sung and past,
> My lute, be still, for I have done.

More vivid still is this freedom carol:

> Tangled I was in love's snare,
> Oppressed with pain, torment with care,
> Of grief right sure, of joy full bare,
> Clean in despair by cruelty,—
> But ha! ha! ha! full well is me,
> For I am now at liberty.

Published along with the ninety-seven poems attributed to Wyatt in *Tottel's Miscellany* (1557) were forty poems attributed to Wyatt's younger contemporary and disciple, Henry Howard, earl of Surrey (1517–47), eldest son of the third duke of Norfolk (lord admiral, lord lieutenant of Ireland, treasurer, and earl marshal of England), and grandson of the hero of Flodden Field. The young and dashing Surrey cut a wide swath through the court life of late-Henrician England. During the family ascendency and especially when his cousin Catherine Howard was queen, Surrey became in quick succession a knight of the Garter, the king's lieutenant in Norfolk, and steward of Cambridge. But with the fall of Catherine in 1542 and the return of the rival Seymours, the Howard star descended fast. Arrested in December 1546 for speaking too openly of his descent from kings, Surrey was peremptorily tried for treason, condemned six days later, and beheaded the same afternoon. He was twenty-nine years old. Whatever apprehensions one might have about Tudor justice, one thing is certain: it was swift. Norfolk was also arrested with his son on the charge of abetting a criminal, and would have met the same end had not the king himself died on January 27, the day before Norfolk was to have been executed.

Surrey contributed substantially to the development of the later Elizabethan literature. His sonnets are more polished and graceful than Wyatt's and he employed the same rhyme pattern later made famous by Shakespeare. Moreover, in his translation of Virgil's *Aeneid*, he introduced blank verse into English for the first time. As a poet, as well as a courtier, Surrey was both versatile and accomplished. Yet on the whole, his poems lack the feeling and the depth that would later characterize the Elizabethan poets. The great age of English literature had not yet begun.

Historiography

The leadership and example of Italy also influenced the writing of history in northern Europe, but not as much as it did the poetry and art of the period. With some exceptions, historiography tended to become more national, because its main objective was to reveal the glory and triumphs of the national past. Nevertheless, especially in the realm of methodology and style, European historians owed much to their Italian counterparts and to the disciplining of humanism.

France

The late fifteenth century saw a flourishing of chronicle-histories after the manner of Froissart and Chastellain, reaching their climax in the colloquial *Memoires* of Philippe de Commines (1445–1509). But with Commines, a new age also dawned in European historiography. A member of the upper nobility of Flanders and a servant of Charles the Bold, duke of Burgundy, Commines had a unique opportunity to observe many of the great events of the time from very close range. In 1472 he abandoned the Burgundian court and entered the service of Charles's rival, the king of France, seeing in the cunning Louis XI rather than in the chivalric Duke Charles signs of the coming times. When he eventually lost favor with Louis's successor for opposing the French invasion of Italy in 1494, Commines set himself the task of recording the great events that had taken place during his lifetime. Less colorful than Froissart's *Chronicles*, Commines's *Memoires* are a clear and vivid narrative account of the people and events of late-fifteenth-century France and Burgundy, disclosing their motives and consequences with acrid insight. Much of Commines's narrative is in the medieval tradition, yet his analytic and objective approach to the period, even though he was an active participant in it, and his interpretation of events in other than religious terms (although he did not rule out the frequent intervention of God), are indications that he was as much the precursor of future historiographical methods as he was a culmination of the medieval. In his moral detachment, penetration into motives, and shrewd power of analysis, Commines was the only northern writer who approached the historiographical skill of Machiavelli and Guicciardini.

Germany

In the German lands, history was a mainstay of humanist writers, although it might be misleading to call these men historians. Wimpfeling, Trithemius, Peutinger, Celtis, and Pirkheimer, whom we have previously met as humanists, were all active chroniclers, along with

Albert Krantz (1450–1517), Johannes Cuspinian (1473–1529), and Johannes Aventinus (1477–1534). Encyclopedic rather than critical, these writers emphasized the heroic deeds of the ancient Germans and elaborated on the teutonic origins of their noble leaders. Rarely did they write about recent times, although Aventinus's efforts to promote cultural and moral reforms in Germany are reflected in his *Bavarian Chronicle*.

Two German humanists stand out from the rest as more critical and discriminating in their use of historical sources and sounder in their judgments based on these sources. Vadianus (Joachim von Watt), a Swiss humanist-historian who wrote the first reliable history of the forest Cantons, was one of these. The other was the Alsacian Beatus Rhenanus (1486–1547), a close friend and associate of Erasmus. Rejecting the tribal myths that had confounded historical study for so long, Rhenanus went to reliable sources, both written records and remaining artifacts, to reconstruct an authentic picture of German history. His *Historia rerum Germanicarum* (History of German Affairs) was published at Basel in 1531. Although fragmentary and sometimes incoherent, it was the most reliable account of early German history produced in the Renaissance age.

England

The best historian in Henrician England was an Italian cleric and humanist, Polydore Vergil (1470–1555), who went to England in 1505 on an assignment from the pope. Born in Urbino and educated at Bologna and Padua, Polydore Vergil was a cultured and respected scholar who soon became a favorite at the court of Henry VII. As royal historiographer, he was assigned the formidable task of writing the history of England from the earliest times to the present. Being the first historian actually to use many of the early English sources, his task of locating, collecting, and evaluating materials was immense. He devoted almost thirty years to the labor of research, even interviewing many of the public officials under Henry VII and Henry VIII for information not contained in the written documents. The result of his labors was the monumental *Anglica historia* (History of England), published in 1534. Although, by his own admission, Vergil intended to write "the great deeds of English kings and those of this noble people," it was only the authentic deeds that interested him, not the many myths and fables that had hitherto colored the story. Not unnaturally, his fable wrecking aroused the wrath of many patriots, who accused him of falsification and even blasphemy. Perhaps this is the reason his history was more popular outside England than it was among Britons, although it did influence subsequent English historiography.

The first native English scholar to write a creditable history was Sir Thomas More, whose *History of Richard III* is remarkable in that it was composed in both Latin and English and was equally eloquent in each.

Unhappily, though, More paid little attention to original sources or to the reliability of his information. The resulting picture of the last Yorkist king was much more vivid than it was true. More's monster was transported, through Shakespeare, into the literature of all the world, whereas the real Richard III had to wait until the present generation to receive some justice from the muse of history.

The New World

The saga of overseas exploration opened up a whole new area of historical writing. The first of the great chroniclers of Portuguese expansion was Gomes Eannes de Azurara (d. 1474), whose masterpiece *The Discovery and Conquest of Guinea* is not only our best source on the voyages of Henry the Navigator but is also the first account of western Africa by any European author. Others continued Azurara's chronicle, giving us both eye-witness and summary accounts of the Portuguese explorations of Africa. The climax of Portuguese historiography came in the literary triumvirate of Gaspar Correa (1490–1565), João de Barros (1496–1570), and Lopes de Castanheda (1500–59). Together, their books cover almost every aspect of the Portuguese expansion into India and the creation of the eastern empire. In his four *Decades* (dealing with expansion from 1420 to 1538), Barros, especially, qualifies as a truly great historian. In objectivity, balance, style, and clarity, he is without peer among the expansion chroniclers, and fully merits the popular epithet of "the Portuguese Livy." In a way, all of these writings are eclipsed, however, as portrayals of heroic expansion literature by the masterpiece of Portuguese epic poetry, Luiz Vaz de Camões's *Os Lusíadas* (The Lusiads—the sons of Lusus, the mythical founder of Portugal), which describes, as no prose account could, the voyage and exploits of Vasco da Gama.

The first historian of the New World was the Italian cleric, courtier, and tutor, Peter Martyr d'Anghiera (1457–1526). Driven by an insatiable curiosity about the New World, he eagerly listened to Columbus's report of his first voyage, adding to the admiral's account bits of information he could obtain from other crewmen and from the leaders of subsequent expeditions. Martyr's work, called *De orbe novo*, (The New World, a term coined by him) was published in installments between 1511 and 1530. A keen intellect and critical eye made Peter Martyr's narrative something more than a mere chronicle of the conquest. His insights into Columbus and the Columbian voyages are particularly valuable. So are the observations of Ferdinand Columbus, the admiral's illegitimate son, who wrote a remarkable history of his father, including a detailed account of the fourth voyage, of which Ferdinand was a participant. An even more important history of the early Spanish expansion is Bartolomé de Las Casas' *Historia de las Indias* (History of the Indies), written about 1552 near the end of the controversial friar's life, but based upon a firsthand knowledge of conditions in the New World and on the acquaintance of many of the early *conquistadores*. He also made a judicious use of many written sources and documents, including Columbus's journals.

The best of the early Spanish historians was Gonzalo Fernández de Oviedo y Valdes (1478–1557). Arriving in the New World in 1514, he spent all but the last ten years of his life there in various capacities from mining inspector to governor of Cartagena. Constantly on the lookout for historical materials, Fernández de Oviedo gathered an impressive number of sources and interviewed many people who had been involved in the early conquests, before he began compiling his two great works. In 1523 he was officially made historiographer of the Indies. Shortly thereafter, his *La natural historia de las Indias* (Natural History of the Indies) was published, and it was followed in 1535 by the first part of his larger *La historia general de las Indias* (General History of the Indies), dealing with all aspects of the discovery and settlement. Two more parts concerning the conquest of Mexico and of Peru were eventually written, but they remained unpublished until the middle of the nineteenth century.

If Fernandez de Oviedo's *Historia general* is the classic contemporary account of the Spanish conquest, the best study of the Indians is the *Historia universal de Nueva España* (Universal History of New Spain) by Bernardino de Sahagun, a Franciscan missionary who came to Mexico in 1529. Intelligent and passionately interested in the Aztec culture, Sahagun religiously devoted himself to discovering and writing down everything he could learn about their history, religion, customs, institutions, and life. He even lived in a native village and learned to speak and write their language fluently. As a result, much priceless knowledge about the Aztecs was preserved and passed on to posterity; unfortunately, not as much as was lost at the hands of other, more zealous, friars and ruthless soldiers.

The conquest of Mexico found its most enthusiastic chronicler in Cortés's later secretary and chaplain, Francisco López de Gómara (1510–55). Based on a knowledge of his patron's exploits, acquired through an intimate association with Cortés for many years, and through repeated use of Cortés's famous letters to the Emperor Charles V, López de Gómara's *Historia de las Indias y conquista de Mexico* (History of the Indies and Conquest of Mexico, 1552) became the most popular history book of the time. It was well written and to the point. But his hero worship of Cortés was more than some of his contemporaries could swallow. Las Casas and others denounced the book, but it remained for one of Cortés's own soldiers to refute it.

Bernal Díaz del Castillo (1492–ca. 1581), according to his word, had fought by the side of Cortés in no less than 119 battles, from the first skirmishes in Yucatan to the final fall of Tenochtitlán. He never denied the valor and leadership of his commander, but he resented López de Gómara's neglect of the footsoldiers and men in the ranks. So, in his seventy-sixth year, the doughty soldier armed himself with pen and parchment and stepped forward to right the wrong that he felt had been done. We are the beneficiaries of that encounter, for whether or not his account is truer than that of his predecessor is secondary to the fact that Díaz's *Historia verdadera de la conquista de la Nueva España* (True History of the Conquest of New Spain) is a classic of its kind. Unpolished and rough, in the colloquial language of the common man (although by the time he wrote he had become a rather prosperous landowner), Bernal Díaz describes in the greatest simplicity and candor the epic story of the fall of the Aztec empire and the unspectacular but dogged heroism of the Spanish soldiers. Literarily less meritorious than most of the other histories of the conquest, it is nevertheless the only one that has become a modern classic. It is the universal soldier's story, simply but powerfully told.

The best chronicles of the Peruvian conquest are also narratives written by some of its participants. The earliest of these was by Francisco Pizarro's secretary Francisco de Xeres, who wrote his short *Verdadera relación de la conquista del Perú* (True Account of the Conquest of Peru) while the action was taking place. He returned to Spain after the fall of Cuzco and had his narrative published in Seville in 1534. A longer, but equally fresh eyewitness account is Pedro Pizarro's *Relaciones del descubrimiento y conquista de los reynos del Perú* (Relations of the Discovery and Conquest of the Kingdoms of Peru), written by a less violent and more literary cousin of the *conquistador*, who retired to Arequipa in southern Peru to write his memoirs after the conquest. In its simple, straightforward style, Pizarro's history most resembles that of Bernal Díaz.

Less pungent and engaging, yet perhaps more authoritative and certainly more objective, are the *Historia del descubrimiento y conquista del Perú* (History of the Discovery and Conquest of Peru) by Augustine de Zarate, and the *Crónicas del Perú* (The Chronicles of Peru) by Pedro Cieza de León. Arriving in Peru as a civil servant after the conquest was over, Zarate soon found himself in the middle of the civil wars between Pizarro and Almagro and then among the Pizarro brothers themselves. Being somewhat less than a Pizarro fan, and having angered others of the *conquistadores*, Zarate found it easier to publish his history outside of Spain, which he did at Antwerp in 1555. Cieza de León was a young soldier who lived and campaigned in Colombia and Peru for seventeen years. After the civil wars, he traveled throughout Peru observing, questioning, listening, and writing about everything he saw, especially the customs and lore of the Indians. Cieza de León has been called the "prince of chroniclers," because of the comprehensiveness of his work and its rich, picturesque language. Covering all aspects of Inca ethnology, from geography and history to the building of their cities and highways, the *Crónicas* did for the Incas what Sahagun's *Historia* did for the Aztecs.

Finally, the work of one more remarkable historian must be mentioned, that of El Inca Garcilaso de la Vega. It is unique because it is the first history of the New World to be written by an American-born author. Garcilaso was born in Cuzco in 1539, the son of a Spanish *conquistador* and an Inca princess. He spent his early years in Peru, where he lived and learned the ways of his mother's people. At the age of twenty, he went to Spain, where he remained the rest of his life, and where he wrote his great work. The first part of the opus is the *Comentarios reales de los Incas* (Royal Commentaries of the Incas), a comprehensive and eulogistic account of the rise and fall of the Inca empire, from its legendary origins until the execution of its last native ruler, Túpac Amaru. Part two, *Historia general del Perú* (General History of Peru), is a detailed history of the conquest. The contrast in the two books—between the description of the tightly governed, orderly, collectivist state of the Incas and the violent, strife-ridden, individualism of subsequent Spanish rule—is most striking.

The Art and Architecture of Western Europe

Flanders

Much of the inspiration and pattern of the artistic style of western Europe can be traced to the influence of the Flemish painters of the early fifteenth century. The early art of Flanders and the Netherlands was, in turn, a composite of Burgundian court style, Parisian miniaturism, and the compositional influence of Renaissance Italy. This blending produced a style characterized by minuteness of detail, richness in color, and a notable preoccupation with the various aspects of daily life. Sometimes it also reflected deep concern with more profound matters involving human nature and people's relationship with God.

The recognized master of Flemish art in the Renaissance was Jan van Eyck (1390–1441). His works (many of which are thought to have been done in collaboration with his brother, Hubert) are characterized by vivid and intimate, although motionless, portraits set against a scenic background or enveloped in rooms filled with countless objects of daily use. The detailed naturalism of his style is as thorough in his religious paintings as in his portraits, giving precision and interest to his work, if at the expense of spiritual conviction. Van Eyck was also a pioneer in the use and development of oil pigments as well as a bold innovator in using color. The *Altarpiece of the Holy Lamb* in the Church of Saint Bavon in Ghent, Belgium (known also as the *Ghent Altarpiece*) is Van Eyck's masterpiece. It is composed of twenty panels depicting on one side (when closed) the story of the Annunciation, with single figures of John the Baptist, John the Evangelist, and the donors, Jodocus Vyd and his wife, kneeling in prayer. When opened, the panels reveal a panorama of New Jerusalem and the Adoration of the Lamb, with a multitude of worshipers surmounted by figures of the Godhead, the Virgin, Adam and Eve, and a chorus of angel-musicians.

The Van Eyckian realism is pronounced in some of his contem-

ROGIER VAN DER WEYDEN, "CRUCIFIXION" DETAIL. *Utter grief and pain are depicted in this picture of Mary embracing the cross that bears her beloved son. (Kunsthistorisches Museum, Vienna)*

poraries, including the mysterious painter known as the Master of Flémalle (usually identified as Robert Campin of Tournai, ca. 1378–1444), whose works include Nativities, Annunciations, and a striking Entombment. His pictures reflect the same minute detail, heavy and crumpled draperies, rich color, and fascinating backgrounds that are characteristic of the early Flemish style. The emotional intensity of his religious works have suggested a connection with Rogier van der Weyden of Brussels (1399–1464), who may have been Campin's pupil. Van der Weyden concerned himself more with human emotion than Van Eyck did, and he especially depicted feeling in a remarkably dramatic way, involving the viewer much more directly than previous artists had. His art reflects the religiosity of the *devotio moderna*. Especially noteworthy are his Prado *Descent from the Cross*, the Uffizi *Entombment* (frequently compared with Fra Angelico's sensitive style), and the Saint Columba altarpiece in Munich, especially its exquisite central panel depicting in vivid color the *Adoration of the Magi*.

In the second half of the fifteenth century, Flemish style was continued, especially at Brussels, Bruges, and Ghent, by the gifted Dieric Bouts, Hans Memling (although with much less success in expressing emotion), Gerard David, and especially Hugo van der Goes (ca. 1440–82), whose virtuosity was remarkable. Van der Goes's *Portinari Altarpiece*, containing an unusual central panel *Nativity*, was painted for Tomaso Portinari, the Medici agent in Bruges. Taken to Florence in 1475, it greatly influenced the spread of the oil-painting technique in Italy. By the beginning of the sixteenth century, Italian influences were being felt more strongly. With the Antwerp School of Gerard David (1460–1523), Quentin Metsys (or Massys, ca. 1464–1530), and Jan Gossaert, called Mabuse (1478–1533), classical themes and Italianized settings became common.

Another facet of Flemish painting is seen in the works of Bosch and Bruegel. Detailed and untocused, they represent highly individual expressions of Northern Renaissance art. Hieronymous Bosch (ca. 1450–1516) was fascinated by the grotesque and bizarre, and his fantastic pictorial imagery has sometimes been classified as a precursor of Surrealism. Yet his famous *Seven Deadly Sins*, the *Temptation of Saint Anthony*, the *Hay Wain*, the *Earthly Paradise*, and the *Ship of Fools* are all clearly defined allegories of well-known social and religious themes, or symbolic representations of common Flemish proverbs. Even his most bizarre, the triptych *Garden of Earthly Delights*, is not the depiction of some mystical rite or the expression of sexual obsession, but a highly moralistic allegory, a lucid and coherent vision of the human dilemma.

The artistic relationship between Bosch and Pieter Bruegel the Elder (ca. 1525–1569) is most evident in the latter's strange Antwerp *Dulle Griet* (Fall of the Rebel Angels) and the Prado's *Triumph of Death*. The mocking figures in his *Adoration of the Kings* are also reminiscent of Bosch's *Adoration*, but this was his way of exposing their inner character, for Bruegel was a master satirist. He was also an expressive landscape painter and, above all, a unique and masterful portrayer of contemporary life, especially the daily life of the peasants. The activities of these country folk, both toilsome and festive, are the subject of Bruegel's most famous paintings, including the *Country Wedding*, the *Wedding Dance*, *Peasants Dancing*, and the great series *Seasons*. Mildly satirical, yet with an obvious sense of understanding and sympathy, Bruegel

depicted, as no one had ever done before, the tone of peasant life in the sixteenth century.

France

Painting did not flourish in Renaissance France as the literary arts did. However, under the auspices of Francis I, a conscious attempt to stimulate art resulted in some noteworthy achievements. The closest France came to a native school of painting in the Renaissance was achieved by the late-fifteenth-century miniaturists, and they were heavily influenced by the Flemish painters. Jean Fouquet (ca. 1415–80) was the most renowned of this school, known not only for his miniaturist portraits and book illuminations but also for several larger works, including a highly sensual *Virgin and the Child* and a remarkable portrait of Charles VII. Hoping to make France the northern center of Renaissance art, Francis I brought many Italian artists to his court, including Andrea del Sarto, Rosso Fiorentino, Francesco Primaticcio, Leonardo da Vinci, and Benvenuto Cellini. Although their individual works were impressive, these artists failed to bear the fruit they were expected to produce toward the cultivation of a native artistic rebirth. In painting, the most fruitful issue from the school of arts founded by Francis at Fontainebleau was Jean Clouet (ca. 1485–1545) who, along with his more renowned son, François, established a tradition of fine court portraiture that lasted until the end of the century.

French architecture underwent remarkable growth and change under the patronage of Francis I, particularly in the construction and decoration of chateaux and stately mansions. By the early years of the sixteenth century, some evidences of Italian influence on French architecture were already appearing, but by and large the structures erected by Charles VIII and Louis XII were typically Gothic, with varying degrees of Renaissance decoration added to the façades. An excellent example of the evolution of French architecture may be seen in the château of Blois, the popular residence and court of the French kings during the sixteenth century, and sometimes referred to as the "Versailles of the Renaissance." Originally a thirteenth-century castle, commanding one of the vital bridgeheads across the Loire River, Blois had been a possession of the dukes of Orléans for over a hundred years when in 1498 the scion of that family became King Louis XII. Louis and his wife, Anne of Brittany, made Blois the center of French government and court life, and added a wing with many decorative features, including dormer win-

PIETER BRUEGEL, "PEASANTS DANCING." *Bruegel was the peasant painter par excellence. In this lively panel he captured both the spontaneity and the pathos of peasant life in the sixteenth century. (Kunsthistorisches Museum, Vienna)*

CHENONCEAUX. *The château proper was built in 1513–21 by Thomas Bohier. The attached gallery-bridge was added later by Philibert de l'Orme for Catherine de' Medici, who loved this château. (Courtesy of French Government Tourist Office)*

dows and Renaissance moldings adopted from Italian buildings. They also had their Italian gardener, Pacello, lay out great terraces and gardens in the Italian manner.

When Francis I succeeded to the throne in 1515, a renaissance of building began. At Blois he added a magnificent wing to the chateau, highlighted by a unique octagonally spiraling exterior staircase. At nearby Amboise, which had been Francis's childhood home, the castle wing begun by Louis XII was completed and Leonardo da Vinci was brought there to work. Resembling these structures, yet with an added mark of femininity and elegance, are the chateaux of Azay-le-Rideau and Chenonceaux. Both built between 1513 and 1529 by great financiers under the intimate direction of their respective artist-wives, these mansions are the finest examples of the French artistic combination of basically Gothic structures with Renaissance ornamentation. Both chateaux were later taken over by the crown, and Chenonceaux became the favorite residence of Catherine de' Medici.

Francis's own building splurge is best illustrated in the grandiose Chambord, under construction throughout his thirty-two-year reign, and the fabulous Fontainebleau, located in the middle of the king's favorite hunting reserve. Gothiclike in appearance, due to the elongation and multiplication of chimneys, spires, and dormer windows, Chambord is nevertheless Renaissance in decoration and proportion, containing no fewer than seventy-four staircases (including one superimposed double spiral), ample courtyards and galleries, and 440 rooms. It was more a monument than a habitat.

Fontainebleau, on the other hand, was the residence par excellence of the Renaissance king. Begun in 1528, it quickly became the center of Francis's artistic and cultural interests. For constructing this complex of buildings, he engaged the best master masons of France, and to give them the interior style and grace of a truly Renaissance palace, he brought Rosso and Primaticcio to supervise and assist the work of hundreds of French builders. The result is a breathtaking panorama of coffered vaulting, multiwood paneling, marble staircases, delicate stuccos and friezes—and a graceful cast-bronze nymph done by Benvenuto Cellini—that mark the zenith of the French Renaissance. Detailed and unfocused like a Flemish painting, Fontainebleau yet reflects the successful accommodation of Italian Renaissance style with the best elements of native French architecture. The fruits of that union can also be seen in Pierre Lescot's façade of the rebuilt Louvre Palace (ca. 1546) and in the individual classical style of Philibert de l'Orme.

Spain

Spanish architecture is even more richly varied and complex as a result of its development through Moslem, Mozarabic (Moslem features in Christian architecture), Romanesque, Mudéjar (a later fusion of Christian and Moslem), and Gothic styles. Toward the end of the fifteenth century, another style emerged, known as Plateresque, a variation of late Gothic with Mudéjar, Flemish, and Burgundian influences, with strong decorative overtones inspired from the wealth of the New World. Corresponding roughly in time with the reign of Queen Isabel in Castile, this style is frequently called Isabelline. Its most recognizable features are elaborate surface ornamentation, with façades embellished with stones, shells, and heraldic devices, windows covered with beautiful iron grillwork, intricately carved and decorated wooden ceilings, and delicately ornamented arches. The castle at Manzanares and the monastery of San Juan de los Reyes in Toledo are examples of the early work of Juan Guas (d. 1496) in this style. Its most exuberant features can best be seen in the façade and patio of the College of San Gregorio in Valladolid (now housing the National Sculpture Museum) and the west front of the Salamanca Cathedral.

The first introduction of Italian Renaissance features into Spain came in the form of marble tombs commissioned in Italy by Castilian nobles and ecclesiastics. Then, as the Spanish political and military presence in Italy became more pronounced and continuous in the sixteenth century, the influence of classical architecture on Spain increased. The Gothic elements in Plateresque gradually gave way to classical columns, Italian pilasters, and Florentine rustication. Yet it was still genuinely Spanish in its harmonious blending of these components, including the continuingly popular Mudéjar plasterwork and ceilings. By the second decade of the sixteenth century, we can speak meaningfully of a Renaissance Plateresque, as in the entrance to the University of Salamanca Library and the Royal Hospital at Santiago de Compostela (both by Enrique de Egas), the Alcazar and the Cathedral Chapel of the New Kings in Toledo (by Alonso de Covarrubias), and the graceful and more reserved façade of the entrance to the University of Alcalá (by Rodrigo Gil de Hontañón).

The boldest attempts at creating a purer classical Renaissance architecture took place at Granada, in the south: first in the serene majesty of the great palace of Charles V—a unique two-storied quadrangle structure enclosing an elegantly colonnaded circular court—designed by Pedro Machuca, a pupil of Bramante and Raphael; and next in the magnificent Granada Cathedral, built by Diego de Siloé over a previous Gothic plan.

Spanish painting in the fifteenth century was strongly influenced by the Flemish school, with the Italian influence growing after the opening of the Italian wars. Renaissance Castile produced two important painters in Fernando Gallego (active 1466–1507) and Pedro Berruguete (ca. 1450–ca. 1504). In its precise rendering of naturalistic detail, Gallego's work reflects the Flemish models, but with the inclusion of familiar scenes of the Castilian countryside. In the 1470s Berruguete went to Italy, where he was employed by Federigo da Montefeltro, duke of Urbino, the illustrious *condottiere*-turned-patron, who was at the same time the employer of Piero della Francesca. Berruguete was the first Spanish artist to achieve a harmonious synthesis of Spanish-Flemish-Italian traditions. His most famous work is the portrait of *Federigo da Montefeltro with His Son Guidobaldo*, while his most important are the

PEDRO DE BERRUGUETE, "AUTO DE FÉ." *This gifted painter represents Saint Dominic punishing the Albigenses, but the scene also depicts the sixteenth-century Inquisition in action. (Derechos Reservados ©️ Museo del Prado—Madrid)*

Altarpiece of Saint Thomas Aquinas, which he painted near the end of his life for the high altar of Santo Tomás at Avila, and the *Auto de fé*, for the altar of the Dominican convent.

Under Charles V, the cultural relationship between Spain and Italy, and between Spain and the Netherlands, increased to such an extent that the demand for native Spanish art declined noticeably. This Italian and Flemish domination lasted until the middle of the sixteenth century, when the conjunction of Spanish assertiveness and the Counter-Reformation produced a burst of artistic creativity in Spain that made her a leader in the art of the later sixteenth century. Sculpture in Spain likewise leaned heavily on Italian models and style, even to the agitated Mannerism of Michelangelo's later works, as introduced into Spain by Bartolomé Ordóñez, Diego de Siloé, and Alonso Berruguete (ca. 1488–1561), Pedro's son and talented pupil of Michelangelo. Burruguete's *Altarpiece of San Benito el Real* in Valladolid is a masterpiece, combining polychromed statues, bas reliefs, and paintings.

Art and Architecture in Northern and Eastern Europe

Gothic art and architecture, which had predominated in most of Europe since the twelfth century, were still in their heyday at the end of the fifteenth century. The soaring vertical lines of the Gothic cathedral, with its mystic statuary and ribbed vaulting were familiar throughout Europe. In the German empire and further east, Gothic architecture continued in popularity until at least the middle of the sixteenth century. Churches and cathedrals that were begun in an earlier period and completed in the late fifteenth or early sixteenth century were as Gothic in style as were those completed 200 years earlier.

Nevertheless, by the end of the fifteenth century, Gothic architecture had a rival in the spacious, classical Italian style, even though the architectural influence from the south remained moderate until late in the sixteenth century, and then turned quickly into baroque. The chief impact of Renaissance architecture on the north was to induce some modification in façades and decoration, but seldom did it dominate local Gothic styles. Often rib vaulting lost its structural function and became a decorative motif, as in the Vladislav Hall of the castle of Prague in Bohemia. In many cases, the Gothic design became wildly flamboyant, as in the elaborate fan vaulting of the Henry VII Chapel in Westminster Abbey and in the hall of Christ Church in Oxford. What we now designate as English perpendicular and, later, Tudor, are a melding of this classical style with English Gothic. Sometimes a complete mixture of the two styles was effected, as in the Palace of Justice (at that time the residence of the regent, Margaret of Austria) at Malines in Belgium, built during the first quarter of the sixteenth century; or in the façade of the Heidelberg Castle, now seen only in semiruin. The Fugger Chapel and Mausoleum in Augsburg, with its Renaissance form and modified Gothic star vault, is an example of a more harmonious blending of the two styles, as is the graceful Belvedere in Prague.

Occasionally, a pure Renaissance structure emerged, but when it did, it was usually the work of Italians. Two striking examples of this are the Residenz at Landshut in Bavaria, built by Mantuans, and the Sigismund Chapel in the Wawel Cathedral of Cracow, built and decorated by Florentine and Sienese artists. Sigismund I was a great admirer of the Italian Renaissance, and through his patronage, many Italian artists came to Poland (he even married an Italian woman, Bona Sforza). Renaissance civic architecture in Poland is represented in the town hall of Poznan, reconstructed in Italianate style but crowned with a typical "Polish attic."

Earlier, in the 1470s, the Hungarian king Matthias Corvinus had introduced Italian Renaissance art into Hungary and made his court the eastern center of Renaissance culture. The court architect of Buda until the king's death in 1490 was a Florentine; and a number of Italian sculptors, painters, goldsmiths, and illustrators, including Giovanni Dalmata and Francesco Rosselli, were patronized by Matthias. A good example of this influence may be seen in the stately Bakócz Chapel in the Cathedral of Esztergom, just north of Budapest. The flowering of Renaissance art in Hungary was short-lived, however. Acute financial problems, political strife, and the invasion of the Turks ended it by 1526.

During the fifteenth century, the art of sculpture was given new life in the Holy Roman Empire by several German artists whose work was strongly influenced by Flemish painting. Hans Multscher (ca. 1400–67) of Ulm and Nicolaus Gerhaerts of Leiden (who worked mainly in Alsace and Vienna) were two of those whose boldly expressive realism and angular, or crumpled, drapery style began the break with International Gothic. The work of the Tyrolean woodcarver and painter, Michael Pacher (ca. 1435–98), is the first to reflect a strong bias toward Italy. That influence, particularly from Andrea Mantegna, is revealed in the power, harmony of space, realism, and grandeur of Pacher's masterpiece, the high altar in the church of Saint Wolfgang, near Salzburg, and in many other parish churches in Austria and Germany. The Renaissance impulse to evoke the "inner life" of the human form is uniquely expressed in the famous *Morris Dancers,* small figures posed in various attitudes of action, created in 1480 by Erasmus Grasser (ca. 1450–1518) for the Rathaus in Munich. Finally, Veit Stoss (ca. 1445–1533), a Nuremberg sculptor, combined the religious symbolism of Gothic forms with the simpler and more realistic Italian techniques to produce some of the most vivid and expressive examples of northern Renaissance sculpture.

Although the Empire produced some outstanding painters during the Renaissance and enriched the western heritage with many woodcuts and priceless portraits, the general level of German painting in the fifteenth century was below that of Flanders. Patronage was less certain and the people seemed to be less appreciative of art than in the western

KONRAD WITZ, "THE
MIRACULOUS DRAUGHT OF
FISHES." *One of Witz's
many distinctive tempera
panels. It is from the Saint
Peter Altarpiece. (Collection Musée d'art et d'histoire, Geneva)*

and southern countries, and more prone to regard artists at best as unnecessary luxuries and at worst as outright parasites (or so Dürer complained). Among the early artists who contributed to the evolution of German painting were Hans Multscher, who was both a sculptor and painter, and Konrad Witz (ca. 1405–45) from Constance and Basel. Witz was especially influenced by the van Eycks and, like Multscher, adopted a more severe, "architectural" style of painting. He also made important use of light and painted realistic landscapes. Indeed, Witz's *Miraculous Draught of Fishes*, from his Saint Peter Altarpiece in Geneva, is regarded as the first true landscape of the northern Renaissance. Stefan Lochner (ca. 1400–51), the best representative of the Cologne school of painting, was strongly indebted to Rogier van der Weyden for the characteristic softness and grace of his work. At Colmar in upper Alsace, Martin Schongauer (ca. 1445–91) also learned much from van der Weyden's emotional intensity and expressed his own feelings not only in paintings but also in many striking engravings.

Two of the notable German painters to be influenced by the style of the High Renaissance, yet who were uniquely German in both the themes and rendition of their art, were Matthias Grünewald (ca. 1468–1528) and Albrecht Altdorfer (ca. 1480–1538). Grünewald's forte was religious painting, which he endowed with great feeling and a mystic quality while, like the Flemish painters, leaving out none of the details and minutiae of "real" life. His masterpiece is the *Isenheim Altarpiece*, completed in 1515 for the chapel of the Anthonite hospital in Isenheim, near Colmar. The topics of the panels range from the *Meeting of Saint Anthony and Saint Paul*; the *Temptation of Saint Anthony*; the *Annuncia-*

tion; the *Nativity* and the *Resurrection* of Christ; to the unforgettable *Crucifixion*, which occupies the central panel. In these, Grünewald's distinct mastery of expressive gesture to effuse pathos and feeling is evident. Altdorfer was also a religious painter but of a very different stamp. More responsive to the artistic breezes from across the Alps, he produced paintings of great elegance and naturalism. Above all, he was fascinated by nature, and most of his paintings, whether of religious or secular subjects, were primarily landscapes, bathed in a natural atmosphere of trees, water, and air.

Albrecht Dürer

The greatest artist of Renaissance Germany, and the most important link between Italian and northern art, was the skilled and perceptive Nuremberg goldsmith-illustrator-painter, Albrecht Dürer (1471–1528). As a young man, Dürer abandoned his father's trade to embark on a career of painting and drawing, a profession that eventually took him to all parts of Europe and brought him the recognition as one of the greatest of all German artists. After extensive travel throughout the Holy Roman Empire, Dürer went to Italy in 1494, the year of the French invasion, and there became thoroughly imbued with the flavor and objectives of Renaissance art. He was particularly impressed by the classical themes of Venetian painting. In 1505 he again returned to northern Italy to learn more of the secrets of Italian art and to become intimately acquainted with the techniques and artistic theory of the great Renaissance painters.

It was soon evident from Dürer's woodcuts, paintings, and engravings, after his return to Germany, that he had caught the spirit and vitality of Renaissance creativity. He was one of the first artists of northern Europe to fully grasp the possibilities of printing and engraving as a medium of artistic expression. Dürer's woodcuts and copper engravings were soon in demand by publishers all over Europe, and still remain as some of the greatest monuments of early-sixteenth-century art. Like Leonardo, Dürer had a searching mind and was eager to discover the meaning and truths of nature. "For truly art is embedded in nature," he wrote. "He who can pull it out will hold it." Yet Dürer lacked Leonardo's confidence that the true essence of art could be learned or discovered by human endeavor. If God alone can endow mortals with such gifts, what then is the purpose of study, searching, and laboring? Can God's endowments be enriched by human effort? Even before Luther began flooding Germany with his ideas, Dürer had struggled with the problems of will and fate. Perhaps this is the meaning of his famous engraving, *Melancholia*. "The lie is in our understanding," he wrote, "and darkness is so firmly entrenched in our mind that even our groping will fail." Likewise his *Knight, Death and Devil* and his *Four Horsemen of the Apocalypse* reveal the deep concern he had, not only for religious issues but for all human dilemmas.

ALBRECHT DURER, "FOUR HORSEMEN OF THE APOCALYPSE." *One of Dürer's most vivid woodcuts, depicting the end of the world: Death, Want, Sickness, and War ravage their helpless victims. (The Metropolitan Museum of Art, Gift of Junius S. Morgan, 1919)*

But Dürer was as much a man of the Renaissance as of the Reformation. He was more likely than most German artists to appreciate classical style and to paint religious themes in the Italian manner, indeed with a devotion to nature that in many respects went beyond the naturalism of the Italian painters. Although he completed over fifty paintings, Dürer's first love remained designing and engraving, which by the last decade of the fifteenth century, had come into great demand as a result of the spread of printing. In this medium, he produced more than a thousand portraits, designs, and illustrations. It is not surprising to find that Dürer was also fascinated by both the practical and mystical qualities of numbers, and that he devoted some very serious thought to the theory of mathematical proportion, publishing a book on measurements and beginning another on human proportions. In this field, he continued the tradition of Brunelleschi, Alberti, and Leonardo da Vinci.

Two contemporaries of Dürer from neighboring Augsburg, Lucas Cranach (1472–1553) and Hans Holbein the Younger (1497–1543), must also be mentioned, for not only were they highly talented synthesizers of German, Flemish, and Italian traditions, they were also great innovators in portrait painting. It is to these two that we are most indebted for the many portraits of the great personalities of the early sixteenth century. Both painters lacked the depth of feeling and thought of Dürer, but they possessed a keen sense of reality and great technical skill—attributes that served them well as portrait painters. Holbein's life from 1532 to 1543 was spent in England (except for occasional visits to Basel and Italy), where he soon became a close friend to Sir Thomas More and court painter to Henry VIII. His presence there helped fill the artistic void in England resulting from the almost total lack of native artists.

Music in the Renaissance

Just as the Burgundian Netherlands set the tone for lyrical poetry in the tradition of the *Grand Rhétoriqueurs* and led all the northern Europeans in the luxury and exhilaration of their painting, so did they dominate in Renaissance music. The sacred music of the Middle Ages, characterized by the Gregorian chant, was monodic (single-voiced or sung in unison), and nonrhythmical. But like most everything else in the Middle Ages, music underwent notable changes in structure and effect. The greatest innovation of the late medieval period was the introduction of polyphony, by which two or more independent voice parts are employed simultaneously to enrich and embellish the musical effect. In the twelfth and thirteenth centuries, fixed rhythms were introduced into some types of church music and an improved system of musical notation developed. The fullest blossoming of medieval music corresponded with the creative period of the great Gothic cathedrals.

In the fourteenth century, music found its greatest literary exponent and theorist in the French composer, poet, and royal householder, Philippe de Vitry, whose influential treatise entitled *Ars nova* (The New Art), popularized to Petrarch's generation the notion of a new birth in religious and secular music. The musical style associated with this early period of the Renaissance is called the *ars nova* and is characterized by further changes in musical notation and harmony, by the growing influence of secular music, and by the more rapid evolution and adaptation of musical instruments, especially in Italy. As instrumental accompaniment increased in popularity, musical instruments underwent changes resulting in the fourteenth-century clavichord and virginal (precursors of the piano), full keyboard organ, trombone, trumpet, and bagpipe—and of course the kettle drum, purportedly introduced into the west in 1457 by a Polish ambassadorial entourage. For solo accompaniment, the viol, flute, and harp were used. But the most popular of all was the lute, which by the fifteenth century had found its way into every part of Europe.

The leading figure of the *ars nova* was Guillaume de Machaut, a prominent French poet and composer, whose compositions include a number of religious motets (named for the "little words," as text, sung by counterpoint voices), a monumental polyphonic mass, and many secular songs. Machaut was a bold innovator, anxious to experiment with new forms and effects regardless of their immediate acceptance. One of his more controversial experiments was with syncopation, which had some popularity in his time. In fourteenth-century Italy, the most talented and prolific composer was the humanist Francesco Landino, blind organist of the church of San Lorenzo in Florence.

The long-standing leadership of the Low Countries was established early in the Renaissance with Guillaume Dufay (1400–74), court singer, composer, and music teacher of the duke of Burgundy. More inventive than creative, Dufay's music was both elegant and colorful, without losing the devotional motif so dear to the Brethren of the Common Life, who greatly admired Dufay's work, as they did the painting of his contemporary, Jan van Eyck. The greatest contribution of the Burgundian and Flemish schools was to choral music, which they enriched with more integrated harmonies and counterpoint, and enlarged with more voices and instruments. The choral masses of several Flemish composers of the late fifteenth century are among the finest of the entire period.

The High Renaissance produced in music, just as in painting and architecture, a culmination and expansion of the art developed over the centuries. More magnificent and on a larger scale than any previous productions, the music of the High Renaissance was lofty, majestic, and varied. Leadership still came from the Netherlands and Flanders, where every form of mass, motet, madrigal, and song was elaborately developed. The most brilliant musical figures of this period were Jan van Ockeghem (ca. 1420–95) and Josquin Deprès (ca. 1450–1521), both gifted choir singers and composers from Hainaut in the southern

Netherlands. Josquin Deprès spent many years in Italy where he was not only influenced by the literature and art of the High Renaissance, but contributed to it his own musical genius. He excelled in every form of musical expression known at the time, and his compositions were always melodious, giving full expression to the feelings of his heart. At the same time, they were appropriately related in both mood and tempo to the religious text or other lyrics being used. His contemporaries considered him the greatest composer of the age, and modern musicologists have agreed with that judgment.

Popular Culture in Renaissance Europe

The literary, artistic, and musical creations that have been described were not equally available or relevant to all levels of Renaissance society. The poorer classes, especially the rural peasants, urban craftsmen, and homeless vagabonds could not share a culture that they neither related to nor understood. For these and many other ordinary people, the poetry of Marot and the paintings of Raphael were out of reach and foreign to their way of life. For them, other cultural traditions existed that historians have only recently begun to study and appreciate.

This "popular culture" had a great many variations and manifestations; shepherd culture, for example, was different from the culture of village craftsmen, and this in turn was distinct from the subculture of soldiers and sailors, or beggars and thieves. There were likewise many regional and ethnic variations in popular culture as local folklore and customs dominated the content of popular art, drama, songs, and celebrations. At the same time, universal themes and traditions also gave a certain unity to the activities and amusements of the people. Some of these themes were drawn directly from the heroes of "learned culture," such as Roland, El Cid, and King Arthur; and of course the upper classes had no monopoly on biblical themes or the lives of the saints. The coincidence of subject matter may also be due in part to the itinerant nature of the professional entertainers, from ballad singers, minstrels, and storytellers to popular preachers and players. Traveling tumblers, jugglers, puppeteers, clowns, and comedians also entertained the people, especially on market days and during fairs. At the fairs, people were likewise amused with bear baiting, horse racing, and many kinds of games.

The singing of folksongs, especially ballads and various narrative songs, was popular in all parts of Europe, as were simple stock-character plays and more involved comedies and farces, culminating in the elaborate Italian *commedia dell'arte*. Serious religious plays were performed alongside parodies of church rituals and practices, while mock weddings, mock funerals, and mock trials poked fun at many other social and legal institutions. Dancing was extremely popular in Renaissance folk culture, in the country as well as in the villages, especially the many group dances that involved both men and women. Frequently these dances depicted common activities such as courting, or portrayed military conflicts prominent in the history of the region or country. Many of these dances have had an amazing longevity and have been introduced into the repertoires of modern folkdancers. Courtship was the main motif of dances for couples, while solo dances were performed principally by the males.

These activities were not confined to the fairs but also frequently took place in the church (especially mystery or miracle plays) and at popular inns and taverns where people gathered to socialize and drink. In warmer climates, the marketplace was the center of almost continuous entertainment, especially in the larger piazzas and plazas of Italy and Spain where plays, puppet shows, acrobatic feats, horse races, football games, bullfights and other spectacles, including executions were performed. In Renaissance Europe, every happening was a social event and became part of the popular culture.

The most important settings for these and many other amusements were the frequent festivals that punctuated the otherwise dreary life of the people. These celebrations included family festivals such as baptisms, first communion, and weddings; community festivals celebrating local patron saints' days; and yearly general festivals like Easter, May Day, Midsummer, Christmas, New Year's, and Epiphany. The greatest extravaganza of all was Carnival, the pre-Lenten celebration running from January until Shrove Tuesday (Mardi Gras), the day before Ash Wednesday, when Lent begins. Carnival season was a succession of mass performances of formal events (processions, competitions, plays) and countless other activities of eating, drinking, singing, dancing, and lampooning the church, the government, and all aspects of orderly society. It was a time of indulgence and license, characterized by the consumption of enormous amounts of food, especially meat (carne, hence carnival), sexual debauchery, and violence. During Carnival, inhibitions and restraints were abandoned. Verbal and pictorial abuse of authorities was condoned; everyone was masked and vented their spirits as they liked; men dressed as women, and women dressed as men; everything was turned upside down.

Not surprisingly in such a prolonged orgy, ritualized violence sometimes turned into riots and bloody rebellion as the people worked themselves into a frenzy. For this reason, and because of its general immorality, Carnival was criticized by the religious reformers: by Catholics because of the excess and overindulgence, by Protestants because they felt that this ceremony, like all idolatry, should be abolished. The church also objected because Carnival had roots in pagan ritual and was consequently unchristian. Pieter Bruegel's famous painting of *The Battle between Carnival and Lent* symbolizes the continuing struggle of the religious to tame and Christianize the popular festivals.

The long-range impact of the reform movement, and the Protestant Reformation in particular, seems to have been less effective in controlling Carnival than it was in changing other features of Renaissance popular culture. The Reformation introduced new elements, such as Bible reading—especially the Psalms—and the singing of hymns, while Catholic reformers emphasized other Christian virtues, thereby giving a more religious flavor to the popular culture of the sixteenth and early seventeenth centuries.

Suggestions for Further Reading

GENERAL

R. Wittkower, et al., "The Arts in Western Europe," *The New Cambridge Modern History*, I, 127–93, is a good introduction. See also Lewis W. Spitz (ed.), *The Northern Renaissance* (Englewood Cliffs, 1972), selected extracts with introductions, and C. S. Lewis, *Studies in Medieval and Renaissance Literature* (New York, 1966). Anne Denieul-Cormier, *A Time of Glory: The Renaissance in France, 1488–1559*, tr. by Anne Freemantle (Garden City, 1968) is a well-illustrated survey of literature and art; also Franco Simone, *The French Renaissance: Medieval Tradition and Italian Influence in Shaping the Renaissance in France*, tr. by H. Gaston Hall (New York, 1969), which is broad and perceptive.

LITERATURE IN FRANCE AND SPAIN

I. D. McFarlane, *A Literary History of France: Renaissance France, 1470–1589* (London and New York, 1974) is an excellent survey. Also suggestive is a much shorter book by Donald Stone, *France in the Sixteenth Century* (Englewood Cliffs, 1969). Barbara C. Bowen, *The Age of Bluff: Paradox and Ambiguity in Rabelais and Montaigne* (Urbana, 1972) is a fast-moving analysis of the two most famous sixteenth-century French writers. The best introduction and guide to Rabelais is Donald M. Frame, *François Rabelais: A Study* (New York, 1977). Also enlightening are Donald Stone, Jr., *French Humanist Tragedy* (Manchester, 1974), and Marcel Tetel, *Marguerite of Navarre's Heptameron* (Durham, 1973). For Spain, see Otis H. Green, *The Literary Mind of Medieval and Renaissance Spain* (Lexington, 1970), and Royston O. Jones, *The Golden Age: Prose and Poetry, the Sixteenth and Seventeenth Centuries* (London, 1971).

LITERATURE IN GERMANY AND ENGLAND

Roy Pascal, *German Literature in the Sixteenth and Seventeenth Centuries* (London and New York, 1968) is a good starting point. Keith L. Roos probes an interesting facet of German literature in *The Devil in Sixteenth-Century German Literature* (Bern, 1972). Gerald Strauss, *Historian in an Age of Crisis: The Life and Work of Johannes Aventinus, 1477–1534* (Cambridge, Mass., 1963) is a thorough study. Harry Levin provides a short interpretive survey of English Renaissance literature in "English Literature of the Renaissance," in T. Helton (ed.), *The Renaissance* (Madison, 1964), 125–51. H. A. Mason, *Humanism and Poetry in the Early Tudor Period* (London, 1959) is a useful inquiry. Also recommended is Maurice Pollet, *John Skelton: Poet of Tudor England*, tr. by John Warrington (Lewisburg, 1971).

Otto Benesch, *The Art of the Renaissance in Northern Europe*, rev. ed. (New York, 1965) is still very useful; also W. Stechow, *Northern Renaissance Art, 1400–1600* (Englewood Cliffs, 1966). Alastair Smart's *The Renaissance and Mannerism in Northern Europe and Spain* (New York, 1972) is an outstanding volume in the Harbrace History of Art series, showing northern Renaissance art as the product of the classical revival in Italy and the medieval art of the north.

For Flemish art, the most succinct summary is John Canaday, "The Flowering of Flemish Art," *Horizon*, 8 (1966), 85–105; on France, see Anthony Blunt, *Art and Architecture in France, 1500–1700*, rev. ed. (Baltimore, 1970); on Spain, B. Smith, *Spain: A History in Art* (New York, 1966), beautifully illustrated. Theodor Müller, *Sculpture in The Netherlands, Germany, France and Spain, 1400–1500*, tr. by Elaine and William Scott (Harmondsworth, 1966) is a very handy little volume. For a lively and succinct look at Grünewald, Arthur Burkard, *Matthias Grünewald: Personality and Accomplishment* (New York, 1976) is more than adequate; on Dürer and his age, see Francis Russell, *The World of Dürer* (New York, 1967). The very best on eastern Europe is Jan Bialostocki, *The Art of the Renaissance in Eastern Europe* (Ithaca, 1978).

RENAISSANCE MUSIC AND POPULAR CULTURE

The authoritative text on Renaissance music is Gustave Reese, *Music in the Renaissance*, rev. ed. (New York, 1959), but it is extremely technical and difficult for the nonspecialist to read. More satisfactory are R. Alec Harmon, *Man and His Music: Mediaeval and Early Renaissance Music* (New York, 1969), and especially Howard M. Brown, *Music in the Renaissance* (Englewood Cliffs, 1975). Isabella Caseaux, *French Music in the Fifteenth and Sixteenth Centuries* (London, 1975) is an informative study, as is Frances H. Ellis, *The Early Meisterlieder of Hans Sachs* (Bloomington, 1974). On popular culture, Peter Burke's recent *Popular Culture in Early Modern Europe* (New York, 1978) is wide-ranging and thought-provoking. Natalie Z. Davis, *Culture and Society in Early Modern France* (Stanford, 1975) gives valuable insights into many aspects of French life.

APPENDIX I
Chronology of Important Events

1337 Petrarch retires to Vaucluse. Beginning of the Hundred Years' War.
1341 Petrarch receives the laurel crown in Rome.
1346 Bardi and Peruzzi banks fail. Battle of Crécy. First use of cannons.
1347 Outbreak of the Black Death. Cola di Rienzo seizes Rome.
1348 The Black Death begins to spread across Europe (1348–50). University of Prague founded.
1349 Persecution of Jews in Germany.

1350 Naval war between Venice and Genoa.
1351 English Statute of Provisors. Zürich joins Swiss Confederation.
1353 Statute of Praemunire. Bern joins Swiss Confederation.
1356 Battle of Poitiers. Emperor Charles IV issues the Golden Bull.
1358 The *Jacquerie* in France. Uprising of Etienne Marcel.
1360 Peace of Brétigny. The Turks take Adrianople.
1364 Niccolò Niccoli born. University of Cracow founded.
1365 University of Vienna founded.
1370 Guarino da Verona born. John Hus born. Treaty of Stralsund between Hansa and Denmark.
1374 Death of Petrarch. Leonardo Bruni born. Last persecution of the Cathari.
1375 Wyclif writes *On Divine Dominion*. Abraham Cresques' *Catalan Atlas* completed.
1377 Brunelleschi born. John Wyclif tried and acquitted.
1378 *Ciompi* revolt in Florence. Beginning of the Great Schism. Vittorino da Feltre born. Lorenzo Ghiberti born.
1380 Poggio Bracciolini born. Thomas à Kempis born. Royal Library of France founded.
1381 Peasant revolt in England, led by Wat Tyler.
1382 Wyclif begins English translation of the Bible.
1386 Donatello born. Ambrogio Traversari born. Heidelberg University founded. Alliance between England and Portugal.
1387 Chaucer begins *Canterbury Tales*.
1388 Flavio Biondo born. University of Cologne founded.
1389 Sultan Murad I defeats Serbian army at Kossovo. Cosimo de' Medici born.
1390 Jan van Eyck born.
1391 Massacre of Jews in Seville.
1394 Expulsion of Jews from France. Prince Henry the Navigator born.
1396 Michelozzo born. Turks defeat Christians at Nicopolis.
1397 Founding of the Medici Bank. Manuel Chrysoloras in Florence. Paolo Uccello born. Union of Kalmar.
1399 Carlo Marsuppini born. Rogier van der Weyden born.

1401 Masaccio born. The *Taula* founded in Barcelona.
1402 Death of Gian Galeazzo Visconti. Tartars defeat the Turks at Ankara.
1405 Leon Battista Alberti born. Veneziano born. Pope Pius II born.
1406 Fra Filippo Lippi born.
1407 Bank of St. George founded in Genoa. Lorenzo Valla born.

1409　Council of Pisa.
1410　Teutonic Knights defeated at Tannenberg. Ptolemy's *Geography* recovered.
1413　Lollard rebellion in England.
1414　Opening of the Council of Constance. Ludovico Gonzaga born.
1415　John Hus burned at the stake. Battle of Agincourt. Portuguese take Ceuta. Prince Henry establishes school of navigation at Sagres.
1416　Piero della Francesca born. Piero de' Medici born.
1418　Portuguese colonize the Madeiras.
1419　The Four Articles of Prague. Beginning of the Hussite wars.
1420　Brunelleschi begins Cathedral dome in Florence.
1421　Andrea del Castagno born.
1424　Cristoforo Landino born. Death of Jan Žižka.
1425　Alliance of Florence, Venice, and papacy against Milan.
1427　Leonardo Bruni becomes chancellor of Florence.
1429　Gentile Bellini born. Joan of Arc breaks the siege of Orléans. Order of the Golden Fleece instituted by Philip of Burgundy.
1431　Giovanni Bellini born. Mantegna born. Opening of the Council of Basel. Joan of Arc burned at the stake. Ercole d'Este born.
1432　Luigi Pulci born. Antonio Pallaiuolo born.
1433　Marcilio Ficino born. Robert Gaguin born.
1434　The Medici come to power in Florence. Matteo Boiardo born. Gil Eannes rounds Cape Bojador.
1435　Alberti writes *On Painting*. Verrocchio born.
1436　Regiomontanus born.
1437　Isaac Abrabanel born. Cardinal Cisneros born.
1438　Pragmatic Sanction of Bourges.
1440　Nicholas of Cusa writes *De docta ignorantia*.
1442　John Hunyadi temporarily expels Turks from Transylvania.
1443　Alberti's *Della famiglia*. Alfonso V moves his court to Naples.
1444　Botticelli born. Bramante born. Antonio de Nebrija born. Rudolf Agricola born. Turks defeat Christian crusade at Varna.
1445　Philippe de Commines born.
1446　William Grocyn born. Battista Sforza born.
1449　Lorenzo de' Medici born. Ghirlandaio born.

1450　Founding of the Vatican Library. Aldus Manutius born. Lefèvre d'Etaples born. Cade's Rebellion.
1451　Josquin Deprès born. Fall of Jacques Coeur.
1452　Leonardo da Vinci born.
1453　Fall of Constantinople. End of the Hundred Years' War.
1454　Peace of Lodi. Poliziano born.
1455　Johann Gutenberg prints the forty-two-line Bible. Wars of the Roses begin. Johann Reuchlin born.
1457　Sebastian Brant born. University of Freiburg founded.
1458　The Pitti Palace begun. George Poděbrady elected king of Bohemia. Matthias Corvinus becomes king of Hungary.
1459　Council of Mantua fails to organize crusade against the Turks.
1460　Death of Prince Henry the Navigator. Thomas Linacre born.
1462　Pietro Pomponazzi born.

1464 Platonic Academy established in Florence. Printing introduced in Rome.
1466 Erasmus born. John Colet born.
1467 Guillaume Budé born. Charles the Bold becomes Duke of Burgundy.
1468 Castilian nobles force Enrique IV to recognize his sister Isabel as heir.
1469 Lorenzo de' Medici begins rule in Florence. Machiavelli born. Marriage of Ferdinand and Isabel.
1470 Nicolas Jenson establishes printing press in Venice.
1471 Albrecht Dürer born. Hernán Nuñez born. Mutianus Rufus born. Elisabetta Gonzaga born.
1472 Lucas Cranach born.
1473 Copernicus born. Printing introduced in Lyon. Caxton prints in Bruges.
1474 Ariosto born. Printing begins in Valencia. Isabella d'Este born.
1475 Michelangelo born. Beatrice d'Este born.
1476 Charles the Bold defeated at Grandson and Murten. Uppsala University founded.
1477 Death of Charles the Bold. Marriage of Maximilian of Austria and Mary of Burgundy. Titian born. Thomas More born. University of Tübingen founded.
1478 Pazzi Conspiracy. Castiglione born. The Inquisition established in Castile. Fernández de Oviedo born.
1480 Portugal cedes Canary Islands to Spain.
1482 Portuguese establish Elmina on the Gold Coast of Africa.
1483 Raphael born. Martin Luther born.
1484 Charles VIII convenes Estates General. Diogo Cão reaches Congo River.
1485 Henry Tudor defeats Richard III at Bosworth Field.
1487 Bartholomew Dias rounds Cape of Good Hope.
1488 Pedro de Covilhão visits Calicut.
1489 Treaty of Medina del Campo.
1490 Aldine Press established in Venice. Vittoria Colonna born.
1491 Ignatius Loyola born.
1492 Death of Lorenzo the Magnificent. Pietro Aretino born. Marguerite of Navarre born. Juan Luis Vives born. Bernal Díaz born. Spanish capture Granada, expel the Jews from Spain. Columbus discovers America.
1493 Papal line of demarcation. Columbus's second voyage. Paracelsus born.
1494 Charles VIII invades Italy, expels the Medici. Correggio born. Georg Agricola born. Rabelais born. Treaty of Tordesillas.
1495 Leonardo begins *The Last Supper*. Holy League formed against France.
1496 Marot born. João de Barros born. Forced conversion of Jews in Portugal.
1497 Cabot reaches North America. Da Gama sails for India. Holbein born.
1498 Death of Savonarola. Columbus embarks on third voyage. Da Gama reaches Calicut.
1499 Cesare Borgia campaigns in the Romagna. Erasmus makes first trip to England. Da Gama returns from India.

1500 Cabral discovers Brazil. Columbus returns to Spain in chains. Treaty of Granada. Tartaglia born. Cellini born.
1501 Vespucci's voyage to South America. Garcilaso de la Vega born.
1502 Columbus's fourth voyage. University of Wittenberg founded.
1503 Erasmus publishes the *Enchiridion*. Thomas Wyatt born. Casa de Contratación founded.

1504 Thomas More elected to Parliament.
1505 Amerigo Vespucci becomes pilot major of Castile.
1506 Reuchlin publishes Latin-Hebrew grammar. Philip the Handsome dies.
1507 Waldseemüller's *Cosmographiae introductio.*
1508 League of Cambrai against Venice. Patronato Real. University of Alcalá founded.
1509 Erasmus writes *The Praise of Folly.* Etienne Dolet born. Battle of Diu.
1510 Albuquerque made viceroy of India. López de Gómara born. Ambroise Paré born.
1511 Council of Pisa. Thomas Wolsey appointed lord chancellor of England.
1512 The Medici return to Florence. Battle of Ravenna. Michelangelo completes the Sistine Ceiling.
1513 Machiavelli writes *The Prince.* English victory over the Scots at Flodden Field. Balboa reaches the Pacific Ocean.
1514 Complutensian Polyglot New Testament completed. Vesalius born. Wolsey becomes archbishop of York. Ponce de León discovers Florida.
1515 Battle of Marignano. Treaty of Fribourg. Saint Teresa of Avila born. Juan de Solis explores Río de la Plata estuary.
1516 Concordat of Bologna. Ariosto's *Orlando Furioso.* More's *Utopia* published. Erasmus's *New Testament* published.
1517 Luther's Ninety-Five Theses. Henry Howard born.
1518 Thomas More joins king's council. Vives publishes *Fabula de Homine.*
1519 Charles V elected Holy Roman Emperor. Magellan begins his voyage. Cortés begins the conquest of Mexico.
1520 Michelangelo begins the Medici tombs. Pieter Bruegel born. Meeting at the Field of Cloth of Gold. *Comunero* revolt in Spain.
1521 Diet at Worms. French besiege Pamplona. Magellan killed in Philippines. Secret treaty between Charles V and Henry VIII.
1522 Cortés completes the conquest of Mexico. Del Cano completes the first circumnavigation of the world. Ottoman Turks take Rhodes.
1523 Lefèvre's *New Testament* translation. Vasa dynasty in Sweden. Pedro de Alvarado begins conquest of Guatemala.
1524 Verrazano explores North American coast, enters New York harbor.
1525 Battle of Pavia. Francis I taken prisoner. Tyndale's *New Testament.*
1526 Battle of Mohács. Turks conquer most of Hungary. Treaty of Madrid. League of Cognac.
1527 Sack of Rome. Florentine Republic established (lasts until 1530). Death of Machiavelli.
1528 Castiglione's *Book of the Courtier* published. Paolo Veronese born. Fontainebleau begun.
1529 Peace of Cambrai. Fall of Wolsey; Thomas More becomes lord chancellor of England. Turks repulsed from Vienna.
1530 Charles V crowned by pope in Bologna. Collège de France founded. Pizarro begins final assault on Inca Empire.

APPENDIX II
Rulers of European States

The Papacy

Florence

Florence (continued)

1512–1516 Giuliano and Lorenzo de' Medici
1516–1519 Lorenzo de' Medici
1519–1523 Giulio de' Medici
1523–1527 Alessandro de' Medici
1527–1530 Republic

Doges of Venice

1382–1400 Antonio Venieri
1400–1413 Michele Steno
1414–1423 Tommaso Mocenigo
1423–1457 Francesco Foscari
1457–1462 Pasquale Malipiero
1462–1471 Cristoforo Moro
1471–1473 Niccolò Trono
1473–1474 Niccolò Marcello
1474–1476 Pietro Mocenigo
1476–1478 Andrea Vendramini
1478–1485 Giovanni Mocenigo
1485–1486 Marco Barbarigo
1486–1501 Agostino Barbarigo
1501–1521 Leonardo Loredano

Milan

1378–1402 Gian Galeazzo Visconti
1402–1412 Gian Maria Visconti (part of territory)
1412–1447 Filippo Maria Visconti
1447–1450 Ambrosian Republic
1450–1466 Francesco Sforza
1466–1476 Galeazzo Maria Sforza
1476–1494 Gian Galeazzo Sforza (Regency by Bona of Savoy &
           Ludovico Sforza)
1479–1499 Ludovico Sforza, il Moro
1499–1508 Louis XII of France
1508–1515 Massimiliano Sforza
1515–1525 Francis I of France

Naples

1343–1382 Joanna I
1382–1384 Charles III (Charles II of Hungary)
1382–1384 Louis I of Anjou*
1386–1414 Ladislas
1384–1417 Louis II*
1414–1435 Joanna II
1417–1434 Louis III*

*Rival claimant to the throne

Naples *(continued)*

1435–1458 Alfonso the Magnanimous (of Aragon)
1458–1494 Ferrante
1494–1495 Alfonso II
1495–1496 Ferdinand II
1496–1501 Frederick

England

1327–1377 Edward III (Plantagenet)
1377–1399 Richard II (Plantagenet)
1399–1413 Henry IV (Lancaster)
1413–1422 Henry V (Lancaster)
1422–1461 Henry VI (Lancaster)
1461–1483 Edward IV (York)
1483   Edward V (York)
1484–1485 Richard III (York)
1485–1509 Henry VII (Tudor)
1509–1547 Henry VIII (Tudor)

France (Valois)

1328–1350 Philip VI
1350–1364 John II, the Good
1364–1380 Charles V, the Wise
1380–1422 Charles VI
1422–1461 Charles VII
1461–1483 Louis XI, the Spider King
1483–1498 Charles VIII
1498–1515 Louis XII (Valois-Orléans)
1515–1547 Francis I (Valois-Angoulême)

Spain

CASTILE

1350–1369 Pedro the Cruel
1369–1379 Enrique II (of Trastámara)
1379–1390 Juan I
1390–1406 Enrique III
1406–1454 Juan II
1454–1474 Enrique IV, the Impotent
1474–1504 Isabel, the Catholic
1504–1516 Juana, the Mad
1516–1556 Charles I of Castile
           and Aragon (Holy Roman
           Emperor Charles V, 1519–1556)

ARAGON

1336–1387 Pedro IV
1387–1395 Juan I
1395–1410 Martin I
1412–1416 Ferdinand I
1416–1458 Alfonso V, the
           Magnanimous
1458–1479 Juan II
1479–1516 Ferdinand, the
           Catholic*

*From 1506 (when Juana's husband, Philip the Handsome, died) until 1516, Ferdinand was regent in Castile during the madness of Juana and the minority of her son Charles.

Portugal

1357–1367 Pedro I
1367–1383 Fernão I

HOUSE OF AVIS

1385–1433 João I, the Great
1433–1438 Duarte
1438–1481 Afonso V, the African
1481–1495 João II
1495–1521 Manoel I, the Fortunate
1521–1557 João III

Scandinavia

1340–1375 Waldemar III (Denmark)
1343–1380 Haakon VI (Norway)
1365–1387 Albrecht of Mecklenburg (Sweden)
1376–1387 Olaf V (Denmark; also Norway, 1380–1387)
1387–1412 Margaret (Denmark, Norway, Sweden)
1412–1439 Eric (Denmark, Norway, Sweden)
1440–1448 Christopher III (Denmark, Norway, Sweden)
1448–1481 Christian I (Denmark, Norway; intermittently in Sweden)
1448–1457 Karl VIII (intermittently in Sweden)
1481–1513 Hans II (Denmark, Norway, Sweden)
1513–1523 Christian II (Denmark, Norway, Sweden)

Holy Roman Emperors

1346–1378 Charles IV (House of Luxembourg; Charles I of Bohemia)
1378–1400 Wenceslas of Bohemia (Luxembourg)
1400–1410 Rupert of the Palatinate (House of Wittelsbach)
1411–1437 Sigismund of Hungary and Bohemia (Luxembourg)
1438–1439 Albert II (also of Bohemia and Hungary; Albert V of Austria)
1440–1493 Frederick III of Austria (Habsburg)
1493–1519 Maximilian I of Austria (Habsburg)
1519–1556 Charles V (Habsburg-Burgundy-Castile-Aragon)

Bohemia

1346–1378 Charles I, the Great (Holy Roman Emperor Charles IV)
1378–1419 Wenceslas IV (Holy Roman Emperor Wenceslas I)
1419–1437 Sigismund (also of Hungary and Holy Roman Emperor)
1438–1439 Albert (Habsburg; also of Austria, Hungary, and Holy Roman Emperor)
1440–1457 Vladislav Posthumus (Habsburg; Ladislas Posthumus of Hungary)
1458–1471 George of Poděbrady

Bohemia *(continued)*

1471–1516 Vladislav II (Jagiellonian; Ladislas II of Hungary)
1516–1526 Louis II (Jagiellonian; also of Hungary)

Hungary

1342–1382 Louis I, the Great (also of Poland)
1382–1385 Marie (Anjou)
1385–1386 Charles II (Charles III of Naples)
1387–1437 Sigismund (also of Bohemia and Holy Roman Emperor)
1437–1439 Albert (also of Bohemia and Holy Roman Emperor)
1440–1444 Ladislas I (Jagiellonian; Wladyslaw III of Poland)
1444–1457 Ladislas Posthumus (Habsburg; Vladislav Posthumus of Bohemia)
1458–1490 Matthias I Corvinus
1490–1516 Ladislas II (Jagiellonian; Vladislav II of Bohemia)
1516–1526 Louis II (Jagiellonian; Also of Bohemia)

Poland

1333–1370 Casimir III, the Great (Last of the Piast dynasty)
1370–1382 Louis I, the Great (Anjou; Louis I of Hungary)
1383–1399 Jadwiga (Princess, then Queen)

JAGIELLONIAN DYNASTY

1386–1434 Wladyslaw II (Jagiello of Lithuania; married Jadwiga)
1434–1444 Wladyslaw III (Ladislas I of Hungary)
1447–1492 Casimir IV
1492–1501 John Albert
1501–1506 Alexander
1506–1548 Sigismund I

Ottoman Turks

1361–1389 Murad I
1389–1402 Bayazid I
1413–1421 Mohammed (Mehmed) I, the Restorer
1421–1451 Murad II
1451–1481 Mohammed (Mehmed) II, the Conquerer
1481–1512 Bayazid II
1512–1520 Selim I
1520–1566 Suleiman I, the Magnificent

APPENDIX III
Genealogical Charts

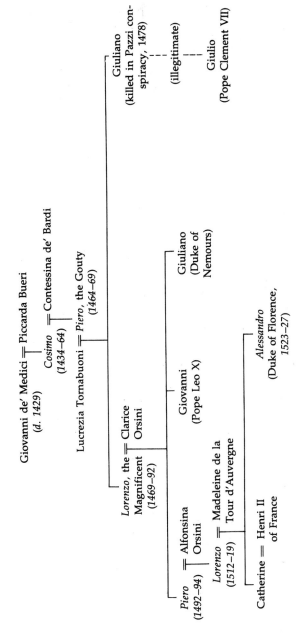

THE MEDICI

Giovanni de' Medici ⊤ Piccarda Bueri
(d. 1429)

Cosimo ⊤ Contessina de' Bardi
(1434–64)

Lucrezia Tornabuoni ⊤ *Piero*, the Gouty
(1464–69)

Lorenzo, the ⊤ Clarice
Magnificent Orsini
(1469–92)

Giuliano
(killed in Pazzi con-
spiracy, 1478)

(illegitimate)

Giulio
(Pope Clement VII)

Piero ⊤ Alfonsina
(1492–94) Orsini

Lorenzo ⊤ Madeleine de la
(1512–19) Tour d'Auvergne

Giovanni
(Pope Leo X)

Giuliano
(Duke of
Nemours)

Alessandro
(Duke of Florence,
1523–27)

Catherine = Henri II
of France

385

ENGLAND

(Houses of Plantagenet, Lancaster, York, and Tudor)

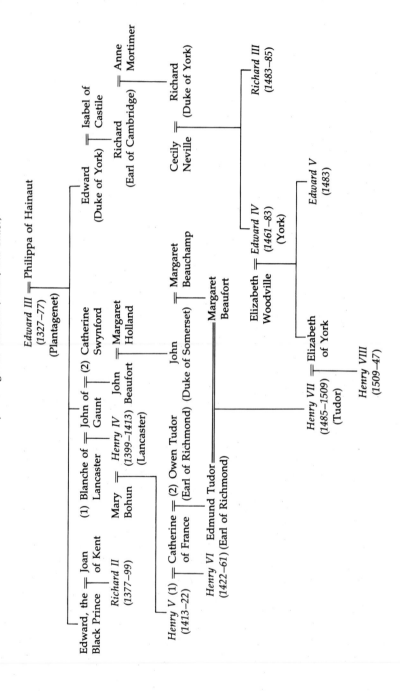

FRANCE

(House of Valois)

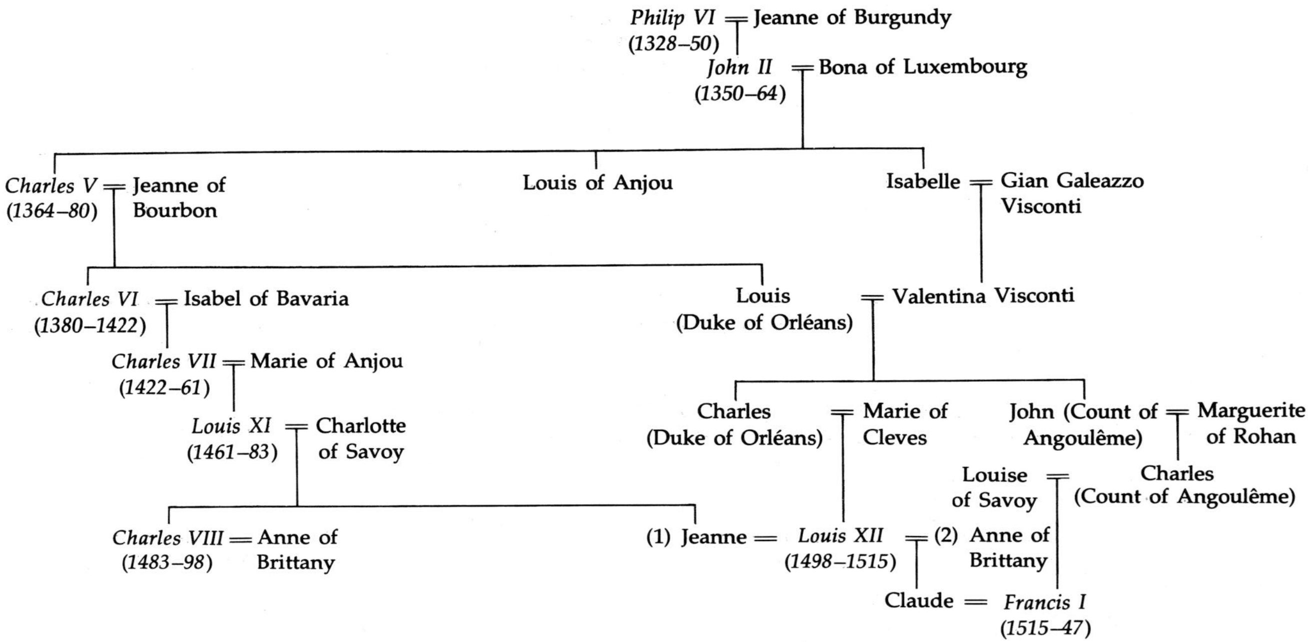

Philip VI = Jeanne of Burgundy
(1328–50)

John II = Bona of Luxembourg
(1350–64)

Charles V = Jeanne of
(1364–80)   Bourbon

Louis of Anjou

Isabelle = Gian Galeazzo
              Visconti

Louis
(Duke of Orléans) = Valentina Visconti

Charles VI = Isabel of Bavaria
(1380–1422)

Charles = Marie of
(Duke of Orléans)   Cleves

John (Count of = Marguerite
Angoulême)   of Rohan

Charles VII = Marie of Anjou
(1422–61)

Louis XI = Charlotte
(1461–83)   of Savoy

(1) Jeanne = Louis XII = (2) Anne of
                (1498–1515)   Brittany

Charles = Louise
(Count of Angoulême) of Savoy

Charles VIII = Anne of
(1483–98)   Brittany

Claude = Francis I
             (1515–47)

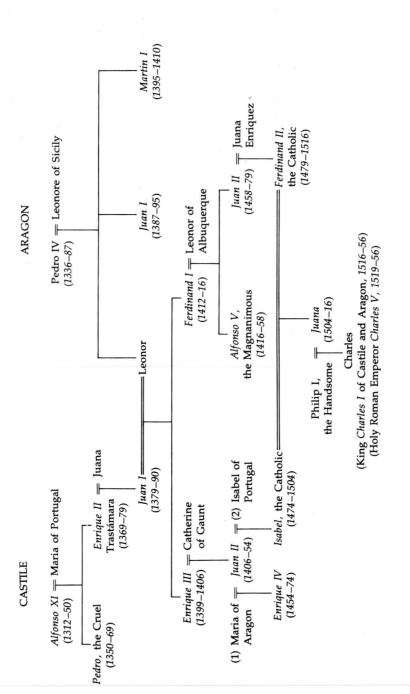

CASTILE

ARAGON

Alfonso XI = Maria of Portugal
(1312–50)

Pedro, the Cruel
(1350–69)

Enrique II = Juana
Trastámara
(1369–79)

Juan I
(1379–90)

Enrique III = Catherine
(1399–1406)   of Gaunt

(1) Maria of = Juan II = (2) Isabel of
Aragon   (1406–54)   Portugal

Enrique IV
(1454–74)

Isabel, the Catholic
(1474–1504)

Pedro IV = Leonore of Sicily
(1336–87)

Martin I
(1395–1410)

Juan I
(1387–95)

Leonor

Ferdinand I = Leonor of
(1412–16)   Albuquerque

Alfonso V,
the Magnanimous
(1416–58)

Juan II = Juana
(1458–79) Enriquez

Ferdinand II,
the Catholic
(1479–1516)

Philip I, = Juana
the Handsome (1504–16)

Charles
(King Charles I of Castile and Aragon, 1516–56)
(Holy Roman Emperor Charles V, 1519–56)

HABSBURGS OF AUSTRIA

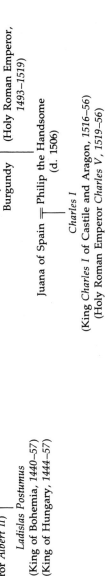

Albert II ═ Johanna von Pfirt
of Austria
(d. 1358)

Beatrice of ═ *Albert III*
Brandenburg   of Austria
               (1365–95)

Albert IV ═ Johanna of Bavaria
of Austria
(1395–1404)

Albert V ═ Elizabeth (daughter of
of Austria   Emperor Sigismund)
(King of Hungary, 1437–39)
(King of Bohemia, 1438–39)
(Holy Roman Emperor Albert II)

Ladislas Postumus
(King of Bohemia, 1440–57)
(King of Hungary, 1444–57)

Leopold III ═ Virida Visconti
(d. 1386)

Ernest ═ Cimburca of Masovia
(d. 1424)

Frederick III ═ Eleanor of
(Holy Roman Emperor,   Portugal
1440–93)

Mary of ═ *Maximilian I*
Burgundy   (Holy Roman Emperor,
(d. 1506)   1493–1519)

Juana of Spain ═ Philip the Handsome

Charles I
(King *Charles I* of Castile and Aragon, 1516–56)
(Holy Roman Emperor *Charles V*, 1519–56)

Index

Cynocephali, 280
Cyprus, 18, 34, 78

Dalmata, Giovanni, 364
Dalmatian coast, 58, 77, 246
Damascus, 18, 31, 78, 248
Dante, 25–26, 51
    Divine Comedy, 25, 119, 339
    On Monarchy, 25, 197
Danzig, 12, 77, 220
Datery, 20
Datini, Francesco, 88, 90
David, Gerard, 357
De re metallica (Agricola), 177
Decades (Barros), 353
Decades, The (Nebrija), 319
*Decades of History since the Decline
    of the Roman Empire* (Biondo),
    127
Decameron (Boccaccio), 107, 119,
    340
Defensor Pacis (Marsiglio of
    Padua), 197, 276
Delft, 187, 198
Della famiglia (Alberti), 97
Della Scala family, 51
Demesne, 10, 37
Denmark, 36, 244
Deprès, Josquin, 369
Desconhout (Lull), 25
Deventer, 187, 198, 315, 331
Devotio moderna, 198
Dialogues (Plato), 115
Diana, la (Montemayor), 344
Diaries (Sanuto), 74
Dias, Bartholomew, 287, 290, 294
Dias, Dinis, 286
Díaz del Castillo, Bernal, 354–55
    *Historia verdadera de la conquista
    de la Nueva España*, 355
Diplomacy, 60–61, 266–71
Discourses, The (Machiavelli), 275
*Discovery and Conquest of Guinea,
    The* (Azurara), 353
Disputationum Camaldulensium
    (Landino), 117
Diu, battle of, 290
Divine Comedy (Dante), 25, 119,
    339
Docta ignorantia, De (Cusa), 162
Doge of Venice, 53, 58, 61, 74, 153
Doges' palace, 145
Dolet, Étienne: *Commentaries on
    the Latin Tongue*, 317
Dominican Order, 21, 304, 306
Donatello, 140–41
Donation of Constantine, 111
Duccio, 141
Dufay, Guillaume, 369
Dumas, 246
Duns Scotus, John, 23
Dürer, Albrecht, 366–68
Dushan, Stephen, 248
Dutch, 176, 310

Eannes, Gil, 286
Education, 111–13, 314–15
Edward I (king of England), 40
Edward III (king of England), 199
Edward IV (king of England), 229

Edward, the Black Prince, 41
Egas, Enrique de, 361
Egloga primera (Garcilaso de la
    Vega), 345
Egypt, 75, 77, 89, 287
    conquered by Ottoman Turks,
    248
    conquered by Seljuk Turks, 33
El Cid, 24, 370
Eleanor of Austria, 228
Elegancies of the Latin Tongue
    (Valla), 111
Elizabeth of York, 229
Elmina, 287, 292
Emilia-Romagna, 58, 99, 256, 258
Encina, Juan del, 344–45
Enchiridion (Erasmus), 321, 333–35
Encomienda, 304–305
England, 26, 39–40, 220, 268, 276,
    279, 321, 338
    banks in, 82
    cities of, 51
    Erasmus in, 333
    fairs in, 12
    and the Great Schism, 193, 197
    under Henry VII, 229–30
    humanism in, 325–31
    and the Hundred Years' War,
        40–42
    Jews in, 32
    Jews expelled from, 201
    law in, 272
    literature in, 349–51
    Peasants' Revolt in, 87
    Petrarch in, 106
    textiles and wool from, 77,
        83–85
    trade of, 78–79, 91
    war fleet of, 265–66
    Wyclif and the Lollards in,
        199–200
Enrique IV (king of Castile), 43
Epistres de l'amant vert (Lemaire
    de Belges), 339
Erasmus, 198, 316, 328, 332–35, 338
    Adages, 333
    Colloquies, 334
    Enchiridion, 321, 333–35
    Institutio principis Christiani, 333
    The Praise of Folly, 333
    Querela pacis, 335
    in Spain, 321
Erfurt, University of, 323
Ergang, Robert, 2
Ernest (elector of Saxony), 239
Estates General, 37, 221, 225
Este, Beatrice d', 64
Este, Ercole d' (duke of Ferrara),
    323
Este family, 51, 112, 120, 203, 252
Este, Isabella d', 63–64, 96
Este, Niccolò d' (duke of Ferrara),
    112
Estienne, Henri, 187
Estienne, Robert, 187
Estissac, bishop Geoffroy d', 341
Estremadura, 300
Esztergom, 364
Eucharist. *See* Catholic liturgy
Eugenius IV (pope), 208–11

Fabriano, papermakers of, 183
Fabrica (Vesalius), 171
Fabula de Homine (Vives), 320
Familiar letters (Cicero), 108
Families and family life, 10–11,
    95–100
Felix V (anti-pope), 210
Feltre, Bernardino da, 204
Feltre, Vittorino da, 112
Ferdinand II (king of Aragon), 43,
    128, 202, 230, 232, 234–37,
    241, 253, 255–56, 258–59, 292,
    294, 319
    diplomacy of, 266
Ferguson, Wallace K., 2
Fernandes, Alvaro, 286
Fernandez de Oviedo y Valdes,
    Gonzalo
    La historia general de las Indias, 354
    La natural historia de las Indias, 354
Ferrante (king of Naples), 252
Ferrantino (king of Naples), 253
Ferrara, 51, 63, 112, 173, 203, 252,
    258
    duke of, 120
    University of, 120, 323
Ferrara-Florence, council of, 210,
    248
Feudalism, 14–19, 48, 52, 221
Fevre, Raoul le: *Collection of the
    Histories of Troy*, 187
Fichet, Guillaume, 187
Ficino, Marsilio, 114–16, 118, 318,
    325
Fiefs, 15, 19, 37, 43, 48
Figgis, J.N., 273
Filelfo, Francesco, 213
Filocol, Il (Boccaccio), 119
Filostrato (Boccaccio), 119
Fiorentino, Rosso, 359–60
Fiume, 258
Flanders, 40, 42, 80, 91, 193, 220,
    225, 331, 342, 351
    art of, 356–59, 364
    cloth of, 18, 77, 83, 230
    printing in, 187
Flanders Fleet, 77–78, 80
Flemish language, 242
Flemish League, 85
Florence, 49, 52, 86, 103, 169, 210,
    213, 256
    architecture and sculpture in,
        135–38, 140–41
    art and painting in, 133, 141–43
    banking center, 82
    foreign relations of, 58–59
    and the French invasion, 253
    government of, 52–55
    humanism in, 107–10, 117–18
    Jews and Jewish studies in, 203
    Leonardo in, 147–49
    Machiavelli and, 275–77
    and the Medici, 64–69, 90–91,
        113, 260, 262
    Michelangelo in, 150–51, 153
    Pico in, 116
    Platonic Academy of, 114, 326
    Savonarola and, 254–55
    textile industry in, 83–85, 87–89
    University of, 110, 115, 324

3 4 5 6 7 8 9 10